SCHOOL OF PROPHETS

A Bicentennial History of
Colgate Rochester Crozer
Divinity School

JOHN R. TYSON

JUDSON PRESS
PUBLISHERS SINCE 1824
VALLEY FORGE, PA

School of Prophets: A Bicentennial History of Colgate Rochester Crozer Divinity School
© 2019 by Judson Press, Valley Forge, PA 19482-0851
All rights reserved.

Judson Press has made every effort to trace the ownership of all quotes and pictures. In the event of a question arising from the use of a quote, we regret any error made and will be pleased to make the necessary correction in future printings and editions of this book.

Unless otherwise noted, Bible quotations in this volume are from the New Revised Standard Version of the Bible, copyright © 1989 by the Division of Christian Education of the National Council of the Churches of Christ in the United States of America. Used by permission. All rights reserved. Other quotations are from *The Holy Bible*, King James Version (KJV).

Pictured on the front cover: Top row left to right: Augustus H. Strong, Walter Rauschenbusch, William Colgate, Martin Luther King Jr. Bottom row left to right: Joanna P. Moore, Isabel Crawford, Howard Thurman, Ruth Hill. William Colgate photo is from the Colgate family papers, Special Collections and University Archives, Colgate University Libraries. Martin Luther King Jr. photo provided by Boston University Photography. Walter Rauschenbusch, Augustus H. Strong, and Howard Thurman provided by Colgate Rochester Crozer Divinity School.

Interior design by Crystal Devine.
Cover design by Lisa Delgado.

Library of Congress Cataloging-in-Publication data

Names: Tyson, John R., author.
Title: School of prophets : a bicentennial history of Colgate Rochester
    Crozer Divinity School / John R. Tyson.
Description: Valley Forge, PA : Judson Press, [2019] | Includes
    bibliographical references.
Identifiers: LCCN 2019010977| ISBN 9780817018047 (pbk. : alk. paper) | ISBN
    9780817082000 (epub)
Subjects: LCSH: Colgate University. Theological Seminary--History. | Colgate
    Rochester Divinity School--History. | Colgate Rochester Divinity School,
    Bexley Hall--History. | Crozer Theological Seminary--History. | Colgate
    Rochester Divinity School, Bexley Hall, Crozer Theological
    Seminary--History.
Classification: LCC BV4070.C66 T97 2019 | DDC 230.07/36174789--dc23 LC
record available at https://lccn.loc.gov/2019010977

Printed in the U.S.A.
First printing, 2019.

Contents

Foreword

My first encounter with the Rochester schools was in the late 1960s when I was in search of a seminary to prepare for the Baptist ministry. Ultimately, I landed elsewhere, but in graduate school, my dissertation research was focussed on western New York in the Burned Over District era. I studied in Rochester at the American Baptist Historical Society and the University of Rochester, roomed in the Mount Hope area, and took many of my meals in the Divinity School Refectory. I became deeply enamored of the bricks, stone, people, and great ideas that occupied the Hill, not to speak of my growing appreciation for Rochester as a premier progressive American city.

My next intersection with the Rochester schools was to attend a nearby lecture at Alfred University School of Theology by the esteemed Winthrop S. Hudson, who was the defining character of the Divinity Schools for an entire generation. I had devoured his works in American religion and Baptist studies, and because Dr. Hudson was a gracious person, our meeting at that event began a friendship that lasted to his senior years.

In 1978, I was elected Executive Director and Curator of the Samuel Colgate Baptist Historical Collection of the American Baptist Historical Society, the largest assemblage of "baptistiana" in the world. It was housed on the ground floor of Strong Hall in Colgate Rochester Divinity School (CRDS). Day after day for almost a decade, I sat amid hundreds of years of Baptist and Free Church literature, supplemented by the vast CRDS Ambrose Swasey Library, then one of the top five theological collections in North America. Though not an alum, I found a collegiality at the Divinity School that was productive and gratifying. To my delight, I was subsequently elected to the faculty as Associate Professor of Baptist Studies and Bibliography and taught the basic course in Baptist life and thought, once developed by Professor Hudson.

In addition to my interest in the Colgate and Rochester narratives, I also took a keen research interest in Crozer. The Crozer family, its early faculty and connection to the Revival tradition, the bridge status of the school between northern and southern Baptists, the bold reorganization of the faculty in light of contemporary developments in theological studies, and its open racial and ethnic stance provided a unique chapter in American Baptist educational history. Of course, Crozer was also the heart of Baptist historical research, for many years being the home of the American Baptist Historical Society.

In a comprehensive history of North American Baptists in higher education, I determined that the Hamilton/Madison/Colgate, Rochester, Crozer, and Baptist Missionary Training schools played seminal roles in the development of Baptists in theological education.[1] Their influence was deep and cast a long shadow over the entire family of Baptists, and beyond. The Colgate tradition exemplified a unique type of school, the blended literary and theological institution, suitable for the uneven needs of the growing frontier Baptist community. It took first place in so many developing trends, as this present book shows. Rochester Seminary quickly became the leading Baptist seminary of its time, urban-defined, missionary-oriented, ethnically diverse, and nurtured by a great university. Crozer exhibited the outer boundaries of a philanthropic tradition, a freestanding, progressive, denominational school. Its academic acceptance by local research universities gave it a unique reputation in its southeastern Pennsylvania environment. Chester, Pennsylvania, became a seedbed in civil rights consciousness and the emergence of the black church, to be blessed by the reputations of Martin Luther King Jr., J. Pius Barbour, and Samuel DeWitt Proctor. The Baptist Missionary Training School, first in Chicago and later in Rochester, opened opportunities for women to seek Christian vocations around the world. The marriage of BMTS in Rochester in 1961 united the strands in American Baptist educational and gender history.

---

1. William H. Brackney. *Congregation and Campus: Baptists in Higher Education* (Atlanta: Mercer University Press, 2008).

Four characteristics of a great tradition continue to commend the heritage of these schools. The first is **diversity in learning and experience**. None of the schools that came to live together in Rochester were monolithic. Early in their histories, diverse racial, gender, nationality, and religious outlooks were witnessed in the classrooms and faculty rosters. Learning strategies and outcomes were deliberately diversified. Graduates found placement in both parish-based and corporate social life.

A second characteristic is **ecumenism**. Witnessing the cluster of denominations in places such as Toronto, Berkeley, Chicago, Atlanta, and Boston, Rochester took on its own challenge by bringing five schools and five denominations together to comprise something fit for the Rochester community. The Rochester Center for Theological Studies brought together Baptists, Episcopalians, United Methodists, Roman Catholics, and several African American traditions in a daring experiment.

A third enduring characteristic is the **incarnation of the Social Gospel** at Rochester. With the coming of Walter Rauschenbusch and his internationally recognized new interpretation of the gospel, Rochester will be forever associated with this movement and vice versa.

And finally, there is the **Liberal theological tradition** unashamedly advanced at Rochester. The educational community of Rochester identified itself with the Chicago School, Union Seminary in New York, Yale Divinity School, and Toronto School of Theology, making a robust, self-defined contribution to North American culture. Here the theological disciplines truly interacted with the social sciences. Sometimes the interaction was prophetic and painful, but always faithful to its place in the American Liberal tradition.

On the occasion of the bicentennial of the founding of the Hamilton Literary and Theological Institution in 1819, we are indebted to the schools for supporting this project and to well-known scholar Dr. John Tyson for the labor and spirit he brings to the narrative. My personal gratitude is expressed over four decades to my former colleagues and friends in helping to define the great tradition of the divinity schools: W. Hudson, J. Ashbrook, J. C. Wynn, G. Wilmore,

J. Carey, K. Smith, W. K. Cauthen, C. Nielson, W. E. Saunders, O. H. Baker, L. Pacala, L. Greenfield, H. D. Lance, L. Sweet, P. Vander-berge, H. Trickett, T. Weeden, and K. Dean.

Ut traditionem durare!

William H. Brackney BA, MA, MAR, PhD
Millard R. Cherry Distinguished Professor of
Christian Thought and Ethics, *Emeritus*
Acadia University
Wolfville, Nova Scotia, Canada

Preface

The current work began almost four years ago. As the Divinity School anticipated its two hundredth anniversary, there was interest in the development of a bicentennial history to commemorate and celebrate the event. About that same time, Ms. Sally Dodgson, who had served the Colgate Rochester Crozer Divinity School (CRCDS) as director of public relations and then as assistant to the president for institutional research (1984–1999), walked into my office with two large shopping bags filled with books and pamphlets. Sally, who had recently been diagnosed with a terminal illness, was the unofficial institutional historian and had published one of the few narratives of the Divinity School or its constituent bodies.[1] Our conversation that day, and the delivery of those resources, amounted to a passing of the mantle of the bicentennial history from Sally Dodgson to me. Little did I know or imagine the difficulties, both personal and academic, that lay ahead as I sought to bring the CRCDS history book to fruition.

Much to my surprise, no previous history of CRCDS had been written. There were a few partial accounts, such as the reminiscences left by early presidents like Augustus Strong and George Eaton about the founding years. The eminent Colgate Rochester Divinity School (CRDS) church historian Dr. Winthrop Hudson was commissioned to develop a volume for the sesquicentennial anniversary of the school—but that never appeared. Sally Dodgson had written a brief but well-researched article on the early years of Rochester Theological Seminary. There was also a brief

Sally Dodges

---

1. Sally Dodgson, "Rochester Theological Seminary: 1850-1928," *American Baptist Quarterly* 20, no. 2 (June 2001): 114-29.

history, written by Faith Coxe Bailey,[2] of the Baptist Missionary Training School, which was originally located in Chicago and which merged with CRDS in 1962, along with similar small works on Bexley Hall by Richard Spielmann[3] and St. Bernard's Institute by Robert McNamara.[4]

The relocation of the American Baptist Archives from CRCDS to the campus of Mercer University in Atlanta, Georgia, along with the disorder among much of the material that remained in the CRCDS archives, further complicated the task of creating a reliable paper trail where none had previously existed. My friend and colleague, Ms. Marge Neade, current director of the Ambrose Swasey Library at CRCDS and archivist, was of immeasurable assistance in this process. It is to these two women, Sally Dodgson and Marge Neade, who have been so passionate about the prophetic legacy of the Divinity School, that this work is gratefully dedicated.

Marge Neade

Additional and heartfelt thanks are also extended to Ms. Debbie Diederich and Ms. Lisa Bors in the Institutional Advancement Office, who helped supply documents and photos for this bicentennial history, as well as to Mr. Thomas McDade-Clay, who heads that area. I am deeply indebted to my colleagues Dr. Marvin McMickle, Dr. Melanie Duguid-May, and Dr. Stephanie Sauvé who, along with Ms. Neade and Ms. Gertrude (G.P.) Dickerson-Hanks, read all or portions of my manuscript in its early stages and provided helpful suggestions. My gratitude also extends to Dr. William H. Brackney, professor emeritus of Arcadia Theological College, for his careful and helpful reading of an earlier version of this book. Clearly, however, whatever shortcomings may exist in this work belong to me alone.

---

2. Faith Coxe Bailey, based on research done by Margaret Noffsinger Wenger, *Two Directions* (Rochester, NY: Baptist Missionary Training School, 1964).
3. Richard M. Spielmann, *Bexley Hall: 150 Years—A Brief History* (Rochester, NY: CRCDS Bexley Hall, 1974).
4. Robert F. McNamara, *St. Bernard's Seminary: 1893-1968* (Rochester, NY: The Sheaf Press, 1968).

Introduction

This bicentennial history of Colgate Rochester Crozer Divinity School (CRCDS) chronicles the story of one of the oldest and most influential theological seminaries in the United States. It is tempting, perhaps, to view the legacy of this or any educational institution as being, to borrow the words of Dr. Augustus Strong, who was president here from 1872 until 1912, a story about "brains, bricks, and books." It is that, but also so very much more.

This book is also the saga of the rich legacy established by many dedicated Christian women and men who strove to respond to the call of God upon their lives. It is the story of several constituencies and their respective institutions: Colgate Theological Seminary (Hamilton Institute), Rochester Theological Seminary, the Baptist Missionary Training School, Bexley Hall Theological Seminary, Crozer Theological Seminary, and St. Bernard's Institute. It is a richly ecumenical story begun by American Baptists, who were soon joined by Episcopalians, Methodists, Presbyterians, and Roman Catholics, among many others—who embraced the task of proclaiming the gospel of Christ in word and deed, through inclusion and care for those who stood on the margins of society, thereby seeking to build a better world. It was a task which they understood as preparing the way for the kingdom of God (Walter Rauschenbusch) and establishing "the beloved community" (Martin Luther King).

Beneath the heroic acts of individuals and their institutions, there was a galvanizing vision and point of view clearly present in the hearts and minds of the thirteen men who gathered in the parlor of Samuel Payne's home in Hamilton, New York, in May 1817. After long and prayerful conversations, they dedicated themselves to the task of establishing "a school for prophets" in rural western New

1

York, because God's work was seriously hampered by a dramatic shortage of educated pastors. As if to seal the deal, each man contributed $1.00, a significant sum in those days, to establish a circle of correspondence and a committee to push the plan forward.

The vision of the founders has lived on in various forms and in the lives of various people down through the two centuries of the Divinity School's existence. Hence, Colgate Rochester Crozer has long been a place where the gospel of Christ was deeply understood, engaged, and fearlessly incarnated—even when that task took it and its constituency to the margins of society to stand alongside of those whom Jesus called "the least of these my brethren" (Matthew 25:40, KJV). These were women and men who not only championed the gospel of grace and inclusion but also dared, using prophetic words and action, to "speak truth to power"[1] in ways epitomized by the ministry of CRCDS alumni Martin Luther King Jr.

This point of view was ably described by one of its most illustrious professors, Walter Rauschenbusch, when he told a young candidate for a teaching position at Rochester Theological Seminary, Justin Wroe Nixon, "We build prophets here." Like countless others, Nixon enthusiastically accepted the invitation and the challenge of being a part of the enterprise of building prophets for the kingdom of God. This same vibrant legacy lives on in the mission statement of CRCDS's current faculty:

> We are committed to the ministry as we engage the theological disciplines in an ecumenical Christian community of teaching, learning and worship that prepares students for Christian ministries that are learned, pastoral and prophetic.
> We are committed to theological education that embodies acts of radical hospitality, in our classrooms, and in chapel, in our churches and communities.
> We seek the integrity of living faith and intellectual inquiry by which women and men are prepared for local, national and global Christian ministries dedicated to a life-giving future for all God's people.[2]

The CRCDS story is one of academic excellence, pastoral relevance, and innovation, as well as Christian social engagement. It is the story of Augustus Strong seeking to establish a systematic theology that is both evangelical and progressive; it is William Newton

---

1. This phrase was coined and popularized by a pamphlet by the African American Quaker Baynard Rustin, *Speak Truth to Power: A Quaker Search for an Alternative to Violence* (Philadelphia: American Friends Service Committee, 1955), and epitomized the approach of Martin Luther King Jr, and many others engaged in the struggle for civil rights.
2. *Colgate Rochester Crozer Divinity School Catalogue*, 2017-2019, 10. Hereafter, publications of the Divinity School, such as catalogues and bulletins, are abbreviated CRCDS.

Clarke chronicling his own and the school's fifty-year pilgrimage through the Bible and approaches to its interpretation; it is Walter Rauschenbusch pointing out the impending social crisis due to extreme economic disparity in America; it is Howard Thurman rising up out of conditions of poverty and oppression to help others find a way to view the world through the eyes of Jesus; it is Joanna P. Moore educating freed men and women in the reconstructionist American South; it is Isabel Crawford spending her life living and working among the Kiowa; it is Martin Luther King Jr. announcing a new and dramatic stride toward freedom for all people.

The CRCDS story is one of faithfulness, empowerment, and inclusion. It is Charles Hubert, a black man, who graduated with a bachelor of divinity degree from Rochester Theological Seminary in 1912, beginning a rich legacy that continued on in the lives and work of Mordecai Wyatt Johnson, Howard Thurman, Martin Luther King Jr., Wyatt T. Walker, Samuel Proctor, and Johnny Youngblood, to name but a few African American alumni whose contributions to church and society are incalculable. It is epitomized by the work of Rumah Alvilla Crouse, Mary Burdette, and the heroic women who established the women's Baptist Missionary Training School, thereby opening an educational and missional door for women that was closed to them for centuries. It is Ruth Hill, who entered the Divinity School to study Christian ministry a full four years before women were given the right to vote in the United States; or Betty Bone Schiess, who was among the first female Episcopalian priests in the land; or Marjorie Matthews, the first woman to become a bishop in a mainline Protestant church. It is the strong witness of CRCDS students, alumni, and faculty in standing with the poor and the disenfranchised, be they indigenous people, immigrants, racial minorities, or those striving for gender equality—understood in the broadest sense.

The structure of this book is essentially twofold: it is partly the story of a great theological seminary—an institutional history seasoned by the developments, changes, and issues that have shaped CRCDS through the years. It is also a dramatic story of women and men, from each period of the two-hundred-year history of the school, who both embodied and contributed to its rich legacy. Hence, while this is a history of an institution, it is really the history of the people who have epitomized, shaped, contributed to, and furthered its heritage and legacy. This twofold aspect is easily discerned in the composition of CRCDS's narrative, since it includes chapters about institutional growth and development, as well as cameo biographies of key people who epitomized the spirit of that same period. President Strong was correct to call this a story of "bricks, brains, and books," but in a larger sense it is a story about the lives of many dedicated women and men and the galvanizing prophetic Christian vision that bound them together for the enterprise that came to be known as Colgate Rochester Crozer Divinity School.

It is said that the past can function as a distant mirror by which we take a fresh look at ourselves and our past to see ourselves and our present situation more clearly. My hope is that this work causes us to look at ourselves and our past in a way that also sets our feet upon a Christ-like and transformative path that impels us forward into the deepening years of the twenty-first century. Dramatic challenges lie ahead of us at all levels of life; having a better sense of our identity as followers of Christ and our heritage as bequeathed to us through the legacy of the Divinity School, will better equip us to meet and transcend them.

My hope and prayer are that upon looking into this mirror, readers will find themselves encouraged and empowered by the witness of the women and men who have gone on before, who have lived out this legacy of faithfulness to the full-orbed gospel of Jesus Christ, and who seem to bid us to do likewise. I also hope that we will see in the illustrious example of this "cloud of witnesses" (Hebrews 12:1) an unspoken call both to do likewise, and perhaps, in some instances, to do even better.

1

Thirteen Men with Thirteen Dollars

Our saga begins with the religious expansion following the War of 1812, and the explosion of religious fervor that came to be known as the Second Great Awakening. The Christian religion, particularly in its Protestant varieties, moved from the Eastern Seaboard into the rural, western lands, along with the steady march of much of the population. Because of their spontaneity, independence, and ability to adjust themselves to the new media of revivalism and camp meetings, Baptist churches drew adherents in unprecedented numbers during the pre–Civil War period. After this rapid growth and expansion of the denomination, a shortage of trained ministers soon followed. This was particularly the case in western New York.

In 1817, for example, the Baptist denomination in the state of New York numbered about 310 congregations, staffed by 230 ministers, with about 28,000 members. The ministers were pious and diligent men who "were lacking in nothing except education"; in fact, only three New York Baptist ministers west of the Hudson River possessed a college education.[1] All the while, the congregants became better educated, and it seemed that an educated ministry was needed. But there were no provisions for educating ministers in this region, the nearest theological school being Newton Theological Seminary in Massachusetts. The humble beginnings of Colgate University and Colgate Theological Seminary reach back to this period, as New York Baptists began to look for ways to develop an educated ministry to serve their growing church.

1. B. F. Bronson, ed., *The First Half Century of Madison University (1819-1869) or, The Jubilee Volume Containing Sketches of Eleven Hundred Living and Deceased Alumni with Fifteen Portraits of Founders, Presidents, and Patrons. Also The Exercises of the Semi-Centennial Anniversary* (New York: Sheldon and Co., 1872), 25.

Theological education was a progressive and forward-looking idea at this time, and not all Baptists favored ministerial education; indeed, some openly opposed it because it "lacked Scriptural sanction."[2] At the fiftieth anniversary of the Hamilton Literary and Theological Institution, located in Hamilton, New York, its president, George Eaton, explained, "An *Institution* for the special purpose of educating ministers, many good and influential brethren, when the Society was formed, [was] considered as a human device, and to be regarded with suspicion, as if dispensing with the necessity of the gifts of grace, and so likely to inflict upon the churches the curse of a coldly intellectual and graceless ministry."[3] Illustrating this point, the New York *Baptist Register* reported that for more than thirty years the Hamilton school functioned under "prejudices [that] were mountain-high in the churches" against the "minister factory."[4]

In this climate, and with a pressing need for ministerial education, Baptists often turned to voluntary associations and informal societies as a means of consolidating their limited resources and implementing a process that would lead to the education of ministers and eventually to the establishment of Baptist seminaries. One of the first of these educational associations was the Baptist Education Society of the Middle States, which was founded in 1812. In these early days theological education was often received through tutorials given by well-trained senior ministers. In this case, the society sought to raise up students and funds to be sent to William Staughton, who had opened his home and pulpit to students beginning in 1807. In 1813 an auxiliary society was established by Baptists in New York City. It, too, would send students and funds to Staughton's makeshift school. A similar school soon emerged in New York City under the leadership of John Stanford. By 1817 New York Baptist Theological Seminary incorporated the New York group and was planning to establish its own theological seminary within the year.

At this same time in New England, Jeremiah Chaplin, the Baptist pastor of Danvers, Massachusetts, began a circle of correspondence that strongly advocated for an educated ministry. Chaplin argued

---

2. Howard D. Williams, *A History of Colgate University* (New York: Van Nostrand Reinhold, 1969), 2.
3. George W. Eaton, "Historical Discourse Delivered at the Semi-Centenary of Madison University, Wednesday, August 5th, 1869," in Bronson, *First Half Century*, 40.
4. Jesse Rosenberger, *Rochester and Colgate: The Historical Backgrounds of Two Universities* (Chicago: University of Chicago Press, 1925), 30–31.

that ministers would need to be educated in subjects like history, geography, rhetoric, logic, mathematics, philosophy, and astronomy, as well as in theology and the biblical languages, to meet fully the needs of the current age. Chaplin bewailed the fact that Brown University, which was initially established by the Baptists to provide the church with an educated ministry, no longer offered a divinity course, and the majority of the students were, in his words, "destitute of the grace of God."[5] Chaplin's letter urged that at least four new regional Baptist seminaries were required to meet the needs of the rapidly growing church: one in the West, one in New England, one in the middle states, and one in the South.

Jeremiah Chaplin's letter struck a responsive chord in the heart and mind of Daniel Hascall (1782–1852), pastor of the First Baptist Church at Hamilton, New York. Located on the Hamilton-Skaneateles Turnpike in rural Madison County, Hamilton had only recently incorporated in 1816. Soon the village grew to the point that a private school called the Hamilton Academy was established, along with a newspaper named *The Hamilton Gazette*. Pastor Hascall had been serving the First Baptist Church of Hamilton since 1813. He was a graduate of Middlebury College in Middlebury, Vermont, and was well in touch with the educational endeavors of Baptists in New England and New York City. Hascall was utterly convinced that the Western Baptist Seminary, which Jeremiah Chaplin's encyclical called for, should be established at Hamilton, New York.

Hascall soon discussed his idea about the location and establishment of the Western Baptist Seminary with another sympathetic listener, Nathaniel Kendrick, of Middlebury, Vermont. Kendrick was an educated Baptist minister who had studied informally with Samuel Stillman of Boston. He was enthusiastic about the idea, and in 1817 Kendrick relocated to the village of Eaton, New York, not far from Hamilton. Several others in the Hamilton area were also enthusiastic about the seminary, so in May 1817 these "Ministers and Brethren" met in the Hamilton home of Samuel Payne (1782–1852). They met to establish a "school of prophets" and "to consider the propriety and importance of affording assistance to young men, in obtaining a competent education, who are called of God to preach."[6] A committee of four was established for that purpose, and they issued a

5. Ibid., 4.
6. Williams, *History of Colgate University*, 7.

public notice published on the cover of the November edition of the *American Baptist Magazine*. The notice reported that "after prayerful deliberation on the subject, it was the unanimous opinion of those present that to promote the future usefulness of those whom God is raising up to be Ministers of the New Testament, some provision should be made for their instruction."[7] The group pledged to gather more information, spread the word about their intentions, and meet again at the end of September.

The public notice was signed by Joel W. Clark, Nathaniel Kendrick, Charles W. Hull, and Daniel Hascall, all notable leaders in the community in and around Hamilton. Joel Clark was pastor at the Sagerfield Baptist Church, which was a few miles east of Hamilton. Charles Hull was a local physician and a member of Kendrick's church in Eaton.

The Ostego Baptist Association, from Ostego County, New York, seems to be the only other group that responded to the call for the meeting. In all, thirteen men arrived for the programmatic meeting: Jonathan Olmstead, Daniel Hascall, Nathaniel Kendrick, Samuel Payne, Elisha Payne, John Bostwick, Joel W. Clark, Charles W. Hull, Thomas Cox, Samuel Osgood, Amos Kingsley, Peter Philathropos Roots, and Robert Powell.[8] Of these thirteen men, nine were members of Hascall's Hamilton Baptist Church. Most of the men were middle-aged, prominent civic leaders in their respective communities; the only exception was Robert Powell, who was twenty-seven. Only Hascall, who had attended Middlebury, and Roots, who had attended Dartmouth, were formally educated ministers.

When it was clear the group would number only thirteen men, the meeting was momentarily adjourned and then reconvened in the more comfortable surroundings of the parlor of Deacon Olmstead's home, located about a mile south of the village of Hamilton. Powell, who left a recollection of the meeting, remembered it as "a solemn and impressive occasion."[9] After stating the purpose of the meeting, there was a period of ominous silence, during which Kendrick led in prayer, as the others all joined in. They implored God's strength and insight as they charted a new and potentially disruptive course that would alter the direction of both church and society. The intention of

---

7. Ibid.
8. Bronson, *First Half-Century*, 38.
9. Williams, *History of Colgate University*, 9.

the group was to begin a school especially designed and exclusively operated for the education of the rising ministry. They reported that the new school, while dedicated to the education of "those young men whom God calls to the ministry of the gospel," would be of a different sort than its predecessors. This school would care for "the means of defraying their expenses, as well as to the preservation of their morals and the promotion of their piety." Recognizing the need for broadly based ministerial education, the new school would be "an institution in which they shall be assisted in the pursuit both of literary and theological knowledge, and in which they shall be directed to such a course of studies as shall be deemed most conducive to their usefulness."[10]

The committee, which had been appointed the previous May, presented a draft of a constitution to the Baptist Education Society of the State of New York, which they suggested the group should form. The preamble to their constitution reads,

> Impressed with the vast importance of the Christian ministry as connected with the conversion of sinners and the edification of the church, and desirous to furnish young men of piety and gifts the means of acquiring an education with a view to their public usefulness, we do hereby associate and adopt the following constitution.[11]

The constitution went on to describe the aim of the society by reporting, "The object of this Society shall be to afford means of instruction to such persons of the Baptist denomination as shall furnish evidence to the churches of which they are members, and to the Executive committee hereafter named, of their personal piety and call to the gospel ministry."[12]

The group would, therefore, identify suitable candidates, approve them for ministry, and raise monetary support for them. The committee also presented an address, "To the Baptists of New York State," which both explained the reasons for forming the Baptist Education Society and solicited support on behalf of the project. Both documents were heartily accepted by the group, and it was ordered that five hundred copies of each document should be printed for distribution. A board of trustees was established, which elected Roots as

---

10. S. W. Adams, *The Memoirs of Rev. Nathaniel Kendrick D.D. and Silas N. Kendrick* (Philadelphia: The American Baptist Publication Society, 1860), 122.

11. Bronson, *First Half-Century*, 38.

12. *The Baptist Education Society of the State of New York, Annual Reports: 1818-1828*, 81.

president, Clark as secretary, and Olmstead as treasurer of the group. Those present agreed to pay $1.00 each as an annual membership fee, to help defray costs. Thus, it was with thirteen men, $13.00, and thirteen prayers that the ambitious project was launched.

The first year of inception for the Baptist Education Society of New York was more successful than its founders probably anticipated. More than $2,400 was raised in donations, and another $55 in annual subscriptions. One student, Jonathan Wade of Hartford, New York, was received and approved as their first candidate for ministerial studies.[13] In his ardent anticipation to begin his ministerial studies, Wade walked the 141 miles from his home to Hamilton. He arrived and was accepted for studies by February 2, 1819.[14] Wade was the beneficiary of the society's first scholarship, receiving $27.12 for fifteen and one-half weeks' tuition to study Latin with Daniel Hascall, as well as $1.75 per week toward his room and board. The committee was so pleased with the progress of the project that they directed their trustees to seek a charter from the state legislature. A committee to determine where the society's institution would be located also commenced during this time.

When the trustees petitioned the New York State legislature for a charter, they learned that a powerful assemblyman named General Erastus Root opposed the proposition on the grounds that it would effectually be chartering a religious society and hence blurred the line of separation between church and state. Ebenezer Wakeley, a member of the committee and of the New York State Assembly, introduced a bill of incorporation for the society in the January assembly session of 1819. After strenuous debate and quiet diplomacy, the bill passed on its third reading before the assembly, 62–35 and then made it through the state senate without much opposition. The bill of incorporation became law on March 8, 1819, and the new charter gave the Baptist Education Society of New York the usual privileges granted to corporations. The society did encounter obstacles after the establishment of the charter, such as a restriction to ownership of

---

13. He was described in the 1930 edition of the Colgate Divinity School catalogue in the following manner: "Jonathan Wade, D.D. born at Otsego, Dec. 10, 1798; graduated 1822; student of the Burnam language 1822-23; ordained at Broadathin, Feb. 23, 1823; missionary of the American Baptist Foreign Mission Society to the Karens, Burma, 1823-1872). Died Rangoon, Burma, June 10, 1872. Author: "Vocabulary of the Sgau Karen Language." From Glenn B. Ewell, "Baptist Theological Education in New York State," *Colgate Rochester Divinity School Bulletin* 10, no. 2 (1937): 73 (hereafter *CRDS*).
14. Glenn Blackmer Ewell, "Colgate-Rochester Divinity School: 1817-1942," *CRDS Bulletin* 15, no. 1 (October 1942): 7.

property of no more than $5,000, and was expressly prohibited from making "any law or regulation affecting the rights of conscience."[15]

The committee that worked on the site for the society's institution in 1818 had difficulty reaching an agreement as to where it should be located. They investigated venues in the villages of Elbridge, Throopsville, Skaneateles, Fabius, Sagerfield, and Hamilton. In each location concerns such as the climate, soil, accessibility, economic conditions, and the spiritual state of the local Baptist church were taken into consideration. A bid was also received from Peterboro, but there does not seem to have been an on-site visit to that location. When the committee was hopelessly deadlocked, a second committee was appointed. They decided upon Skaneateles, providing that the village would raise $10,000 to help support establishment of the school. The agreement was breached, however, when the trustees found that the people of Skaneateles anticipated that the seminary would operate as a school open to local students not intending for the ministry. The board rejected this idea and began looking for an alternative site. Confronted with the same problem still another time, the committee once again wavered between Peterboro and Hamilton. Ultimately, however, Hamilton was selected as the more appropriate location.[16] The minutes of that meeting, dated November 3, 1819, survived and report the following:

> After mature deliberation, on receiving ample securities from Hamilton, that they will furnish by the first of May next, the upper story of the academy in the village of Hamilton, well-furnished for the use of the Society, and in four years procure the whole building or one equal to it, estimated at $3500, and $2500 to be paid in board at 12 shillings per week in five equal annual payments provided the Society shall require it in that time or in a longer period.
>
> *Voted* unanimously, that the Theological Seminary be permanently located in or near the Village of Hamilton, Co., of Madison and State of New York.[17]

By the following spring, on May 1, 1820, the Hamilton Literary and Theological Institution formally opened. It was housed in the third story of the brick school building in Hamilton, New York. The first floor of the same building was occupied by the local public school, and Hamilton Academy took up residence on the second floor of the same building. While the seminary had no formal name at this time, it was generally known as the Hamilton Literary and Theological

---

15. Williams, *History of Colgate University*, 13.
16. Eaton, "Historical Discourse," 42.
17. Williams, *History of Colgate University*, 13.

Institution. This title bespoke its founders' concern for a liberal arts foundation for proper ministerial studies. After a few false starts in their search for a suitable instructor, the committee turned to Hascall, "whose services thus far [had] been acceptable."[18] While students had been receiving tutorials from Hascall for two years, this marked the first term of the institution. Beginning with ten students, Hascall and his third-story classroom represented the fruition of the ideals cherished by the New York State Baptist Education Society and its ardent labors for many years.

Nathaniel Kendrick (1777–1848) was added to the teaching faculty in 1821. He had already served many functions for the society, including secretary of the board of trustees from 1819 to 1848, and gradually developed that office into the most influential and responsible role in the society. Kendrick had a vigorous personality and an intimate knowledge of the challenges facing the fledging institution. As an officer of the Baptist Triennial Convention and the Home Missions Society, he was well connected within the Baptist denomination and carried on a wide correspondence on behalf of the school. A commanding figure, endowed with the qualities of leadership, Kendrick quickly became the dominant force in the society. "He ruled in every position," one early colleague recalled, "not with an arbitrary power, but by natural authority."[19] The school found in him a leader who was able to combine the forces that had given birth to the institution and consistently fashion them into concerted pattern and constituency. Kendrick was, as Williams described him, "the architect who shaped most of the foundations and also one of the builders who gave the edifice permanent form."[20]

Formal recognition of Kendrick's visionary and diligent leadership finally came in 1836 when, at the request of the faculty, the board of trustees recognized him as president of the institution. It was an honor he accepted with hesitation and a title he used only less than a year, yet he carried on the duties normally associated with the presidency from 1819 until his death in 1848. He was assisted in the day-to-day governance of the school by a five-member executive committee who were local members of the board of trustees. Their responsibilities ranged from crucial issues like struggling to pay

18. Ibid., 14.
19. Williams, *History of Colgate University*, 16, citing a manuscript source from Philetus B. Spear, class of 1836.
20. Ibid.

faculty salaries to mundane matters like voting that students who chewed tobacco needed to provide their own "spit boxes."[21]

George Eaton (1804–1872), the second president of Hamilton Institute, who knew both men, fondly remembered the contributions of his predecessors:

> To Hascall is undoubtedly due, more than any one man, the origin of the Institution. The praise of founder, by common consent, is accorded him, but to Kendrick, more than any other, is due the massive structure in its peculiar form as originally shaped and constructed. Both alike clearly comprehended and absorbingly felt the vast importance of the sacred enterprise; both gave their whole hearts in the work—nay, they lived in it and it in them. They embodied the Institution in their own individualities, and would have sacrificed their own lives for it, if necessary, to keep it in life and power.[22]

Theologically, both men were strong Calvinists, although Hascall affirmed general atonement while Kendrick adhered to particular election. Hascall was a man of "restless and impatient energy," and Kendrick was "more steady, slow and concentrative." But they "moved together in their common work amicably and harmoniously, having 'one mind and one way.'"[23]

Meanwhile, in its meeting on March 24, 1823, the New York City group resolved to send Hamilton Seminary as much money as could be spared and as many students as would be expedient. By April 15 they were able to send $350 to Hamilton to help with the educational expenses of a young man they recommended to the institution. On December 31, 1824, they resolved to send all the books in their library to Hamilton. From this point forward, the board of New York City and the education society in Hamilton were for all practical purposes one. The New York group kept their legal existence and retained their own charter, but they gradually assumed the role of a strong financial arm upon which the Hamilton Institution could lean in frequent times of difficulty.[24] One of the ancillary but extremely important benefits of this growing partnership between the two Baptist educational societies was that it brought the Hamilton group into contact with William Colgate of New York City.

William Colgate (1783–1857) was born in Hollingbourne, Kent, England, on January 25, 1783. He was the second child of Robert

---

21. Ibid., 17.
22. Eaton, "Historical Discourse," 86.
23. Ibid.
24. Ewell, "Baptist Theological Education in New York State," 77.

and Sarah Bowles Colgate. He relocated to the United States with his parents, due to his father's political radicalism. A revolutionary and friend of Prime Minister William Pitt, Robert Colgate was warned of his impending arrest for anti-Tory agitation in England. Since he had lobbied for the American colonies throughout the Revolutionary War, Robert Colgate felt America was a logical destination for him and his family. They arrived in Baltimore on May 28, 1795. In 1804 William relocated to New York City, where he learned the business of soap manufacture. In 1806 he opened his own starch, soap, and candle-making business in Manhattan. In 1820 he would later open a large factory across the Hudson River in Jersey City, New Jersey.

Brought up in a Christian home, William found himself feeling bereft of Christian nurture when he moved to New York, so he joined a Bible study associated with the Presbyterian Church. He soon became uncomfortable with the Presbyterian practice of infant baptism because he could find no reference to it in the Bible, and this prompted William and his future wife, Mary Gilbert, to join the First Baptist Church of New York City, which was located on Gold Street. They were baptized as members of that fellowship in February 1808. After their wedding on April 25, 1811, they transferred their membership later that year to the Oliver Street Baptist Church, located near the Bowery in lower New York City. Colgate's pastor there, Dr. W. W. Everts, summarized the character of William Colgate: "(1) Benevolence; (2) Devotion to parents; (3) Conviction concerning right observance of the Sabbath Day; (4) Belief in the Divine authority of the Bible; (5) Consecration of prayer; and (6) thorough Commitment to the church."[25]

William Colgate became a trustee of the New York Baptist Theological Seminary at its inception in April 1817. When this organization joined forces with the Hamilton Institution in 1823, Colgate transferred his allegiance to the new school, and its well-being became one of the causes closest to his heart.[26] The board of trustees at Hamilton constantly called upon Colgate for various forms of help:

> He was often asked to finance the buying of groceries for the boarding house, to advance money to pay for books, to canvas for funds in the New York City area, to obtain legacies left to the school, to assist in collecting taxes on certain lands

---

25. Shields T. Hardin, *The Colgate Story* (New York: Vantage Press, 1959), 36.
26. Ibid., 122.

owned by the university, to serve on numerous committees, to contribute to salaries of the professors, to help raise money to pay on the school debt, to contribute
to scholarships and endowments, and to serve on committees seeking ways to
finance the institution more advantageously, and to give advice on many other
important matters.[27]

As a result of his undisputed control over the soap and candle market
during the War of 1812, Colgate became quite wealthy, and as his
wealth grew, Colgate resolved to give one tenth of his income to
Christian causes. The first donation William Colgate made to the
Hamilton Literary and Theological Institution was for $210, but that
was only the beginning of what would later prove to be a series of
donations running into the millions of dollars given by himself and
the Colgate family through three successive generations.[28] In honor
of this leadership, benevolence, and generosity, the Hamilton Institution was renamed Colgate University in 1890.

After the first three years of holding classes in the third story of
the same brick building that housed Hamilton Academy, in 1822
the institution began to plan for the building of its own structure.
Under Daniel Hascall's tireless leadership, the building was ready for
occupancy in 1823. The building project came in over the budgeted
costs, and Hascall was forced to involve his own personal finances,
leaving him in debt more than $1,100 even a decade later.[29] Two
years after the completion of the new "stone academy," enrollment
in the Hamilton Institution jumped to fifty students. This prompted
Hascall and the executive committee to propose the construction
of a four-story structure, but the trustees proposed another idea.
They urged the purchase of a farm near Hamilton, where students
could work the land for the benefit of themselves and the institution.
Jonathan Olmstead and Seneca Burchard were set to work on this
project in February 1826, and in less than a month they purchased
the 123-acre farm of Samuel Payne and his wife for $2,000, less than
one half of its market value.[30] Hascall and a committee of six raised
funds and built a new structure on the Payne farm. The New York
City Baptist Seminary association raised $2,000 for this project, and
another $1,000 was raised through the efforts of Nicholas Brown
and Pastor Stephen Gano of Providence, Rhode Island. An additional

27. Ibid., 123.
28. Ibid., 122.
29. Williams, *History of Colgate University*, 26.
30. Ibid, 28..

$1,000 was borrowed at 7 percent interest. By May 28, 1827, the second new building, known as West Hall, was completed on the Payne farm site.[31]

Initially, the academic program at Hamilton lasted three years, with the first two years devoted to sacred languages and general studies. In 1829 this program was extended to four years, and then, in 1832, to six years. A typical student day in 1831 began at 5:00 a.m. with chapel and set times for private devotions, reading, and studying before breakfast (6:30 to 7:00 a.m.). A similar pattern was followed after breakfast, with the addition of "exercise by manual labor." More manual labor followed after dinner (the noontime meal) and then formal "studies and recitations" between 1:30 and 5:00 p.m.; the day continued with chapel, supper, private devotions, and study, and ended with sleep at 9:30 p.m.[32]

The academic program for each student consisted of several years of liberal arts studies followed by specialized studies in divinity. Establishing theological studies upon a solid liberal arts foundation was an innovative and forward-looking idea at a time when many pastors saw no need for an educational alliance between theology and the liberal arts. In 1832 there were more than a hundred students in the institution, and by 1834 the academic program extended to eight years. This consisted of two years in the academic department, four years in the literary department, and two years in the theological department.[33]

In 1839, the Hamilton Literary and Theological Institution made a radical change in its admissions policy. The trustees decided to admit students who did not "have the ministry in view."[34] This proposal originated among the friends of the Institution who thought the admission of nonministerial students would not do disservice to the original plan of training minsters. After long hours of discussion and deliberation at the trustees' meetings of June and August 1839, this admissions policy was approved over the one opposing vote of Professor Dr. Kendrick. He foresaw this step as a fundamental shift in the program that would ultimately shift its focus away from ministerial education. He further opined that the addition of non-ministerial students would impede the piety of the others. "Can your young

31. Ibid., 31.
32. Ibid., 50.
33. Eaton, "Historical Discourse," 45–46.
34. Ibid., quoting the resolution of the board of trustees, 50.

men," he asked, "preparing for the ministry, in the incipient state of their piety, before their religious habits are formed, become the companions of prayerless youth, to room and study and lodge with them for a term of years, and not be retarded in the cultivation of their Christian grace?"[35] The chronically empty treasury, in addition to the prospect of serving a larger student body, made the new enrollment policy attractive to the trustees. This decision was a significant turning point in the academic journey of the Hamilton Institution, which was now on its way to becoming a major university.

Prior to the Hamilton Institution receiving a charter to grant university degrees, a special arrangement with Columbia University stipulated that Hamilton graduates, when certified by the faculty, could also graduate with Columbia University degrees.[36] After several legislative rebuffs in their attempt to achieve a university charter from the state of New York, Hamilton was finally successful in 1846. A charter was granted under the name "Madison University," honoring the county in which the institution was located. It defined the purpose of Madison University as "promoting literature and science" and made no reference to the training of ministers. This meant that the hamlet of Hamilton now technically housed a theological institution, with its own charter, as well as Madison University, both of which operated under the direction and support of the New York Baptist Education Society.[37] In reality, these were simply two academic departments functioning under the same roof. The close alliance symbolized by the physical location of the divinity and liberal arts departments signaled an educational innovation that soon invited theological assessment of contemporary issues and would pave a prophetic path toward their resolution.[38]

---

35. Williams, *History of Colgate University*, 81.
36. Eaton, "Historical Discourse," 51.
37. Williams, *History of Colgate University*, 103–4.
38. William H. Brackney, *Congregation and Campus: North American Baptists in Higher Education* (Atlanta: Mercer University Press, 2008), 64–103, on the strategic importance of the blending of liberal arts and theological education.

2

The Removal Controversy

Located 121 miles northwest of the village of Hamilton, New York, the city of Rochester was bustling and thriving by 1850. It stood astride the Genesee River, which flowed north from the Pennsylvania border and emptied into Lake Ontario. As early as 1812, land speculators from Maryland, including Colonel Nathaniel Rochester, occupied the site near the falls that began about three miles below Lake Ontario. The population grew steadily until 1825, when the Erie Canal, which transversed New York State, connected Albany on the Hudson with Lake Erie and opened the way to destinations further west. The combination of the water power from the falling Genesee and the Erie Canal, with its broad access to markets, turned Rochester into an infant industrial giant. It soon became known as the "Flour City." For a time, it was a boom town with a somewhat transient population, many of whom stayed less than six months on their trek farther west.

During the 1830s and 1840s, religious fervor had come to Rochester through the revivals of Charles Finney (1792–1875). His "new measures" played a significant role in the Second Great Awakening in the American West, and they returned to this region with such frequency that western New York became known as "the burnt-over district" because the fires of religious reform burned so brightly and so frequently there.[1] Education was a significant part of the Second Great Awakening. From 1830 to 1861, 122 denominational colleges were founded throughout the American West as a result.

---

1. Whitney R. Cross, *The Burned-Over District: The Social and Intellectual History of Enthusiastic Religion in Western New York, 1800-1850* (Ithaca, NY: Cornell University Press, 1950).

By 1850 the population of Rochester had grown to exceed thirty-six thousand, many of whom were transplants from New England.[2] The population was further augmented by the arrival of immigrants from England and Germany, as well as by African Americans from Maryland and Pennsylvania, many of whom may have arrived in Rochester via the Underground Railroad which was very active in the region.[3] The religious identification of citizens varied and became further stratified through the impulses of revivalism. No fewer than twenty-eight churches coexisted in the city as this time; Roman Catholicism claimed the largest number of adherents, closely followed by the Presbyterians who, with eight churches, were the largest Protestant denomination. They were also the most prosperous and prestigious group at that time. The Presbyterians were closely followed by the Baptists, Methodists, and Episcopalians in numerical predominance. Religious growth continued, and by 1855 there were more than fifty established churches in town.[4] While religious strife impeded the growth of some congregations and led to divisions within the various religious communities, the Baptists escaped doctrinal controversy. The First Baptist Church prided itself in its Sabbath school and other educational endeavors, while the Second Baptist Church adopted a reformist posture and was the first church in Rochester to welcome African Americans to nonsegregated Sunday worship.[5]

Writing thirty years later, in 1880, Rochester newspaper publisher Henry Alvah Strong reflected upon the sentiments of this period by noting, "All denominations of Christians had long felt that, owing to our favored location and surroundings, a college of some sort ought to be founded in Rochester."[6] The first attempt at building a college in Rochester stemmed from a Presbyterian group of ministers and laity who came together to discuss establishing a college to train Presbyterian ministers and laymen. The group took their plans so seriously that they applied to the New York legislature for a charter to found the University of Rochester and were granted a temporary charter for

---

2. Blake McKelvey, *Rochester on the Genesee: The Growth of a City* (Syracuse, NY: Syracuse University Press, 1973), 43.
3. Frederick Douglass, a former slave turned abolitionist spokesman, was a resident of Rochester at this time and published his abolitionist newspaper, *The North Star* (1847-1848), there. Harriet Tubman (1822-1913), known as "the Moses of her people," lived in nearby Auburn. Elizabeth Cady Stanton (1815-1907), an ardent abolitionist and staunch advocate for the full equality of women, took up residence in Seneca Falls. The Seneca Falls Women's Rights Convention (July 19-20, 1848), which met "to discuss the social and religious condition and rights of women," was the direct result of the efforts of Elizabeth Cady Stanton, Lucretia Mott, and several others.
4. McKelvey, *Rochester on the Genesee*, 67.
5. Ibid., 57.
6. Jesse Rosenberger, *Rochester and Colgate: The Historical Backgrounds of Two Universities* (Chicago: University of Chicago Press, 1925), 21.

a nondenominational school in 1846. Their plans, however, did not come to fruition, due in part to denominational wrangling among the Protestants of the city. The Baptists of Rochester, represented by Pharcellus Church, pastor of the large First Baptist Church, were alienated by what they deemed to be the Presbyterian control and aims of the college.[7] This adventure, however, sparked an interest in Church and others for a Baptist-sponsored college in Rochester.

Meanwhile, things seemed to steam ahead quite well at Madison University, in the village of Hamilton. By 1846 the enrollment swelled to 146 students, the vast majority of whom intended to pursue parish ministry at home or missionary work abroad. The small but vital faculty were close-knit and highly devoted to their cause. They met frequently to discuss the business of the college, for academic conversation, and for worship at the local Baptist church. Beneath the surface of pastoral tranquility, however, there lurked dissatisfaction. Hamilton, with a population of roughly fifteen hundred in 1847,[8] was not easily accessible by rail or water, and it lacked many of the conveniences that larger cities could provide: for example, libraries, museums, music halls, theaters, and public lectures, as well as a sizable professional class of educated men and women with whom the Madison University faculty and students might fellowship. One Madison professor, John H. Raymond, gave voice to these sentiments when he wrote that he "had a depression of feeling from the extreme loneliness and inactivity of our secluded place."[9] He soon proposed moving Madison University to a more populous location. There was ample precedent for this sort of action; Brown University recently relocated, and Yale had moved twice prior to settling down in a thriving city.

In its short history, Madison University was chronically short of funds. The professors, who were dedicated and talented men, were drastically underpaid and often paid only sporadically. The Baptist Education Society and the Hamiltonians had failed to raise the endowment promised when the institution first started. In fact, the society carried a $20,000 debt on behalf of the university. In 1846 the university board in its "First Compact" agreed "to make earnest and extended efforts for the collection of an endowment sufficiently large, to exempt [the university] from the necessity of continued appeals to

7. Arthur May, *A History of the University of Rochester 1850-1962* (Rochester, NY: University of Rochester Press, 1977), 9.
8. Rosenberger, *Rochester and Colgate*, 23.
9. May, *University of Rochester*, 10.

the Churches, but never so increased as to foster inaction in the Faculty, or independence of the Churches."[10] They set the goal of raising $50,000, one half of which would be used to pay the professors' salaries, with the remaining amount going into the general fund. But a full year later almost no progress had been made on this goal and the financial crisis continued. This was when considerations about moving the university to a more populous area began.

Other tensions began to emerge as well. Relations between the university faculty and the local Baptist church were strained. After changing pastors several times in the 1840s, the Hamilton Baptist Church called revivalist Jacob Knapp to become pastor, and the congregation grew significantly under his leadership. Knapp proclaimed a "free gospel" that ran counter to the staunch Calvinism advocated by the faculty of the institution.[11] There was also a conservative contingent in the church that reacted negatively to what they viewed as the liberal social tendencies of the university faculty. In 1845 several of the faculty and a few others withdrew from the village church to form the Seminary Church on the Hill. A particular point of contention was the social life of some of the faculty, about whom unfriendly rumors had circulated even to the northern parts of the state. Kendrick received communications stating that it was difficult to raise funds for the university because there was an impression that the professors lacked personal piety and that their wives "pattern too much after the vain and fashionable [styles] of the world."[12] This ecclesiastical schism contributed to the removal controversy insofar as it undermined the Christian unity and cohesion of the Hamilton community. But Professor John S. Maginnis, who held the chair of biblical theology at the seminary, was at the storm center of these controversies.

Advocacy for removal found sympathetic ears among the trustees of Madison University, notably John N. Wilder of Albany and Pharcellus Church of Rochester. Wilder was a wealthy merchant in his early thirties and a staunch supporter of the university. His interest and commitment stemmed, in part, from the fact that he lacked a college education and, therefore, keenly felt the importance of having an education. Wilder wrote,

10. Howard D. Williams, *A History of Colgate University* (New York: Van Nostrand Reinhold, 1969), 110.
11. Jesse Rosenberger, *Rochester: The Making of a University* (Rochester, NY: University of Rochester Press, 1927), 4–5.
12. Williams, *History of Colgate University*, 110.

Rochester we advocate as the center of a large, wealthy and intelligent population numbering 5 or 600,000 without any local college excepting the little affair at Geneva, as having a population itself ¾ as large as the whole of Madison Co., as easy of access via the lakes from Vermont, the Canadas, and the northern part of our own state, by lake and R.R. From the Western states and the North River, and by Erie R.R. from the southern tier of counties, the [Baptist] denomination in its vicinity probably better off than in any other part of the state and decidedly favorable to education.[13]

Church had long advocated for a university in Rochester and was bitterly disappointed when previous plans had come to naught.

These subterranean tensions came abruptly to the surface in 1847, when it came time for the education society to formally approve and appoint the theological faculty under the new charter. Knapp and others saw this as an opportunity to remove the troublesome John Maginnis, who "had aroused their enmity by his intellectual approach to religion and his uncompromising Calvinism."[14] Knapp had also not forgotten that Maginnis was his chief critic in an inter-church quarrel a few years earlier. Only thirteen of the thirty-one society members were present for this crucial meeting, and these were most likely dominated by the local residents of Hamilton. Professors Conant and Eaton were both unanimously approved for continuing with the school, but only four votes were cast in support of Professor Maginnis. Seven trustees nominated William R. Williams of New York City to replace Maginnis, and two other trustees abstained. This was, in effect, a dismissal of Maginnis, and most likely it was carried out with the intention to restore the harmony that previously existed between the university and the village church.[15]

A special meeting of both boards (trustees of the university and the educational society) was called for September 1, 1847, to iron out the difficulties caused by the previous session. Trustee Elisha Tucker, who was a member of both boards, wrote to Dr. Kendrick expressing his disapproval of the previous action, which he argued would deprive the institution of friends and funds it could not spare. Dr. Williams also emerged as a strong supporter of Maginnis. The tumultuous meetings lasted two full days. In the end, the earlier vote of the board of the education society was deemed illegal because Professor Maginnis was already approved and voted tenure at the June 9,

13. May, *University of Rochester*, 12.
14. Williams, *History of Colgate University*, 107.
15. Ibid., 107–8.

1847, meeting of the board of trustees. A resolution "expressing their undiminished confidence in the ability & competence & diligence of Prof. Maginnis, and their solicitude to retain for this Institution the benefit of his experience, influence, and high endowments" was passed.[16] Those who voted earlier not to continue Maginnis withdrew their rejection, and the broader and more inclusive views of non-resident trustees like John Wilder predominated.

Soon after this stormy meeting, Tucker traveled to Rochester, where he was pastor of the Second Baptist Church, to report these developments to Church, who was a university trustee, an alumni of the institution, and a strong advocate for starting a university in Rochester. Wilder, and Maginnis and Conant, soon arrived in Rochester and agreed with Tucker and Church that relocating the institution to that city was a good idea. This informal meeting bore such fruit that a second meeting was planned for September 12, 1847, at the First Baptist Church of Rochester.

At the September 12 meeting, it was resolved that the financial embarrassment of the university and its "out of the way" location suggested that relocation of Madison University was necessary. Hence, when Church stated "that it is regarded as the sense of this meeting that Madison University be removed to Rochester" there was no dissent. A committee of eight was appointed to canvass the churches of western New York for their opinion about the proposed removal. At a subsequent meeting on September 20, a resolution was passed to urge the board of Madison University to petition to the state legislature for permission to relocate to Rochester. It was further resolved that the Baptists of Rochester and Monroe County should raise $30,000 toward endowment for the new university. "Let not the idea of losing our investments in the buildings at Hamilton deter you," the Rochesterians (not all of whom were from Rochester) wrote; "we shall gain ten dollars where we lose one."[17] The Removalists sent out a circular letter to the Baptists of the state in October, which outlined the reasons for relocation, the pressing need for endowment, and the advantages of the Rochester location.[18] It was published under the title *Circular to the Friends of Madison*

---

16. Ibid., 109.
17. Augustus H. Strong, *Historical Discourse Delivered as a part of the exercises in connection with the celebration of the Fiftieth Anniversary of the Rochester Theological Seminary* (Rochester, NY: E. B. Andrews, 1900), 8.
18. Strong suggested that a goodly portion of the Removalists were from Hamilton and were weary of living there (*Historical Discourse*, 8), but Williams suggests that the circular letter was "probably written by Dr. Church" (*History of Colgate University*, 112).

University. Writing fifty years later, Augustus Strong reported, "As we read their address we cannot fail to be impressed by the zeal and enthusiasm of those who signed it, and by their evident sense of a divine mission. It rang through the State like a trumpet call."[19] By late October the news of a possible relocation of Madison University began to appear in the newspapers of Utica, Syracuse, Auburn, and Rochester, as well as *The Baptist Register* of Utica and *The New York Recorder*, a Baptist organ in New York City.[20]

Initially, a stunned silence emanated from Hamilton on the topic of relocating Madison University. By November 25, 1847, however, the Hamiltonians held a public meeting to discuss the matter and a committee was appointed to study the reasons for and against removal. A few days later, an article by a concerned citizen appeared in the Hamilton *Democrat Reflector* newspaper that pointed out how deeply the removal of Madison University would injure all members of the community.

Professor George Eaton soon emerged as a staunch and articulate opponent to removal. In his subsequent "Historical Discourse," written in 1869 after he had become president of Madison University, Eaton acknowledged that there were honest and sincere motives on both sides of the "Removal Controversy," but "removal was resisted mainly on the following grounds; (1) it was unnecessary; (2) inexpedient; (3) perilous; (4) wrong; and (5) sacrilegious. Every one of these grounds became a conviction in the minds of the opponents of removal, intense and absorbing as their mental and moral nature admitted of. They believed and therefore spoke and acted."[21]

By January 11, 1847, Eaton had published a *Candid Appeal* against removal, and it became the chief topic of conversation at the meeting of the Western New York Baptists in Wyoming, New York. Church replied to the treatise in the lengthy and sharply written *Address to the Baptist Churches of the State of New York*. These publications both expanded and sharpened the dispute, and a war of words ensued. Several faculty memebers wrote letters and columns either supporting or condeming removal of the university that were carried in the *Reflector*, *The Baptist Register*, and *The New York Recorder*;

19. Strong, *Historical Discourse*, 8.
20. Williams, *History of Colgate University*, 112–13.
21. George W. Eaton, "Historical Discourse," in B. F. Bronson, ed., *The First Half Century of Madison University (1819–1869) or, The Jubilee Volume Containing Sketches of Eleven Hundred Living and Deceased Alumni with Fifteen Portraits of Founders, Presidents, and Patrons. Also The Exercises of the Semi-Centennial Anniversary* (New York: Sheldon and Co., 1872), 65–66.

this had the effect of making the disupte very public.[22] Both factions sent representatives to New York City to meet with and attempt to gain support from William Colgate and other prominent friends of Madison University. Initially, Colgate took no position, but he eventually threw in his lot with Eaton and those who opposed removal.

Several leading Baptists of Albany sided with John Wilder and the others who opted for the removal of Madison University. Among these were Ira Harris, judge of the state supreme court, Friend Humphrey, mayor of Albany, Bartholomew Welch, pastor of Pearl Street Baptist Church, and Smith Sheldon, all of whom were trustees of the univerisity. Because of their knowledge of and connections to the state government, these trustees were able to sponsor a bill in the legislature, authorizing removal in February 1848. Faculty and trustees lined up as lobbyists and spokesmen for both sides of the issue. When it was discovered that the whole board had not been officially consulted, the bill stalled and a compromise was worked out, in which it was stated that the university could relocate only if the promised endowment of $50,000 had not been raised by August 1848. This compromise was accepted, and the opponents of removal busied themselves in a strenuous fund-raising campaign throughout the summer of 1848.[23]

The agreed-upon funds were not raised, and the acrimonious debate contined on for another two years. Both sides canvassed the Baptist churches for support and thought they heard the voice of Providence in their plans. Over the course of three years, a small majority of the Baptist Education Society and the Madison trustees gradually decided in favor of removal, providing the various financial and legal obstacles could be. This proved to be a difficult matter, however, because the Hamiltonians had applied to the state supreme court for an injunction against removal, and a temporary injunction was granted on January 23, 1849. Later the next year, a permanent injunction against removal was granted.[24]

A statewide meeting of Baptists, held in Albany in October 1849, met for the purpose of proceeding with the plan to establish a new university and theological seminary in Rochester. In December 1849

22. George W. Eaton, "History of the 'Removal Controversy,'" in Bronson, The First Half Century, 53–79.
23. Williams, History of Colgate University, 118–21.
24. May, University of Rochester, 12–13.

a committee of nine met at the First Baptist Church of Rochester to craft a plan for facilitating the institution's relocation to Rochester. After conferring with the Regents of the State of New York, this group was granted a provisional charter, and at a meeting at Second Baptist Church on May 11, 1850, a new education society, the New York Baptist Union for Ministeral Education, was formed as well as and along with the University of Rochester and Rochester Theological Seminary. Like the Hamilton institution before them, the sister schools of Rochester maintained a close alliance between the liberal arts and theological education, albeit in distinct institutions, and each maintained a "unique Baptist identity."[25] The Baptist Union made its mission quite clear: "The object shall be to furnish means of instruction to such young men of the Baptist denomination as shall give satisfactory evidence to the Churches of which they are members, and to the trustees of the Society, of their personal piety, and their call to the Gospel Ministry."[26] This meant that the Baptists of New York State were responsible for two education societies, two universities, and two theological seminaries.

The two Rochester schools, though founded by Baptists for Baptists, would not be narrowly sectarian and would be sister institutions, each maintaining a separate identity.[27] They would be, in the words of Augustus Strong, "twins, —they came into the world together. They were not Siamese twins, organically and inseparably united."[28] Both schools were launched in November 1850, in the building formerly occupied by the old United States Hotel on Buffalo Street in Rochester.[29] The university had sixty students and the theological school had twenty-five.[30] The Regents were informed that at least $130,000 would be raised as start-up funds, and three-quarters of that amount would be placed in a permanent endowment for the new school. A list of prominent New Yorkers was submitted as trustees, who would subsequently appoint a president and professors and confer academic degrees upon graduates of university and seminary. A provisional charter was granted on January 31, 1850,

---

25. William H. Brackney, *Congregation and Campus: North American Baptists in Higher Education* (Atlanta: Mercer University Press, 2008), 198–202.
26. *The Thirtieth Annual Report of the New York Baptist Union for Ministerial Education: Proceedings of the Annual Meeting, Held at Rochester, May 19, 1881* (Rochester, NY: E. E. Andrews, 1881), 1.
27. Sally Dodgson, "Rochester Theological Seminary," *American Baptist Quarterly* 20, no. 2 (June 2001): 118.
28. Strong, *Historical Discourse*, 22.
29. McKelvey, *Rochester on the Genesee*, 60.
30. Rosenberger, *Rochester and Colgate*, 137.

and the Rochester group was given two years to raise the stipulated funds—or the charter would expire.[31]

The Rochester group began raising interest and funds in earnest. A fund-raising committee of six Baptists vowed to call upon "every Baptist in this great State" in support of the university, and accepted donations of money or merchandise. An editorial in the Rochester press urged financial support for the cause, suggesting, "For the honor of our city we ought to establish an institution that will compare with Yale and Cambridge and furnish in the coming generation her share of Poets, Orators, and Statesmen." John Wilder was joined by William Sage, a Brown graduate and the son of a Rochester shoe manufacturer, to write and publish *The Annunciator* from 1850 to 1851. It was chiefly an apologetic organ for the University of Rochester project, which rebutted the disputing claims still pouring forth from the imperiled Madison University, and urged, "Farmers, Educate Your Sons."[32]

Rochesterians like newpaper publisher Henry Alvah Strong joined Wilder and church deacon Oren Sage (1787–1866) in vigorous fundraising. There were many gifts and pledges, both small and large, which totaled $142,000. This amount was close enough to the financial goals and stipulations of the provisional charter, that the Regents were willing to issue, on February 14, 1851, a charter valid for five years. Within that five-year period, the founders were to accumulate at least $100,000 of actual endowment. When the conditions of that charter were not met in 1856, the trustees petitioned for and received a five-year extension on the charter on the grounds that successful instruction was going on and good progress with procuring funds continued. By January 10, 1861, the trustees disclosed assets valued at $190,000, only $53,000 of which was in investments, but the Regents accepted this report as fulfilling the conditions of the provisional charters and declared the university charter permanent.[33]

Initially, the University of Rochester was legally constituted as a body of trustees, without a president or faculty. Twelve of these men (and all of them at this time, unfortunately, were men) transferred from Madison University; the others were prominent men from across the state. Wilder, who led the board of trustees of the university and

---

31. May, *University of Rochester*, 13.
32. Ibid., 13–14.
33. May, *University of Rochester*, 15.

chaired the executive committee, relocated from Albany to Rochester to be more involved in university affairs. As chairman of the board, he often functioned as president of the university, though when offered that position, he refused, saying that his business interests precluded it. David R. Barton, Elon Huntington, Edwin Pancost, William N. Sage, and Elijah F. Smith—Rochesterians who had all donated $1,000 or more during the subscription campaign—also became trustees. These were men of Baptist piety, business accumen, and financial substance. Three other Rochesterians who were not Baptists were also added to the fold: Frederick Whittlesy and William Pitkin, who were Episcopalians, and Everard Peck, a Presbyterian.[34]

Among those faculty elected by the trustees at their first meeting were the nephew of Nathaniel Kendrick, Asahel C. Kendrick, professor of Greek; John F. Richardson, professor of Latin; and John H. Raymond, an early critic of the relocation to Rochester and professor of rhetoric. A native of New York City and graduate of Columbia University, Raymond was remembered as a man of "broad culture and good humor." He emerged as an ardent abolitionist who delivered numerous public addresses on the evils of slavery and in support of the "under-ground railroad" which was flourishing in Rochester at this time.[35] He also chafed under the crushing course load of the fledgling institution, and after five years in Rochester, Raymond relocated to Brooklyn, where he continued to be involved with new educational ventures. He subsequently became the second president of Vasser College for women and was chiefly responsible for the innovative academic curriculum established there.

Oren Sage served as chairman of the seminary board of trustees, and Henry Alvah Strong was treasurer. Both were Baptist deacons and men of deep piety, with great energy and commitment to the school. Augustus Strong remembered,

> Many a time in those early days the meeting of the Committee found bills accumulated, but no money in the treasury. The question stared the brethern in the face: "Shall we send away our students and close our doors?" Then Deacon Sage would say, "First, let us pray." All would kneel, while the Deacon poured out his soul in prayer and tears to God. Then, they would rise, and brother Sage would put his name to a note at the bank, and the money would be borrowed to carry the institution on.[36]

---

34. May, *University of Rochester*, 16-17.
35. Ibid., 19.
36. Strong, *Historical Discourse*, 20.

Alvah Strong, Augustus's beloved father, remembered as "not a profound thinker nor a skilled writer, nor a practiced speaker, nor a
master of social graces, . . . was a modest and honest man, careful of
the feelings of others, with great persistency of purpose, some inven-
tive and organizing ability, and the inflexible determination to use
what gifts he had for the glory of God and the good of the world."[37]

In his *Historical Discourse*,[38] written fifty years after the founding
of the Rochester institutions, President Augustus Strong (1836–1921)
supplied an apt conclusion for this section:

> So the University of Rochester and the Rochester Theological Seminary were, in the
> providence of God, launched for their voyage. The people of Hamilton predicted
> that these new institutions would soon suffer shipwreck, and the people of Roches-
> ter in their turn half expected to hear that Madison University had been destroyed
> by fire from heaven. Neither event has taken place. . . . We must recognize, with all
> this, the good hand of God which has gradually smoothed down the asperity of
> feeling, has made each institution a means of stimulus to the other, and has made
> the two . . . the means of accomplishing some things for the cause of education
> and for the Kingdom of Christ which neither one of them singly could have done.[39]

Turning to James 1:20, Strong concluded: "There was something of
wrath in our beginnings, and the 'wrath of man does not work the
rightouesness of God.' Yet this seems to be a case in which God has
made the wrath of man to praise him, while with the remainder of
wrath he has girded himself."[40] The birth of Rochester Theological
Seminary through the travail of the Removal Controversy did, in
time, "work the righteouness of God" as the prophetic vision that
was at the heart of the Madison Institution, a vision that was both
theologically sound and culturally relevant, was transplanted in the
far-reaching environment of Rochester without extinguishing it in
rural Hamilton, New York.

---

37. Ibid., 21.
38. Ibid.
39. Ibid., 16.
40. Ibid.

3

The Colgate Theological Seminary Story (1850-1920)

If those who exited Madison University and gave birth to the twin institutions in Rochester expected the Hamilton Institution to close, they were sorely mistaken. The Hamilton Institution struggled through three years of controversy because professors were frequently away on legal business and academic instruction, then seemed to take a back seat to the ensuing controversy. Despite these many difficulties, Madison University opened in the fall of 1850 with a full faculty and thirty-three students. The theological seminary teaching staff consisted of George W. Eaton and Edward Turney, with Eaton serving as professor of theology and Turney, who graduated from Madison Seminary in 1838, as professor of biblical criticism and interpretation. Professor Philetus Spear (1811–1901) stayed on as professor of Hebrew and Latin.[1] Eaton, Spear, and Turney also served on the faculty of the university, where they were joined by six others. As Eaton subsequently reported, "Every class was represented, from the senior theological down to the junior academic. The organization was unbroken throughout."[2]

The postremoval seminary faculty was soon joined by three seminary alumni: Alexander M. Beebee, Ezra S. Gallup, and Ebenezer Dodge. The most able and notable of the new hires, however, was Ebenezer Dodge, who came in 1853 as professor of biblical criticism and interpretation.

---

1. Colgate University Libraries Catalogue, http://deoacveritati.colgate.edu/early-faculty/.
2. George W. Eaton, "Historical Discourse," in B. F. Bronson, ed., *The First Half Century of Madison University (1819-1869) or, The Jubilee Volume Containing Sketches of Eleven Hundred Living and Deceased Alumni with Fifteen Portraits of Founders, Presidents, and Patrons. Also The Exercises of the Semi-Centennial Anniversary* (New York: Sheldon and Co., 1872), 80.

Ebenezer Dodge was born on April 22, 1819, in Salem, Massachusetts. He earned a bachelor's degree from Brown University in 1840, studied at Newton Theological Institution, and was ordained in Salem on September 3, 1845. He earned a doctorate of divinity from Brown in 1861 and a doctor of laws degree from the University of Chicago in 1869. He was the author of several important books, including *Evidences of Christianity* (1869, 1876) and *Lectures on Christian Theology* (1875, 1883). Dodge was a longtime professor and administrator at Madison University. He served as professor of biblical criticism and interpretation from 1854 to 1861, professor of Christian theology from 1861 to 1890, and president of the university from 1868 until his death in 1890.[3]

In the fall of 1851, Dr. Stephen W. Taylor left Lewisburg University (now Bucknell) to become president of Madison. Eaton remembered Taylor quite well: "He brought with him great strength and popularity. . . . His reputation as an educator and a disciplinarian was second to that of no other—he had for years previously been connected with the Institution, and knew minutely all its history."[4] During the first year of Taylor's leadership, Madison University's enrollment grew from 33 to 84, and the endowment swelled to over $60,000. Within the next three years, enrollment reached 216 students. Madison University was, by 1854, larger than it had been prior to the "removal agitation."[5] The institution not only revived but also grew and thrived.[6] Eaton recalled, "In four years after the session to Rochester, the University and Theological Seminary were stronger in men and means than for many years previous to the conflict."[7]

Taylor sometimes came into conflict with Turney over the governance of the seminary; the substance of the matter was that Turney and the seminary faculty had become accustomed to a significant degree of independence from the governance structures of the university, and Taylor viewed both schools as functioning under his authority. The Education Society board passed a resolution that gave the seminary a degree of independence but placed most governing authority of the seminary in the hands of the university board and president. Turney subsequently left the institution in the fall of 1853. After a

3. Colgate University Libraries Catalogue, http://deoacveritati.colgate.edu/early-faculty/.
4. Eaton, "Historical Discourse," 80.
5. Ibid.
6. Ibid.
7. Ibid., 81.

brief though painful illness due to a fall, Taylor died on January 7, 1856. Eaton eulogized him by writing, "In short, Dr. Taylor was the synonym of massive and unadorned mental power. His character was a Doric pillar of marble for solidity and simplicity."[8] After much prayer and prodding, Eaton accepted the board's invitation and, in August 1856, became the third president of Madison University.

George Washington Eaton was born on July 3, 1804, in Huntington, Pennsylvania. He received his bachelor of arts degree in 1829 from Union College, his doctorate of divinity in 1844, and his doctor of laws degree from Union University, Tennessee, in 1861. He had a long and distinguished career at Madison University, where he held virtually every academic chair in the seminary at one time or another. He was president of the seminary at Madison University from 1861 to 1871 and professor emeritus of practical theology from 1871 to 1872. Eaton also served as president of the university from 1856 to 1868.[9]

The stress of the office wore on President Eaton significantly. While he is not remembered as a strong leader, Eaton helped the university navigate the troubled waters of the American Civil War and significantly increased the circle of Madison University's friends through the "social leadership" provided by him and his wife.[10] He offered his resignation to the university board in July 1865, which was reluctantly accepted with the provision that he would stay in office until a suitable successor could be selected. When the board failed to induce three successive candidates to accept the office, Eaton continued on as president until August 1868, when Professor Ebenezer Dodge was called to the post.

During this period, the Madison University and Seminary also gained financial ground. Following the death of William Colgate in 1857, his son Samuel, who had worked in the thriving family soap and candle business since 1838, took over operations. Both Samuel and his brother, James B. Colgate (1818–1904), were staunch supporters of Madison University. In 1865, for example, James and his business partner, John B. Trevor, gave $70,000: $40,000 was designated for scholarships for Civil War veterans, and the remaining $30,000 was placed at the discretion of the president for the operation of the

8. Ibid., 100.
9. Colgate University Libraries Catalogue, http://deoacveritati.colgate.edu/early-faculty/.
10. Howard D. Williams, *A History of Colgate University* (New York: Van Nostrand Reinhold, 1969), 147–48.

university. The next year, the brothers gave an additional $10,000 for campus improvements.[11] Shields Hardin reported that James Colgate, "like his father before him, was the personification of honesty in its very highest sense. He was a humble man, and he looked with great disfavor upon pride and self-exaltation." James was an active member of the Oliver Street Baptist Church, and for more than thirty years he served on the board of trustees of Madison University, making sizable, annual contributions to the university.[12] By 1869 the endowment rose to more than $180,000, and Madison University experienced no indebtedness. Giving from Baptist churches through the Education Society also rose significantly from $1,000 in 1865 to more than $13,000 in 1869.[13]

Samuel Colgate was also active in the affairs of Madison University. He had been a trustee since 1857. His particular interest, however, was that of the seminary and its supporting organization, the Baptist Education Society of the State of New York, of which he served as president from 1861 to 1897.[14] Samuel, who entered the family business at the age of sixteen, was raised in Oliver Street Baptist Church in New York City. Following his marriage (March 30, 1853) to Elizabeth Ann Morse, Samuel and his wife moved to Orange, New Jersey, in 1857, where he initiated a new church planting. It began as a Sunday school led by Samuel Colgate himself. The North Orange Baptist Church was the result of these and other meetings, and Samuel served as Sunday school superintendent there for more than forty years. He also served intermittently as deacon and trustee of the church, as well as president of the board of trustees. "No task was too small," wrote Shields Hardin, "for this great soul to perform in the work of the church."[15] From its inception in 1857, the North Orange Church and Samuel Colgate made regular and substantial subscriptions in support of students at the seminary of Madison University.[16]

The years of Ebenezer Dodge's presidency, from 1869 to 1890, were years of growth and stability for Madison University. He became a particularly close friend of James B. Colgate, and the two worked as "yokefellows" in the leadership of the university. Through

---

11. Ibid., 150–51.
12. Shields T. Hardin, *The Colgate Story* (New York: Vantage Press, 1959), 93–94.
13. Williams, *A History of Colgate University*, 150–51.
14. Ibid., 176–77.
15. Hardin, *Colgate Story*, 165.
16. Ibid.

its friendship with the Colgate family and the generosity of many others, Madison University reached financial equilibrium. Dodge brought a pastoral style of leadership to his post and demonstrated both diligence and Christian compassion. He also had harmonious relationships with the faculty.

Under Dodge's leadership, campus buildings were renovated, and the campus grounds were given careful attention. Prior to the Dodge era, Professor Taylor reported the campus looked like "a third class farm" compared to other institutions. Initially, President Dodge and Treasurer Spear were averse to the idea of bringing in external consultants to make improvements, but they were gradually won over, and Taylor was appointed superintendent of buildings and grounds due to his advocacy. In the fall of 1883, James B. Colgate brought Frederick Law Olmstead, the designer of Central Park in New York City and Prospect Park in Brooklyn, to the Madison campus for suggestions about renovations and the location of proposed buildings and gardens.[17]

The university saw the construction of four new buildings during the Dodge era. The first of these was to house the Grammar School, which was a gift from James B. Colgate, named the Colgate Academy in his honor. The second edifice was the chemistry building, which went into use in 1885. Beginning in 1881, Professor Hezekiah Harvey began to urge for a separate seminary building. Eaton Hall, or "the angel factory," as it was sometimes called in those days, was dedicated in 1886. The last of these four additions was arguably the most impressive: the James B. Colgate Library. The Romanesque-American structure cost more than $140,000 and went into service in January 1891. The university faculty also grew significantly during the Dodge era. There were thirteen faculty members in 1869, and by 1890 it numbered twenty-two, six of whom were ministers. This growth in faculty was necessitated by rising enrollments, and it allowed for greater specialization among the teaching faculty. Thanks to endowments and matching gifts from James B. Colgate, faculty salaries were being paid on time and had risen significantly.[18]

Dodge, as one meets him in his published works, was a liberal-minded conservative. In the popular nomenclature of our day, he would be thought of as "a liberal-evangelical." He was pious and

17. Williams, *A History of Colgate University*, 180.
18. Ibid., 179–86.

steeped in the classical doctrines but unafraid of the new progressive overtures in biblical criticism and science. Writing and teaching during the opening decades of what would later be called the Fundamentalist-Modernist controversy, Dodge's work represented a moderating position in which conservative doctrines were affirmed in concert with progressive developments in science and religion. He wrote and taught theology in service of the church and in hopes of winning souls to faith. Hence, in his primer on Christian evidences and classical doctrines, he stated, "If this volume shall prove of any service to the youth of my country, and to the ministry of my Lord, I shall be amply rewarded."[19] His book *The Evidences of Christianity* (1869) was a full-scale introduction to Christian belief, written from the standpoint of one answering the challenges to faith mounted by the new intellectual developments of the late nineteenth century. In this text, Dodge affirmed the full authority of the New Testament documents[20] over and against contemporary theories that undermine it. He urged, "The New Testament has been transmitted to us in its essential integrity allows us no doubt whatsoever."[21]

At this time, Darwin's *Origin of the Species* (1859), which studied the role of evolution in science, generated tremendous interest in evolutionary theory and its pertinence to other fields like religion. Although Dodge's *Evidences* did not mention Darwin directly, it evidenced none of the antipathy between the Christian religion and science that characterized many theologically conservative works of the era. In Dodge's work, modern science was seen as supporting Christianity while also allowing intellectual room for the miraculous and supernatural, upon which classical Christianity depends. In an age open to intellectual agnosticism about the divinity of Jesus, Dodge urged, "Christianity is gathered and centered in the incarnation of the only Son of God. . . . With the truth of this assumption, Christianity stands or falls."[22] Hence, Christianity, as Dodge understood it, requires a belief in the miraculous and the supernatural, because, as he stated, "Jesus himself is the miracle of the ages."[23]

In his *Lectures on Theology* (1883), Dodge acknowledged that divine inspiration is a crucial element for properly understanding

---

19. Ebenezer Dodge, *The Evidences of Christianity and an Introduction on the Existence of God and the Immortality of the Soul* (Boston: Gould & Lincoln, 1869).
20. Ibid., 48–49.
21. Ibid., 70.
22. Ibid., 105.
23. Ibid.

the Christian Scriptures. He wrote, "Inspiration is both a divine im-
partation and a human reception; and these two interpenetrate each
other, and constitute the same mental state and movement, and make
up one and the same divinely human process. Thus we see that the
authorship in the Scriptures is a double one. The energizing Spirit
secures infallibility; and the soul, working according to its own laws,
secures intelligibility."[24] He considered the "dynamic theory" of biblical inspiration "preferable, because it calls attention to God's action on and in the human soul. Here the divine and human elements
blend together in inspired thought and expression as we find them
in the Word of God."[25] Dodge was a progressive evangelical theologian, and under his leadership the Colgate Theological Seminary
began to show evidences of liberal thinking alongside its evangelical
foundations.

The biblical studies faculty were a good example of this development. Dr. Sylvester Burnham, who was appointed to the seminary
faculty in 1875, offered a course on the Bible as the national literature of Israel, in comparison with that of other cultures in 1887.
Having studied in Germany after his graduation from Bowdoin College in 1802, Burnham learned and employed literary criticism in the
study of the Scriptures. He served as professor of Semitic languages
and Old Testament interpretation at Colgate University from 1875
to 1918 and authored several important books on interpreting the
Hebrew Scriptures, including *A Manual of Old Testament Interpretation* (1882) and *Elements of Biblical Hermeneutics* (1916).[26]
Known as a passionate and energetic teacher, a student remarked,
Burnham's "raven locks and beard, his large features, his vigor of
body, mind, and spirit, made him a veritable Elijah as he stood before
his classes."[27]

Walter Brooks, who joined the faculty in 1874, gave a series of
lectures on the relationship between religion and science from 1887
to1888. These lectures were so successful that Brooks's widow maintained funding for the series in his memory until 1900. Dr. Alexander
Winchell, an eminent geologist who was expelled from Vanderbilt
University for his liberal views, lectured at Colgate in 1889 and 1890.

---

24. Ebenezer Dodge, *Lectures in Theology* (Hamilton, NY: University Press Print, 1883), 97.
25. Ibid., 110.
26. Colgate University Libraries Catalogue, http://deoacveritati.colgate.edu/early-faculty/.
27. Ibid., 195.

His lectures, titled "The Place of Man in Creation" and "The The-istic Interpretation of Evolution" evidenced a liberal point of view.[28] Progressive thinking was also echoed in the Seminary Catalogue of 1885, which reported that the goal of its religious instruction "has been, not to impress a common stamp upon the minds of its students, but to secure the best development of individual power consecrated to Christ."[29]

These developments, along with Dodge's progressive and irenic spirit, may have caused some concern within the Baptist Education Society, because the trustees appointed a committee in 1888 to visit the seminary and its classes in order to make a report to the whole board. But no problems were identified, and the report was over-whelmingly positive. Hence, his friend and theological successor William Newton Clarke (1841–1912) recalled that Dodge was "swift in spirit, and cautious in step."[30] Dodge's style of leadership permitted wide academic freedom in class discussion and investigation, as well as patience for the various intellectual vacillations to which students are sometimes prone.

In 1889 Dodge began the process of changing the institution's name from Madison University to Colgate University. Following Dodge's sudden death in the spring of 1890, however, Madison of-ficially became Colgate University on May 26, 1890.[31] The name change from Madison to Colgate University and Seminary symbol-ized the significant changes in administrative structure, academic in-struction, curriculum, and the physical plant that were under way at both institutions: new academic structures, new faculty, new courses, a more innovative curriculum, and several new buildings all seemed to appear at the same time. Younger scholars who were experts in their fields were hired, and the curriculum was modernized.

Dodge's death in 1890 did not slow the engine of change at Col-gate University. His former student, William Newton Clarke, stepped into his seminary classes in systematic theology and ably filled the vacuum, eventually eclipsing his mentor as a prominent theolo-gian with an international reputation. But the passing of Ebenezer Dodge reminded the trustees how irreplaceable he was as president of the university. Two tension-producing issues loomed large in the

---

28. Williams, *A History of Colgate University*, 195.
29. Ibid.
30. Ibid., 196.
31. Ibid., 195-99.

institution's immediate future: the poorly defined relationship between the university and the Baptist Education Society, and the similarly ill-defined relationship between Colgate University and Colgate Theological Seminary.[32]

Of the developments following the passing of President Dodge, perhaps the most significant one was the establishment of the Dodge Memorial Fund by James B. Colgate. One half of the annual income of the Dodge Fund was to be paid to the trustees for the operation of the university, and the other half of the annual income was to be added to the principal; in this way the Dodge Memorial Fund increased both the operating funds of the two schools and their endowment.[33] James Colgate imposed no particular limitations upon the use of this income, stating that he was "confident that this University will continue to be in the true sense of the term, a Baptist University where the ruling purpose is to discover and teach truth in order that it may be fearlessly, yet reverently, followed wherever it may lead."[34] This statement had an ominous ring to it because it assumed, wrongly, that both the university and the seminary would continue their identity as distinctly Baptist institutions into the distant future.

When it was founded as the Hamilton Literary and Theological Institution, the educational philosophy of the institution was geared toward training educated Christian ministers (chiefly Baptists), as well as an educated and effective laity for the church. By the 1890s, however, it was clear that the educational goals of the university had changed and significantly broadened over the years. In an address given at the dedication of the new library in 1891, Samuel Colgate reflected this shift: "It always seems to me to be a lack of faith, rather than indication of reverence when people are afraid to have their beliefs examined in the broad light of day. A university should be a source of light. Where we make no boast yet we believe that the principles for which this university stands . . . need never fear the white light of keenest criticism."[35] In 1896 he further defined the chief aim of the college course as "culture," which Colgate understood to be "a passion for knowledge" combined with the ability to use knowledge intelligently. Hence, the educated person should be able "to reason rightly, to judge correctly, to perceive the beautiful and recognize the

32. Ibid., 218.
33. Ibid., 219.
34. Ibid.
35. Ibid., 225.

true."[36] While not antithetical to the earlier emphasis upon Baptist identity, these new aims did not clearly enunciate it either.

The modernist attitude toward the positive and noble effects of modern science and philosophy, which Colgate called "culture," along with the willingness to try to reconcile these developments with historical Christian teachings, was also reflected in the new, analytical approaches of younger professors on the faculty of the university and the seminary. The growing secularization of the university was a particular point of concern for the faculty of the theological seminary, who reminded their colleagues of the institution's original intent. The alumni, too, complained of a loss of "the old spirit" of former days when a greater percentage of the university's enrollment was comprised of ministerial students.[37] The connection between the university and the theological seminary, which was quite natural and fluid in the earlier days, seemed to be declining; in 1898, for example, only six Colgate University students entered the theological seminary upon graduation.[38]

Joining William Newton Clarke (who will be examined at length in the next chapter) as seminary faculty in the 1890s were David Estes, who began teaching New Testament in 1891 and became the university librarian in 1892. Arthur Jones succeeded Beebee in the instruction of homiletics in 1891. George Berry came in 1896 to teach Semitic languages, and in 1897 Edward Judson joined the faculty on a part-time basis while simultaneously pastoring the large Judson Memorial Baptist Church in New York City. During these years, a progressive attitude toward the modern higher criticism of the Bible, emanating from Europe, began to affect the outlook and methods of American theologians, including American Baptists. This began an intense conversation among them about the nature and proper methods for interpreting the Scriptures. These conversations occasionally led to heresy trials and dismissals as conservatives sought to protect denominational institutions from what they considered heretical and/or disreputable approaches to the Bible.

In 1891 the twenty-nine-year-old professor of Semitic literature and languages, Nathaniel Schmidt, became the lightning rod for these conversations at Colgate Theological Seminary. As he built

36. Ibid.
37. Ibid., 233.
38. Ibid.

a substantial academic reputation for his scholarly attainments in Scripture study and languages, it was also rumored that Schmidt denied the divine inspiration and inerrancy of the Bible. These were hallmark tenets of the faith among conservative Baptists and Fundamentalists.

Schmidt's position in a Northern Baptist theological seminary made his fidelity to those cardinal doctrines a paramount concern to the Baptist Education Society of New York. Through responding to questions from Samuel Colgate, president of the education society, Schmidt defended his views on the Bible as being in accordance with Baptist beliefs and the best modern methods. In his letter dated May 25, 1895, addressed to Samuel Colgate, Schmidt asserted that the issue at stake is not only the phraseology of one person's understanding of the authority of Scripture but rather "whether there is room in the Baptist denomination for a consistent application of scientific principles in the interpretation of the Bible and for progressive theology to which it invariably leads and what is the true conception of the duty of a theological professor in a Baptist seminary."[39]

Upon the explication of his colleague's views, Dean Burnham, who had himself studied in Germany and was no archenemy of the new biblical criticism, asserted that Schmidt's views were more consistent with Unitarianism than Baptist beliefs, and that he would resign if Schmidt remained on the faculty. These developments brought matters to a head at the June 1896 meeting of the university board and the education society trustees. A joint committee recommended that Nathaniel Schmidt be dismissed from the faculty due to his views, which tended "to weaken the confidence of young men in the Scriptures and to alienate the sympathy of our churches from the institution."[40] While the university board of trustees had already adjourned at this point, the education society's trustees unanimously approved the committee's recommendation to dismiss Schmidt.

Just as Samuel Colgate informed Schmidt of the trustees' action and advised him to look for another position, a chair in Semitic languages was established at nearby Cornell University. In September 1896, Schmidt resigned at Colgate Seminary to take the newly established position at Cornell.[41] Nathaniel Schmidt went on to have an

---

39. Ibid., 232.
40. Ibid.
41. Ibid., 233.

illustrious career at Cornell, leaving dissenion and division among the seminary faculty and, to a lesser degree, at Colgate University at large. Hinton Lloyd, executive secretary of the Baptist Education Society, reported that Schmidt "was sent away because he was a troubler of the peace."[42]

The journey of the Hamilton Literary and Theological Institution toward becoming first Madison University and then Colgate University and Theological Seminary, was one of growth, financial stability, and development. Herculean efforts of men like George Eaton, James Colgate, Ebenezer Dodge, and Samuel Colgate laid this solid foundation, and Hamilton-Madison became Colgate University. With stability and growth, there also came a gradual broadening of the faculty, curriculum, and the overall outlook of the school. While still affiliated with the Northern Baptist Convention, the school was discernibly moving away from a distinctively Baptist theological perspective and a corresponding openness to modern ideas about the alliance between historic Christianity and new developments in science, philosophy, and theology. On the eve of the controversy between Fundamentalist and Modernist perspectives about the nature of Christianity, Colgate's sympathies were with the progressives. The irenic spirit of Dodge and the progressive theology of William Newton Clarke exemplified this gradual theological transition from evangelicalism toward liberalism, just as the dismissal of Nathaniel Schmidt showed that Colgate University's progressive outlook also had its limits and there were boundaries that dared not be crossed.

---

42. Ibid.

4

William Newton Clarke: Prophet of Progressive Theology

William Newton Clarke (1841–1912), introduced in the last chapter as the successor of Ebenezer Dodge as professor of systematic theology at Colgate Theological Seminary, was, as Robert Handy described him, "the first American christocentric evangelical liberal theologian to write a major systematic work."[1] Up until this time, most Baptists in America embraced the older, so-called New England theology pioneered by Jonathan Edwards, which was a combination of Calvinism and revivalist impulses.[2] In Clarke's work, a wholesale change in the theological landscape is evident. He affirmed and embraced traditional Baptist beliefs but reinterpreted them in the light of new research methods of higher criticism and the evolutionary ethos of the day. In this sense, then, his work epitomized an important transition under way in American theology: the emergence of new modernist theology and evolutionary ethos from older, more traditional approaches. Clarke not only epitomized this transition but also was a great facilitator of it through his publications, lectures, and preaching.[3] Thus, William Brackney described him as "a pivotal figure not only in the Colgate tradition, but also among American theologians in general. . . . He was creative in his thinking. The first true 'liberal' among Baptist theologians."[4]

---

1. Robert T. Handy, "The Ecumenical Vision of William Newton Clarke," *Journal of Ecumenical Studies* 17, no. 2 (January 1980): 84.
2. See Frank Hugh Foster, *A Genetic History of the New England Theology* (New York: Russell & Russell, 1963).
3. Progressive theology had reached a general consensus by the time Clarke wrote his *An Outline of Christian Theology*. It included the following: "1. The acceptance of evolution. 2. The application of evolutionary method of study to historical investigation. 3. The acknowledgment of Biblical criticism in principle and in some results. 4. Various modifications of doctrine here and there." See Frank Hugh Foster, *The Modern Movement in American Theology* (New York: Books for Libraries, 1969), 144.
4. William H. Brackney, *A Genetic History of Baptist Thought* (Macon, GA: Mercer University Press, 2004), 305.

Clarke was an evangelical liberal who operated from the presuppositions of modern, progressive theology while affirming the traditional Christian doctrines and the centrality of the gospel of Jesus Christ. In its own day, this approach was called "progressive orthodoxy."[5] Clarke's modernism was signaled by his starting point, which was located in human experience, as he explained: "The theology of any age is largely an expression of the Christian experience of that age. The general experience of any given time, with its characteristic peculiarities, grows up into a style of thinking, a moral and spiritual consciousness, from which there is no escaping."[6] Claude L. Howe summarized Clarke's approach (as demonstrated in his *Outline of Theology*) in this manner:

> The immediate reception and appropriation of the basic tenets of Clarke's theological system by liberal theologians can easily be understood. He accepted without question both biblical criticism and theistic evolution, while the place of primacy he gave to Christian experience accorded with the liberal outlook. In fact, this theological system was basically a traditional orthodoxy, modified by new views of the Bible and the universe, and re-interpreted in the light of Christian experience.[7]

Clarke's willingness to theologize within the matrix of lived human experience signaled his commitment to the methods of theological liberalism just as his affirmation of "a basically traditional orthodoxy" that was "modified by new views of the Bible and the universe" evidenced that his was an evangelical liberalism that sought to enervate historical Christian verities with exciting new developments.

Clarke was born in Cazenovia, New York. He was raised in a devout Christian home, where he learned to love and study the Bible. He recalled, "My father, a minister of the gospel, was constantly in communion with the book . . . for him, and for my mother, the Bible was the last word."[8] His mother "carried the Bible in mind and heart. She was not always quoting it, but for guidance of her life, and ours, it was always with her."[9]

Clarke attended the Oneida Conference Seminary in Cazenovia, operated by the Methodist Episcopal Church, for his secondary education. William experienced evangelical conversion during one of the revivals that frequented campus, an experience he mentioned in a

5. James Tull, *Shapers of Baptist Thought* (Macon, GA: Mercer University Press, 1972), 156–58.
6. William Newton Clarke, *An Outline of Christian Theology* (New York: Charles Scribner's Sons, 1899), 19.
7. Claude L. Howe, "William Newton Clarke: Systematic Theologian of Theological Liberalism," *Foundations* 6, no. 2 (1963), 123.
8. William Newton Clarke, *Sixty Years with the Bible* (New York: Charles Scribner's Sons, 1909), 15.
9. Ibid.

retrospective letter: "I have sweet remembrance of the tender and beautiful religious revival that occurred in the spring of 1858, in my last term. My own religious experience then began, in meetings of the young men in the old western building."[10] This event brought with it thirst for new religious inquiry, and William wrote to his father to ask where he should begin reading his Bible in earnest. The elder Clarke recommended concerted study of the eighth chapter of Romans. He explained, "It is certain that from that day began the selection of my personal Bible. From day to day and from year to year I went on finding what in the Bible was precious to me, and making it my own."[11] This began what can only be termed a sixty-year love affair with the Bible, which Clarke chronicled, decade by decade, in his major autobiographical work, *Sixty Years with the Bible* (1909).

Clarke graduated from Madison University in 1863, while the American Civil War raged and the majority of Clarke's fellow graduates enlisted in the Union Army. William was unable to go to war due to his physical frailty caused by polio during his childhood. He enrolled in Hamilton Theological Seminary instead and answered the call to Christian service.

Clarke's theological development at what would become Colgate Theological Seminary revolved around the impact of two diverse but influential professors: Hezekiah Harvey in biblical studies and Ebenezer Dodge in systematic theology. William described Harvey as "a good scholar, though I do not know that he was an exceptionally great one. But I do know that he was a man of strong convictions, of a most beautiful devoutness, of absolute sincerity, and of perfectly unconquerable industry. . . . His Christian character held my love and admiration, his scholarship commanded my respect, and his industry was contagious."[12] More than his personality and scholarship, however, Harvey passed on to him a great love for the Bible and its message. As Clarke recalled, "His aim was to bring out the meaning of the Bible, and to train us in ability to do the same. For him the voice of the Bible was the voice of God, and therefore he bent his ear to listen. . . . No labor too great if he could understand the message."[13] The love and enthusiasm for the Bible with which Clarke was raised were met and extended through the influence of Harvey.

---

10. Ibid., 17.
11. Ibid., 24-25.
12. Ibid., 34.
13. Ibid., 35.

"His influence and example," Clarke later wrote, "made me a Bible student."[14] Hence, Clarke confessed, "I was a firm Biblicist."[15]

It was precisely his love and enthusiasm for the Bible that made Clarke somewhat suspicious of his professor of systematic theology, Ebenezer Dodge, who had just returned from a study leave in Europe. "My teacher in that department was a man of a different mould of mind from my teacher in the Bible," Clarke wrote. "He ranged more widely, he was more mystical in his vein, and he was more of a philosopher, thinking for himself and outreaching far and wide. One was searching in the Bible to discover the truth of God; the other was using truth that he had found there or anywhere else, in the broad expression of a reverently exploring spirit."[16] Dodge was, at this early stage of his personal development, objectionable to the young Clarke. "To this speculative work of the theologian I felt deep objection," Clarke declared, "because it was not biblical enough: it was not built on proof-texts, or buttressed by them, as I thought it ought to be: it was too speculative, I thought, and grounded everywhere than in the word of God. In this judgment I was sincere, but I was wrong."[17] Indeed, one of the genuine ironies of his history is that within thirty years Clarke not only succeeded Dodge as professor of systematic theology at the same seminary but also adopted his mentor's formerly objectionable approach to theology.[18]

Clarke's theory of biblical inspiration was not inherited from either Harvey or Dodge, though he had studied the current theories under their direction. His theory, rather, was a development flowing from his own heritage and thinking. Soon he moved beyond a belief in verbal inspiration or the dictation of the biblical text because he had too much experience in the various readings offered by textual criticism "with its uncertainty as to the very words, and constantly called my attention to the human element in the Scriptures."[19] Yet, at this point, Clarke reported, "I looked upon the Bible as so inspired by God that the writers were not capable of error. I did not feel myself at liberty to dissent from its teachings, to doubt the accuracy of its statements, or to question the validity of its reasonings. This was not

---

14. Ibid., 36.
15. Ibid., 40.
16. Ibid.
17. Ibid., 40–41.
18. Claude L. Howe, *The Theology of William Newton Clarke* (New York: Arno Press, 1980), 11.
19. Clarke, *Sixty Years with the Bible*, 42.

the result of a theory of the manner of inspiration: it was my working principle in the use of the Bible, inherited from earlier times."[20]

Such was the shape of Clarke's mind when he graduated from the seminary at Madison University in the summer of 1863. By the following January, his father preached his ordination sermon, and Clarke assumed the duties of the pastorate in Keene, New Hampshire. It was a time of fruitful learning, work, and study for him. This began more the twenty-five years of pastoral work that preceded his return to Madison University.

Sixty Years with the Bible reported a series of significant transitions which, over time, brought Clarke to a progressive view of the Bible, in which his allegiance was focused not so much upon the individual words of Scripture but upon its grand and enduring principles. He was asked to rebut the evolutionary philosophy of Hebert Spencer, which he did with all his might through a barrage of proof-texts. But Clarke was dissatisfied with his own approach: "Any great array of good texts it was not possible to find. Moreover, I found that . . . some other kind of refutation would be better suited to the case if refutation were proposed."[21]

A second jarring event emerged in this early pastorate of Clarke: his church was wracked by the chiliastic Millerite delusion in 1868, when "Father Miller" predicted Christ's return and the end of the world. After meeting Father Miller, Clarke sought to dissuade him from his biblical prognostications. "But all in vain," he wrote, "I saw him last about 1870. The date of hope had moved on, and the end was still coming soon."[22] These two events conspired in Clarke's own thinking to begin the process of his own gradual movement away from a literalist, proof-texting approach to the Scriptures. He wrote, "I was beginning to know . . . how much it means that the Bible is a genuinely historical book, having its rise and habitat in the human world, recording vital dealings between God and men, and to be understood in the light of its historical origins, intentions, and development. . . . It was thus becoming more intimately my own because it was more alive, and was more available for my use in the ministry of Jesus Christ."[23] Clarke's pastoral experience contributed as much or more to his new approach to the Bible than anything he read.

20. Ibid., 42–43.
21. Ibid., 57–58,
22. Ibid., 64–65.
23. Ibid., 68–69.

During this same period Clarke's thinking about the kingdom of God began to undergo reexamination and change. A conversation, conference, and subsequent intensive study of both the premillennial and postmillennial views of the advent brought him to the conclusion that neither view was, in the strictest sense of the term, scriptural. This discovery pushed Clarke to continue his own intensive study of the Bible's teaching about the return of Christ, and he came to believe that the New Testament witness was one of a "disappointed expectation" of the soon-coming visible return of the Lord. It was a discovery that had far-reaching consequences for Clarke: "The discussion showed that upon one point at least the early Christians, including the apostles and writers of the New Testament, were mistaken—not only could be mistaken, but were."[24] This realization brought him to an important conclusion: "From all this it followed," Clarke recalled, "that I was not obliged to agree with these writers in all that they had written, or to look upon them as infallible guides. It did not follow, therefore I ought to throw the Bible away. . . . But it did follow that I was not required to accept all statements in the Bible as true and all views it contained as correct."[25]

During this period, Clarke studied *The Vicarious Sacrifice*, written by Horace Bushnell in support of the moral influence theory of the atonement. His wife, Emily Smith Clarke, reported that "the genius and personality of the author impressed him more than his teaching, yet Clarke could never afterward see the doctrine of the atonement in precisely the same light as before."[26] Thus, Clarke's study of *The Vicarious Sacrifice* engendered another important conclusion that was based upon his own analysis and spiritual reflection about the atonement. Clarke reported, "I now saw clearly in what region the question lay. It lay in the realm of ethics. The decisive fact is the character of God. . . . In this work [on the cross] he has acted out his real self. It was morally impossible for me to believe that he has done anything for our salvation that does not accord with and express his own character."[27] The interconnection he saw between soteriology and ethics became a liberating event for Clarke. After several months of personal study and reflection, Clarke produced a paper he then presented to a group of fellow ministers, titled "The

24. Ibid., 105.
25. Ibid.
26. Emily Clarke, ed., *William Newton Clarke: A Biography* (New York: Charles Scribner's Sons, 1916), 44–45.
27. Clarke, *Sixty Years with the Bible*, 114.

Saving Interposition of God." What was revolutionary and liberating in this inquiry, for Clarke, was not only the theological verities that he came to accept but also, perhaps more fundamentally, the freedom and excitement he found in the methodology he came to employ. He recalled: "I had entered upon freedom of inquiry, and a broad world was before me, which I was sure that I should find to be the world of God. And the Bible had become the instrument of my liberty."[28]

During the next decade, this liberation began to make itself felt in pronounced ways through Clarke's ministry. An example of this development includes his changed approach to the prevailing interpretation of Paul "as laying a heavy hand upon the activities of women."[29] For a long time, the Pauline prohibitions against women's leadership shaped his thinking and pastoral leadership. But, as Clarke writes, "gradually there was a dawning upon me the improbability of God's intending to govern our movements in America through Paul's directions to the church in Corinth two thousand years ago. The method did not seem like the reasonable God."[30] By the time Clarke reached his third parish, "all was changed. . . . The women were taking part in the meetings of the church, as many of them as wished to do so, with perfect freedom. They knew all about the arguments for reading Paul's prohibition as local and temporary . . . and so had no fear that they were sinning against the Scriptures."[31] Clarke reveled in the God-given gifts these women displayed as they found their ecclesial voice: "Some of them had fine gifts for speaking and something to say, and would have found some way to speak their minds if Paul himself had been there with all the weapons that he was supposed to carry."[32]

In a similar way, in the late 1880s Clarke said, "Higher criticism began to influence my thinking about the Bible."[33] In this pursuit, Clarke found, "The Bible was commended to me by its spiritual character as exceedingly precious, but it . . . claimed neither inerrancy nor perfection of any kind. It was simply itself, and asked for no privileges."[34] This approach both unified and Christianized Clarke's reading of the entire Bible. He explained, "I commend this experience of mine to the many Christians who have been led to suppose that the

---

28. Ibid., 123.
29. Ibid., 149.
30. Ibid., 153.
31. Ibid., 154.
32. Ibid.
33. Ibid., 173.
34. Ibid., 179.

higher criticism can be nothing else than a weapon of unbelief. For me it has made the Bible to be far more consistently a Christian book than it had ever been before, and has placed it in my hands more ready for all Christian use."[35]

In January 1890, Ebenezer Dodge, president of the university and professor of systematic theology at Colgate Theological Seminary, died suddenly. William Newton Clarke, then, was called upon to replace his beloved mentor in a class on systematic theology. Since the textbook his predecessor authored and used for the class was out of print, there was no clear way forward but for him to make his own. As he undertook this task, and in the light of his changing views on biblical inspiration and authority, Clarke hit upon his own systematic principle: "My own experience here was very simple. I found that the Bible set before me the historical and spiritual figure of Jesus Christ, and showed me the principle on which he taught us to live the true life of men: it showed me the Saviour, and the salvation. In this twofold vision I had the key to Christian theology. . . . I had the light which it was my privilege to hold up for illumination of the field."[36]

This discovery of the living experience of Christ and salvation caused Clarke to eschew "the ancient and familiar proof-texting method" and emphasize the great principles of the Bible beyond its particular words. It also focused his interpretive lens upon "a system of Christian theology [that] has God for its centre, the spirit of Jesus for its organizing principle, and congenial truth from within the Bible and from without for its material."[37] It was on this methodological foundation, then, that Clarke constructed his epoch-making *An Outline of Christian Theology* (1898). Clarke's *Outline* was a theological watershed; it was the first major American reconstruction of Christian theology from a modern, progressive perspective.[38]

Clarke's work focused upon a reinterpretation of six basic theological categories: God, humanity, sin, Christ, the Holy Spirit, the divine life in man, and the life to come. In these subsections, he discussed "central doctrine of the Christian faith in the light of modern knowledge, but quite cautiously, always striving to understand and follow the teachings of Jesus Christ."[39] Ironically, even as he charted

35. Ibid., 192.
36. Ibid., 199.
37. Ibid., 210.
38. William H. Allison, "William Newton Clarke," in *The Dictionary of American Biography* (New York: Charles Scribner, 1928), 4:164.
39. Handy, "Ecumenical Vision," 85.

his own progressive approach to Christian theology, several of his contemporaries who espoused more radical positions pointed to the "unconquerable conservativism" of Clarke's views.[40] Yet his mixture of progressive methodology and traditional Christian affirmations made Clarke an important transitional figure who could rightly be characterized as an "evangelical liberal."[41] He used liberal or progressive methodologies and assumptions to ascertain and affirm traditional, gospel-based theological verities. Thus, as historian Claude Howe concluded, "His theological system was basically a traditional orthodoxy, modified by his new views of the Bible and the universe, and reinterpreted in the light of Christian experience."[42]

Clarke's wife, Emily, reported that social and political matters were lifelong concerns for her husband. She wrote, "He was deeply interested in public affairs and his opinions on social and political questions were clear and decided and freely expressed. He was in sympathy with efforts for the removal of unjust and injurious conditions and worked throughout his life for the uplifting of humanity."[43] Hence, Clarke began to emerge as a significant social theologian when other progressive theologians, like Albert Schweitzer, were going on a *Quest for the Historical Jesus* (1909). Merging Christology with social concerns, Clarke addressed himself to the principles, vision, and social teachings of Jesus in *The Ideal of Jesus* (1911).

While at Rochester Theological Seminary Walter Rauschenbusch was making a similar discovery, Clarke came to see the kingdom of God (or the "reign of God") "as the embodiment of the ideal of Jesus."[44] The kingdom of God became the basis for Clarke's social theology, a theology that found its basis in the teachings and example of Jesus. As he wrote, "The kingdom of God is a reign of mutual service and help, with our unselfish devotion to others for its impelling power."[45] Or again, "Whatever graces may be gathered into it, the kingdom of God and the ideal of Jesus, is a reign of unselfish service, seeking all good for all."[46]

Refusing to accept the false dichotomy drawn by some of his contemporaries in distinguishing the work of the of the kingdom of God

---

40. Frank Hugh Foster, *The Modern Movement in American Theology* (New York: Fleming H. Revell, 1939), 149.
41. Handy, "Ecumenical Vision," 85.
42. Howe, "William Newton Clarke," 123.
43. Emily Clarke, *William Newton Clarke*, ii.
44. William Newton Clarke, *The Ideal of Jesus* (New York: Charles Scribner's Sons, 1911), 71.
45. Ibid.
46. Ibid., 90.

(choosing to "save souls or save society"), Clarke saw the kingdom of God as being both personal and social, but he believed that "the kingdom of God has to be a kingdom of individual renewal before it can be a kingdom of social power."[47] Jesus' values and teachings, such as the Golden Rule and the value of human life, combine to raise realization among people of faith about the vast and oppressive presence of social sin all around us.[48] This, in Clarke's view, brings us back to the heart and soul of Jesus' teaching: "The further we go into the teaching of Jesus, the more does the great social question open about us on every side. Plainer and plainer it grows that his ideal was a social idea. We may enter the kingdom of God by the individual door, but the kingdom itself is a social realm."[49] For it to be prophetic, relevant, powerful, and revolutionary, Christianity must be both personally appropriated and socially embodied. As Clarke wrote, "Christianity is revolutionary in power and revolutionary in purpose. It is in the world to make its assault upon the evils that prey upon the human race, and put in their place the fulfillment of the ideal of Jesus. And if this is to be done at all it must be done in the large. Society is the field of Christianity."[50]

William Newton Clarke's health had never been robust, and following a series of falls beginning in 1883 that left him increasingly infirm, he resigned his professorship at Colgate Theological Seminary in 1908. He died suddenly, four years later, at his winter home in Deland, Florida, on the forty-eighth anniversary of his ordination. He left a lasting and prophetic legacy, however, in this many books and lectureships that espoused a theology that was both evangelical and progressive, one that was squarely focused on Jesus' ideals for personal renewal and profound social change.[51]

Clarke's many contributions also signaled that an important transition had occurred in "the Colgate tradition." As William Brackney reported, "Colgate was known in its earlier period for training pastors and missionaries. Over time it developed a reputation as a center for the emerging New Theology under the long-term influence of William Newton Clarke. Till later, the Colgate School became synonymous with the liberal tradition in American theology."[52]

---

47. Ibid., 92.
48. Ibid., 225.
49. Ibid., 204.
50. Ibid., 305.
51. For further exploration of William Newton Clarke's theology, see Brackney, *Genetic History*, 305–12.
52. Ibid., 293.

5

Rochester Theological Seminary: The First Twenty Years

Rochester in 1850 was a bustling place, poised on the edge of fulfilling the great economic and social promise of its advantageous geographic location. Writing about this era, Blake McKelvey reported,

> The early 1850s brought to fruition many of Rochester's early aspirations and opened new vistas. The measure of achievement experienced in several fields matched the fullness of years enjoyed by the scattered pioneers who remained. Fresh ventures interested their sons, some already in the prime of life, who shared with able newcomers the direction of the city's economic, civic and cultural affairs, while vigorous younger men [and women] were rising to positions of influence. The influx of newcomers from abroad who brought new cultural patterns foreshadowed the transformation of the Yankee city into a more cosmopolitan community.[1]

Economically, the city had not yet arrived at its full potential. The enlargement of the western section of the Erie Canal progressed haltingly toward Buffalo, and the extension of the valley canal gave Oswego and other cities on Lake Ontario greater advantages as shipping centers. Even the completion of the Rochester and Lake Ontario Railroad in 1853 did not bring the anticipated economic results, and the cholera epidemic of 1852 painfully pointed out the city's shortcomings with respect to sewage, sanitary conditions, and public health.[2]

The addition of a dozen new churches brought their number to fifty by 1855.[3] With new religious fervor and growth came the danger of divisiveness and schism, but the Rochesterians were relatively free from these. There was some friction among the Presbyterians

1. Blake McKelvey, *Rochester on the Genesee* (Syracuse, NY: Syracuse University Press, 1973), 62-63.
2. Ibid., 62-63, 66.
3. Ibid., 67.

between the "Old Lights" and "New Lights" of revivalism, and a new "Old School Synod" was formed in the Rochester area. The Presbyterians were still viewed as leaders among the Protestants, but the Baptists also grew in numbers and prestige through their association with the new University of Rochester and Rochester Theological Seminary (RTS). These two institutions began their function in the refurbished American Hotel on Buffalo (later West Main) Street. While they shared many things in common, including their inception, their building, and several of the same professors, the two Rochester institutions were, as Augustus Strong recalled, "twins, but not Siamese twins."[4] In this, the Rochester institutions differed from those in Hamilton; as Sally Dodgson wrote, "Although birthed by Baptists, the [Rochester] schools would not be narrowly sectarian in approach and although the two would be sister institutions, they would maintain separate corporate identities."[5]

Classes for the University of Rochester and Rochester Theological Seminary started on the first Monday in November 1850. There were sixty-six students in the university and twenty-four in the seminary.[6] The schools began with a coachload of professors who had relocated from rural Hamilton, as had many of their incoming students. The first seminary graduating class of 1851 was comprised of six students: Joseph Bailey, Erastus Burr, Peter Irving, Charles Keyser, Henry Richardson, and William Sawyer, three of whom had come from Hamilton.[7] The teaching staff of RTS consisted of John Maginnis, professor of biblical and pastoral theology, and Thomas Jefferson Conant, professor of biblical criticism and interpretation. Strong stated that Maginnis "held tenaciously to the stiffest Princeton [Calvinistic] theology, and like Dr. Hodge declared it to be not only the doctrine of the Scripture but the doctrine of the Church of God."[8] Conant was a talented biblical linguist who translated Genesius's *Hebrew Grammar* into English, and through this and other works "he had made for himself already the reputation of being one of the greatest Hebrew scholars in America."[9] RTS was loosely organized, having no president or dean until 1868, and it was governed by the Baptist Education Society and the trustees and officers elected

4. Augustus H. Strong, *Historical Discourse* (Rochester, NY: Press of E. R. Andrews, 1900), 16.
5. Sally Dodgson, "Rochester Theological Seminary: 1850–1928," *American Baptist Quarterly* 20, no. 2 (June 2001): 118.
6. Strong, *Historical Discourse*, 23.
7. *Rochester Theological Seminary: General Catalogue: 1850–1910*, 11.
8. Ibid., 25.
9. Ibid.

by it.[10] When Maginnis died suddenly in 1852, he was replaced by Ezekiel G. Robinson in April 1853.

Born at Attleboro, Massachusetts, and educated at Brown, Ezekiel Gilman Robinson (1815–1894) graduated from Newton Theological Institution. After serving several pastorates, and a brief stay as professor of biblical interpretation at Western Theological Seminary, he assumed professorship of theology at RTS in the spring of 1853. Augustus Strong, who had studied under Robinson, remembered him vividly: "Our greatest man was Ezekiel G. Robinson. He did most to impress upon the Seminary a definite character. Commanding in figure and somewhat austere in manner, there was yet a heart within that chilling exterior."[11] Robinson stood out in Strong's recollection because of his ability and style as a teacher; "it was in the class-room that he most shone," he wrote. [12] Soon after he assumed the professorship at RTS, Robinson was pressed to fill the pulpit of the local Baptist church as well. Although this was a blessed burden, in terms of the additional workload, it provided a much-needed financial supplement to the sporadic salary he received from RTS.

In a day when pedagogy was made up largely of rote memorization and copying down notes from professor to student, Robinson used the Socratic question-and-answer approach. This was a drastic departure from the typical seminary classroom in which there was "no opportunity for question and free discussion." Augustus Strong reported approvingly, "He put himself side by side with his students as an inquirer; together they fought their way toward fixed convictions. This gave a freshness to his teaching. . . . He was more critical than constructive; his chief merit is that he taught his pupils to think for themselves; so he put life and reality into the ministry."[13] As he explained in his autobiography, "It has always seemed to me that no greater wrong could be done to theological students than to require them to accept without scrutiny any principle or sentiment avowed by their teacher. They should, on the contrary, be encouraged, with an humble reliance on Divine guidance, to inquire, think, and decide for themselves."[14] Robinson's emphasis upon the ability to analyze important ideas and to think for oneself became hallmarks of a RTS

10. Dodgson, "Rochester Theological Seminary," 119.
11. Strong, *Historical Discourse*, 25.
12. Ibid., 26.
13. Ibid.
14. E. H. Johnson, ed., *Ezekiel Gilman Robinson: An Autobiography: With a Supplement by H. L. Wayland and Critical Estimates* (New York: Silver, Burdett, and Co., 1896), 49.

theological education and a significant part of CRCDS's continuing legacy.

When he assumed the chair of theology at Rochester, Robinson found himself amid division within the churches and suspicions of heresy. He steered a course between these two dangers by stressing the centrality and unifying vitality of Christian experience. As he wrote in his memoirs, "The jealousies created by the abortive attempt to transfer the institution bodily from Hamilton to Rochester had divided the churches into two opposing camps. Even a suspicion of heterodoxy, it was feared, would be fatal to the Rochester interest. I accordingly prepared an address on the need of Christian experience to a right understanding of theological doctrine. . . . That enabled me to steer clear of both Scylla and Charybdis."[15] Since he had no predetermined "system of theology" in mind as he taught systematic theology, Robinson reported, "As I entered upon the special work of instruction in Systematic Theology, I was filled with constant solicitude as to how I was to teach the great doctrine of Christianity. . . . In all that was given, either in dictation or discussion, I was most distinctively and guardedly orthodox: but the question continually before us all was, not what is the orthodox of the sect, but what is the truth?"[16] Robinson's spirit of discovery and inquiry also shone forth as he directed his students to prepare sermons on each of the Christian doctrines they studied. As he reported, "In the absence of all provision for homiletical instruction, it became my duty to train the class in sermonizing."[17] The interface between theological study and powerful proclamation gave the RTS experience a second lasting hallmark and legacy that would continue into CRCDS.

As a theologian, Robinson, at least as we meet him through the pages of his *Christian Theology* (1896), was an irenic evangelical. Attempting to locate Robinson among the prevailing schools of his day, Strong recalled, "As a theologian, he was at this time critical rather than constructive. He represented the tendencies of Brown and Newton, rather than those of Hamilton, from which his predecessor, Doctor Maginnis, had come."[18] Writing more recently than Strong, William Brackney described Robinson's theology as "Critical

---

15. Ibid., 51.
16. Ibid.
17. Ibid.
18. Augustus H. Strong, *Miscellanies*, vol. 2, *Chiefly Theological*, 2 vols. (Philadelphia: Griffith & Rowland Press, 1912), 59.

Orthodox."[19] The content of Robinson's theology was indeed orthodox, but he approached the theological task with an analytical and penetrating mind, using the same Socratic method that characterized his teaching style.

Robinson's theology was based on and drawn from the Bible. As he noted, "Christian Theology builds on the Christian Scriptures."[20] Eschewing all the various theories of biblical inspiration, including plenary inspiration, which were popular with conservative evangelicals of his day, Robinson turned directly to the Scriptures in order to describe the Scriptures: "Discarding then every theory of Inspiration, and declining any attempt to state by what method the Spirit must have fulfilled the Divine will in the writing of the Scriptures, we turn at once to the Scriptures themselves."[21] His theology was both evangelical and irenic, as he explored the traditional doctrines in conversation with the Bible as well as with contemporary theologians like Schleiermacher and John Henry Newman.[22] But Robinson was not foreclosed to the current developments in natural science: "The demonstrable conclusions of a real science must certainly have a positive authority so much the explicit declaration of the divine word," he wrote. "But these two authorities cannot clash. God cannot contradict in his word what he has already declared in his works."[23]

Robinson was also influenced by Reformed theology. Although he explained the doctrines of predestination and particular election, he did not argue for them.[24] Ironically, Robinson's Baptist roots were not strongly lauded in his *Christian Theology*. While he described baptism as "the visible representation" of the subjective change that regeneration brings upon a person, he did not stress baptism by immersion.[25] Baptism and Communion were ordinances for him but not sacraments or "means of grace" through which "Romish notions of churchly and sacramental efficacy" are substituted for spiritual regeneration by the Holy Spirit.[26]

Between 1857 and 1859, RTS passed through dire financial straits. The school was unable to meet the payroll of $1,200 for the salaries of its teaching faculty. The school had $50,000 in endowment for student scholarships and had just raised funds to purchase the extensive

19. William H. Brackney, *A Genetic History of Baptist Thought* (Macon, GA: Mercer University Press, 2004), 318.
20. Ezekiel Robinson, *Christian Theology* (New York: Silver, Burdett, and Co. 1896), 33.
21. Ibid., 37.
22. Ibid., 15.
23. Ibid.
24. Ibid., 310–11.
25. Ibid., 318.
26. Ibid., 319.

theological library, comprised of more than forty-six hundred volumes, of a German theologian, Johann August Neander (1789–1850), but not a dollar of those funds could be used to support faculty salaries. A person of action, Robinson shouldered the responsibility of raising the necessary funds: "There was but one thing to do, and that was for me to go to New York and raise the $1200. I left my class in the hands of my colleagues, spent a Sunday with Madison Avenue Church, receiving a contribution of several thousand dollars, and the remainder I picked up in various places, hat in hand."[27]

In 1860, the seminary restructured the entire curriculum and added a third year of study to its program. At this same time the trustees officially elected Robinson as the first president of RTS, in addition to his teaching, pastoral, and academic duties. It was an unmanageable burden that, in 1863, resulted in Robinson's serious illness.[28] As the seminary continued to grow to the extent that it no longer seemed practical to share space with the University of Rochester, the trustees and many of the administration hoped that the seminary would be located on the new campus of the University of Rochester. Ultimately, that also proved impractical, insofar as the trustees of the seminary refused to construct a new building upon land they could not own. Thus, tensions arose between the "sister schools" as they became separate entities and competitors in fund-raising and influence. "Inevitably," President Robinson reported, "some coolness arose between the immediate friends of the Seminary and those of the University. As president of the Seminary a little more than due share of odium fell upon my shoulders."[29]

1n 1853 the university received the gift of a parcel of eight acres of land east of the city's center, in Pitkin's Woods. The gift was officially received by the trustees on July 14, 1853, and an additional seventeen acres adjoining the original gift was purchased for $1,000 per acre. By September 1859, the architectural design for a new academic building was approved and ready for occupancy in December 1861.[30] The seminary continued in the refurbished American Hotel until 1868 when it relocated to its own building, named Trevor Hall in honor of its philanthropic benefactor John Trevor of Yonkers, New York.[31]

27. Ibid., 63.
28. Ibid., 70–71.
29. Ibid.
30. Arthur May, *A History of the University of Rochester: 1850-1962* (Rochester, NY: University of Rochester Press, 1977), 47–49.
31. Johnson, *Robinson*, 163.

In an attempt to put RTS on more secure financial footing and to terminate the scandal that had developed due to the Baptists' two rival theological schools in the same locality, Robinson wrote to Dodge at Hamilton suggesting they consider merging the two schools in a new location in some major eastern area, such as Albany, New York, Pennsylvania, or New Jersey (this was before Crozer was established). But, Robinson recalled, "Dr. Dodge replied that the proposed movement could not fail to be abortive, and would, instead of uniting two institutions, result in the formation of a third. The only alternative, so far as I could then see, was to take off our coats and go to work in earnest to put the Rochester Seminary into a home of its own, and to place it on a foundation where it could do its work more effectively than had been possible in its preceding years."[32] While he raised funds in New York City in 1865, Robinson was befriended by "Mr. Coffin, who for many years been at the head of the mailing department of the Post-Office of New York City." After a casual conversation, Coffin resolved to send him to England carte blanche: "I can send you and your family to England," he said," without a dollar of expense to you."[33] After an extensive tour of England, with stops in Italy and Germany, Robinson returned to Rochester in January of 1868 to find the seminary in complete shambles.[34] "When I came back," he wrote, "the Seminary was, in fact, but little more than half manned in its teaching force. But before we could venture to fill vacancies, long strides need to be taken toward completing an endowment. It seemed insane to invite professors, with no money to pay their salaries."[35] These funds were soon raised by the dedicated efforts of Robinson and many others, and RTS was able to hire George Whittenmore teach Hebrew and Old Testament in 1868, and Joseph Buckland came to teach ecclesiastical history in 1869.[36]

At the same time, President Gilman recalled, "An addition to our endowment, on which I had confidently calculated, was lost to us through the inexperience and maladroitness of one of the Seminary's functionaries."[37] Financial shortages dogged the seminary almost from its inception. " Strong estimated the seminary's capital assets, when it began, at about $1,000. It took ten long years to accumulate

---

32. Ibid., 75.
33. Ibid., 77.
34. Ibid., 101.
35. Ibid., 101–2.
36. *Rochester Theological Seminary: General Catalogue*: 1869, 4.
37. Johnson, *Robinson*, 103–4.

$75,000 in endowment, and eight years later their funds stood at $80,000. When Robinson resigned his position at RTS to take a similar one at Brown in 1872, the RTS endowment stood at only slightly more than $100,000.[38] Strong recalled: "It is still true that to Dr. Robinson the institution at Rochester owes more of its character and success than to any other single man. The seminary, which at the beginning of his administration in 1853 was destitute of property or endowments, had in 1872, resources amounting to $224,000. This increase represents an amount of personal and skillful work on the part of one man."[39] Despite these fiscal challenges, the seminary labored diligently to make much out of a little investment and to meet the ever-changing challenges of its holy mission.

One shining example of the seminary's passion for relevancy and mission was the establishment of the German department in 1851. German immigrants streamed into America since the 1770s, and by 1830 German immigration had increased tenfold. In 1832, for example, more than ten thousand German immigrants arrived, and by 1854 that number had jumped to nearly two hundred thousand per year.[40] To answer this influx of German-speaking people, RTS established a German-language-based track for ministerial education, termed the German department. The 1852 board minutes of the New York Baptist Union for Ministerial Education, the seminary's governing body, indicated a resolution to establish a program aimed at "the speedy evangelization" of the waves of German immigrants, as well as "the means of providing for them an educated gospel ministry," by the University of Rochester and RTS.[41]

It soon became evident that a full-time professor and administrative head for the German department at RTS was needed, and in 1858 a recent graduate from the University of Berlin, Augustus Rauschenbusch, who had just arrived in America as a missionary and preacher among the Germans, was hired. Rauschenbusch had an unbelievable workload, as Sally Dodgson pointed out; he "taught English, German, Latin, Greek, geology, botany, astronomy, natural history, grammar, rhetoric, homiletics and theology, Old and New

38. *Rochester Theological Seminary Bulletin: The Anniversary Volume* 75, no. 1 (May 1925): 11.
39. Strong, *Miscellanies*, 2:62.
40. Immigration, Library of Congress, http://www.loc.gov/teachers/classroommaterials/presentationsandactivities/presentations/immigration/german4.html.
41. *The Third Annual Report of the Board of Trustees of the New York Baptist Union for Ministerial Education* (Rochester, NY: 1852), 9.

Testaments, history of the world and history of the church, and manners and morals—all for an initial salary of $600 per year."[42]

The development of the German department not only evidenced the curricular dexterity of its head but also spoke volumes about the seminary's commitment to minister to people who stood at the margins of American society. This too would become part of the continuing legacy of CRCDS. The German department continued preparing ministers for many years, as the 1929 seminary *Bulletin* reported, "German speaking churches and mission stations, now scattered over the entire country and Canada, have increased to 283, having a membership of 33,689. With very few exceptions all of these missionary centers are manned by pastors trained in Rochester Seminary."[43] While the elder Rauschenbusch spent thirty years on the German faculty of Rochester Theological Seminary, it was the work of his illustrious son, Walter, who would subsequently bring RTS to national prominence as the citadel of the social gospel.

As Rochester Theological Seminary grew beyond its inauspicious beginnings in the United States Hotel in bustling downtown Rochester and moved to Trevor Hall, its future was being shaped by several verities. The cosmopolitan religious climate of the city of Rochester both enabled and necessitated that RTS would move beyond the more narrowly sectarian approach that was characteristic of the Hamilton Institution.[44] President Ezekiel Gilman, to whom "the institution at Rochester owes more of its character and success than to any other single man,"[45] began building a solid academic foundation for RTS by attracting a nationally prominent faculty, as well as an extraordinary library despite chronic financial shortages. But even more importantly, perhaps, he imbued RTS with the spirit of devout and open theological inquiry in which both God's Word and God's works in the contemporary world were embraced.[46] With equal emphasis, Gilman established at RTS a broad view of ministry and a theology that preached well; in the face of the conspicuous needs of newly arrived immigrant people, it was a message that was proclaimed in English as well as in German.

---

42. Dodgson, "Rochester Theological Seminary," 122.
43. "The German Department," *The Colgate-Rochester Divinity School Bulletin* 1, no. 3 (January 1929): 236.
44. Dodgson, "Rochester Theological Seminary," 118.
45. Strong, *Miscellanies*, 2:62.
46. Ibid., 15.

6

The Strong Years

Augustus Hopkins Strong (1836–1921) succeeded Ezekiel Robinson as president and professor of systematic theology at Rochester Theological Seminary after Robinson resigned in 1872 to take the helm of Brown University. Strong was a native Rochesterian and RTS was already in his bloodline. His father, Henry Alvah Strong (1809–1885), was a local newspaper magnate who was converted to vital faith during Charles Finney's first revival in the city (1830).[1] The elder Strong was one of the early supporters of the emigration from Hamilton and served as treasurer of RTS for many years.

"Gus," as Augustus was known as a young man, was raised in a devoutly Christian home. One of his earliest religious recollections comes from when he was six; his mother led him into "a large and dimly lighted closet," where she taught him how to pray.[2] He worked various jobs for his father's newspaper, *The Rochester Democrat*, prior to going to Yale University.[3] During his spring break of 1856 in Rochester, the younger Strong also experienced conversion under Finney's preaching.[4] "It was like a thunder bolt hit me," he told the students of RTS in a chapel talk years later.[5] Soon thereafter he was baptized:

> On the third day of August, my twentieth birthday, I was baptized by Rev. J. R. Scott in the First Baptist Church of Rochester. I was not at that time fully convinced that Baptist doctrine was absolute truth. But I knew that I must make a public profession

---

1. Crerar Douglas, ed., *Autobiography of Augustus Hopkins Strong* (Valley Forge, PA: Judson Press, 1981), 32-33.
2. Augustus Strong, *One Hundred Chapel Talks to Theological Students* (Philadelphia: Griffith & Rowland Press, 1913), 5.
3. Strong, *One Hundred Chapel Talks*, 7.
4. Douglas, *Autobiography of Strong*, 83-86.
5. Strong, *One Hundred Chapel Talks*, 12-13.

of religion and must connect myself with some body of believers. I argued that, if I were immersed, I certainly should never be obliged to be baptized again.[6]

After a broad liberal arts education at Yale University, where he studied the philosophical idealism of Noah Porter (1811–1892),[7] Strong returned to Rochester for seminary. At RTS Strong came under the powerful influence of Ezekiel Robinson. "To my teacher and predecessor," Strong recalled, "I owe more than I owe any one else outside my own family circle."[8] Those three figures, then, Finney, Porter, and Robinson, were each formative for the young Augustus Strong, but the most influential by far was Robinson.[9]

After graduation in 1859, Strong pastored Baptist churches in Haverhill, New Jersey, and Cleveland, Ohio—the latter being one of the largest and most prosperous churches among the American Baptists. In the Cleveland church, Strong befriended John D. Rockefeller, who would become a significant participant in the governance of RTS and a major financial contributor during the "Strong years." Their friendship strengthened when Strong's son, Charles, married Rockefeller's daughter Bessie in 1889.[10] But their friendship also became strained when Rockefeller declined to support Strong's decade-long dream to establish a Baptist graduate university in New York City, with himself at the helm. Rockefeller's sizable financial support went, instead, to the University of Chicago and Dr. William Rainey Harper.[11]

For one to describe the personality of Augustus Hopkins Strong is to engage in a study of opposites. He was, as Grant Wacker reported, "lovable and autocratic, affable and grave. All these labels fit. Augustus Strong's personality was not simple, nor was any other aspect of his life. His faculty appointments, his denominational alliances, even the friends he chose, defy categorization."[12] Strong was the sort of person who could be friends with both the likes of John D. Rockefeller and Walter Rauschenbusch, who "vigorously defended Rauschenbusch's right to assail the capitalist system yet just

---

6. Douglas, *Autobiography of Strong*, 92.
7. LeRoy Moore, "The Rise of American Religious Liberalism at the Rochester Theological Seminary, 1872-1928," PhD diss. Claremont Graduate School, 1966, 31.
8. Augustus Hopkins Strong, "Ezekiel Gilman Robinson as a Theologian," in *Miscellanies Chiefly Theological*, vol. 2, (Philadelphia: Griffith & Rowland Press, 1912), 58.
9. While Strong never published a statement on his indebtedness to Porter, the latter is cited forty-six times in his *Systematic Theology*. Cf. Moore, "Rise of American Religious Liberalism," 32-33.
10. Douglas, *Autobiography of Strong*, 261.
11. Ibid., 249-51.
12. Grant Wacker, *Augustus Strong and the Dilemma of Historical Consciousness* (Macon, GA: Mercer University Press, 1985), 4.

as vigorously solicited endowments from John D. Rockefeller and other robber barons."[13] As a leader and chief executive, Strong was "somewhat autocratic and absolute"; a firm and benevolent ruler, he was "by nature, training, and bearing" a true aristocrat, and those who met him "felt it."[14] In his eulogy, RTS president Dr. Clarence Barbour remembered Strong's incredible diligence on behalf of the school and his field of study: "Dr. Strong's industry was a marvel to all who beheld it. He was a man of ceaseless and tireless toil."[15]

Augustus Hopkins Strong was a progressive evangelical theologian whose three-volume *Systematic Theology* became the standard Baptist theological text for decades. In 1906, a time when theological conservatives began to battle modernist ideas like higher criticism of the Bible and evolution, the irenic Strong wrote, "Neither evolution nor the Higher Criticism has any terrors to one who regards them as parts of Christ's creating and educating process."[16] Very much a "shrewd man of the world" when it came to financial and administrative matters, Strong was also a devout churchman who attended church three times a week, taught Sunday school, and offered a daily devotional at the seminary for nearly forty years.[17]

Strong agreed to take the presidency at Rochester only if he could be excused from fund-raising duties for the first two years of his tenure. He explained, "I knew that I needed those two years for unbroken study if I were ever to evolve an original scheme of theology. But I had hardly been settled in my chair for three months when I found that my salary was not paid."[18] Despite his personal distaste for fund-raising—"Begging I hated almost as much as being hanged," he wrote[19]— Strong proved to be very effective at it. He went to New York City and raised the necessary funds for his own salary and that of others. In a subsequent fund-raising campaign in May 1875, Strong urged, "To endow our institutions is a part of our Christian duty. We are not rationalists; we do not believe that man unaided from above can attain to a knowledge of religious truth. Yet we are not mystics; we do not believe that without outward means we can reach the truth. There must be an objective revelation.

---

13. Ibid.
14. Justin Wroe Nixon, "Dr. Strong as Friend and Counselor of His Students," *Rochester Theological Seminary Bulletin* 73 (May 1922): 20–22.
15. Clarence Barbour, "The Funeral Service," *Rochester Theological Seminary Bulletin* 73 (May 1922): 9.
16. Douglas, *Autobiography of Strong*, 339.
17. Wacker, *Augustus Strong*, 4–5.
18. Douglas, *Autobiography of Strong*, 235.
19. Ibid.

We must educate, in order that Christ and his Truth may be better known."[20] When he arrived in the office of the presidency at RTS, the total endowment stood at about $200,000. When Strong retired in 1912, at the age of seventy-five, the school had an endowment and total assets equaling more than $2 million.[21]

In 1880, Rockefeller Hall was built, largely through financial support given by its namesake. It contained a library, lecture halls, and a chapel. A president's house was constructed for Strong in 1896, and the RTS campus reached its full size with the addition of Alvah Strong Hall, which was added in 1907. Strong Hall was an addition to Trevor Hall, making it into a U-shaped building that included student rooms and faculty offices. Additionally, the $125,000 donated by Henry Alvah Strong paid for extensive remodeling of Trevor Hall. It was named for the father of Augustus and Henry Strong, who had been a trustee of the seminary for fifty years. During the Strong years, RTS did indeed become strong and experienced forty years of steady growth in faculty, student body, facilities, financial stability, and the national reputation.[22]

Three main elements comprise the priorities of an educational institution: brains, books, and bricks. While Strong recognized the importance of "bricks," or physical facilities, these were always secondary in his mind to the other two priorities. As we shall see, he spent himself freely in building an extremely capable faculty and superior library. Strong rightly recognized that a good library is instrumental to attracting good students and a notable faculty. During his administration, nearly $150,000 was spent on library acquisitions, and the holdings of the library quintupled to more than thirty-nine thousand volumes.[23] He clearly recognized the importance of an excellent library for the purpose of sustaining the educational and spiritual life of RTS.

"Brains" were also of inestimable importance to the success of the institution, and Strong presided over three very capable faculties during his forty-year reign as president. The first faculty was assembled by Robinson, but within a decade Strong was forced to begin building his own faculty. The first to come, in 1875, was Howard Osgood (1831–1911). A native of Louisiana, Osgood taught

20. *Rochester Theological Seminary Bulletin: The Anniversary Volume 75*, no. 1 (May 1925): 37.
21. Ibid., 27.
22. Sally Dodgson, "Rochester Theological Seminary: 1850–1928," *American Baptist Quarterly* 20, no. 2 (June 2001): 122.
23. Glenn B. Ewell, "Dr. Strong in His Care for the Library," *Rochester Theological Seminary Bulletin*, May 1922, 26–27.

Hebrew language and literature. Two years later, William Arnold Stevens (1839–1910) joined the faculty in New Testament. Albert Henry Newman (1852–1933) came with Stevens in 1877 to teach church history but stayed only three years. He was replaced by Benjamin Osgood True (1845–1902) in 1881, the same year that Thomas Harwood Pattison (1838–1904), an Englishman, came to RTS as professor of homiletics and pastoral theology. These four—Osgood, Stevens, True, and Pattison—along with Strong, comprised "The Big Five," as they were known in those days. It was a faculty that brought the seminary academic stability and national prominence through nearly two decades of their shared labors. These men were theological moderates, like Strong himself, but they were not, perhaps with the exception of Osgood, who was the most conservative of the group, closed minded toward modern developments in theology, philosophy, and science.

Strong's third faculty was his most famous, and also his most progressive. They began succeeding "The Big Five" around 1900. The first replacement was Walter Robert Betteridge (1863–1916), a recent RTS graduate who replaced Osgood as professor of Hebrew language and literature and as librarian. The second, also a son of RTS, was Walter Rauschenbusch (1861–1918), who was brought back to RTS in 1897 to fill a position in the German department but, in 1902, was elevated to the chair of church history in the seminary. Joseph William Alexander Stewart (1852–1948) came as professor of ethics and pastoral theology in 1903. Two years later, Cornelius Woelfkin (1859–1928) came to teach homiletics. The third faculty rounded out with the addition of Conrad Henry Moehlman (1879–1961), another RTS graduate who taught biblical studies for several years prior to his occupancy as chair of church history. Several others joined the faculty, including John Henry Mason (1850–1929) in English Bible and John Philips Silvernail (1851–1930), who taught elocution.[24] This third faculty, which Strong both led and participated in with gusto, was much more liberal than its predecessors.

As a theologian, Augustus Strong is chiefly remembered by the impact of his voluminous *Systematic Theology*. Carl Henry, who made Strong's theology the focus of his doctoral dissertation, remarked, "Among Northern Baptists, no theological treatise has been more

24. Moore, "Rise of American Religious Liberalism," 42–45.

influential than Strong's *Systematic Theology*."[25] Strong's personal theology went through three distinct phases. This pattern was observed by several commentators, including his friend and colleague Moehlman: the first period was characterized by his inherited orthodox evangelical conservatism; the second period was marked by his development as a progressive thinker who developed a posture Strong called "ethical monism"; and the last was a reactionary return to conservativism.[26]

The voice of Strong's initial posture of received orthodoxy was given permanent expression in his *Lectures on Theology*, which were first printed for his classes in 1876. LeRoy Moore aptly described Strong's approach "as Protestant scholasticism" and "another late Calvinistic system."[27] True to his evangelical heritage, Strong held that the Scriptures are "a revelation from God,"[28] but he departed from earlier conservatives who held a mechanical theory of scriptural inspiration and viewed the Bible as inspired "dynamically" in a way that has more to do with the thoughts of God than with words dictated from on high. Inspiration was not thought of as dependent upon biblical inerrancy, though no scientific, historical, or ethical errors were found to exist in the Bible;[29] hence, Strong affirmed that the Bible is an "infallible and sufficient rule of faith and practice."[30] Looking back on his earlier thoughts (in 1899), Strong recalled his early naiveté and simplicity: "When I was a novice I . . . knew much more theology then than I do now. . . . I think I hold the ancient faith today more firmly than ever, but I recognize the fact that modern science and philosophy have thrown great light upon the world's problems, and that it is the duty of the theologian and of the preacher to bring forth out of his treasure things new as well as old."[31]

While his openness to new ideas, hinted at in the citation directly above, signaled a movement into the second and more creative phase of Strong's theology, sweeping changes do not appear so clearly in Strong's magisterial *Systematic Theology*. What changed in Strong's theology was the fundamental point of view from which the various

25. Carl F. H. Henry, *Personal Idealism and Strong's Theology* (Wheaton, IL: Van Kampen Press, 1951), 11.
26. C. H. Moehlman, "Dr. Strong as Teacher," *Rochester Theological Seminary Bulletin*, May 1922, 19. This pattern of noting three periods has been followed by Moore, "Rise of American Religious Liberalism," and Henry, *Personal Idealism*.
27. Moore, "Rise of American Religious Liberalism," 47. Cf. Noah Porter, *The Human Intellect* (New York: Charles Scribner, 1869).
28. Augustus H. Strong, *Lectures on Theology* (Rochester: E. R. Andrews, 1876), 17ff.
29. Moore, "Rise of American Religious Liberalism," 47.
30. Strong, *Lectures on Theology*, 50.
31. Strong, *Miscellanies*, 2:251.

points of systematic theology were viewed. Writing in reaction to "Ritschl and his Kantian relativism," through which "many of our teachers and preachers have swung off into a practical denial of Christ's deity and of his atonement,"[32] Strong attacked "a second Unitarian defection, that will break up churches and compel secessions."[33] In the face of this wholesale threat from modernity, Strong reconstructed traditional theology on a foundation of ethical monism.

Strong defined ethical monism in this way: "Ethical Monism is that method of thought which holds to a single substance, ground, or principle of being, namely God, but which also holds to the ethical facts of God's transcendence as well as his immanence, and of God's personality as distinct from, and as guaranteeing, the personality of man."[34] In one of his chapel talks, titled "Theology and Experience," Strong described how he discovered the Christ-centered focus of his ethical monism:

> Saviour. I now learned that Christ is *the life of the universe*, as well as the life of the believer; that in him all things consist, or hold together; that he is the one and only medium through whom God creates, upholds, and governs the world. This discovery of Christ's creatorship was my fifth great lesson in doctrine. My studies in science gave me inspiring views of the wisdom and power of God, and I drew from science a multitude of illustrations for my preaching.[35]

Strong's new emphasis upon development, progress, and science fit well with the intellectual climate of the late 1880s and the early 1890s, and his movement toward ethical monism is discernible in his writings from the same period. By 1894 his views changed to the degree that felt he must add a brief disclaimer to the preface of the fifth edition of his *Systematic Theology*: "For substance . . . the book remains unchanged—but with four exceptions . . . where the principle of Ethical Monism is adopted, and application of it made to the explanation of the doctrine of Preservation and of the Atonement."[36]

The year 1894 was pivotal in the development of Strong's thinking. In June he read Ezekiel Robinson's *Christian Theology*, and although he constructed his theology without conscious influence from his former mentor, it was then clear to Strong just how much he had learned from Robinson. He wrote, "I am humbled to find how much of my

32. Ibid., 2:ix.
33. Ibid.
34. Ibid., 1:105.
35. Strong, *One Hundred Chapel Talks*, 28.
36. Ibid., 95.

own thinking that I have thought original has been an unconscious reproduction of his own. . . . The ruling idea of his system—that stands out as the ruling idea of mine; I did not realize until now that I owned it almost wholly to him."[37] In 1899 Strong published a series of essays under the title *Christ in Creation and Ethical Monism*. At this point, his approach to salvation and renewal had broadened to include all of creation, not just the human creation. Summarizing what theology had taught him in the last fifty years, Strong wrote:

> I have found these newly apprehended or new emphasized truths to be: first that God is immanent in his universe; secondly, that this immanent God is none other than Christ; thirdly, that Christ's method is that of evolution; fourthly, that this evolution is characteristically and predominantly ethical; fifthly, that the ethical meaning of the universe is summed up in the historical Jesus; sixthly, that the central principle of this ethical system is the supremacy of righteousness in the nature of God; and seventhly, that this principle of ethical development is to be applied to the understanding and interpretation of Holy Scripture.[38]

While exploring how Christ works God's will in the universe, Strong asserted, "Christ is the principle of evolution,"[39] and so God comes to us in Christ, as well as through nature, as Strong affirmed: "This living God whom we see in nature is none other than Christ. Nature is *not* his body, in the sense that he is *confined* to nature. Nature is his body, in the sense that in nature we see him who is *above* nature, and in whom, at the same time, all things consist."[40] This vison of the cosmic Christ, described as "the larger Christ," was one that shaped Strong's later theology and was never completely abandoned.[41] Indeed, it is precisely this "larger Christ" who is "the Christ who is behind and in the process that guarantees the unity, sufficiency, and the authority of Scripture."[42]

For his part, Strong wanted to be both traditional and progressive at the same time. As he wrote in "Fifty Years of Theology," "I have hoped that this statement of the gains of the last half-century might answer a pacific purpose and might show us that some of the divisions of the past were needless and might now be healed."[43] But the fallout from his new theological developments was widespread. His

---

37. Strong, *Miscellanies*, 2:64. Henry questions whether Robinson embraced ethical monism. But a foray into that question is beyond the scope of our concern here. See Henry, *Personal Idealism*, 96–97.
38. Augustus H. Strong, *Christ in Creation and Ethical Monism* (Philadelphia: Roger Williams Press, 1899), 206–7.
39. Ibid., 10.
40. Ibid., 14.
41. Moore, "Rise of American Religious Liberalism," 57.
42. Strong, *One Hundred Chapel Talks*, 31.
43. Strong, *Christ in Creation*, 207.

own son, C. A. Strong, while correcting the proofs of his father's later works, lost his faith in God and gave up studying divinity in order to pursue a career in psychology.[44]

The delicate balance between orthodox Christian foundations and new theological ideas, which Augustus Strong both advocated for and exemplified, proved difficult to maintain. Soon the progressive posture of RTS eclipsed Strong's own views; and although Strong was no longer president after 1912, he continued to serve as a trustee of the seminary, and several faculty members, including Dr. George Cross, were elected over his strenuous opposition.[45] The "practical Unitarianism" that Strong bewailed in his earlier writings seemed to be a real a possibility at his own beloved seminary. In public Strong remained silent about his fears, but privately he took a more conservative and reactionary course.[46] He began to doubt the orthodoxy of his former student and friend Walter Rauschenbusch.[47]

In his last publication, *What Shall I Believe*, published posthumously in 1922, Strong expressed himself as still striving for the middle ground that seemed to have eluded RTS. "I hold," he wrote, "middle ground between the higher critics and the so-called fundamentalists, and believe it is possible for them both to reconcile their differences by a larger view of the deity and omnipresence of Christ."[48] Scripturally nuanced, Strong's mature theology continued to place Christ at the center. He affirmed both the continuity between Christ and other humans, as well as the utter uniqueness of Christ: "The difference between Christ and common men is two-fold: first, that his life is the *source* of all other lives, while our life is only *derived* from him; and secondly, that in him was 'all the *fullness* of the Godhead bodily' (Colossians 2:9) which common men are only *sparks* from the divine flame."[49] Strong maintained his high view of Scripture through this same Christocentric emphasis: "We come now to the consideration of Christ's relation to Holy Scripture," he wrote. "The whole matter is summed up in the statement that *the written word is the expression of the eternal Word*."[50] Yet this statement was not seen as antithetical to evolution (as it would have been for

---

44. Henry, *Personal Idealism*, 193.
45. Douglas, *Autobiography of Strong*, 357.
46. Wacker, *Augustus Strong*, 104–7.
47. Dodgson, "Rochester Theological Seminary," 124.
48. Augustus H. Strong, *What Shall I Believe?* (New York: Fleming H. Revell, 1922), 8.
49. Ibid., 30.
50. Ibid., 48.

many conservatives), since "evolution is simply the ordinary method of Christ's working. He uses the past in his building of the future, as he uses the seed in his bringing forth of fruit (Gen. 1:12)."[51]

Scripture itself, as a written book, evidences the evolutionary process: "In this evolution of Scripture, Christ may use all the methods of literary composition which are consistent with truth—poetry as well as prose, proverb as well as history, parable as well as dogmatic teaching, apologue and drama as well as legislative enactment."[52] Strong affirmed, "Christ [is] the Sufficient Guarantor of Scripture";[53] therefore, "this superintendence of Christ makes the written word, with all its literary and human shortcomings, an expression of the eternal Word, and gives it unity, sufficiency, and authority, as a rule of faith and practice."[54] As an authoritative, sufficient rule of faith and practice, Strong viewed Scripture as both inspired and inspiring, but it was not infallible, error-free, or dictated from on high. Here we see Strong seeking a balance between conservative and progressive theological impulses—this irenic spirit characterized his work.

Augustus H. Strong's contribution to the CRCDS legacy was huge, but chiefly threefold. In his presidency of forty years, he brought significant strength and stability to RTS through his emphasis upon "brains, books, and bricks." In this regard, he sought to produce ministers who were both adept scholars and good preachers; this, too, would become part of the CRCDS legacy.[55] Through his own example, efforts, and administrative style, Strong kept the relationship between the seminary and the churches vital. This fundamental concern was echoed in the "closing sentiment" of his retirement speech: "The church and the seminary, now and forever, one and inseparable."[56] He was a talented and creative theologian who championed the delicate balance between orthodox, biblical theological foundations and progressive ideas with social concerns as one of the hallmarks and aims of the school.

---

51. Ibid., 49.
52. Ibid., 50.
53. Ibid., 54.
54. Ibid., 55.
55. Moore, "Rise of American Religious Liberalism," 132.
56. Rochester Theological Seminary, *The Record,* May 1912, 11.

7

Walter Rauschenbusch: Prophet of the Social Gospel

"What do you want to be when you grow up?" a good-natured adult asked the primary school-aged "Wally." "John the Baptist!" came young Walter Rauschenbusch's (1861–1918) reply.[1] There must have been something prescient in that moment, because both men were prophets of the kingdom of God. It was an answer that, as Paul Minus points out, must have been gratifying to "all good Baptists."[2] Such an outlook, however, might not be too surprising coming from a young man raised in the home of Walter's father, August.

August Rauschenbusch was a Baptist missionary-pastor and seminary professor who left his native Germany to serve God and immigrants in America. His was a bilingual, middle-class household, in which the family lived close to the claims of the Christian gospel as well as to the needs and challenges of poor immigrants. Fifteen years prior to Walter's birth in 1861, August arrived in America to work among the tidal wave of German immigrants who wound up laboring in urban sweatshops or standing in unemployment lines. While Walter was raised in Rochester, where August became a seminary professor and the director of the German department at Rochester Theological Seminary. The Rauschenbusch home was a Christian home where daily devotions and regular attendance at worship were highly esteemed.

It must have been difficult being the son of a pastor and seminary professor, and for a time young Walter tried to outdo his peers

---

1. Dores Robinson Sharpe, *Walter Rauschenbusch* (New York: Macmillan, 1942), 25.
2. Paul M. Minus, *Walter Rauschenbusch: American Reformer* (New York: Macmillan, 1988), 8.

in swearing and other kinds of adolescent rebellion. At the age of seventeen, however, he had a religious experience that changed his entire outlook and vocational goals. He later described this conversion: "Such as it was, it was of everlasting value to me. It turned me permanently and I thank God with all my heart for it. It was a tender, mysterious experience. It influenced my soul down to its depths."[3] Subsuquently, Rauschenbusch reported that "very soon the idea came to me that I ought to be a preacher and to help save souls. I wanted to go out as a foreign missionary—I wanted to do hard work for God."[4]

Walter's early education was carried out both in Rochester and in Germany. In 1879 he went abroad to travel and to study at the Evangelical Gymnasium in Gütersloh, Westphalia. Despite initial academic and adjustment struggles, Rauschenbusch soon became Primus, or top student of the school. In the gymnasium, he mastered Latin, Greek, French, German, and Hebrew. After finishing the German equivalent of high school in the spring of 1883, Walter spent several weeks studying at the University of Berlin and visiting Munich and Hamburg. He returned home to America by way of England.

Upon returning to Rochester, Rauschenbusch plunged deeply into academic life again, this time simultaneously attending the University of Rochester and Rochester Theological Seminary. At this time, Walter had a second conversion-like experience in which "one of the great thoughts that came upon me was that I ought to follow Jesus Christ in my personal life, and to die over again his death. I felt that every Christian ought to participate in the dying of the Lord Jesus Christ, and in that way help to redeem humanity, and it was that thought that gave my life its fundamental direction in doing of Christian work."[5] This event may have occurred during his study of the "Life of Christ" with Dr. William Arnold Stevens. His seminary experience also brought about an intellectual conversion. Rauschenbusch explained, "My inherited ideas about the inerrancy of the Bible became untenable. I determined to follow the facts as divine, and let my man-made themes go if they conflicted."[6]

Rauschenbusch graduated from the University of Rochester in 1884, from the German department of RTS in 1885, and from

3. Sharpe, *Walter Rauschenbusch*, 43.
4. Minus, *Rauschenbusch*, 17.
5. Sharpe, *Walter Rauschenbusch*, 57.
6. Minus, *Rauschenbusch*, 40.

the English department of RTS in 1886. Upon graduation he felt a strong pull toward foreign missions and offered himself to the American Baptist Foreign Missions Society for service abroad. After considering him for the presidency of Telugu Theological Seminary in India, the missions society rejected his application, reporting that they wanted him to have more pastoral experience. But Walter subsequently learned that his appointment was blocked by a negative reference letter from his former RTS professor Howard Osgood that expressed concerns that Rauschenbusch did not fully affirm "the Divine Authority of the Old Testament."[7]

Forgoing his dream to become a foreign missionary, Rauschenbusch accepted a call from the Second German Baptist Church in New York City. Paul Minus captured the social and economic climate at this time: "Factories were multiplying, immigration was accelerating, cities were expanding, wealth was piling up for a few, urban poverty was gripping more and more, tensions were mounting between owners and workers, and traditional religious symbols were losing their power to guide the American people."[8]

While the writings of social reformers like Washington Gladden and Josiah Strong[9] were influential for Walter during his early pastorate,[10] Christopher Evans noted that his "early social awakening" occurred primarily through his own pastoral experience.[11] His extended encounter with the plight and problems of poor, immigrant, urban working people became the maternity ward in which Rauschenbusch's awareness of the grim realities of the social crisis was born. Walter described this period poignantly in an address he gave before the Central YMCA in Cleveland, Ohio, in 1913:

> My social view did not come from the church. It came from outside. It came through personal contact with poverty and when I saw how men toiled all their life long, hard toilsome lives, and at the end had almost nothing to show for it; how strong men begged for work and could not get it in hard times; how little children died—oh the children's funerals! They gripped my heart—that was one of the things I always went away thinking about—why did the children have to die? . . . A single human incident of that sort is enough to set a great beacon fire burning, and to light up the whole world for you—if you only have the right mind in you.[12]

7. Ibid., 52. Cf. Sharpe, *Walter Rauschenbusch*, 58.
8. Minus, *Rauschenbusch*, 37.
9. Christopher H. Evans, *The Kingdom Is Always Becoming: The Life of Walter Rauschenbusch* (Grand Rapids: Eerdmans, 2004), 56.
10. Minus, *Rauschenbusch*, 62-64.
11. Ibid., 57ff.
12. Sharpe, *Walter Rauschenbusch*, 418-19.

His social awakening began to bear fruit almost immediately. Not only did it begin to emerge in his preaching, which caused some consternation among his conservative parishioners,[13] but it also exploded into passionate essays and publications about the social crisis he observed every day. His essay "Beneath the Glitter," which was published first in the daily press and then in *The Christian Inquirer* in 1887, invited his readers to look beneath the opulence of New York's fashionable stores and theaters to see the suffering of exploited workers bent low beneath their load of cares.

Rauschenbusch, along with Elizabeth Post, J. E. Raymond, and Leighton Williams, soon established a journal, *For the Right*, in 1889 that sought to cultivate the church's sympathy for the horrible plight of urban working people. *For the Right* announced its opening issue (November 1889): "This paper is published in the interests of the working people of New York City. It proposes to discuss, from the standpoint of Christian socialism, such questions as engage their attention and affect their life."[14] In an early 1890 edition of *For the Right*, Rauschenbusch explained,

> Most people look only to the renewal of the individual. Most social reformers look only to the renewal of society. We believe that two factors make up the man, the inward and the outward, and so we work for the renewal and Christianization of the individual *and* society. Most Christians demand the private life for God and leave business to the devil. Most social reformers demand justice for business life, in order that private life may be given to pleasure. We plead for self-sacrifice in private life, in order to achieve justice in business life; and for justice in business life that purity in private life may become possible.[15]

Rauschenbusch wrote twenty-one articles in sixteen months for *For the Right*. It was a pace that his editors could not maintain, and the short-lived publication project came to an end in March 1891. But it drew Rauschenbusch into the emerging Christian criticism of the values of the Gilded Age and soon catapulted him into prominence.

In May 1892, Walter and his ministerial colleagues, Leighton Williams and Nathaniel Schmidt, traveled to Philadelphia for the tenth annual session of the Baptist Congress. It was his first opportunity to announce his newfound message before an international audience. "The whole aim of Christ," he proclaimed, "is embraced in the words 'the Kingdom of God.' In that idea is embraced the sanctification

---

13. Evans, *The Kingdom*, 79, 126.
14. Sharpe, *Walter Rauschenbusch*, 86.
15. Ibid., 82–83.

of all life, the regeneration of humanity, and the reformation of all social institutions."[16] Samuel Batten, a young Baptist pastor from the ghetto in Philadelphia, was among those who heard Rauschenbusch's speech and sought him out after the session. Meeting with Rauschenbusch, Schmidt, Williams, and two others, Batten urged them to create an organization to implement what Rauschenbusch proposed in his speech. Batten suggested they should meet regularly for study and mutual encouragement in their respective efforts to serve Christ and the kingdom of God. The little group agreed to meet again on July 9, 1892, in Rauschenbusch's New York apartment. At that time, six young Baptist ministers agreed, in Batten's words, to form "some association which would serve as a bond of union and a strengthener of convictions." Samuel Batten proposed a name for the group: "The Brotherhood of the Kingdom."[17] This fellowship of progressive pastors became a center of spiritual refreshment, academic reflection, and empowering motivation for Rauschenbusch.

At a second meeting, on December 19, 1892, the founders were joined by several others to approve a statement of aims and organization. Their charter described both their ethos and aims quite well: "The Spirit of God is moving men in our generation toward a better understanding of the idea of the Kingdom of God on earth. Obeying the thought of our Master, and trusting in the power and guidance of the Spirit, we form ourselves into a Brotherhood of the Kingdom, in order to re-establish this idea in the thought of the church, and to assist in its practical realization in the world."[18] They agreed to publish essays on aspects of "the social interpretation of the gospel"[19] and to meet again that next summer.

As the group continued to grow, Leighton Williams's summer home on the Hudson was chosen as the location for the next meeting of the Brotherhood of the Kingdom. They met for five days in August 1893. The original founders were joined by several others, including William Newton Clarke, Baptist theologian from Hamilton Theological Seminary. Each participant addressed the social gospel from their own academic perspective, and a formidable collection of essays was compiled and circulated as leaflets. Walter Rauschenbusch penned an essay titled "The Ethics of Jesus" and a leaflet called "The Kingdom

---

16. From the Annual Report of the Baptist Congress, 1892, 127. Quoted in Minus, *Rauschenbusch*, 84.
17. Minus, *Rauschenbusch*, 98.
18. Batten's minutes, as quoted in Minus, *Rauschenbusch*, 86.
19. Ibid.

of God." It was the social gospel equivalent of Martin Luther nailing his Ninety-Five Theses to the door of Christendom.[20]

The twofold task of the reformation of church and society became more of a challenge as Rauschenbusch's hearing began to fail suddenly to the point where he contemplated leaving the pastorate. Describing this development in his diary, Walter wrote, "My hearing, which had steadily decreased since I first discovered it failing in 1885, took a sudden drop downward, so that I could hear only what was spoken directly to me and very near to me. I saw then that I should have to resign my position."[21] After a period of study and a failed attempt at restorative treatment in Europe, Rauschenbusch accepted the invitation of his friend and former teacher Augustus Strong to return to RTS to serve as the head of the German department, but the experience of his New York years would never leave him.[22]

When the invitation came in May 1897, Strong alerted Walter that his socialist leanings would pose a problem for a few of the trustees who would have to approve his appointment. Rauschenbusch responded by sending a copy of an article he published the previous year that evaluated both the strengths and weaknesses of socialism; that article, along with Strong's assurance that Walter advocated "no revolutionary action, but only legal changes as would result from mutual sympathy of rich and poor,"[23] secured his position at RTS.

Rauschenbusch's Rochester years were extremely productive ones, despite initial misgivings about his growing deafness. Student secretaries wrote down and handed Rauschenbusch class comments and questions in writing to keep him in the give-and-take of class dialogues, chapels, and public addresses.[24] In 1902 he accepted the Pettingill Chair of Church History at RTS, a position he held for sixteen years. He fit in well and was well appreciated by students and faculty. As an "evangelical liberal," with roots in both the older conservativism and the new liberal theology, Rauschenbusch seemed well-equipped to bridge the gap between the two opposing approaches represented on campus and among the faculty. As Heinz Rossol reminded the readers of his essay "More Than a Prophet,"

20. Ibid., 88.
21. Ibid., 69–70.
22. Evans, The Kingdom, 126.
23. Ibid., 33.
24. John E. Skoglund, "Edwin Dahlberg in Conversation: Memories of Walter Rauschenbusch," Foundations 18, no. 3 (July 1975): 209. Dahlberg, who was Walter's student secretary in 1917, described the role and reported that by then Rauschenbusch was "stone-deaf."

Rauschenbusch "did not reject his Pietist heritage, but built upon it and expanded and enlarged it."[25]

Rauschenbusch was soon joined on the faculty by other progressive theologians, such as J. W. A. Steward, who was named academic dean in 1903, and Cornelius Woelfkin, who followed in homiletics. The school's gradual conversion from conservativism to progressivism was completed after Strong's retirement as president in 1912, when George Coats joined the theology faculty. Justin Wroe Nixon taught Old Testament, and Rauschenbusch's own student and protégé Conrad Moehlman came to replace him in church history. Rauschenbusch personally wrote to encourage his former student Justin Wroe Nixon to accept the Old Testament position at Rochester: "We want to breed prophets here," he explained. "We need you for just that thing."[26]

As a church historian, Rauschenbusch taught the whole span of Christian history, but he had a particular interest in socially reformist groups like the early church, Waldensians, Lollards, and Anabaptists.[27] He spent considerable care in demonstrating that Jesus' mission was focused on the kingdom of God and that this mission was compromised by the institutional church due to the pressure of alien influences. He also stressed that recent developments revealed that God was still at work in human affairs and that a promising change was under way as Christians began to recognize that they were called by Christ to construct a new social order in which the kingdom of God prevailed.[28]

Rauschenbusch's first major theological writing was never published in his lifetime. In this 450-page unfinished manuscript he laid the theological foundation for his subsequent lectures and more famous publications.[29] The manuscript was, as Minus described it, "a searing indictment of the church, but it was rendered by a man who loved it, and believed that change was possible."[30]

The kingdom of God is the central theme of the manuscript and the lens through which Rauschenbusch assessed and sought to correct contemporary Christianity. The author's introduction begins with the person and teachings of Jesus: "It would be a mistake to represent

25. Heinz Rossol, "More Than a Prophet," *American Baptist Quarterly* 19, no. 2 (June 2000): 132.
26. Minus, *Rauschenbusch*, 143.
27. Cf. Sherman B. Barnes, "Walter Rauschenbusch as Historian," *Foundations* 12, no. 3 (July 1969).
28. Minus, *Rauschenbusch*, 159-60.
29. Cf. Max Stackhouse, *The Righteousness of the Kingdom* (Nashville: Abingdon, 1968).
30. Minus, *Rauschenbusch*, 78-79.

Jesus merely as an ethical teacher. His purpose above all things was to make God known and loved among men. To leave the Father out of Christ's teaching is to blot the sun out of the sky," Rauschenbusch wrote, "but on the other hand he was not merely a guide to mystical religion. He came to found a new society on earth, and he laid down the principles of conduct which were to govern men in this new society."[31] Rauschenbusch broke step with many of his scholarly contemporaries who found only an ethical teacher in Jesus through scientific research. Rauschenbusch saw in Jesus and his teachings the same emphasis upon personal transformation and social reform that was so important to his own assessment of the gospel.

The manuscript proceeds from the assertion, demonstrated in the first chapter, that "Christianity is revolutionary. Its revolutionary character is apparent from the spiritual ancestry to which it traces its lineage. Jesus was the successor of the Old Testament prophets."[32] After a thorough examination of the teachings of the prophets and the expansion and refinement of the theocratic ideal of the Hebrew Scriptures that became the basis of Jesus' kingdom theology, Rauschenbusch noted, "While Jesus began his work in the inward and spiritual side of human life, he did not propose to let it end there. That is the falsity of the conception of the Kingdom current among Christians today. They have learned so thoroughly the lesson that the Kingdom of God is righteousness and peace and joy in the Holy Ghost, that they are ready to close the book there."[33] But the kingdom Jesus preached and inaugurated was also an outward and social entity based on an "inward communion with God and in outward obedience to him. . . . By the power of the spirit dwelling in it, it was to overcome the spirit dominant in the world and thus penetrate and transform the world."[34] This inward (personal) and outward (social) transformation taken together, Rauschenbusch termed the "revolutionary" aspect of Christianity.[35] Walter located both of these impulses within his theology of the kingdom of God:

> This is the program of the Christian revolution: the Kingdom of God on earth. It includes a twofold aim: the regeneration of every individual to divine sonship and eternal life, and the victory of the spirit of Christ over the spirit of the world in every

31. Stackhouse, *Righteousness of the Kingdom*, 63.
32. Ibid., 79.
33. Ibid., 86.
34. Ibid., 87.
35. Cf. Bill Pitts, "Personal and Social Christianity in Rauschenbusch's Thought," *The American Baptist Quarterly* 26, no. 2 (Summer 2007): 138–60, on these two dimensions of Rauschenbusch's gospel.

form of human society and a corresponding alteration of all institutions formed by human society. These two are simultaneous aims. Every success in one is a means for a new success in the other.[36]

This, in its earliest form, is the prophetic message Walter Rauschenbusch would preach, teach, lecture on, and publish throughout the rest of his illustrious career.

The event that brought Walter Rauschenbusch to national fame and prominence was the publication of his *Christianity and the Social Crisis* in 1907. A well-thought out and compelling manifesto of the social gospel, it had, as Minus described it, "a gestation period of sixteen years."[37] He dedicated the book to his former parishioners on the west side of New York City, "to discharge a debt" he owed them for sharing their lives and hopes with him.[38] The contents and insights of the book drew heavily upon Rauschenbusch's unpublished work on "Revolutionary Christianity" and other earlier publications. It was immensely popular and sold more than fifty-five thousand copies.[39] *Christianity and the Social Crisis* was a clarion call for contemporary Christians to follow Christ and create a new social order that corresponded to the ideals of the kingdom of God. The book's popularity can be attributed to the cogency of its argument, as well as to the timing of the work, coming in the midst of the progressive era and on the eve of the First World War.

Christianity and the Social Crisis drew together the new theological insights about Jesus and the kingdom of God with the reform spirit of the age; it merged these into a passionate plea for a social reformation that challenged the values and practices of the Gilded Age and modern, urban, industrial society. The first four chapters formed the foundation of the book; chapter 1 explored the historical roots of christianity in the Hebrew prophets. Here we meet Rauschenbusch's argument that Christianity is a prophetic, revolutionary faith, rooted in the teachings of the great prophets of the Hebrew Scriptures.

Chapter 2 examined the social aims of Jesus in order to show Jesus' continuity with and extension of the work of the Hebrew prophets, as well as the truly social character and implications of

36. Stackhouse, *Righteousness of the Kingdom*, 110-11.
37. Minus, *Rauschenbusch*, 157.
38. Walter Rauschenbusch, *Christianity and the Social Crisis* (New York: Macmillan, 1907), xxxviii.
39. Minus, *Rauschenbusch*, 162.

Jesus' teachings about the kingdom of God. Rauschenbusch argued persuasively that "Jesus [was] not a social reformer, but a religious initiator." Hence,

> no comprehension of Jesus is even approximately true which fails to understand that the heart of his heart was religion. No man is a follower of Jesus in the full sense who has not through him entered into the same life with God. But on the other hand, no man can share his life with God whose religion does not flow out, naturally and without effort, into all relations of his life and reconstructs everything that it touches. *Whoever uncouples the religious and the social life has not understood Jesus.*[40]

In his final chapters, "The Stake of the Church in the Social Movement" (chapter 6) and "What to Do" (chapter 7), Rauschenbusch moved from diagnosis to prescription. These chapters called for a wholesale reenvisioning of the church and the church's mission in the world.[41] The book was written in evangelism–social gospel style. It is a wake-up call for the church to look around and carefully assess the social problems that assail people and to create new energy, efforts, and institutions to undertake the difficult task of social change. Rauschenbusch depicted the institutional church as standing at a critical juncture. If the church follows contemporary society into decay, disintegration, and self-destruction, then "the Church will be carried down with it."[42] But in "doing the will of God it will have new visions of God. [And] with a new message will come a new authority."[43] Doing the will of God in a faithless and unjust world does not guarantee a path of ease or immediate success, but, as Rauschenbusch stated, "If the Church fulfills its prophetic functions, it may bear the prophet's reproach for a time, but it will have the prophet's vindication thereafter."[44]

After a thorough exploration of social, economic, and political realities, like private ownership of all property and rampant capitalism—all of which need to be transformed—Rauschenbusch urged his readers to look within themselves; the roots of social crisis run deeper—to the corruptions of the human heart. Rauschenbusch relayed that there is no real hope for humanity short of seeking the "mind of Christ" about our individual and corporate lives, so that

---

40. Ibid., 48.
41. Ibid., "Contents," viii–ix.
42. Ibid., 341.
43. Ibid.
44. Ibid., 341–42.

our entire lives are lived with a profound sense of stewardship and responsibility under God.[45] In Rauschenbusch's view, the root causes of social crisis are moral and spiritual at its basis; they can be dug out only through religious regeneration.

Rauschenbusch fled to Europe just prior to the release of *Christianity and the Social Crisis*, partly because of his justified trepidation about how the book would be received. While it hit the American religious scene like a bombshell, the book was widely acclaimed, and its popularity catapulted him into a position of national prominence, making him the tacit leader of the social gospel movement. As Christopher Evans pointed out, "The years between 1908 and 1912 witness the institutional ascendency of the social gospel in American Protestantism and Walter Rauschenbusch was at the center of that movement."[46]

Rauschenbusch's next major publication, *Prayers of the Social Awakening* (1910), was, as the title suggests, a book of prayers that were shaped by the perspective of the social gospel. They emphasized Christian collective consciousness and social responsibilities. Because they embodied a synthesis of Rauschenbusch's earlier evangelical piety with the concerns of the social gospel, these prayers both "reflected the devotional side of his faith and symbolized for later generations the distinctive evangelical-liberalism of the social gospel."[47]

The year 1912 saw the emergence of Rauschenbusch's *Christianizing the Social Order*. The production of this book was thrust upon him by the popularity of *Christianity and the Social Crisis*. As he explained in the preface to his second major published work, "I had urged a moral reorganization of social institutions, a Christianizing of public morality. Men asked 'what must we do?' And 'what must we undo?'"[48] Where his first major work was a searing diagnosis of the illness of contemporary society, the second one was a prescription for its healing.

In reply to his own question, "What next?"[49] Rauschenbusch undertook a scathing analysis of "Our Present Economic Order" in which he reported, "Business life is the unregenerate section of our social order."[50] The necessary economic and social changes demanded a

45. Ibid., 386–87.
46. Evans, *The Kingdom*, 208.
47. Ibid., 214–15.
48. Walter Rauschenbusch, *Christianizing the Social Order* (New York: Macmillan, 1913), vii.
49. Ibid., 155.
50. Ibid., 157.

wholesale regeneration of society. "We must begin at both ends simultaneously," he wrote. "We must change our economic system in order to preserve our conscience and our religious faith; we must renew and strengthen our religion in order to be able to change our economic system. This is a two-handed job; a one-handed man will bungle it."[51]

The years between the publication of *Christianity and the Social Crisis* and the outbreak of World War I marked the most satisfying and productive period of Walter Rauschenbusch's professional life. They were, as Dores Sharp described them, "the happiest years of Rauschenbusch's life."[52] His happiness evaporated quickly, however, as the world marched steadily toward all-out war. Rauschenbusch's love for Germany and his own ethnic heritage, as well as his commitment to the gospel mandate for peace, caused him to harbor deeply ambivalent feelings about World War I when hostilities erupted in 1914. In a climate strongly charged by American patriotic jingoism, even on the part of the church, Rauschenbusch persistently urged American political neutrality.[53] His posture drew questions about his personal patriotism and his loyalty to America. Despite considerable public pressure, even from his colleagues at RTS, Rauschenbusch did not make a public denunciation of German militarism until the war wound down in 1918.[54] In the context of his own serious illness and relentless public criticism, he wrote in March 1918, "Since 1914 the world is full of hate, and I cannot expect to be happy again in my life time?"[55]

During these sad times, Rauschenbusch wrote two small works books directed to the general public. The first, *Dare We Be Christians?* was published in 1914, just as the war broke out. It was an extended exposition of Paul's and Jesus' teachings about *agape*, which challenged his fellow Christians to live an authentic life of love. "Our capacity to build society depends on our power of calling out love," he wrote. "Our faith in God and Christ is measured by our faith in the value and workableness of love."[56] It was a volatile message for a world at war, and yet love was absolutely essential to Rauschenbusch's larger proposal for social reform: "Every step of social progress demands an increase in love. The history of evolution is

51. Ibid., 459–60.
52. Sharpe, *Walter Rauschenbusch*, 75.
53. Evans, *The Kingdom*, 288.
54. Minus, *Rauschenbusch*, 184.
55. Sharpe, *Walter Rauschenbusch*, 356.
56. Walter Rauschenbusch, *Dare We Be Christians?* (New York: Beacon Press, 1914), 35.

a history of the appearance and the expansion of love."[57] Rauschenbusch viewed the breakdown of love and a corresponding loss of
"fellow-feeling" as the reason for the current social crisis and class
strife in America; this was especially obvious in the selfish exploitation that was so much a part of big business.[58] Written as it was, on
the eve of World War I and the context of the tumultuous events that
led up to it, *Dare We Be Christians?* was both socially relevant and
prophetically challenging.

The Social Principles of Jesus was published in 1916 as a "personal study" for college students. Arranged in short daily readings,
the contents are comprised of biblical texts with exposition and analysis, as well as study questions designed to help the reader understand
"the connection between the principles of Jesus and modern social
problems. . . . It challenges college men and women to face the social convictions of Jesus and to make their own adjustments."[59] The
book concludes with "A Review and Challenge," in which the college
women and men were urged to join the struggle for social justice: "If it
can win the active minds of the present generation of college students,
it will swing a part of the enormous organized forces of the Christian
Church to bear on the social tasks of our American communities, and
that will help to create the nobler America which we see by faith."[60]

Rauschenbusch's last major work, which provided both the
foundation and summation for the others, was *Theology for the
Social Gospel*. This work emerged just prior to his death in 1918.
Rauschenbusch had called for the production of a new theology
for the new social gospel since 1899, when he urged cogently, "We
need a theological basis for our social intent."[61] Traditional theology was too individualistic to be of much use to the social gospel;
more consideration needed to be paid to the collective aspects of
Christian faith. But Rauschenbusch's *Theology for the Social Gospel*
was not so much a repudiation of the older theology as it was an
enlargement of it. The older theology also needed to be energized
and broadened by the new insights and new progressive spirit that
was emerging at this time. "Theology," he wrote, "needs periodi-
cal rejuvenation. Its greatest danger is not mutilation but senility."[62]

57. Ibid., 35.
58. Ibid., 40-43.
59. Walter Rauschenbusch, *The Social Principles of Jesus* (New York: Association Press, 1916), i.
60. Ibid., 196.
61. Sharpe, *Walter Rauschenbusch*, 321.
62. Walter Rauschenbusch, *A Theology for the Social Gospel* (New York: Macmillan, 1917), 12.

Later in the same work, Rauschenbusch summed up the failure he saw in traditional, individualistic theology: "Theology has not been a faithful steward of the truth entrusted to it. The social gospel is its accusing conscience."[63]

Theology for the Social Gospel was dedicated to Rauschenbusch's friend and former mentor, Augustus H. Strong. Despite his conflicted relationship with Strong, the dedication evidenced Walter Rauschenbusch's enduring friendship, as well as his attempt to build his new social theology upon the doctrinal foundation that Strong had bequeathed to him. Rauschenbusch later said he wrote not only out of gratitude toward Augustus Strong but also in an attempt to "clasp hands through him with all those whose thought has been formed by Jesus Christ."[64] Yet, on several significant matters, including the atonement of Christ and eschatology, Rauschenbusch made significant departures from the older approach, but he also understood and advocated for the deep interconnection between the old gospel and the new. "We have a social gospel," Rauschenbusch declared. "We need a systematic theology large enough to match it and vital enough to back it. . . . The social gospel needs a theology to make it effective; but theology needs the social gospel to vitalize it."[65] He urged, "In short, we need a theology large enough to contain the social gospel and alive and productive enough not to hamper it."[66]

Walter Rauschenbusch was a prophet of the kingdom of God; that he was indeed a prophetic figure is made clear by his own definition of a prophet:

> These men were so alive to God and felt his righteousness so overpoweringly that they beat their naked hands against jagged injustice and inhumanity. They were centers of religious unrest, creators of divine dissatisfaction, and the unsparing critics of all who oppressed and corrupted the people. The prophets were religious reformers demanding social action.[67]

Ethicist William Ramsey rightly termed this definition of a prophet "a kind of unconscious self-portrait by Walter Rauschenbusch."[68]

Walter Rauschenbusch's many contributions to the turn-of-the century theological scene loomed large in the founding and shaping

---

63. Ibid., 53.
64. Ibid., i.
65. Ibid., 1
66. Ibid., 9.
67. Rauschenbusch, *Christianizing the Social Order*, 51.
68. William Ramsey, *Four Modern Prophets* (Atlanta: John Knox Press, 1986), 10.

of the social gospel and progressive theology.[69] The "father of the social gospel," as some have called him, was a Christ-centered man whose life and values were indelibly shaped by *The Social Principles of Jesus*. He was also a deeply spiritual man whose inner strength was as evident in his *Prayers for the Social Awakening* as it was in his overcoming ethnic prejudice and disabling deafness to issue a clarion call for American middle-class Christians to renew and mobilize to take up the task of redeeming society. His years in Hell's Kitchen taught him lessons that could not be learned entirely in the classroom and gave Walter a particular sensitivity to the burdens of the poor and the working class, and a deep awareness of the pain and exploitation that came with economic disparity. He was, by his own definition, a prophet; that is, "a center of religious unrest, creators of divine dissatisfaction, and the unsparing critic of all who oppressed and corrupted the people."[70]

Rauschenbusch understood and proclaimed the wholeness of the gospel of Christ: "Whoever uncouples the religious and the social life," he wrote, "has not understood Jesus."[71] And so it was a matter of *Christianity and the Social Crisis* and not, as it was for so many contemporary people of faith, Christianity or the current social crisis. For him, Christianity—authentic Christianity—was by nature intimately involved in ameliorating all the problems that assailed the children of God, even as people of faith were called to create a new and better future together. Hence, in the face of the militarism, jingoism, and prejudices that impelled his world toward all-out war, Rauschenbusch prophetically asked *Dare We Be Christians*? That is, dare one live by the *agape* of God that was manifest in Jesus?

Walter Rauschenbusch exemplified what was best in the legacy of the Divinity School and summarized well its mission when he wrote, "We want to breed prophets here."[72] His advocacy for personal transformation and social reform rooted in the gospel of Jesus and the presence of the kingdom of God is the vital legacy of CRCDS, and indeed of all Christians, as we look upon the crises plaguing our modern society.

---

69. The fuller vision of the Rauschenbusch legacy has recently been made more accessible through the prodigious efforts of William H. Brackney and the publication of *Walter Rauschenbusch: Collected Works and Selected Writings*, 3 vols. (Macon, GA: Mercer University Press, 2018).
70. Rauschenbusch, *Christianizing the Social Order*, 51, slightly modified for tense agreement.
71. Minus, *Rauschenbusch*, 48.
72. Ibid., 143.

8

An Era of Change

When Augustus H. Strong announced his retirement in May 1911, it marked the end of an era. The trustees appointed a search committee for the difficult task of finding his replacement. Strong hoped that his youngest son, John Henry Strong (1866–1960), would succeed him.[1] After studying at Harvard and RTS, John Strong joined the Rochester faculty as professor of New Testament interpretation. He was a man of deep piety but not deep scholarship, and he ultimately left RTS in 1914 to assume a pastorate in Baltimore. With John went his father's hopes of retaining the school's delicate balance of traditional and liberal theology. And while Augustus Strong professed a willingness to stay out of the search for his successor, his towering presence continued to cast a long shadow over the presidential search and other events at RTS. Walter Rauschenbusch, who served on the search committee, nominated two of his friends as potential candidates: William H. P. Faunce, who was president of Brown University, and a young Colgate Theological Seminary graduate, Harry Emerson Fosdick, who was serving as professor of homiletics at Union Theological Seminary.[2] But neither nomination panned out. While the committee searched for three years, J. A. Stewart, who joined the faculty as professor of ethics and acted as dean in support of Strong since 1903, served as both dean and interim president.

The vacancies caused by the retirement of Augustus Strong were twofold, since he held the chair of systematic theology in addition to

---

1. LeRoy Moore, "The Rise of American Religious Liberalism at the Rochester Theological Seminary, 1872-1928," PhD diss., Claremont Graduate School, 1966, 164.
2. Christopher H. Evans, *The Kingdom Is Always Becoming: The Life of Walter Rauschenbusch* (Grand Rapids: Eerdmans, 2004), 257.

the presidency. While Stewart served as interim president, significant theological and curricular changes began to occur at the seminary. As Stewart himself noted in a retrospective address, "Change had already begun in Dr. Strong's time, and after his retirement in 1912 it went forward rapidly. It has not been a revolutionary change; it has rather been an inevitable and wholesome evolution. . . . Transition was inevitable."[3] In 1915, at the end of his stint as acting president, Stewart told the trustees, "It is difficult to realize how greatly and in how many ways the seminary has changed at this time."[4]

One of those changes appeared in the theological perspective of the faculty. The swing toward a more progressive faculty, which began in the waning years of Strong's regime, became complete. Most notable among the new additions were Henry Burke Robins (1874–1949), who came to RTS to teach the history and philosophy of religion (among other things); Ernest William Parsons, who taught English Bible and biblical languages; and George Cross (1862–1929), who filled Strong's chair in systematic theology. Each of these men was more progressive than his predecessor. The only faculty chair that remained vacant under Stewart's leadership was homiletics, and that position would be filled by the incoming president.[5]

The appointment of George Cross was probably the most influential of these new appointments. He was the first of the liberal theologians who came to RTS during Stewart's tenure and was hired at the same board meeting that approved J. A. Stewart as acting president. Cross earned a PhD in systematic theology from the University of Chicago in 1900, having spent a year studying abroad in Edinburgh and Berlin. Prior to joining the RTS faculty in 1912, Cross taught at McMaster Divinity College in Hamilton, Ontario, and Newton. In 1911, just prior to his time at RTS, Cross published his first major theological work, *The Theology of Schleiermacher*. It was a significant work on the thought of "the father of modern liberal theology" and remains in print to this day.[6] It is a careful translation and distillation of Friedrich Schleiermacher's main theological work, *Die Christliche Glaube* (1889). Cross's admiration for the work of the German theologian was immense. Cross wrote, "It remains the

3. *Rochester Theological Seminary Bulletin*, May 1925, 45.
4. *Rochester Theological Seminary Bulletin*, June 1915, 34.
5. Moore, "Rise of American Religious Liberalism," 171-72.
6. George Cross, *The Theology of Schleiermacher: A Condensed Presentation of His Chief Work "The Christian Faith"* (Chicago: University of Chicago Press, 1911).

imperishable honor of Schleiermacher that he grasped the whole problem of theology in a new way and compelled theologians of all schools to follow him. He vindicated for the religious life the claim to utter supremacy in any theory of the relations of God, man and the world. He has gradually forced modern theology to attempt the radical reconsideration of every traditional doctrine."[7]

So significant was Schleiermacher's willingness to start the theological task with lived human experience that Cross stated that "every theologian of the present day is his debtor."[8] That George Cross intended to follow Schleiermacher in this task of theological reconstruction and revision was made clear in an address he gave at RTS at the beginning of his second year:

> The theologian of the present is not specifically called upon to destroy or repair the doctrinal forms of former times. If he is worthy of his calling he will revere these forms, for he will find in them monuments of a great Christian past, indispensable for the interpretation of our history and our present relation to the past. . . . But let us of this new age set ourselves to the task of building for our own times structures in which a living man can be at home with his God and do his work.[9]

What Cross learned from Schleiermacher was the willingness to locate the starting point of religious inquiry squarely in universal human experience. He wrote: "Schleiermacher discovers religion to be an ultimate element of the self-consciousness. Accepting the common division of ultimate psychic facts into feeling, thought and will, he finds that religion is a universal human experience in the form of feeling."[10] Taking this starting point and task as his own, Cross wrote,

> the materials of theology are . . . human experiences. It turns to the inner life, the self-conscious life, of men . . . and seeks to know what is there. It is interested in the religious experience of *all* men and with *all* their religious experiences of men which have shown themselves to be the most valuable. . . . Modern theology is thoroughly humanistic. It seeks to know God and to interpret his ways, first of all, by discovering his ways in the souls of men.[11]

The theological project Cross inherited from his German mentor, Schleiermacher, was undertaken in several of the influential works he developed during this Rochester years; perhaps most notably was Cross's *What Is Christianity?* (1918). In this seminal work, he

7. Ibid., 333–34.
8. Ibid., 334.
9. George Cross, "The Call of the Day to the Religious Thinker," *Rochester Theological Seminary Bulletin*, January 1914, 10.
10. Cross, *Theology of Schleiermacher*, 310.
11. George Cross, *Rochester Theological Seminary Bulletin*, May 1916, 43–44.

offered a wholesale reinterpretation of the Christian faith from the standpoint of its essence as universal human religious experience. Cross's preface clearly spelled out the need for this sort of doctrinal revision in order for the person of faith to keep abreast with modern sensibilities and concerns. "The aim of this work," he wrote, "is to assist the intelligent layman and the minister of the gospel who have felt the need of revising their doctrinal inheritance to reach a more satisfactory interpretation of the Christian faith."[12]

After a painstaking analysis of six separate, historical interpretations of the essence of Christianity, Cross sought to answer the question posed by the title of the book: *What Is Christianity?* This, too, led to a thorough analysis on his part, but the basis of his argument was clear: "Christianity is the religion whose whole character is determined by the personality of Jesus Christ."[13] Becoming "like him [Christ]" was for Cross not merely imitating the actions of Jesus, or even trying to implement his words; rather, "since we must see our Christ with our own eyes, we must make our own interpretation of the Christian faith as we seek to fulfill the meaning of life. For us, there can be no set rules or fixtures for faith, for Christianity is free realization by the self-conscious spirit, of the kind of life Jesus Christ brought into the world."[14]

The life of Christ among us brings "the practice of the most perfect human fellowship."[15] According to Cross, this deep fellowship is also the essence and nature of Christianity: "Christianity is the religion of the most perfect fellowship because it magnifies every human life and enhances the worth of every factor that goes into the exaltation of it. Thus it teaches men to bring all the good things of the world into their service, and it makes the whole order of things a regular medium of the communion of men with one another."[16] But fellowship among Christian people is not to be construed as mere empathy, emotional attachment, or intellectual agreement; rather, "it is fundamentally constituted by moral action."[17] In his emphasis upon solidarity with the life of Jesus, in consecration toward God and solidarity with one's fellow humans through concerted moral action, based in God's assessment of human self-worth, Cross's social

---

12. George Cross, *What Is Christianity: A Study of Rival Interpretations* (Chicago: University of Chicago Press, 1918), vii.
13. Ibid., 193.
14. Ibid., 196.
15. Ibid., 197.
16. Ibid.
17. Ibid., 198.

vision proved to be an apt and able guide to the path previously marked out by Walter Rauschenbusch.

Augustus Strong, who was familiar with the work of Cross prior to Cross's coming to RTS, strongly opposed his election to the chair of systematic theology. Strong confided in his memoirs, "I regard that election as the greatest calamity that has come to the seminary since its foundation. It is the entrance of an agnostic, skeptical, and anti-Christian element into its teaching, the results of which will be only evil."[18] The election of Cross was soon followed by that of Henry Burke Robins and Ernest William Parsons, who were also liberal theologians. Their presence at RTS, along with that of Rauschen-busch and Conrad Moehlman, caused Strong to lament that "a veritable revolution had taken place."[19] But Stewart looked upon these developments with much more favor. Comparing the new additions to "the Big Five" of Strong's era, he remarked,

> Anyone who knew the teachers of other days and who knows their successors knows perfectly well that these men will not walk in the identical tracks of the former, but will make paths of their own. They too, equally with their predecessors, are Christian scholars and thinkers, men of conviction and power. They too must teach as God gives them to see the truth; the work of each will bear the stamp of his individuality.[20]

Stewart observed that a progressive attitude toward new, modern developments was necessary to keep up with changing times. Hence, in addition to an awareness of new developments in biblical studies, science, and philosophy, Dean Stewart believed, "Students in the Seminary must be trained to face the questions which will confront them in their ministry in order that they may be real pastors and teachers, and helpers of those who look to them. All this does not mean that Christian truth is ever in a state of flux; whatever the changes the Seminary stands, as it ever stood, an unchanging witness to Christ and His redeeming grace."[21]

A second place where significant changes were made under the leadership of Dean Stewart was in the curriculum. Developed under the guidance of Professors Betteridge, Rauschenbusch, and Cross, the new curriculum of 1913 abolished the old departments and grouped

18. Crerar Douglas, ed., *The Autobiography of Augustus Hopkins Strong* (Valley Forge, PA: Judson Press, 1981), 357.
19. Ibid.
20. Joseph William Alexander Stewart, "More Recent Days: 1912-15," *Rochester Theological Seminary Bulletin: The Seventy-Fifth Anniversary Record* 75, no. 1 (May 1925): 47–48.
21. Ibid., 48.

courses under four types: biblical, historical, systematic, and practical. New courses were added in the psychology of religion and religious education and sociology, and the offerings in biblical theology, biblical criticism, English Bible, missions, and ethics increased. The large number of required courses was reduced to allow for more selection on the part of the students. Moehlman described the new curriculum as "a creative adventure, and the most progressive action thus far taken in the history of the seminary."[22]

Even more progressive steps were taken along the lines of racial inclusion in 1912 as, beginning with Charles Hubert, African Americans began to be admitted to RTS, though with a limitation of two persons a year. In the vanguard of these early African American pioneers was Mordecai Wyatt Johnson (1890–1976). Born in Paris, Tennessee, the son of a former slave, Johnson was named for his father, Wyatt Johnson, a bivocational laborer and Baptist minister. The name Mordecai came from the book of Esther. In the spiritual dynamics of the biblical account and the powerful example and influence of his father and mother, Mordecai began to feel a call to Christian service even as a young man. He attended Roger Williams University in Nashville, but a fire destroyed so much of the campus during his junior year (1904–1905) that the school was unable to resume operations for nearly three years. Johnson then went from Nashville to Atlanta Baptist College (subsequently known as Morehouse College), where he excelled in academics, music, and athletics.

Upon graduating from Morehouse, Johnson attended the University of Chicago, taking courses there until he accepted a call from Morehouse to return to his alma mater to teach. Soon, however, Johnson responded to a growing call to Christian ministry and applied for admission to Newton Theological Seminary; he was, however, refused admission there because of his race. Johnson then applied and was admitted to Rochester Theological Seminary in 1913. He felt comfortable applying to RTS, in part, because one of his classmates from Atlanta Baptist College, Charles Hubert, graduated from RTS in 1912.[23]

At RTS Johnson was, once again, an outstanding student. Arriving near the end of the career of Walter Rauschenbusch, Johnson was able to study with the father of the social gospel, and as

22. Conrad Moehlman, "The Story of the Curriculum," *Rochester Theological Seminary Bulletin*, November 1926, 276.
23. Richard I. McKinney, *Mordecai: The Man and His Message* (Washington, DC: Howard University Press, 1997), 25–31.

a result, he was "imbued with a deeper sense than ever before, of the social implications of Christianity."[24] Johnson's own experience of the racial situation in America, coupled with his Christian faith and passion for social reform, fueled in him a holy impatience for social change, which he voiced to his friend John Hope, president of Morehouse College: "Sometimes I get very impatient at my studies. I long to be in the thick of the fight! Religion is going to be a great factor in the new adjustment. There never was such a reformation as we now are on the verge of. This religion reemphasized with new aspects to suit the modern needs will bring forth great moral and spiritual engineers. God grant that I may be one of these among my own people."[25]

Shortly after his graduation from RTS in 1915, Johnson was ordained into the Christian ministry at the Second Baptist Church in Mumford, New York, where he served as a student pastor for three years. RTS president Dr. Clarence Barbour was present at his ordination and prayed the ordination prayer. Johnson soon married his college sweetheart, Anna Ethelyn Gardner, and they settled in Mumford.

In 1917 Johnson enthusiastically accepted a position with the International Committee of the YMCA, expecting it to be a part of the dramatic social change he anticipated for America. He soon resigned, however, because when he attended an important YMCA staff conference in Atlantic City, Johnson found that the organization had succumbed to segregationist and discriminatory attitudes in eating and lodging. He promptly resigned in protest of this lack of Christian brotherhood in an organization that was professedly Christian. This was a bold and dangerous step for Johnson to take, because his wife, Anna Ethelyn, was three months pregnant.[26] But he was soon offered a call to serve as pastor at the First Baptist Church in Charleston, West Virginia, which he accepted. He had a very successful ministry there that embraced both the personal and social aspects of the Christian gospel. The church tripled in membership in his first three years there and was placed upon a solid financial foundation by his institution of a planned giving program. Johnson established a department of social services in the church, expanded its educational

24. Ibid., 34.
25. Ibid., 33. McKinney cities a letter of Mordecai Wyatt Johnson to Dr. John Hope, dated March 29, 1914, from the manuscript.
26. Ibid., 36.

programs, and developed a library. Among his social accomplishments in Charleston was the establishment of a local chapter of the NAACP to meet the needs and protect the rights of the more than one thousand African Americans in Charleston.[27]

After four years of energetic and intense pastoral work, Mordecai Wyatt Johnson requested and was granted a sabbatical leave during which he attended Harvard University Divinity School to earn a master of sacred theology degree in 1922. Once again, he graduated at the top of his class and was invited to deliver a commencement address. The topic he chose was "The Faith of the American Negro." In his remarks Johnson detailed the extensive black contribution to the establishment of America, as well as the disenfranchisement of African Americans from their well-earned rights of full citizenship. His assessment was that most blacks are "completely disillusioned," because

> they see themselves surrounded on every hand by a sentiment of antagonism which does not intend to be fair. They see themselves partly reduced to peonage, shut out from labor unions, forced to inferior status before the courts, made subjects of public contempt, lynched and mobbed with impunity, and deprived of the ballot, the only means of social defense. . . . And now they can no longer believe . . . that their own efforts after intelligence, wealth, and self-respect can in any wise avail to deliver them from these conditions unless they have the protection of a just and beneficent public policy in keeping with American ideals.[28]

The impact of this address was dramatic. It was received as both a challenge and a call to action. Among the outcomes stemming from this address was an offer from Harvard for Johnson to stay on in order to study with Dr. George Foot Moore for a PhD degree. But Johnson did not feel free to accept this offer due to his prior commitment to return to the Charleston church following his sabbatical year. There, in the midst of the Bible Belt, he continued to proclaim personal and social salvation along with personal and social ethics.

His sermons established Mordecai Wyatt Johnson as a nationally sought-after pulpit orator and lecturer. Among the venues where he frequently appeared as a guest preacher and lecturer was Howard University in Washington, DC, where he preached and lectured frequently over a five-year period. In token of their appreciation and approval, Howard awarded him an honorary doctor of divinity degree in 1923. By 1926, at the age of thirty-six, he was invited to serve

27. Ibid., 38-42.
28. Ibid., 46.

Howard University as president; he was the first African American president of that prestigious, historically black institution. During Johnson's thirty-four-year tenure at the head of Howard University, he established a pattern of academic excellence and leadership that affected several generations of able and well-prepared students. Under his leadership the enrollment at Howard grew from two thousand in 1926 to ten thousand in 1960, the year of his retirement. The size of the faculty tripled and faculty salaries doubled. But his most enduring legacy, it seems, was the influence Mordecai Wyatt Johnson had upon the lives of those who served or studied with him. They invariably absorbed his Christian, social reformist vision, and among them are preacher and theologian Howard Thurman, Supreme Court Justice Thurgood Marshall, and nonviolent Christian social reformer Martin Luther King Jr.[29]

After a three-year hiatus, in 1915, Clarence A. Barbour (1867–1937) became the third president of Rochester Theological Seminary and professor of homiletics. Barbour served as pastor of Lake Avenue Baptist Church in Rochester from 1891 to 1909 and was well known to the seminary, having served on the board of trustees since 1896. RTS was also well-known to Barbour. After graduating from Brown University in 1888, where he studied under Ezekiel Gilman Robinson, he attended RTS and graduated in 1891. Following graduation, he was called to Lake Avenue Baptist Church in Rochester, where he had an illustrious ministry and grew it into one of the city's foremost churches. Emphasizing the social gospel he learned at RTS, Barbour was also a "forceful and effective leader in campaigns for temperance, good government and efficient operation of the public schools."[30] In 1909 he resigned from Lake Avenue Church to accept an executive position with the International Committee of the YMCA. In this capacity, he traveled far and wide, largely in connection with the "Men and Religion Forward Movement." During his six years with the YMCA, Barbour became widely known and acclaimed as a public speaker and pulpit orator. In recognition of his successful ministry and public service, he was awarded an honorary doctor of divinity degree from the University of Rochester in 1901 and Brown University in 1909 prior to his leadership at RTS.

29. Dianne Washington, "Johnson, Mordecai Wyatt," in *An Online Reference Guide to African American History*, http://blackpast.org/aah/johnson-mordecai-wyatt-1890-1976, accessed September 28, 2017.
30. Moore, "Rise of American Religious Liberalism," 228.

LeRoy Moore characterized President Barbour as "an evangelical liberal who made a great deal of experienced religion and very little of the subtleties of dogma."[31] Under his leadership, RTS's transition into a progressive seminary was completed. Describing the "Educational Attitude of the Seminary" in 1925, Barbour wrote,

> The seminary has endeavored to maintain a progressive attitude. Her passion is for truth and reality. She has fearlessly faced the facts which call for a reinterpretation and restatement of our Christian faith. She is keenly alert to the quests and the needs of humanity today. Her attitude is likewise constant in the exaltation of the spirit above the letter and in the development of the free prophetic spirit and vision. To stimulate the consciousness of a divine urge and a divine dynamic and mission within her sons is her constant aim.[32]

As an able administrator and much sought-after speaker, President Barbour traveled widely on behalf of the seminary, logging an estimated forty thousand miles per year in days prior to passenger air travel.[33] He was also very active in the Northern Baptist Convention, having been elected its president in 1916.

Under Barbour's leadership, RTS made further strides toward financial stability, and curricular innovations continued. Robert Kelly's exhaustive study in *Theological Education in America* (1924) noted that "the program of 1921 is characterized by electives. Only about one-third of the advertised courses and about two-thirds of the total number of hours required for graduation are prescribed."[34] Kelly also reported a proliferation of courses in new, modern subjects and fields. Hence, he concluded, "The above analysis shows this seminary to have made a marvelous development during the last half century in its struggle to meet the needs of changing conditions."[35] The school was staffed by ten full-time faculty members and attended by sixty-six "regular" (full-time, residential) students.[36]

Among those progressive steps were the full and equal admission of women in 1920, the same year in which women's suffrage was enacted through the Nineteenth Amendment. Kelly reported, "Men and women are admitted to the seminary on precisely similar terms. The seminary was opened to women by vote of the trustees in

31. Ibid., 234.
32. Clarence A. Barbour, "The Future of the Seminary," *Rochester Theological Seminary Bulletin* 75, no. 1, May 1925: 76.
33. Moore, "Rise of American Religious Liberalism," 235.
34. Robert Kelly, *Theological Education in America* (New York: George Doran Co., 1924), 80.
35. Ibid., 81.
36. Ibid., 322.

1919."[37] This development drew criticism from conservative Baptists and their publications.

The first of the women to graduate from RTS with a Bachelor of Divinity was Ruth von Krumreig Hill in 1922. Ms. Hill was also a graduate of the Baptist Missionary Training School in Chicago (1916) and Shurtleff College in Alton, Illinois (BS, 1918). Her college yearbook, *The Retrospect,* remembered Hill as "an earnest worker. Unassuming, with soft, well-modulated voice, and quiet, zentle 'rays, Ruth is one of those persistent persons who holds to her purpose tenaciously until she obtains her ideal. Studious to the point of disregarding her health, but she wills to finish with this class and she will."[38] Ordained to Christian ministry on February 20, 1925, Hill served as an associate pastor in Ferndale, Michigan, then as pastor at Park Church in McKeesport, Pennsylvania, and the Baptist Temple, in Logansport, Indiana.[39] Hill eventually earned a PhD from the University of Chicago Divinity School in 1933.

During this same period African Americans, such as Howard Washington Thurman (1899–1981) from Daytona, Florida, continued to be represented among the student body. He came to RTS through the challenges of the Jim Crow South and a stellar career at Morehouse College in 1923. He was at the head of his class of twenty-nine students in 1926 and graduated with a bachelor of divinity degree as valedictorian. Thurman became an internationally famous preacher, teacher, writer, and spiritual guide.[40]

Another prominent African American of the newly unified Colgate Rochester Divinity School was Joseph H. Jackson (1900–1990), who graduated in 1932. Jackson served as pastor of Olivet Baptist Church in Chicago (1941–1990) and as the secretary of the Foreign Missions Board of the National Baptist Convention (NBC) from 1935 to 1941. In 1953 Jackson was elected president of the NBC, a position he held for twenty-nine years. As a conservative political and theological voice within the African American community, his advocacy for "civil rights through law and order" ran counter to the social activism and civil disobedience of Martin Luther King Jr. and others. Jackson's long presidency of the NBC and conservative views

---

37. Ibid., 323.
38. The Junior Class of Shurtleff College, ed., *The Retrospect* 7, Upper Alton, IL, (1917), 46.
39. *CRDS Bulletin* 3, no. 1 supp. (October 1930): 222.
40. See chapter 9 of the present work for a fuller treatment of Howard W. Thurman.

led to schism within the NBC and the formation of the Progressive National Baptist Convention in 1961.

Meanwhile, significant changes also occurred in Hamilton, New York, at Colgate Theological Seminary. In 1893 the seminary became a department of Colgate University, thereby resolving the question of its relationship with the university. In 1907 an Italian department was established in Brooklyn, New York, in order to serve the burgeoning immigrant population. The seminary was staffed by five full-time faculty members and had a student population in 1922 of forty-five students. It offered two degree programs: the traditional bachelor of divinity, which at Colgate ran six years and included baccalaureate education at the university, and the bachelor of theology degree, which was a four-year course that blended a collegiate education and seminary training into one program.[41] Faculty continued to turn over with great frequency at Colgate as Dr. John Vichert became a professor of theology and dean after William Allison's resignation in 1910. Frank Starratt also joined the theology faculty, and William Lawrence became lecturer in Christian ethics in 1912.[42] While Baptists predominated on the faculties of both Colgate and Rochester, neither school required adherence to a formal faith statement from its teaching staff.

In the aftermath of World War I, fundamentalism emerged as a vocal, conservative force in the mainline American denominations. The Northern Baptist Convention was convulsed by theological controversy more than most.[43] In fact, it was a Northern Baptist and editor of the *Watchman Examiner*, Curtis Lee Laws, who gave the fundamentalist movement its name when he wrote in 1920 "We suggest that those who still cling to the great fundamentals and who mean to do battle royal for the fundamentals shall be called 'Fundamentalists.' By that name the editor . . . is willing to be called. It will be understood therefore when he uses the word it will be in compliment and not in disparagement."[44] While there was significant variety as to what specific Christian beliefs constituted "the fundamentals," it became almost universally accepted among conservative Protestants that the "fundamentals" were all derived from the belief in an inerrant Bible. Biblical inerrancy was a proposition that was popularized

41. Kelly, *Theological Education*, 313–14.
42. Howard D. Williams, *A History of Colgate University* (New York: Van Nostrand Reinhold, 1969), 273.
43. Cf. S. C. Cole, *The History of Fundamentalism* (New York: Smith, Inc. 1931), N. F. Furniss, *The Fundamentalist Controversy, 1918-1931* (New Haven, CT: Yale University Press, 1954), and Ernest R. Sandeen, *The Roots of Fundamentalism* (Grand Rapids: Baker Book House, 1978).
44. Curtis Lee Laws, *Watchman Examiner*, July 1, 1920, 834.

by the nineteenth-century Princeton theologians A. A. Hodge (1823–1886) and B. B. Warfield (1881–1921) as a hedge against emergent theological liberalism. The "fundamentals" typically included matters like a six-day creation, the Mosaic authorship of the Pentateuch, the virgin birth of Jesus, the deity of Jesus, and his bodily resurrection. These doctrines were all established from and built upon belief in an inerrant Scripture. This conservative reaction to modernism was particularly potent among conservative Baptists who assumed, in the words of W. R. Riley, that "Baptists believe the Bible to be inspired, and hence inerrant."[45] Progressive theological developments in Baptist seminaries, such as those under way at Colgate and Rochester, drew both suspicion and criticism from Baptist fundamentalists.

At Colgate Theological Seminary, William Newton Clarke had already chronicled his own intellectual pilgrimage away from biblical inerrancy and toward progressive liberalism in *Sixty Years with the Bible*. At Rochester, Augustus Strong, the irenic evangelical, did not speak of the Bible as inerrant but preferred the more flexible term "infallible." He dropped use of the later term in the final edition of his *Systematic Theology*, where he preferred to speak of the Bible as "sufficient for its intended purpose."[46] This movement away from the conservative terminology and a conservative approach to the Bible became even more pronounced at RTS through the work of George Cross, Henry Robins, Ernest Parsons, and others of this era.

Fundamentalists within the Northern Baptist Convention sought to curb what they viewed as the dangerous tide of modernism in the Baptist seminaries. Laws conducted his own editorial survey of the Northern Baptist schools in order to determine their fidelity to what the conservatives viewed as a list of key Bible doctrines. This survey was sent to each of the Baptist seminaries, and their replies were to be published in the *Watchman Examiner*. No reply to the doctrinal survey was forthcoming from Colgate, Rochester, or Crozer theological seminaries, and the answers that were supplied by Newton were deemed unsatisfactory to the critics.[47] When he was president, Barbour explained Rochester's noncompliance to the RTS board of trustees in May 1920 in this way: "We have not responded to what

---

45. *Baptist Fundamentals: Being Addresses Delivered at the Pre-Convention Conference at Buffalo, June 21 and 22, 1920* (Philadelphia: Judson Press, 1920), 169.
46. Augustus Strong, *Systematic Theology*, 3 vols. (Philadelphia: Griffith & Rowland Press, 1907), I:196.
47. Moore, "Rise of American Religious Liberalism," 264.

we deem an unwarranted demand for a specific and detailed statement of creed. We believe that we would be misrepresenting your desire were we to make such a statement."[48] In support of his position, Barbour quoted Strong as saying the "duty of private judgment" was a Baptist tenet of faith and led to the impossibility of "absolute uniformity of thinking . . . among differently constituted men."[49] The fundamentalists, however, did not see this reply on behalf of the seminaries as being either positive or helpful. C. H. Fountain, in a work whose subtitle clearly suggests its content (*Should Our Schools Be Investigated?*), explained the seminaries' failure quite simply: "They fell down."[50] These tensions, then, inspired the calling of a general conference on "The Fundamentals of our Baptist Faith," in Buffalo on June 21and 22, 1920, immediately prior to the regular stated meeting to the Northern Baptist Convention.

The opening address at the Buffalo Conference, given by J. C. Massee of Brooklyn, New York, set the tone for the entire meeting: "The situation in our schools and seminaries is critical," he reported. The problem, as he saw it, was "the presence in our schools of the radical, scientific attitude of mind toward the Bible, of the materialistic evolutionary theory of life, and the extreme propaganda of the gospel of social betterment in substitution for the gospel of individual regeneration."[51] When W. R. Riley presented his report on "Modernism in Baptist Schools," he lamented, "Many of the Baptist seminaries of the North are hot-beds of skepticism."[52] The University of Chicago drew most of Riley's ire, but Cross, professor of systematic theology at Rochester, was also singled out for particular criticism.[53] Massee analyzed several of the published works by Crozer professors A. S. Hobart and Henry C. Vedder and concluded, "All of Crozer needs a denominational disinfecting."[54]

These speeches and charges produced an important impromptu resolution at the national meeting of the Northern Baptist Convention that was subsequently adopted. The resolution was comprised of three parts: the trustees and faculties of all the Northern Baptist seminaries were requested "carefully to examine their work, to correct

---

48. C. A. Barbour, *Rochester Theological Seminary Bulletin* (June 1920), 42.
49. A. H. Strong, *Philosophy and Religion* (Philadelphia: Griffith and Rowland, 1912), 327.
50. C. H. Fountain, *The Denominational Situation: Should Our Schools Be Investigated?* (Plainfield, NJ: n.p., 1921), 23.
51. J. C. Massee, "Opening Address," in *Baptist Fundamentals: Being Addresses Delivered at the Pre-Convention Conference at Buffalo, June 21 and 22, 1920* (Philadelphia: Judson Press, 1920), 4-5.
52. W. R. Riley, "Modernism in Baptist Schools," in *Baptist Fundamentals*, 178-79.
53. Ibid., 180-81.
54. Ibid.

evils which they may discover, and put forth a statement of their purpose of work"; second, a provision was made for an investigation committee to "inquire into the loyalty of our Baptist schools to Jesus Christ and his Gospel, and to the historical faith and practice of the Baptists, and their efficiency in producing men and women of Christian character and capacity for Christian service"; and, finally, this committee was instructed to report to the convention on "the entire question of the control of these institutions."[55] The report of this committee was to be presented to the entire convention at its next meeting in Des Moines in 1921.

The next year, the committee gave their investigative report, which was received with significant heat and controversy. A resolution was passed that said, "It is the duty of the Baptist communities throughout the country to displace from the schools men who impugn the authority of the Scriptures as the Word of God and who deny the deity of our Lord."[56] But no concrete action was taken against the theological schools or their faculties. After another year of pamphleteering and editorializing from conservatives and progressives, the convention met again in Indianapolis in 1922. Controversy erupted once again as a proposal was made for the entire convention to pledge itself to the moderately conservative New Hampshire Confession of Faith. At this point, RTS professor Cornelius Woelfkin rose to offer a substitute proposal: "that the New Testament is the all-sufficient ground of faith and practice, and we need no other statement."[57] The overwhelming support for and passage of Woelfkin's motion defeated those conservatives who sought to establish a formal standard of theological orthodoxy for the Northern Baptist Convention that would purge their seminaries of progressives. Woelfkin's proposal formed a new consensus to build a more harmonious future based on trust and academic freedom. By 1925 the trustees of RTS were able to remove a statement from the by-laws indicating that it is "the duty of the Committee on Instruction to visit from time to time the classrooms of the several professors."[58]

It was in this new climate that the Baptist seminaries at Colgate and Rochester began to move beyond their previous painful history

55. *Annual of the Northern Baptist Convention, 1920*, 60–61, 183.
56. *Annual of the Northern Baptist Convention, 1921*, 93.
57. *Annual of the Northern Baptist Convention, 1922*, 133.
58. "Minutes of the Board of Trustees," May 12, 1915, cf. C. H. Barbour and A. W. Beaven, "The Future of the Seminary," *Rochester Theological Seminary Bulletin*, May 1925, 75–81.

of division and separation to take steps of cooperation. In 1913, for example, when Colgate Theological Seminary began a summer school program, it soon became a joint venture shared by the two schools. This continued for a number of years, alternating locations between both schools, which allowed the faculty of the two schools to become better acquainted. These cooperative measures, and others like them, provided some foundation upon which the reunion of Colgate and Rochester seminaries could be built. But the final impetus for their merger came from beyond either school.

Talk of a merger, or reunion, of Colgate and Rochester went back to 1919, when President George Cutten (1874–1962) of Colgate University stated the

> inadvisability of maintaining a theological course at Colgate . . . when the curriculum was changed; that in order to better serve the denomination, Colgate Seminary volunteered to train men who, by reason of age or other handicaps, were unable to spend seven years in the full college course and seminary course subsequently, and to combine both in a course leading to the degree of Bachelor of Theology in four years.[59]

President Barbour of RTS recalled, "President Cutten urged the merger and consolidation, and gave weighty reasons why, in case of such a merger and consolidation, Colgate should move to Rochester rather than Rochester to Hamilton."[60] Similar sentiments were voiced by Dr. Albert Beaven, chairman of the board of trustees of New York Baptist Union for Ministerial Education, who also added other reasons in support of a merger.

In 1925, in response to an appeal from RTS to make a sizable contribution to its endowment in celebration of the seminary's seventy-fifth anniversary, John D. Rockefeller suggested that he would be willing to make a significant financial contribution if RTS, Colgate Theological Seminary, Newton, and Crozer Theological Seminary (all Northern Baptist seminaries functioning in the same geographic region) were willing to unite.[61] In March of that same year, Frank Padleford, secretary of the Northern Baptist Convention and a trustee of RTS, issued an unofficial invitation for representatives of the aforementioned four theological schools to meet in Albany on

59. Clarence H. Barbour, "Yesterday, Today, and Tomorrow," CRDS Bulletin 1, no. 1 (October 1928): 24.
60. Ibid.
61. This is reported by Orin Judd in an unpublished manuscript, "An Historical Sketch of Colgate Rochester Divinity School," 1963, who states this report came to him from Dr. Winthrop Hudson of CRCDS.

April 9, 1925, to discuss this merger. Three seminaries responded with representatives: Colgate, Rochester, and Newton. After several productive meetings in February 1926, the group concluded that a merger of the three schools was not feasible, but productive discussions continued between Colgate and Rochester. On March 30, 1926, plans for reunion were formalized in a meeting at Utica, New York, and the so-called Utica Agreement, outlining the conditions to merge Colgate and Rochester seminaries, was constructed. By June of the next year, a final agreement was reached.

The new corporation sponsoring Colgate Rochester Divinity School had its first meeting on July 26, 1928. It elected a board of trustees and appointed faculty; Ambrose Swasey of Cleveland became president of the Baptist Education Society, and Beaven, a 1909 alumni of RTS and pastor of Lake Avenue Baptist Church in Rochester, was elected chairman of the newly constituted, unified board of trustees. Dr. Thomas Wearing of Colgate was named dean of the new school, and four former Colgate Seminary professors were appointed along with him.

The new CRDS faculty was comprised of George Ricker Berry, John Benjamin Anderson, and John Frederick Vichert, all of whom came to CRDS from Colgate. They joined former RTS professors Conrad Henry Moehlman, George Cross, Glen Blackmer Ewell, Henry Burke Robins, Ernest William Parsons, Earle Bennet Cross, Frank Otis Erb, and Leland Foster Wood. At their first meeting, on July 31, 1928, the new CRDS faculty issued a new mission statement:

> We must maintain a progressive attitude, our position being for truth and for reality. We must fearlessly face the facts which call for a reinterpretation and restatement of our Christian faith, and we must place renewed emphasis upon practical training. The intellectual disciplines are important, but the primary objective of the school must be to send forth, not speculative scholars, but vital workers, in school and parish.[62]

Barbour was named president of CRDS, and the new seminary was born. On September 19, 1928, Colgate Rochester Divinity School formally opened its doors on the old Rochester Theological Seminary campus. It was, as Colgate archivist and historian Harold Williams concluded, an auspicious event: "Instead of two declining Baptist

---

62. *CRDS Bulletin* 1, no. 1 (October 1928): 27.

seminaries there was one strong one admirably fitted to educate young men for the ministry."[63]

At the November 7, 1928, board of trustees meeting, it was announced that CRDS had received "An Amazing Gift" from John D. Rockefeller, amounting to $1,250,000 "toward the purchase of a site, its development, and erection thereon of buildings for the new institution."[64] The Rockefeller gift was contingent upon the new seminary raising $250,000 in good-faith pledges and donations from other sources. Rockefeller also stipulated that his name not be directly associated with any of the campus buildings.

In 1929 Barbour left CRDS to assume the presidency of Brown University. Barbour was succeeded by Dr. Albert Beaven (1882–1943). A 1909 alumni of RTS, Beaven had been awarded the doctor of divinity degree from the University of Rochester in 1920. Under his leadership, the Lake Avenue Church grew to more than twenty-eight hundred members and developed such innovative programs of community service that it gained a national reputation.[65] In its attempts to sever the "personal gospel" from "the social gospel" and its reformist implications, Beaven clearly embraced the legacy of his prophetic predecessors. In his sermon "Religion: A Privilege or a Responsibility," for example, he lamented,

> A great deal is said in contemporary discussion about the individual and the social elements in religion, as though they were two separate things. . . . Indeed, there are those who insinuate that religion gets out of hand when it attempts to go beyond the individual and affect broader human relations. . . . "Let the preacher preach the gospel," we constantly hear; "Let the churches stick to their business, and not bother about the things of the world."[66]

After delineating the nature of the "Christianizing Process," Beaven concluded, "It is the normal expectation that the individual experience of surrender to Jesus Christ will be followed by an ever-expanding attempt on the part of those who profess faith in him to square their various relationships, in politics, in business, in all human relations, to the ideals of Jesus Christ."[67] The two schools' long heritage of producing analytical, thinking Christians was also enunciated and embraced by the new unified Divinity School, and

---

63. Williams, *History of Colgate University*, 290.
64. A. W. Beaven, "An Amazing Gift," *The Colgate-Rochester Bulletin* 1, no. 2 (November 1928), 82.
65. "The History of Lake Avenue Baptist Church," www.lakeavebaptist.org/history, accessed March 3, 2017.
66. Albert Beaven, *The Lift of a Far View* (Philadelphia: Judson Press, 1936), 43–44.
67. Ibid., 48.

in his first chapel address as president of the new CRDS, Beaven promised the student body,

> We shall not dogmatically tell you what you must think nor what you must preach, but we will insist that you must know God, that you must have a constant vital experience with Jesus Christ, that you face the truth without fear or favor, and think your way through it, and go out from here, not as echoes of what we have said, but as fearless prophets of your faith, convinced that in God, and in Christ, you have the greatest conceivable answer to the deepest needs of all those whom you will meet.[68]

As the new president of CRDS, Beaven immediately faced the enormous task of raising funds and building the campus. A twenty-four-acre site adjacent to Highland Park, in the Mt. Hope section of Rochester, was purchased, and Mr. James Gamble Rogers of New York City was hired as the architect for the new buildings. Construction on the new campus facilities began on April 1, 1931. The complex of new buildings was completed in July 1932, and the new campus was occupied for its first session in September 1932. It included Montgomery House, the president's residence, which was a specific gift from William Montgomery, a trustee of the Education Society, and his wife. Strong Hall, named after all three members of the Strong family, was the main academic facility. The building was divided into three adjoining units: at the west end of the building is the Ambrose Swasey Library, named for the president of the Baptist Education Society. The east end of the building, including the refectory and lounges and physical plant, was named John J. Jones Hall after the single largest contributor to CRDS The large center section housed classrooms and offices. The naming of the dormitories was symbolic of the union of the two schools; one section was named Trevor Hall for John B. Trevor, a longtime supporter of RTS, a continued name from the former campus. The other section was called Eaton Hall, named for President George Eaton of CTS, a dormitory name from the former Colgate campus.

The new campus was dedicated with "impressive ceremonies on October 21, 1932."[69] More than five thousand people attended the auspicious events of that day.[70] "The ceremonies," wrote one observer,

---

68. Albert W. Beaven, "President Beaven's First Chapel Address," September 17, 1929, from the manuscript in the CRCDS archives.
69. Albert W. Beaven, "Colgate Rochester Divinity School," in *The Centennial History of Rochester*, ed. Edward R. Foreman (Rochester, NY: Rochester Public Library, 1931–1932), 4:167.
70. Oren H. Baker, "Beautiful New Buildings at Rochester Dedicated with Impressive Ceremonies," *The Baptist* 13, no. 26 (July 2, 1932): 990.

"were made impressive by the simplicity, dignity, and appropriateness of every part of a tastefully prepared order of services."[71] Dr. Harry Emerson Fosdick, a 1900 graduate of Colgate who studied under William Newton Clarke, delivered the dedicatory address.

Reverend Fosdick was then pastor of the prestigious Park Avenue Baptist Church in New York City, and one of the most notable liberal preachers of the day. His address, contextualized in the difficult economy of the early 1930s, was titled "What Can a Christian Minister Do?" Fosdick urged that "the Christian minister can help build personalities strong in faith and character, so that inwardly steady they can do what they think they ought to do and endure what they have to stand."[72] "In the second place," he continued, "the Christian minister can help build the church of the future."[73] Finally, the Christian minister must, in a nonpartisan but prophetic manner, address the current social and economic crisis ("the Great Depression") by inculcating Christian virtues that will supplant those selfish values that fuel the problem: "We thought that we could make more money for ourselves by producing more goods to sell . . . forgetting that in our thirst for private profit, we practiced mass production without providing for mass consumption."[74] Fosdick urged his hearers, and particularly the young ministers assembled before him, to "go out with a high spirit into this three-fold ministry, to be builders of the spiritual life, builders of the church for the new day, and builders of social righteousness."[75]

Among the many dignitaries who attended the ceremonies was Dr. Helen Barrett Montgomery (1861–1934). She was not herself an alumna of the CRDS, but her father, Rev. Amos Judson Barrett, graduated from RTS in 1876 and served as pastor at Lake Avenue Baptist Church in the city from 1876 to 1889. She often joined the divinity school in reformist activities in Rochester and beyond. She was, for example, the first woman elected to the Rochester Public School board. Montgomery was an internationally known scholar, educator, social activist, and religious reformer. A longtime member of Lake Side Baptist Church in Rochester, Montgomery served as president of the American Baptist Convention in 1921 and was deeply engaged in

71. Ibid.
72. Harry Emerson Fosdick, "What Can the Christian Minister Do?" CRDS Bulletin 5, no. 1, 2 (November1932): 82.
73. Ibid., 83.
74. Ibid., 88.
75. Ibid.

church life and reformist activities throughout the region. Along with her friend and reformist colleague, Susan B. Anthony, Montgomery challenged the University of Rochester to open its doors to women in 1898, a challenge that finally came to fruition in 1909, after Montgomery helped raise more than $50,000 in support of that venture.

Helen Barrett Montgomery's motives and talents as a Christian educator, scholar, and social reformer all coalesced in her work as a Bible translator. It was a task she felt was thrust upon her by her experience of trying to teach street-boys Scripture from the dated phrases of the King James Version. This holy frustration combined with her passion for learning to compel Montgomery to make the Bible plain to the "ordinary" reader. When her *Centenary Translation of the Bible* was published in 1924, she was the first woman to translate and publish a version of the New Testament in English, and her translation is still the only English version of the Bible ever published by a Baptist woman. And so, as the aged and venerable American Baptist leader, educator, and social reformer rose to lead the congregation in a benediction at the dedication of the new campus, Dr. Oren Baker remarked, "The ceremony was closed in prayer, by Dr. Helen B. Montgomery, whose presence was a benediction."[76]

The development of the new physical plant of CRDS continued through the 1930s as a formal chapel structure and was added and dedicated in the fall of 1936. It was built, in large part, due to a gift from Russell and Sydney Colgate in honor of their father, Samuel Colgate, who was president for thirty-four years of the board of trustees of Baptist Educational Society of New York, a sponsor of Colgate Theological Seminary. During this same time, housing for married students, as well as apartments for missionaries, was erected and occupied. Additional student housing was developed in 1946, when Eaton Hall was converted into apartments for married students, and again in 1957 when Andrews House was built.

The new divinity school, with its new campus, soon developed a new curriculum as well. New elective courses were added, and all the courses of instruction were gathered under four specific heads: Christian Origins, Christian Progress, Christian Interpretation, and Christian Leadership. In addition to offering the bachelor of divinity degree, CRDS was also authorized to offer advanced courses that

---

76. Baker, "Beautiful New Buildings," 991.

led to the development of master of theology and doctor of theology degrees.[77] The ongoing expansion and development of the academic program was thoroughly consistent with the mission of CDCS to train pastors who were learned, pastoral, and prophetic. As President Beaven pointed out in 1934, "Although the first objective of the Divinity School is the training of young men for the pastoral care of Protestant churches, it is fully recognized that the scope of Christian leadership has greatly advanced in the century since the founding of the school in Hamilton. Many new forms of religious and social ministry have developed, each requiring specialized training for its leaders. . . . The present program of the Divinity School provides for an expansion, rather than a restriction of this development."[78]

Reporting on the dedication ceremonies for the new campus, Oren Baker reminded the readers of *The Baptist* that it was not the new buildings and new programs that were celebrated. Rather, it was the rich spiritual legacy of the two schools and the many devout people who embodied it:

> It was now made clear that the most significant thing about the new Colgate Rochester Divinity School was not the exquisite buildings, but the dedication of life which had made them possible and the spirit of devotion which had finally found for itself a permanent shrine in them. Generations of students who pass through these halls in days to come, if sensitive to all that lies around them, will not be content to read the poem in brick and stone but will discover through deeper appreciations the true epic of life which the whole structure is the symbol.[79]

And so, CRDS opened the 1933–1934 academic year with a full-time enrollment of 143 students, who were graduates of 57 different colleges and universities and hailed from 31 different states and foreign homelands.[80]

The two decades that separated the presidency of Augustus Strong and the reunion of the Rochester and Colgate schools were marked by dramatic changes. These were changes that both reflected and anticipated changing tides in American society and churches. As the theological landscape became polarized by the Fundamentalist-Modernist controversy, both RTS and CDS tilted toward modernism. The progressive spirit was as evident in the theological composition

77. Beaven, "Colgate Rochester Divinity School," 168.
78. Albert W. Beaven, "Colgate Rochester Divinity School," in *The Centennial History of Rochester, New York*, ed. Edward R. Foreman (Rochester, NY: Rochester Public Library, 1931-1934).
79. Baker, "Beautiful New Buildings," 991.
80. Fosdick, "What Can the Christian Minister Do?," 166.

of both schools as it was in their push for the inclusion of African Americans and women, just as immigrants had been embraced before them. And as conservatives fought for control of the Northern Baptist Convention through doctrinal examinations aimed at theological purity and ultimate exclusion of progressives, the progenitors of CRDS answered by noncompliance and by envisioning a broader and more inclusive church, which in the words of Woelfkin, believed: "that the New Testament is the all-sufficient ground of faith and practice, and we need no other statement."[81]

In both with its words and deeds, the new CRDS showed that the prophetic Christian legacy that had been prayerfully conceived in Jonathan Olmstead's parlor had survived the turmoil of schism and rebirth and reunion. It had clung tenaciously to the gospel message of Jesus Christ and refused to sever the gospel of personal renewal from its obvious social implications as the schools expanded their vision and ministry to include immigrants, African Americans, and women and began to challenge social structures like militarism and economic inequity that bred their oppression. The longevity of this legacy had been nurtured and sustained by what President Augustus Strong termed "brains, bricks, and books," but even more so, in the words of Oren Baker, "but the dedication of life which had made them possible and the spirit of devotion which had finally found for itself a permanent shrine in them."[82] It was fitting that on the day of the formal beginning of the new CRDS, one of the leading exponents its legacy, Harry Emerson Fosdick, urged a new generation "to go out with a high spirit . . . to be builders of the spiritual life, builders of the church for the new day, and builders of social righteousness,"[83] while one of its leading practitioners, Helen Barrett Montgomery, earnestly prayed that it would be so.

---

81. *Annual of the Northern Baptist Convention, 1922*, 133.
82. Baker, "Beautiful New Buildings," 991.
83. Fosdick, "What Can the Christian Minister Do?," 166.

9

Howard Thurman: Prophet of Inner Strength

Howard Washington Thurman (1900–1981) was born in West Palm Beach, Florida, and spent his childhood in the segregated Waycross section of Daytona where he encountered the deep challenges and soul-straining situations of being black in the Jim Crow South. As he would later recall, "The fact that the first 23 years of my life were spent in Florida and in Georgia has left its scars deep in my spirit."[1] Black life in the face of segregation, oppression, and injustice sustains an ongoing assault upon one's selfhood, which Thurman described poignantly in *The Luminous Darkness*. "It is clear," he wrote, "that for the Negro the fundamental issue involved in the experience of segregation is the attack that it makes on his dignity and integrity."[2] He came to see that however great was the tremendous evil done to African Americans through segregation, oppression, and prejudice, there was a deeper and more insidious evil involved:

> The real evil of segregation is the imposition of self-rejection! It settles upon the individual a status which announces to all and sundry that he is of limited worth as a human being. It rings him round with a circle of shame and humiliation. It binds his children with a climate of no-accountness as a part of their earliest experience of the self. Thus it renders them cripples, often for the length and breadth of their days. . . . What does it mean to grow up with a cheap self-estimate? There is a sentence I copied many years ago, the source of which I have forgotten: "We were despised so long at last we despised ourselves."[3]

---

1. Howard Thurman, *The Luminous Darkness: A Personal Interpretation of the Anatomy of Segregation and the Ground of Hope* (New York: Harper and Row, 1965), x.
2. Ibid., 5-6.
3. Ibid., 24.

Thurman would later reflect upon the "scars" he bore from his experiences of those early and painful years. He wrote about the path he took toward self-acceptance and affirmation, that it was paved in part by the embrace of tremendous familial strength, the fellowship of his local church, and the development of his own profound Christian faith. Thus, Thurman wrote, "Looking back, it is clear to me that the watchful attention of my sponsors in the church served to enhance my consciousness that whatever I did with my life *mattered*. They added to the security given to me by the quiet insistence of my mother and especially my grandmother that their children's lives were a precious gift."[4]

In his early life, Thurman also experienced a deep sense of solace and self-affirmation through his love for nature and his ability to sense the presence of God through nature. Looking back on this time from the distance of many years, he recalled, "The great contribution religion made to my life as a boy growing up in Florida, was this: it gave me a sense of worth, an intrinsic sense of being credible to myself—a sense that God, who had created the ocean, which I loved, and the eclipses and all the other things in nature, also created me."[5]

Thurman was born into a poor, religious, and strongly determined family. He remembered, "My mother [Alice Ambrose Thurman] was a devout, dedicated praying Christian. My father [Saul Solomon Thurman] was a good man, but the church was not for him."[6] In many instances the dynamic strength of the African American community and Mount Bethel Baptist Church were stabilizing forces in young Thurman's life, but the early death of his father also occasioned one of his first experiences of significant disillusionment with organized Christianity. Seven-year-old Howard Thurman "listened with wonderment, then anger, and finally mounting rage as [a visiting evangelist named] Sam Cromarte preached my father into hell."[7] "One thing is sure," Howard resolved to himself, "when I grow up and become a man, I will never have anything to do with the church."[8]

This youthful pledge, while honestly and deeply felt, would eventually prove to be untenable. Thurman gradually overcame some of

---

4. Howard Thurman, *With Head and Heart: The Autobiography of Howard Thurman* (New York: Harcourt, Brace, Jovanovich, 1979), 20.
5. "An Interview with Howard Thurman and Ronald Eyre," in "The Critic's Corner," *Theology Today* 38, no. 2 (July 1981): 208.
6. Thurman, *With Head and Heart*, 5.
7. Ibid., 6.
8. Ibid.

his earlier ambivalence about the Christian church, and in 1913, when he was twelve years old, he joined Mount Bethel Baptist Church and was (according to Baptist custom) immersed in the Halifax River. Ultimately, Howard Washington Thurman would become, according to *Life* magazine, "one of the twelve Great Preachers of the Twentieth Century."[9] He held significant teaching and preaching posts at several of the nation's leading academic institutions. He authored more than twenty religious books and became one of the paramount spiritual guides and mentors of his generation. But there was much to overcome with this deep ambivalence in his soul about organized religion in general and about American Christianity (as it was then understood and presented to him) in particular.

Both before and after the death of Thurman's father, his maternal grandmother, Nancy Ambrose, played a significant mentoring role in his youth. Born into the horrors of slavery, Nancy Ambrose could neither read nor write, and so, as a child, it fell to Howard to read the Bible to her. She recalled, however, that during her years of enslavement, she all too frequently heard preaching from the writings attributed to the apostle Paul: "Slaves, be obedient to your masters, for this is right in the Lord" (Colossians 3:22). Thurman recalled:

> My grandmother said that she made up her mind then and there that if she ever learned to read or if freedom ever came she would never read that part of the Bible. So all the years that I was growing up and had the job of reading to her every day, I could never read any of the Pauline letters, except now and then the 13th chapter of 1 Corinthians. Maybe this experience unconsciously influenced my thought when I wrote *Jesus and the Disinherited*.[10]

Nancy Ambrose had tremendous inner strength, rooted in her faith in God. Looking back many years later, Thurman described her as "a strong, positive, self-contained human being. Her life was full of tragedies—hunger, cold, the death of some of her children. But she had built-in controls."[11] Her tremendous strength came, as Thurman understood it, from the ability to stand inside Jesus and look out upon the world through Jesus' eyes. As he recalled in subsequent reflection, "She couldn't read her name if it was as big as this

9. Mark Kaufmann, "Great Preachers: These 12—And Others—Bring America Back to the Church," *Life*, April 6, 1953, 128.
10. Mary E. Goodwin, "Racial Roots and Religion: An Interview with Howard Thurman," *The Christian Century* 90 (May 9, 1973): 533.
11. Ibid.

chapel. But she had stood inside of Jesus and looked out on the world through his eyes. And she knew by heart what I could never know."[12]

This same vantage point on life was made evident to Thurman when his grandmother told him stories about the proclamation delivered by slave preachers during her youth:

> When the slave preacher told the Calvary narrative to my grandmother and the other slaves, it had the same effect on them as it would later have on their descendants. But this preacher, when he had finished, would pause, his eyes scrutinizing every face in the congregation, and he would tell them, "You are not slaves! You are God's children." When my grandmother got to that part of her story, there would be a slight stiffening in her spine as we sucked in our breath. When she had finished, our spirits were restored.[13]

It was precisely this same inner strength that Thurman found in his own heritage and faith through the "Negro Spirituals" and shared with others through his earliest publication, *Deep River: Reflections on the Religious Insight of Certain of the Negro Spirituals* (1945): "It was this sense of being a child of God," he wrote, "that the genius of the religious folk songs was born."[14]

The steps, both great and small, that took young Howard Thurman to international prominence and great usefulness for God were many and varied. While he was a junior at Florida Baptist Academy, Thurman was invited to attend the YMCA King's Mountain Conference in 1917, where he met and was befriended by Mordecai Wyatt Johnson. After their brief meeting at the King's Mountain Conference, Thurman, who missed an opportunity to speak with him at length (despite waiting forty-five minutes in the dark after one session), wrote Johnson a long and impassioned letter on June 28, 1918: "I wanted to know you and wanted you to know me, . . . I yearned to tell you [of] my hopes, ambitions, and discouragements, but each time something hindered."[15]

Taking his letter as an opportunity, Thurman recounted his life story in a few poignant paragraphs, beginning, "Listen while I tell you my soul."[16] After a half page of autobiography, Thurman moved to the specific reason he wrote to Johnson: "I want to be a minister

---

12. Howard Thurman, "Standing Inside with Christ," a lecture given at Bishop College, April 21, 1970. Cited in Luther E. Smith, *Howard Thurman: Mystic as Prophet* (Lanham, MD: University Press of America, 1981), 40.
13. Thurman, *With Head and Heart*, 21.
14. Howard Thurman, *Deep River and the Negro Spiritual of Life and Death*, 2nd ed. (Richmond, IN: Friends United Press, 1975), 18.
15. Walter E. Fluker, ed., The *Papers of Howard Washington Thurman*, 4 vols. (Columbia: University of South Carolina Press, 2009-), 1:1.
16. Ibid., 1:2.

of the Gospel. I feel the need of my people, I see their distressing conditions, and have offered myself upon the altar as a living sacrifice, in order that I may help the 'skinned and flung down' as you interpret. God wants me and His precious love urges me to take up my cross and follow Him. I want advice from you as to how to direct my efforts."[17] With both his graduation from high school and World War I looming in his immediate future, Thurman stood at an important juncture. "I am patriotic," he wrote; "I am willing to fight for democracy, but my friend Rev. Johnson, *my people need me*. I want a thorough training for my work which necessitates my taking a college course prior to Theology, would it not? . . . What would you advise me to do?"[18]

Johnson's generous and supportive reply arrived a few weeks later. "I thank you heartily for your recent letter," he wrote. "I have read the story of your aspirations and your strivings with great interest and sympathy. Your industry, your perseverance under difficulty, your reverence for your mother, and your yearning to serve mark you as a God-chosen man."[19] The best way forward for Thurman, Rev. Johnson advised, was further academic education and spiritual formation:

> By all means go on with your preparatory and college work. Meanwhile make yourself more and more acquainted with the history and biography of the Bible and with the teachings of Jesus and of Paul. It will be far better for you to enter the ministry after you have completed a college course than to make a short cut, putting a shallow course in theology on top of your preparatory work. . . . You should set before you the ideal of thorough preparation—a first class college course plus a first class theological training.[20]

Johnson urged Thurman to "keep in close touch with your people, especially with those who need your service. Take every opportunity to encourage their growth and to serve them. School yourself to think over all that you learn, in relation to them and to their needs. Make yourself believe that the humblest, most ignorant, and most backward of them is worthy of the best prepared thought and life that you can give."[21] Finally, Johnson wisely urged young Thurman to begin the practical work of ministry while he attended seminary. "Many

17. Ibid.
18. Ibid., emphasis added.
19. Ibid., 1:4.
20. Ibid.
21. Ibid.

young men pastor churches while they are doing their theological work," Johnson wrote. "I did that in Rochester."[22] In closing, he left young Howard Thurman with one clear word of advice: "Prepare! Prepare! This is the only word for you. You need have no fear about work; you will find plenty to do both while you are in school and afterwards."[23]

Despite great hardship and through much diligence both inside and outside the classroom, Thurman graduated as valedictorian from his high school in 1919 as the first black child from Daytona to earn a high school diploma.[24] Thurman was admitted to Morehouse College in Atlanta that same fall. When he graduated from Morehouse in the spring of 1923, Thurman was described in the yearbook as "our most brilliant classmate."[25] He graduated with a bachelor of arts in economics and many academic honors. Morehouse then offered him the opportunity to stay on as an instructor and have his degree "validated" by also attending the University of Chicago. By this time, however, Thurman's career path was well set in his heart and mind, and he applied for admission to Newton Theological Seminary in Newton, Massachusetts, for the fall of 1923. He heard about the school "from high school days," but as he reported, "I received a very cordial letter from the president expressing his regret that the school did not admit Negroes."[26] He then applied to Rochester Theological Seminary, since "certain things commended the school to me. Dr. Charles Hubert, a graduate of Rochester, taught a course in religion at Morehouse and was a solid, pervasive influence on the life of all the college men of my generation. Mordecai Johnson was also a graduate of Rochester. Morehouse men had established a reputation for high scholarship there that challenged those who followed."[27] Although African Americans were eligible for admission at RTS, at that time there was also a quota that limited their enrollment to no more than two persons at any given year. This meant, for Thurman, that he would almost always be a minority and would rarely have the fellowship and support of faculty and students of his own race. As he wrote, "When I entered seminary, I experienced the most radical

22. Ibid.
23. Ibid.
24. Mark S. Giles, "Howard Thurman: The Making of a Morehouse Man, 1919-1932," *Educational Foundations* 20, no. 1–2 (Winter–Spring 2006): 105–22; citation on 107.
25. Fluker, *Papers of Howard Washington Thurman*, 1:28–29.
26. Thurman, *With Head and Heart*, 45.
27. Ibid., 46.

period of adjustment of my life up to that moment. I was living for the first time in a totally white world. The impact of this fact alone was staggering."[28]

The entire culture of the seminary felt foreign to Thurman; he observed "the general atmosphere at Rochester contrasted sharply with the more personal and responsive ambience of Morehouse College."[29] These difficult social and cultural adjustments were exacerbated by his concern about whether he could measure up to his fellow students. "The majority of my classmates were, from eastern and mid-western colleges. At first my classmates seemed more broadly educated than I, and more widely read, and I felt intimidated by this. But as the weeks wore on I discovered that this was not the case and I could hold my own very well; my anxiety diminished."[30]

Thurman found both spiritual solace and intellectual excitement in the large RTS library. "The library was my refuge and my joy," he wrote. "The librarian . . . took a special interest in me. She responded to my eagerness, which I made no effort to conceal. . . . At last the world of books was mine for the asking."[31] He browsed the open stacks by the hour, "familiarizing myself with writers across the centuries who would in time become as closely related to me as my personal friends."[32]

The Divinity School had a pattern of putting African American students in single rooms, perhaps to ease the cultural clash between black and white cultures, but it also resulted in tacit segregation and, for Thurman, the prospect of being more alone in an already lonely and isolated life. When a suite of rooms across the hall from Howard's single room had a vacancy, two of his white classmates, Red Matthews and Dave Vos, "invited me to move out of my single room and join them. Instinctively, I knew that if I were to make the move I could never be as I was before; a lifetime of conditioning would have to be overcome. I asked for time to think it over so that we could be sure that this was what we wanted. I knew also that if I moved in with them we would be breaking the long-established separate housing policy of the seminary. When I mentioned this to Dave and Red they said that they knew of no such policy and would, in any

28. Ibid.
29. Ibid., 47.
30. Ibid.
31. Ibid.
32. Ibid.

case, ignore it."[33] Ultimately, Howard decided to join Red and Dave, and there were minor repercussions; "officially, not a word was said directly to me," Thurman recalled, "but both my roommates were called to the office; they did not discuss with me the substance of their interview. And that was that."[34]

Life beyond campus in Rochester was also a new, exciting, and challenging place for Thurman. "The city of Rochester," he wrote, "seemed fabulous to me. . . . Generally, I was not troubled by the question of race; I was never refused service or otherwise insulted in any of the stores."[35] He also benefited from the opportunity to occasionally see a movie and various types of concerts around town. He began to receive invitations for speaking engagements around the city and nearby towns where Thurman generally spoke on a religious subject, "but increasingly," he recalled, "I was asked to discuss the race question. Often, before the meetings, I would be the guest of the minister's family at dinner. Most of them had never had any contact with black people before. The experience was always educational and somewhat awkward for us all."[36]

As his off-campus speaking opportunities increased, Thurman's skills and scope of insight increased as well, but with this increase of insight and speaking opportunities came an increase of contact with racism and the hostile white supremacy represented by the Klu Klux Klan. He had his first brush with the KKK, almost unbeknownst to himself"

> During my first year there, I spoke in almost every town in the area around Batavia and Rochester. After my last scheduled talk of the year, a man came up to me saying, "Well, this is your last talk until next fall because the seminary closes this week. I have heard practically every sermon you have preached since last fall. I know where you went, what your subjects were, and how many people were in your audiences."[37]

With that, the mystery man produced a small notebook and showed it to Howard. "Instantly, I knew him to be a Klansman," Thurman recalled.[38] He had a second encounter with the Klan that same year.

---

33. Ibid., 51.
34. Ibid., 52.
35. Ibid., 48.
36. Ibid., 49.
37. Ibid., 50.
38. Ibid.

The most formative feature of Thurman's studies at RTS came through his course work and the personal relationships he established with his professors. Of the latter, three stood out in his mind. The first was Conrad Moehlman, professor of the history of Christianity, who, as Thurman reported, "introduced me to the vast perspective of the Christian movement through the centuries, and the struggle for survival of the essential religion of Jesus. He exposed me to the issues surrounding the great creedal battles of the church. His acute observations, massive scholarship, and authentic sense of humor made historic movements seem contemporary, as very often they were."[39]

A second, significant influence came from Dr. Henry Burke Robins, a professor of philosophy of religion and missions described as "silver-haired and somber."[40] Thurman summarized Robins's impact upon him: "It was he who first defined for me the scent that had been in my nostrils a long time; that the spiritual experience of the human race was essentially one single experience."[41] Thurman's Rochester experience gave him categories to describe and build upon a spiritual quest that began deep in his soul long before. This sense of a unifying essence at the basis of all human religious experience was confirmed through Thurman's studies in comparative religion with Robins.[42]

Thurman's sense of the theological role of religious experience, and its essential nature was reinforced through his association with George Cross, professor of systematic theology. In an interview with Jean Burden, given many years later, he recalled that Cross "had a greater influence on my mind than any other person who ever lived. Everything about me was alive when I came into his presence. He was all stimulus and I was all response."[43] Cross pushed Thurman— pushed him hard—because he saw the makings of greatness in the young man. Thurman recalled one of his earliest research assignments from Cross:

> One of my first papers I wrote for him was a study of the doctrine of original sin in *The Confessions of St. Augustine*. Over Thanksgiving recess I wrote my paper, working day and night. The final draft . . . ran well over seventy pages. I could hardly wait to turn in my assignment. In a few days it was returned to me with a long note from Dr. Cross saying that the paper was completely unsatisfactory and would have to be rewritten. I was hurt and angry; I went to see him to express my utter

39. Ibid., 54.
40. Ibid.
41. Smith, *Howard Thurman*, 30.
42. Ibid.
43. Quoted in Smith, *Howard Thurman*, 22.

> confusion. When I had finished, he said to me . . . "Mr. Thurman, that paper is not worthy of your mind and ability. For some other men in the class the paper would be more than satisfactory, but from you, it is not enough. I insist that you start over again and give me a paper that is worthy of you!"[44]

In Cross's capable hands, Thurman acquired the tools and attitudes that prepared him for his bright future. Cross met with Thurman early on Saturday mornings for mentoring conversations and urged him to think his own thoughts and find his own path into the essence of Christianity. The task of theological reinterpretation and the willingness to see Christian faith "through our own eyes," which Cross explicated in *What Is Christianity?*, was also written on Howard's own heart and mind: "[Cross] was the man who challenged every concept that I ever had and patiently taught me."[45]

Thurman's academic and intellectual development can be traced through several research papers, essays, speeches, and publications he developed during his Rochester years. In one of his earliest research papers, "On the Virgin Birth," written in the spring term of 1924, Thurman used historical and comparative religions analysis to examine the essence and enduring significance found in the traditional affirmation from the Apostles' Creed, that Jesus was "born of the Virgin Mary."[46] A brief essay Thurman penned later that same summer, "The Sphere of the Church's Responsibility in Social Reconstruction," evidenced the impact of Rochester's social gospel on his thinking. After a concise analysis of the appalling social conditions following World War I, Thurman concluded,

> That the Church has a very definite responsibility in the face of the conditions outlined above is obvious. But just what this responsibility is, no one seems to know. In this regard there is a vast medley of confusion. . . . Even the leaders of the Church are far from agreed as to just what its business in the world really is. Many believe that its only aim is to save the individual soul—to give men a simple bliss capsule so as to fire their souls with earnest zeal for the life to come. Jesus is a mistake when he is taken out of the sacraments and altars and becomes the daily companion in the home, in business, and in life generally, they seem to think. They insist that the Church's aim alone is to save men's souls, but it has nothing to do with economic ills, political corruption and social injustice.[47]

44. Thurman, *With Head and Heart*, 55–56.
45. Quoted in Smith, *Howard Thurman*, 22.
46. Fluker, *Papers of Howard Washington Thurman*, 1:35.
47. Ibid., 1:42.

Thurman's quest for the essence of Christianity came into sharper focus in an essay he wrote in the spring of 1925 titled "Let Ministers Be Christians!" His paper examined both the attitude that should constitute the inner character of a minister—who would be Christian—and what that personality entails in the real world of economic injustice and racial prejudice:

> The attitude of the minister, must forever be the attitude of Christ. The attitude of every Christian must be the attitude of Christ. He must recognize and emphasize: 1) the sacredness of human personality; 2) the interdependence of men; 3) Supremacy of righteousness as the quality of life which gets Divine approval; [and] 4) the necessity for all acts to be motivated and actuated by passionate good-will or love. The Story of the Good Samaritan is a matchless example of the Christian attitude *geared to the road of life.*[48]

Thurman's final formative encounter with his RTS mentor, Cross, came soon after he had accepted the call to Mount Zion Church in Oberlin, Ohio. "He was smiling and enthusiastic as I told him my plans," Thurman remembered. The tone of their conversation suddenly changed, however, and Cross's "demeanor became sober, even grave."[49] Cross said to Thurman,

> You are a very sensitive Negro man and doubtless feel under great obligation to put all the weight of your mind and spirit at the disposal of the struggle of your own people for full citizenship. But let me remind you that all social problems are transitory in nature and it would be a terrible waste for you to limit your creative energy to the solution of the race problem, however insistent its nature.[50]

He continued, "Give yourself to the timeless issues of the human spirit."[51]

When his words were met with stunned silence, Cross continued, "Perhaps I have no right to say this to you because as a white man I can never know what it is to be in your situation."[52] "I pondered the meaning of his words," Thurman recalled, "and wondered what kind of response I could make to this man who did not know that a man and his black skin must face the 'timeless issues of the human spirit' together."[53] Thurman's unspoken inner assessment described extremely well the intersection of his personal identity and sense of

---

48. Ibid., 1:44.
49. Thurman, *With Head and Heart*, 60.
50. Ibid.
51. Ibid.
52. Ibid.
53. Ibid.

self-worth as a black Christian with his pursuit of the essential questions that shape the lives of all people. However ill-formed they were at the time, Cross's words did, in one sense, mark out the trajectory of Thurman's subsequent career and the shape his future ministry would embody. Thurman's future interracial and interfaith efforts for justice and his practical experiments in developing a deep sense of community among diverse people (as exemplified by the Church for the Fellowship of all People that he established in San Francisco in 1944), dealt squarely with the "timeless issues of the human spirit."[54] But clearly, as Thurman himself pointed out, he did so from the distinctive social and theological location of being a Christian man in "black skin."[55]

In subsequent years, Howard Thurman continued to study, preach, teach, write, and mentor fellow Christians. From 1932 to 1944 he served as dean of Rankin Chapel and professor of religion at Howard University. From his successful work at Howard, he went to establish the Fellowship of All People, and from there assumed his role as dean of Marsh Chapel at Boston University from 1953 to 1965. At Howard University he worked with his own former mentor, Mordecai Wyatt Johnson, and in the latter role at Marsh Chapel, he was able to touch the life of a young doctoral student named Martin Luther King Jr.

In 1935 Thurman was invited to undertake a mission to India, Burma, and Ceylon by the YMCA and YWCA International Committee on behalf of the World Student Christian Federation. Many formative influences and events were in store for Thurman and his team while visiting India. Among these was a particularly transformative moment that Thurman experienced while visiting the Khyber Pass and overlooking Mount Everest on February 7, 1936. He recalled, "More than forty years have passed since that morning. It remains for me a transcendent moment of sheer glory and beatitude, when time, space, and circumstance evaporated and when my naked spirit looked into the depths of what is forbidden for anyone to see. I would never, never be the same again."[56]

A second transformative event came through a conversation with Mahatma Gandhi on February 21 in his compound in Barodli, India.

54. Ibid.
55. Ibid.
56. Ibid., 128.

During this memorable conversation, the Mahatma described the cause of the lack of vitality among the people of India; the first was obvious, he said, and was that they were hungry. But the second reason was even more revealing: "The second reason for the lack of vitality was the loss of self-respect."[57] This was a challenge Thurman encountered lifelong, and so he smiled a bit knowingly. Gandhi's response was, "You are thinking that we have lost our self-respect because of the presence of the conqueror in our midst. That is not the reason. We have lost our self-respect because of the presence of untouchability in Hinduism."[58] What the foreign conqueror and oppressor could not do, the Indian people had done to themselves for religious reasons—robbed many of their companions of self-respect by declaring them "untouchables." The second struggle Gandhi described was more difficult to overcome than the first, but it was also more debilitating for people. Gandhi tried to remake the Hindu caste system symbolically by adopting an "untouchable" into his family and by changing the word for "outcaste" or "untouchable" into a new phrase that means "child of God." Thurman concluded, "His theory was that if he could make every caste Hindu, whenever he referred to an outcaste, call him a 'Child of God,' in that act he would create within him an acute moral congestion that could not be resolved until his attitude was transformed."[59] Thurman may have also recalled the affirmation his grandmother, Nancy Ambrose, brought with her out of slavery through her own attitude of liberation: "You are not slaves. . . . You are a child of God."[60]

The most revelatory experience, perhaps, in terms of the formation of his own spirituality, occurred in Ceylon, on the team's journey to India. After he presented a lecture at a law college there, Thurman was asked, rather pointedly, by the chairman of the Law Club: "What are you doing here? Your forefathers were taken from the west coast of Africa as slaves, by Christians." After recounting the horrible but also truthful litany of the racial failures of Western Christianity, the law student said pointedly, "I think that an intelligent young Negro such as yourself, here in our country on behalf of a Christian enterprise, is a traitor to all of the darker peoples of the earth. How can

57. Ibid., 133.
58. Ibid.
59. Ibid., 134.
60. Ibid., 17.

you account for yourself being in this unfortunate and humiliating position?"[61]

It was a poignant and pointed question that voiced some of the same challenges Thurman had asked himself. Thurman's reply was especially revealing as it illustrated how his grandmother's ability to "live inside Jesus" and the analytical training he received at RTS allowed him to clearly distinguish "the religion of Jesus" from the segregated and unjust configuration of Christianity in Western organized religion. This then urged him to push deeper beyond the flawed and temporal manifestation of Christianity to its real genius and essential form as manifested in Jesus. Hence, Thurman replied,

> I make a careful distinction between Christianity and the religion of Jesus. My judgment about slavery and racial prejudice relative to Christianity is far more devastating than yours could ever be. From my investigation and study, the religion of Jesus projected a creative solution to the pressing problem of survival for the minority of which He was a part. . . . The minority in my country that is concerned about and dedicated to experiencing that spirit that was in Jesus Christ is on the side of freedom, liberty, and justice for all people, black, white, red, yellow, saint, sinner, rich or poor. They, too, are a fact to be reckoned with in my country.[62]

The development of prophetic self-consciousness, which reached back to the earliest years of his youth in Waycross in the wise, mentoring words of the church and of Nancy Ambrose, gradually came to fruition in Thurman through many challenging but spiritually enriching experiences. Among these refinements were those developments that occurred in and through his studies and sojourn at Rochester Theological Seminary. Walter Rauschenbusch passed from the scene in 1918, but his legacy lived on in the RTS ethos during Thurman's time there. This ethos came to expression in Thurman's own creative thought and transformative ministry. Thurman was fond of quoting Rauschenbusch, the prophet of the social gospel, to the effect that "there are many, many good people around, but very few who are good enough to disturb the peace of the devil."[63]

The wisdom, spiritual growth, and practical experience Thurman learned from Conrad Moehlman, George Cross, Henry Robins, and his formative years at RTS was significant and inestimable. But it also built upon the spiritual foundation that was earlier laid in Waycross by his mother and Nancy Ambrose, Mt. Bethel Church,

---

61. Ibid., 114.
62. Ibid.
63. Vincent Harding, "Dangerous Spirituality," *Sojourners*, January-February 1999, 31.

Morehouse College, and other mentors like John Hope and Mordecai Wyatt Johnson. RTS supplied Thurman with many of the tools
and categories he used to plumb the depths of Christianity to find
and articulate its essence in the religion of Jesus. That essential message, "You are a child of God," would become the heart and soul of
his own self-understanding and spiritual insights. This development
is chronicled in his many literary works, including arguably his most
famous, *Jesus and the Disinherited* (1949), in which he drew specific
parallels between the life challenges faced by Jesus of Nazareth and
"the man who has his back up against the wall," namely, African
Americans and other people oppressed by racial and economic circumstances. Like Nancy Ambrose and his enslaved ancestors, Thurman sought and found the real essence of Christianity as he "stood
inside of Jesus and looked out on the world through his eyes."[64]
By "standing inside Jesus," Thurman found a transformative and
prophetic self-consciousness that overcame the dangerous dichoto-
mies of faith and good works, and individual transformation versus
social reform.

Thurman described this intersection of the religious experience of
the individual, the idea of Jesus, and social character of human existence in *The Creative Encounter*, which both dramatically elevated
the individual and energized the church for social change:

> The ideal that is fundamental to the Jesus idea . . . is a vision of all men as children
> of God, and the church as a social institution formally entrusted with this idea in our
> society cannot withhold it from any man because of status, of class, of any social
> definition whatsoever. A part of its instrumentality in society is to a commitment
> of attack on any binding social classification that takes precedence over the in-
> trinsic worthfulness of the individual as embodied in the centrality of the religious
> experience.[65]

Thurman was sometimes viewed as standing apart from the social
struggle against segregation, prejudice, and social injustice. Vincent
Harding, for example, remembered meeting a young, African American man in the 1930s who, upon meeting Thurman, told Harding, "I
am disappointed in him. We thought we had found our Moses, and
he turns out to be a mystic."[66] But for Thurman it was precisely the
mystic's inner strength and spiritual self-consciousness that fueled the

64. Thurman, "Standing Inside with Christ," cited in Smith, *Howard Thurman*, 40.
65. Howard Thurman, *The Creative Encounter: An Interpretation of Religion and the Social Witness* (New York: Harper and Brothers, 1954), 146.
66. Harding, "Dangerous Spirituality," 30.

fires for social reform. He described the deep interconnection he saw between personal mysticism and social action in this way:

> Social action . . . is an expression of resistance against whatever tends to or separates one from the experience of God, who is the very ground of his being . . . Therefore, the mystic's concern with the imperative of social action is not merely to improve the condition of society. It is not merely to feed the hungry, not merely to relieve human suffering and human misery. If this were all, in and of itself, it would be important surely. But this is not all. The basic consideration has to do with the removal of all that prevents God from coming to himself in the life of the individual. Whatever there is that clocks this, calls for action.[67]

It was in this transformative sense, then, that Catherine Tumber and Walter Fluker described Thurman's main contribution as the formation of "prophetic spirituality."[68]

Howard Thurman's journey from poverty in Waycross to international prominence and acclaim was an extremely challenging and also inspiring one. His Christian faith was mediated to him through his family and church, and he found a new identity; "you are a child of God," Nancy Ambrose told him.[69] RTS broadened and deepened Thurman's religious experience, it also gave him the tools to analyze his faith and powerfully share it with others. The mentorship of Professor Cross and others urged him to find the essense of Christianity, and this quest took him back to the religion of Jesus and the ability to stand "inside of Jesus and looked out on the world through his eyes."[70]

It was precisely from this prophetic vantage point—standing inside Jesus and looking out on the world with his eyes—that Thurman wrote *Jesus and the Disinherited*. It was but the first of his many influential publications. It was through *The Creative Encounter* with God in Jesus that a person came to fully realize one's own identity as a child of God, as well as a "vison of all men as children of God."[71] Thurman viewed the church as the custodian of this luminous vision because of its ability to mediate and engender this transforming encounter with God. For him, the cultivation of one's spiritual life was a powerful force for social change. His was truly a "prophetic

67. Howard Thurman, "Mysticism and Social Action," *The A.M.E. Zion Quarterly Review* 92, no. 1 (October 1980): 9.
68. Walter Earl Fluker and Catherine Tumber, eds., *A Strange Freedom: The Best of Howard Thurman on Religious Experience and Public Life* (Boston: Beacon Press, 1998), xiii.
69. Thurman, *With Head and Heart*, 21.
70. Thurman, "Standing Inside with Christ," cited in Smith, *Howard Thurman*, 40.
71. Thurman, *The Creative Encounter*, 146.

spirituality"[72] because Thurman understood the discovery of one's God-given-identity as a "child of God" as a call for "the removal of all that prevents God from coming to himself in the life of the individual"; spiritual life was basis for profound social reform.[73] In this way, Howard Thurman developed a powerful restatement of the CRCDS legacy, one that enunciated the deep inner connection of cultivating personal spirituality and the transformation of church and society—and he strove to make both a reality.

72. Fluker and Tumber, *Strange Freedom*, xiii. See also Smith, *Howard Thurman*.
73. Thurman, "Mysticism and Social Action," 9.

10

Prophetic but Not Prescient (1930–1960)

As the two Baptist seminaries rooted deeply in the soil of western New York became one institution in 1928, former Colgate Theological Seminary professor of systematic theology, Dr. John B. Anderson, now the new professor of theology and ethics at Colgate Rochester Divinity School, reflected upon the rich heritage of the constituent schools:

> The new school is the heir of the old schools—the heir of their property, their libraries, their trustees, their faculties, their alumni, their great teachers of past decades; heir of their fine traditions, precious memories, noble achievements at home and abroad in the work and progress of the kingdom of God; heir of a richly storied past in the school of prophets at Hamilton and Rochester. It is all ours and it is a truly great inheritance.[1]

The prophetic spirit of CRDS and its able leaders did not, however, allow them to foresee the future. But who could credibly predict the turn of events and challenges that lay almost immediately ahead when the newly reconstituted Divinity School opened its doors for classes on September 19, 1928? The dark days of World War I had passed, and perhaps was "the war to end all wars." It was a message of peace and harmony that large segments of American culture were willing to believe. The aftermath of the war ushered in an era of "good feelings" and increased economic opportunity for many, though not all, Americans. RTS social prophet Walter Rauschenbusch was joined by others, like Henry C. Vedder of Crozer Theological

---

1. John B. Anderson, "Getting Together," *CRDS Bulletin* 1, no. 1 (October 1928): 6.

Seminary, in drawing attention to the growing disparity between the rich and the working poor in industrializing America, and Rauschen-busch's *Christianity and the Social Crisis* (1907) pointed out the deep social and economic inequities that lay beneath the surface of the growing prosperity of modern America. The missional commitment to serving the disadvantaged immigrant populations continued in the new Divinity School, as the German department, which was established by RTS in 1852, and the Italian department, which had been a ministry of CTS since 1907, both continued in new locations.[2] The Italian department was soon discontinued in 1931,[3] while the German department continued on, even through the difficult years of World War II. But by 1949, when it was clear that it had outlived its original function, the school was renamed North American Baptist Seminary and relocated to Sioux Falls, South Dakota.[4]

The Fundamentalist-Modernist controversy, which dominated the theological focus and sapped much of the energy of American Protestantism for almost three decades, seemed to have been resolved with the apparent and public defeat of the conservatives at the Scopes "monkey trial" in Dayton, Tennessee (July 21, 1925). Feeling excluded and banished from mainstream American culture, however, many of the conservatives withdrew from the mainline Protestant denominations and their institutions to set up their own parallel alternatives. This development institutionalized a theological polarization in America that weakened the mainline churches and their seminaries.

Small but also significant strides toward social equality were made by women, who received the vote in 1920, and by African Americans. "The Great Migration," which began in the 1890s, continued to bring large numbers of rural blacks from the South to the North in search of jobs and greater opportunities. Their destination was, invariably, the burgeoning industrial cities of the Northeast and the Midwest. But the significantly growing numbers of blacks arriving in northern cities brought increased racial tensions; for the northern churches in particular, equality and inclusion were more easily achieved in theory than in practice.

---

2. *CRDS Bulletin* 1, no. 3 (January 1928): 173.
3. *CRDS Bulletin* 5, no. 1-2 (November 1932): 131.
4. *CRDS Bulletin* 22, no. 3 (May 1950): 9.

The significant yet unheralded role that both African Americans and women played in World War I led to gradually increasing opportunities for both groups in postwar American culture. The social (nondomestic), hard-drinking, straight-talking, and scantily attired flappers of the Roaring Twenties gradually replaced the proper, domestic, and long-skirted suffragettes as the epitome of liberated American womanhood. The urban centers of America gradually began to take notice of the flowering of black culture epitomized by the Harlem Renaissance.

Whether it was apparent to most Americans in 1928, the nation once again teetered on the brink of crisis, ruin, and war. Certainly none of this was in the minds of the administration, faculty, and students of CRDS when the school opened for classes in the autumn of 1928. But almost precisely one year later, on October 24, 1929—a day forever known as "Black Tuesday"—came the stock market crash that ushered in the Great Depression and brought financial ruin and utter impoverishment to millions of Americans. In a similar way, the "lasting peace" that was forced upon Germany and the Axis powers through their defeat in World War I proved to be an illusion as it was an economically punitive and socially debilitating time for them. The Great Depression in America, despite the New Deal efforts by the federal government, was remedied only by the industrial boom that came with full mobilization for the Second World War in 1941. And so, very soon after the nearly minted CRDS opened its doors in September 1928, world events were about to take an unforeseen and cataclysmic turn of nearly apocalyptic proportions.

The impact of these events already affected the school when Dr. Albert Beaven was inaugurated as president of CRDS on October 21, 1929. In this challenging social and economic context, Beaven urged the graduating class of 1929, only twenty persons, one of whom, Gail Arthur Patterson, was a young woman, to look into the future with both utter honesty and deep faith: "the minister of tomorrow is called to no easy task," Beaven warned. "The ancient writer said, 'Work out your own salvation, for it is God that worketh in you.' The minister is held responsible for his own results, yet paradoxically enough, results are dependent also upon the partnership which he has with God."[5]

5. Albert Beaven, "The Minister's Task," baccalaureate sermon, May 1930, CRDS Bulletin 2, no. 5 (June 1930): 424.

Beaven sounded both confident and hopeful about the future as he announced, "We are hoping, in addition to our regular existing standard course, which leads to a Bachelor of Divinity Degree, and our post-graduate work leading to a Master of Theology Degree, to organize extension work, probably with a Director of Extension, who will be its supervision."[6] There was an immediate surge in student enrollment that next fall, due perhaps in part to these new ventures. The *Bulletin* from May 1930 reports that "the student body this year is the largest in the past nineteen years, with the exception of the year 1926."[7] Enrollment for the next decade fluctuated between the low of 104, in 1930–1931, and the high of 130 in 1939–1940, with the average hovering around 117 students. With the increased enrollment came the opportunity to be more selective in the process of admission, as Beaven told the board of trustees on May 22, 1933, "We have decided to restrict the registration for the new year even more, confining it as nearly as possible to men who we feel certain will have a good opportunity of being located when the course is completed."[8] The fact that Beaven was also still thinking only in terms of "men" being admitted to CRDS suggested that other problems lay ahead.

Seeking to remedy the crisis that came in the aftermath of the crash and the socioeconomic problems accompanying it, Conrad Moehlman, professor of church history, urged his students and his church not to abrogate their leadership role but instead to contemplate with him the question, "If Religion Would Lead." In his chapel address on January 2, 1933, Moehlman proclaimed, "To lead effectively in our time, religion will need to meet these tests."[9] His prescription for what ailed modern American Christianity was this: first, "Religion must be intellectually defensible."[10] Second, "Religion must be both *prophetic and mystical* if it would maintain and accentuate its leadership."[11] Third, "Religion has always been more than personal. . . . It has always been social as well."[12] Fourth, "Religion needs, as never before, a consecrated leadership."[13] This succinct summary of the historic mission and spiritual legacy of the

---

6. Ibid., 127.
7. *CRDS Bulletin* 2, no. 4 (May 1930): 296.
8. Albert W. Beaven, "Report to the Board of Trustees," *CRDS Bulletin* 5, no. 5 (May 1933): 340.
9. Conrad Henry Moehlman, "If Religion Would Lead," *CRDS Bulletin* 10, no. 4 (March 1933): 282.
10. Ibid., 284.
11. Ibid., emphasis added.
12. Ibid., 285.
13. Ibid., 286.

Divinity School, while grounded in the past, guided them forward toward a better future: "Religion *must* face the future, not the past, if it would lead."[14]

The new curriculum, which CRDS launched in 1929, focused on its "primary purpose . . . to prepare men and women for the work of the Christian ministry."[15] It sought to strike a balance between required and elective courses. By 1934 the entire third year of the student's course of study was described as "wholly elective."[16] This curriculum would remain more or less intact until 1947, when it was revised into a new trimester format. Comprehensive examinations were added between the second and third years of instruction.[17] But these exams disappeared from the catalogue and program by academic year 1957–1958.[18] After a brief experimentation with a trimester schedule,[19] another new curriculum was developed in the late 1950s and adopted in 1959. As Dean Oren Baker explained, "Depth rather than coverage was the goal we sought."[20]

The new institution entered the 1930s on a sound financial footing, with a significant endowment, but the unfavorable economic climate soon became detrimental to CRDS's programs and mission. In academic year 1938–1939, the operating budget was reduced by more than $16,000 and still left a deficit of $4,000.[21] The German department, in particular, was plagued by low enrollments and a plummeting income; the latter due in large part to the small return of investments that comprised its endowment.

The Colgate Rochester Divinity School Bulletin was established as a full-scale academic journal "published five times a year," and it served as the voice of CRDS. In its inaugural issue, the editor, Dr. John B. Anderson, explained, "Although the *Bulletin* is in part a journal of theological scholarship and of religious thought and work, yet its chief purpose is to serve as one link between the 'School of the Prophets' and the prophets who go forth from the school."[22] In 1937, however, to cut costs, it was replaced by *The Alumni News Bulletin*. *The Alumni News Bulletin*, which was published in a less expensive

---

14. Ibid.
15. *CRDS Bulletin* 1, catalogue supp. (June 1929): 9.
16. *CRDS Bulletin* 6, no. 3 (January 1934): 120.
17. *CRDS Bulletin* 11, no. 2 (March 1949): 33.
18. *CRCDS Bulletin* 30, no. 1c, "Catalogue" (January 1958): 45.
19. *CRDS Bulletin* 14, no. 3 (February 1947): 41.
20. *CRDS Bulletin* 31, no. 2 (January 1959): 97.
21. Albert Beaven, "President's Report," *CRDS Bulletin* 23, no. 4 (May 1939).
22. John B. Anderson, "Editorial," *CRDS Bulletin*, 1, no. 2 (November 1928): 75.

magazine format, aimed at a more popular readership and was issued only four times a year.

Early in his presidency, Augustus Strong remarked that a solid academic institution was built out of "brains, books, and bricks." While all three aspects were cared for in the merger and relocation through the new campus (the "bricks") and larger combined faculty (the "brains"), "the books" were also extremely important. The RTS library was comprised of about thirty-nine thousand volumes during Strong's tenure, and the collection increased year by year until it exceeded fifty-five thousand volumes at the time of union. An additional seven thousand volumes from the former CTS collection were then added. The new Ambrose Swasey Library was named due to the generosity and foresight of Dr. Ambrose Swasey of Cleveland, Ohio. At the time of its formal opening in the autumn of 1932, the Swasey Library housed more than seventy-five thousand bound volumes, as well as many historically significant manuscripts and rare books. It included, for example, the entire literary collection of the German theologian Johann August Wilhelm Neander (1789–1850). In 1948 the American Baptist Archives, which began as the Samuel Colgate manuscript collection at CTS in 1887, was relocated to CRDS.[23] The Ambrose Swasey collection continued to grow incrementally through this period, arriving at 97,784 volumes by the opening day of classes in the fall semester of 1960.[24]

By 1934 it was clear that the economic depression did not only limit the number of students enrolling in classes but also significantly affected the potential employment of those who graduated and sought full-time pastoral work. That same year, John F. Vichert,[25] director of "external work" at CRCDS, reported a dramatic reduction in the number of student scholarships that were funded by local churches, as well as an "unsettled condition" for the future employment of the graduates "created by some of our churches by the knowledge that there are large numbers of unemployed ministers, many of whom are willing to serve for anything a church can offer. The prospect of serving a full-time position at a minimum salary proves alarming."[26] The prospect of uncertain employment prospects affected both enrollments and placements.

---

23. *CRDS Bulletin* 21, no. 2 (January 1948): 19–20.
24. *CRDS Bulletin* 31, no. 1c (January 1960): 18.
25. Dr. John Frederick Vichert served as the Woelkin Professor of Preaching as well as working in pastoral studies. He joined the CTS faculty in 1921 and that of CRDS at the merger.
26. "Report to the Board of Trustees," May 22, 1934, *CRCDS Bulletin* 7, no. 5 (May 1934): 359.

Because of the increasingly difficult economic situation, in 1935 Auburn Theological Seminary, a smaller institution with Presbyterian roots and a progressive outlook located in Auburn, New York, approached CRDS to begin conversations about affiliation and potential relocation to Rochester.[27] Two years later, however, these plans floundered when Auburn could not raise the funds required to move to Rochester and construct a new facility on the CRDS campus.[28] Ultimately, Auburn cast its lot with Union Theological Seminary in New York City and moved there in 1939.

Despite the harsh financial conditions that nearly forced the closure of Auburn in the spring of 1935, the CRDS board of trustees authorized the construction of the Samuel Colgate Memorial Chapel. It was planned as a part of the original vision for the new campus, but building the chapel was delayed perhaps for financial reasons, as were two additional dormitories.[29] The Colgate Memorial Chapel was completed in 1936 and dedicated that summer in solemn celebration; of particular note are its four beautiful stained glass windows immortalizing Roger Williams, Adoniram Judson, William Newton Clarke, and Walter Rauschenbusch, four heroes of the American Baptist tradition and CRDS's past.[30] In response to the growing number of married students arriving on campus, a special dormitory was constructed for their use in 1936, in addition to a temporary residence that offered six apartments for the use of missionaries on furlough. Both buildings were stand-alone structures disconnected from the larger complex of buildings.[31]

Student enrollment at CRDS fluctuated dramatically throughout the 1930s, which is not surprising given the impact of the Great Depression on the lives of individuals, families, and churches. During this decade, graduating classes ranged from a low of twenty-two in 1930 to a high of thirty-eight in 1934, with the middle range falling at thirty-three. The main costs faced by students were tuition, fees, and housing. As a sign and consideration of the hard economic times facing students, CRDS's tuition and student fees remained constant throughout the entire decade, and furthermore, there was a slight decrease: tuition stood at $175 per year in 1928 and was reduced to $120 in 1931–1932. In fact, at the end of three decades, in 1960 (due

---

27. *CRDS Bulletin* 7, no. 4 (May 1935): 280-81.
28. *CRDS Alumni News Bulletin* 11, no. 2a (November 1938): 1.
29. *CRCDS Bulletin* 7, no. 4 (May 1935): 250.
30. *CRDS Bulletin* 11, no. 3c (March 1939): 15.
31. Ibid., 18.

largely to support from the endowment and the churches), tuition rose only to $375 per year.[32] Dormitory rooms were provided free of charge, but a small fee ($15) was charged for their upkeep.

The composition of the CRDS student body in the 1930s was predominately male, single, white, and Baptist, with a few women, African Americans, and other Protestants seasoned into the mix. During the 1930s, the school's programming, literature, and new physical plant operated under the assumption that this composition of the student body was a constant and unchanging verity—which it was not and would not be. Although the *Bulletin* and its official spokesmen, such as Beaven, refer to the student body as "the men," women were admitted and graduated in small numbers (typically at the rate of one or two a year) throughout the 1930s. There were exceptions to this pattern; in 1935 four women graduated with the bachelor of divinity degree, but there were also several years when no female names appeared on the list of graduating seniors. No special on-campus housing provisions were made for women until 1935, when rooms on the third floor of Strong Hall were converted from office space into dormitory rooms for single women.[33]

The presence of African Americans in the student body is difficult to trace throughout this period because there was no specific consideration of their presence in either the published or unpublished literature. Hints are available, however, as historically black colleges, principally Morehouse and occasionally others, were named among those listed in the "Summary of Colleges" offered in many of the annual CRCDS *Catalogues*. It seems that the policy of admitting no more than four African American students at any one time continued more or less unabated throughout this entire period. Official notice of the importance of black presence at CRCDS manifested through invitations to the school's most notable African American alumni, Mordecai Wyatt Johnson and Howard Thurman, to return to campus to deliver special lectures and addresses. But by 1944 more direct attention was drawn to African American participation in the CRDS legacy though the publication of a study by Floyd Massey (class of 1944) titled "An Outstanding Record." The *Bulletin* of June 1944 reported,

---

32. *CRDS Bulletin* 32, no. 2 (January 1960): 40.
33. *CRDS Bulletin* 8, no. 2 (January 1936): 108.

His findings reveal a remarkable record of achievement [among African American alumni]. All are serving with distinction in various important positions; a few of the more outstanding are: Mordecai W. Johnson ('16)—president of Howard University; Howard W. Thurman ('21)—Dean of the Chapel at Howard University; Joseph H. Jackson—pastor of the Great Olivet Baptist Church in Chicago; Wade Hampton McKinney ('23)—pastor of Antioch Baptist Church in Cleveland; [34] Gordon Blaire Hancock ('20)—Professor of Economics at Virginia Union University; Clarence E. Mc-Fadden ('21)—Dean of the School of Theology at Selma University; Lucas M. Tobin ('38)—Chairman of the Department of Religion at Morris College; Tim Boddie and Chuck Boddie ('36)—pastor at Shiloh Baptist Church in Baltimore, and Mount Olivet Baptist Church, Rochester—respectively.[35]

Mordecai Johnson returned to campus in the autumn of 1933 to deliver an extremely significant address under the mild-sounding title of "Christianity and Occidental Civilization." The occasion of his visit was an inter-seminary conference that not only included greater Rochester's town and gown but also visitors from other regional institutions. It was on this particular occasion that Johnson chose to announce the church's utter failure to deal adequately with the crisis of racial segregation in America. He issued a prophetic call for a "reorientation"[36] of the Christian movement toward its more essential values and spiritual roots to find a resolution to this crisis.

The race question was, in his mind at least, American religion's unfinished business, which both divided churches in the North and South and allowed segregationist attitudes to enter into the body of Christ. He reminded his audience that the problem of race was not simply "a Negro problem";[37] it was a fundamental problem for all American Christians. The prevalence of segregation in American society and religious life was, Johnson reminded his listeners, a ringing indictment of the Christian movement as currently envisioned. The church, he asserted, "is inherently incompetent to work constructively in the sphere of social action."[38] He urged,

I am speaking not as a Negro but as a Christian, deeply concerned about the future of the Christian movement in the world and, therefore unflinchingly confronting

---

34. Interestingly, Rev. Wade McKinney served the Antioch Baptist Church from 1928 to 1964 and was followed there by Dr. Marvin McMickle, who went on to be the thirteenth president of CRCDS. Reverend McKinney's son, Rev. Samuel B. McKinney, earned both the bachelor of divinity and doctor of ministry at CRCDS and was a member of the original class of Martin Luther King Fellows, described in chapter 18.
35. Winthrop Hudson, ed., *The Colgate Rochester Divinity School Alumni News Bulletin* 6, no. 5 (June 1944): 3. *The News Bulletin* was a less expensive, magazine version of the *CRCDS Bulletin*, which was produced chiefly for the alumni during the war years.
36. Mordecai Wyatt Johnson, "Christianity and Occidental Civilization," *CRDS Bulletin* 4, no. 4 (March 1934): 280.
37. Ibid.
38. Ibid., 281.

the most pessimistic aspects of her historic position. It is fundamentally necessary for all healthy thinking that we recognize the elements of strength in the current indictment that she [the church] is inherently incompetent to work constructively in the sphere of social action.[39]

Johnson was not utterly discouraged: "I am convinced," he said, "that her [the church's] weakness is not inherent. She is not a defeated movement. She needs but to re-orient herself and thereby to lay hold on profound resources at her disposal."[40] The path forward was, in Johnson's view, marked out by Jesus' injunction to love God utterly and completely, and in a fashion that both included and celebrated the shared humanity of one's neighbor in that love (as in Matthew 22:27-28). Hence, like Rauschenbusch before him, Johnson was willing to see the current social crisis (represented by the evils of racial segregation) as a defining moment and an opportunity for dramatic change.

One of the new directions, the extension work announced by President Beaven, described the practical, hands-on ministerial work that CRDS students did in Rochester and the surrounding communities. There was a long tradition of students working part-time as student pastors, youth workers, and pastoral assistants throughout the region in the RTS days, but this process was not formally organized or directly supervised. The formalization, organization, and tracking of the pastoral work carried out by the CRDS students indicates the gradual development of what will come to be called "supervised ministry," an emerging field of pastoral theology. Beginning with the catalogue of 1932, it was reported that "practically every student in the Divinity School is engaged in some form of service with churches in and about Rochester. A considerable number teach in church schools, assist in young people's work, or conduct boy's clubs. Others serve as pastors; between forty and fifty churches being cared for in this way."[41] By 1955 emphasizing the importance of practical professional training, the catalogue was emended to read: "All students in the Divinity School *are required* to engage in some form of service with churches as a part of their educational preparation for the ministry."[42]

---

39. Ibid.
40. Ibid.
41. *CRDS Bulletin* 16, no. 3 (January 1934): 112.
42. *CRDS Bulletin* 27, no. 1c, catalogue ed. (1954): 25, emphasis added.

Initially, the supervisory role in this project was divided up among the teaching faculty, but in the fall of 1935 Oren Baker (1894–1982) was hired as assistant professor of applied Christianity and pastoral counseling, beginning his service in the spring semester of 1936.[43] After serving CRDS in various capacities (teacher, counselor, field supervisor), Baker became dean of administration in 1945, following the retirement of Glenn Ewell. The next year, when Thomas Wearing, dean of the faculty, also retired, Baker assumed that second role as well. He held the combined position of dean and secretary of the faculty for another fifteen years until his retirement in 1959.

In addition to Baker's vigorous academic leadership, he was one of the pioneers in the development of the relatively new field of pastoral counseling. Pastoral counseling carved out a distinctive niche between emergent psychiatry on the one hand and pastoral ministry on the other. Baker's *Human Nature under God: The Adventure of Personality* (1958) epitomized his creative synthesis of biblical theology's conception of human nature and the dramatic new insights emerging from the field of social psychology. Commentators heralded Baker's work as "very stimulating" and "a notable addition" to this field of inquiry.[44]

CRDS opened its doors in 1928 with three endowed lectureships that brought nationally known figures to campus for intellectual enrichment and spiritual growth. The first of these, the Trevor Lectures, were used to bring notable preachers and devotional leaders to campus, often to lead worship during the Spring Convocation events. A second significant lectureship was founded in May 1928 by Mrs. Wilfred Fry in honor of her father, the late Francis Wayland Ayer. The Ayer Lectures considered a variety of topics that "fall within the broad field of the history or the interpretation of the Christian Message."[45] Finally, the Rauschenbusch Memorial Lectureship, inaugurated in 1931, was comprised of four lectures "in the field of applied Christianity" and, like the Ayers Lectures, were "subsequently published in expanded form."[46] The coordination of these three endowed lectureships made the annual Spring Convocation an

---

43. *CRDS Bulletin* 7, no. 4 (May 1935): 251.
44. Review of *Human Nature under God*, Kirkus, www.kirkusreviews.com/book-reviews/dr-oren-huling-baker/human-nature-under-god/, accessed January 16, 2018.
45. *CRDS Bulletin* 2, no. 1c (March 1939), 22.
46. Ibid.

extremely significant event for CRDS, as well as its alumni, pastors, prospective students, and scholars who were able to attend.

While all three lecture series were extremely significant in the academic and spiritual life of the CRDS community, the Rauschenbusch Memorial Lectureship in particular carried the legacy of Rauschenbusch and his distinctive synthesis of evangelical liberalism and penetrating social analysis. But this legacy was not merely the subject of special lectures at CRDS; it was also woven deeply into the identity and ethos of the new school. This legacy was mirrored in the classes and instruction, and, perhaps most notably for those who try to discern it after many years, in the school's official publications and celebrations.

The first volume of the *Colgate Rochester Divinity School Bulletin*, in its series of articles titled "Remembering Walter Rauschenbusch," signaled the continuation of the evangelical-liberal, social theology of Rauschenbusch as a constitutive role in the vision and mission of the new school. Two feature articles spelled this out, both written by men who knew and worked with the social prophet of RTS. The first of these articles, "Perpetuating the Memory of Walter Rauschenbusch," by Conrad H. Moehlman, focused on Rauschenbusch's life, work, and significant contributions to their own understanding of Christian faith and its appropriation for living in a new age.[47] Moehlman considered Rauschenbusch's *The Social Teachings of Jesus*, which sold more than two hundred thousand copies in 1916 alone, to epitomize Rauschenbusch and his work.

The second of these articles, "The Religion of Walter Rauschenbusch," written by the "great man's" friend and colleague of fourteen years, Henry Burke Robins, looked at the spiritual life of Rauschenbusch to discern the foundation of his faith, commitments, and motivations.[48] He was, as Robins remembered him, a "[m]ystic and prophet of social righteousness. With him the two were inseparable. He believed in the continuity of inspiration and of the prophetic office, and he kindled that faith in those who knew him best. . . . The power of it is upon many of us still, and will linger with us while we live."[49] In a reflection honoring Rauschenbusch, Robins urged his

---

47. Conrad H. Moehlman, "Perpetuating the Memory of Walter Rauschenbusch," *CRDS Bulletin* 1, no. 1 (October 1928): 32–37.
48. Henry Burke Robins, "The Religion of Walter Rauschenbusch," *CRDS Bulletin* 1, no. 1 (October 1928): 37–43.
49. Ibid., 42.

readers to emulate him instead: "We shall most honor him not by remembering his qualities nor by repeating his words but by taking up the cause which he espoused and allying ourselves freshly with his Master for its accomplishment."[50]

The final contribution to the "Remembering Walter Rauschenbusch" series was written by Justin Wroe Nixon (1886–1958).[51] His essay "The Social Philosophy of Walter Rauschenbusch" focused on the roots of Rauschenbusch's theory of social change; "that philosophy," Nixon asserted, "embodied two fundamental convictions, the one historical and the other sociological."[52] It is rooted, Nixon believed, in Rauschenbusch's appropriation of the example of Jesus and his "forgotten message," which "was primarily a gospel of earthly redemption. . . . He believed that Jesus' authentic message of the Kingdom of God was in essence the old prophetic message of the coming inauguration of the divine rule in human affairs. . . . His gospel was a summons to men to begin living the Kingdom life. As they lived the life the power of God would be released in them and the Kingdom would come more and more."[53] Hence, for Nixon, as with the others, the legacy of Rauschenbusch was an unfinished task.

A decade later, in 1939, the *Bulletin* carried still another significant tribute to Walter Rauschenbusch and his legacy. Titled "Walter Rauschenbusch—A Good Man," it was penned by Dores Robinson Sharpe, who was one of Rauschenbusch's student assistants during his own years at RTS. The article was a distillation of Sharpe's keynote address delivered during Rauschenbusch Week on October 10, 1939. It offered a wide-ranging examination of the man's life and thought viewed through the lens of his conversion and personal faith. As he drew the lecture to a close, Sharpe summarized what he deemed to be the salient features of the "Good Man's" beliefs. The fifth of these features was, perhaps, the most significant:

> When Jesus prayed, "Thy Kingdom come, Thy will be done on earth as it is in heaven," he was not uttering idle words, but outlining a program for his disciples. He meant it. Moreover, if his disciples should take those words seriously and attempt

---

50. Ibid., 43.

51. Reverend Nixon was at this time pastor of The Brick Presbyterian Church in Rochester, where he served from 1924 to 1937. He taught at RTS intermittently from 1916 to 1937 and became acquainted with Rauschenbusch early in the years of this tenure there. In 1937 he became William Newton Clarke Professor of Theology and Ethics at CRDS, a position he held until 1957.

52. Justin Wroe Nixon, "The Social Philosophy of Walter Rauschenbusch," *CRDS Bulletin* 1, no. 2 (November 1928): 104.

53. Ibid.

the seemingly impossible, they would win because all the power of God would be available to them.[54]

When Sharpe's monograph *Walter Rauschenbusch* was published in 1942,[55] it was reviewed by Henry Burke Robins in the *Bulletin* in May of that year. Robins stated,

> If after all these years, Walter Rauschenbusch could stab our souls awake to God's unending concern for the great human majority, and for the common lot, and if we with the Christians of other lands, should catch a vision of that righteous world order in which, under the will of God, humanity should be the touchstone, he might accomplish more, even than those strenuous years when he was with us.[56]

Among the early and notable Rauschenbusch Memorial lecturers was Reinhold Niebuhr of Union Theological Seminary in the spring of 1934. This was an interesting and significant pairing of person and event, not only because Niebuhr was one of the most prominent theological voices in postwar American Protestantism but also because he emerged as a staunch critic of the social gospel as espoused by Rauschenbusch and his successors. The horrors of World War I and its aftermath sapped the optimism out of American theology. It was in that context that the "Christian realism" (based in neo-orthodoxy) of Niebuhr and others emerged. Niebuhr's *Moral Man and Immoral Society* (1932), which might more accurately have been titled *Immoral Man and Even More Immoral Society*, began this process. In Niebuhr's view, defenders of the social gospel were too optimistic about sinful human nature and therefore naïve and unrealistic about the challenges involved in genuine Christian social change.

In his lectures at CRDS, Niebuhr focused his attention upon Christian social ethics and chose "The Ethic of Jesus" as his starting point, which was a common concern he shared with Rauschenbusch and his heirs. Niebuhr's four CRDS lectures were enhanced for publication and appeared as *An Interpretation of Christian Ethics* in 1935. They formed the foundation for Niebuhr's famous Gifford Lectures, given at the University of Edinburgh in 1939, and his magna opus, *The Nature and Destiny of Man* (1943; 2 vols.). At CRDS Moehlman responded to Niebuhr's remarks and offered a sympathetic report

54. Dores R. Sharpe, ""Walter Rauschenbusch—A Good Man," *CRDS Bulletin* 12, no. 2 (December 1939), 63–64.
55. Dores R. Sharpe, *Walter Rauschenbusch* (New York: Macmillan, 1942).
56. Ibid.

of them in the *CRDS Bulletin* in May 1934. "Dr. Niebuhr set over against each other the absolute character of the Ethic of Jesus and the relativities of the present political and economic order," he wrote. "Jesus based his Ethic upon the law of love. This is a principal unqualified and uncompromising. Every act of human being, according to Jesus, stands in relation to God, and therefore the love demand must be absolute. This absolute demand of love of God and the neighbor is directly opposite to all self-love of whatever degree."[57]

In the autumn of 1940, on the eve of another world war, President Beaven both acknowledged the growing tensions and affirmed "the enrollment is about the same as usual, slightly larger if anything. There is a good, sober, and reverent spirit on the campus."[58] A year later, his report was much the same: "I am happy to report a large and promising class entering the school this fall . . . a splendid *esprit de corps* on the campus. While the draft laws may affect the attendance after this year, they have not apparently done so thus far."[59]

But it would all change dramatically with the events of December 7, 1941, and the entrance of the United States into World War II. By September 1942 he reported "The entering class is somewhat smaller this year, naturally, we will have a good group for [the] work ahead." Concern shifted from the impending draft to concerns about the potential for the deferment of military service for ministerial students.[60] In his "Report to the Trustees" on May 18, 1942, Beaven summarized the deep spiritual tensions and reflection that the war brought to the campus and its students:

> The collapse of peace, the recent almost universal adoption of the appeal to force, have come as a tremendous shock to their faith and hope. They have been forced to rethink their own ideas and convictions to see how fully they reflect the reality in life. Some convictions have deepened, some ideas changed, but the intense determination to be hones has frequently caused agony of soul and mind. We who work with them are conscious of many heavy inner struggles going on around us.[61]

Reporting on school finances at the same trustees meeting of May 1942, Beaven revealed that dramatically decreased income caused the need to cut both staff and services at CRDS: "With lowered income

57. *CRDS Bulletin* 6, no. 5 (May 1934): 349.
58. *CRDS Alumni Bulletin* 12, no. 1a (September 1940): 1.
59. *CRCDS Alumni Bulletin* 14, no. 1a (Autumn 1941).
60. *CRDS Alumni Bulletin* 2, no. 1a (September 1942): 1.
61. "President's Report to the Trustees," *CRDS Bulletin* 14, no. 3a (March 1942): 218.

of the last two years," he reported, "we have been forced to curtail our expenditures. We have done this by decreasing the number of professors and more completely consolidating the two faculties into a united faculty. In the second place we have been able to reduce the net expense of our scholarship cost by increasing somewhat the income from student fees."[62] While tuition charges remained constant at $150 per year, the dormitory fee increased from its original $15 to $80 in 1942.[63] It was at this same time that the German department, bowing to external pressures caused by the war and prejudice, was renamed as the Rochester Baptist Seminary.[64] By 1947 ongoing financial challenges drove CRDS tuition up to $335 per year.[65]

In the aftermath of World War II, the Rauschenbusch Lectures turned to a more global focus. Rev. Earl H. Ballou presented four lectures under the general topic "The Church in East Asia." An international note was also sounded in Professor Eduard Lindeman's series titled "Faith for a New World," which explored remaking the postwar future.[66]

Subsequent Rauschenbusch Lectures addressed the horrific political and social problems faced by postwar Americans. Professor Ralph H. Gabriel of Yale, for example, explored the ambiguous relationship of "Protestantism and Democracy In America,"[67] and Dr. William Miller of Smith College examined "The Political Role of American Christianity" in his 1955 lecture.[68] Attuned to the tenor of the times and the African American struggle for civil rights, Dr. Kyle Haseldon explored "The Racial Problem in Christian Perspective" in his 1958 lecture, and the next year, internationally famous theologian Dr. Paul Tillich detailed the connection between "Religious Principles and Political Aspirations" in his lectures titled "Kairos and Utopia."[69]

The fiftieth anniversary of the publication of Walter Rauschenbusch's *Christianity and the Social Crisis* was marked at CRDS by a major conference on September 17, 1957. President Wilbour Eddy Saunders reported,

---

62. Ibid., 220.
63. *CRDS Bulletin* 14, no. 3c, catalogue ed. (March 1942): 39.
64. Ibid., 226.
65. *CRDS Bulletin* 20, no. 3c, catalogue ed. (February 1948): 39.
66. *CRDS Bulletin* 16, no. 3c (March 1944): 23.
67. *CRDS Bulletin* 22, no. 2c (October 1948): 25.
68. *CRDS Bulletin* 28, no. 1c (January 1956): 24.
69. *CRDS Bulletin* 31, no. 1c (January 1959): 25.

The usual formal opening of the school was expanded into a Rauschenbusch Day which was attended by a good-sized and enthusiastic group of alumni and friends. The event was comprised of several key note addresses including one by Dr. Justin Wroe Nixon, who came out of retirement to deliver "Rauschenbusch the Man," which amounted to a series of "impressions about him [which] were modified, underscored and filled out by personal association with him.[70]

Summarizing his impressions of Rauschenbusch in two elements, Nixon recalled "his sympathy with the poor"[71] and "the completeness of his commitment to Jesus."[72] Dr. Henry P. van Dusen, the eminent church historian from Union Theological Seminary (New York), stated, "It is clear, it seems to me, that the greatest single personal influence on the life and thought of the American church in the last fifty years was exerted by Walter Rauschenbusch."[73]

Student enrollment remained strong throughout the 1940s despite the pressures of the economy and the war years. The period opened with a peak enrollment of 131 in 1940–1941. But 1945–1946, in the immediate aftermath of the war, had the lowest enrollment at 77. By the next year, however, total enrollment rebounded to 95, and by 1947–1948 it climbed to 112. The median total for student enrollment for the decade was 111. Declining enrollments brought smaller graduating classes, evidenced by the fact that only 20 bachelor of divinity students graduated in 1945, one of them being Lourinda Marian Rhodes, the wife of Charles Sanford.[74]

In 1942 a request arrived from the federal government for the use of extra dormitory space available on campus: "At the request of the Army and the Navy, the extra rooms which we have had in our single men's dormitories will be used this year to house a group of young cadets who are training for aviation. This will not displace our students but will make use of our facilities to the full."[75] The entering class that fall was "not as large as last year. This was to be expected," Beaven noted, "in view of the war situation. But among the fairly new students are many who give promise of leadership in the Christian ministry."[76]

When Beaven died suddenly in December 1943, he was succeeded the next year by Dr. Edwin McNeil Poteat (1892–1955), with Dr.

70. *CRDS Bulletin* 19, no. 2 (May 1957): 26.
71. *CRDS Bulletin* 21, no. 2 (May 1957): 32.
72. Ibid.
73. *CRDS Bulletin* 29, no. 2 (May 1959): 8.
74. *CRDS Bulletin* 17, nos. 1–4 (May 1945): 15.
75. Ibid.
76. Ibid., 2.

George Cutten coming out of retirement to serve in the interim before Poteat arrived. Poteat came to CRDS with deep roots in the Southern Baptist tradition, and his invitation to come to the helm may have been an attempt to expand the notoriety and student pool of the Divinity School.[77] Poteat came directly from the extremely influential pastorate of Euclid Avenue Memorial Baptist Church in Cleveland, Ohio.[78] President Poteat was inaugurated on April 13, 1944, in an unassuming ceremony because "more elaborate celebration seemed both inappropriate and unadvisable due to war-time conditions."[79]

Poteat's inaugural address, titled "Landscape, Horizon and Sky," came as a challenge that "flung down the gauntlet to the forces of destruction in our day."[80] With World War II behind them, he warned many "lesser wars" lay ahead, issues unresolved in the national corporate life: "In the past thirty years the Christian church has lost spectacularly in four salient [areas] of our corporate life. The war against war was lost: the war against racism was lost; the war against beverage alcohol was lost; and the war against poverty and unemployment was lost."[81] With a view to "the sky," these battles can be undertaken and victory won. "Wherever the Christian testimony is spoken it must present a new synthesis between the dynamics of secular society and the dynamics of the society of God's Kingdom, opposing with the apostle's restlessness, the prophet's wisdom, and the martyr's devotion every external authoritarian bond that would manacle the spirit of humanity."[82]

In 1945, under the title "CRDS prepares for the new age," Dean Baker introduced a new curriculum "for the new age."[83] Mostly, however, it was an attempt to reshape the delivery of what had become a growing program of integral courses. The most dramatic change that came with the new curriculum was a shift from two fourteen-week semesters to three eleven-week trimesters. This approach was heralded as having "improved convenience through better division of time and opportunity for increased concentration of student effort on particular tasks."[84] Fieldwork was then "prescribed for all students

---

77. I am grateful to Dr. William H. Brackney for this assessment, given in his correspondence of June 16, 2019.
78. Poteat was a graduate of Wake Forest (BA, 1881, and DD, 1894), as well as Southern Baptist Theological Seminary (1888). He served as a missionary to China from 1917 to 1929, as well as pastor at Pullen Memorial Baptist Church, Raleigh, North Carolina (1929-1937; 1948-1955), and Euclid Avenue Baptist Church in Cleveland, Ohio (1937-1944).
79. CRDS Bulletin 16, no. 4 (April 1944): 1.
80. Ibid.
81. Ibid.
82. Ibid., 32.
83. CRCDS Bulletin 18, no.1 (October 1945): 2.
84. Ibid.

throughout the entire period of study."[85] In 1948 a program of "Refresher Courses" was also offered to help prepare students whose academic progress was interrupted by World War II.[86]

Following the sudden retirement of Poteat in 1949, Wilbour Eddy Saunders became the fourth president of CRDS. He served a full decade until retiring in 1960. Saunders, a native of Warwick, Rhode Island, was educated at Brown, Columbia, and the Graduate Theological Union. After postgraduate study at Cambridge, he received the doctor of divinity from Colgate in 1936 and a doctor of education from his alma mater, Brown, in 1941.

The political and economic turmoil that preceded and followed World War II was mirrored by a dramatic theological shift, which saw the demise of the earlier liberalism, epitomized and engendered by the work of Schleiermacher, and the emergence of a neo-orthodoxy, most notably embodied in the work of Karl Barth (1886–1962), come to theological prominence. In this "changing theological climate," which Saunders described to the board of trustees in 1954, the social gospel legacy of Walter Rauschenbusch was viewed as either passé or forgotten. Saunders reported: "Among the trends noted is that on the college campuses there is not the social concern of two decades ago. . . . It means that the school whose most distinguished reputation has been for its Rauschenbusch tradition does not find today a former readiness in this appeal to prospective students."[87] Equally evident was the fact that the delicate balance of conservative and progressive theological impulses represented in the evangelical liberalism, and as embodied by Rauschenbusch and others, was difficult to maintain. Later observers, like William Brackney, noted a decided tilt toward the liberal side of that equation as "Colgate Rochester became synonymous with liberal Protestantism."[88]

Looking back on the decade from the vantage point of his report as president in 1959, Saunders aptly characterized the 1950s as "a decade of growth,"[89] and indeed, the economic growth was both steady and dramatic. Annual income and giving increased from $16,342 to $89,875, and the endowment doubled from $4,264,932 to $8,542,046. Dynamic and innovative programs also brought

---

85. Ibid., 3.
86. *CRDS Bulletin* 20, no. 3c, catalogue ed. (February 1948): 30.
87. *CRDS Bulletin* 26, no. 3 (May 1954): 6.
88. William H. Brackney, *Congregation and Campus: North American Baptists in Higher Education* (Macon, GA: Mercer University Press, 2008), 266.
89. *CRDS Bulletin* 31, no. 2 (May 1959): 81.

an increased operating budget, which increased from $203,565 to $415,000 over the same period.[90] Enrollment also grew throughout the 1950s, although sporadic. It fluctuated from a high of 140 in 1951–1952 to a low of 92 students in 1953–1954 (due perhaps to the Korean conflict). The average for the decade was an enrollment of 118 students each year. Graduating classes followed a similar pattern, ranging from a low of 15 bachelor of divinity students in May 1951 to a high of 40 in May of 1959. The presence of women in graduating classes remained quite low, and these women were often the spouses of graduating men.

The composition of the student body, while not changing dramatically in terms of either race or gender during the 1950s, shifted significantly from a single male population—the situation for which the new campus was designed in 1928—toward a much larger proportion of married students. In 1955, for example, 13 of the 29 students matriculated that fall were married. This situation necessitated several renovations of campus housing facilities to better accommodate the influx of married students.[91] By 1959 a total of 74 married students lived on campus.[92]

The official publications of the Divinity School seemed more aware of the ecumenical role CRDS played in the region in the 1940s. In 1943 President Cutten described "Baptist students" as "the primary material with which to deal, and the justification for our existence" but also reported that "students of other denominations, or any women provided they are up to our standards, are welcome, and pay extra dividends in the service which we can render."[93] It was not until early 1951, however, that CRDS began to publish (and perhaps track) the denominational makeup of the student body. While the number of students representing the various Protestant traditions varied from year to year, Cutten's description of the student body as predominately Baptist remained accurate throughout this period. Baptists made up roughly three-quarters of the student body, with the remaining one-quarter comprised of Methodists, Presbyterians, and Congregationalists—in order of numerical predominance. This pattern of Baptist predominance continued more or less unabated throughout the 1950s, with Baptists making up 70 percent of the

90. Ibid., 81–82.
91. *CRDS Bulletin* 27, no. 2: 14.
92. *CRDS Bulletin* 32, no. 2 (June 1960): 94.
93. *CRDS Alumni Bulletin* 15, no. 4a (April 1943), 1a.

student body in 1950–1951 and 71 percent in 1959–1960. By 1956, President Saunders addressed the "distinctive role of the seminary in relation to the ecumenical task."[94]

Student fees, which remained fairly constant after the war, also began to grow by the end of "the decade of growth." Tuition rose slightly from $335 to $375 per year.[95] Dormitory rooms for single students (both men and women) cost $110 per year, and the campus apartments rented by married students ranged from $11 to $15 per week.[96] The "estimated cost" of a CRCDS education in 1959 rose to $800 a year for a single person and to $1,700 for a married person— neither figure included annual tuition or student fees.[97]

At the midpoint of his tenure as president, Dr. Saunders's "Report to the Trustees" posed the rhetorical question "What of the future?" Exploring "why Colgate Rochester is in a unique position to move confidently ahead, Saunders pointed to the strong historical roots and financial stability of the institution, on the one hand, and its ever innovative ethos on the other. Already "two new ventures" designed to move the school into this future were under way: the first was a major expansion of the Supervised Ministry Program, which began in 1951 following the successful campaign to raise $400,000 specifically for that purpose.[98] The second was "the new curriculum which was put into effect in the fall of 1955 after two years of intensive study."[99] The new curriculum was characterized primarily by increased opportunities for seminar and discussion classes in each discipline and for a greater specialization within the broad bachelor of divinity program. As Dean Baker noted in 1955, "the revision represents a broadening of our offerings to young people interested in preparing for Christian vocations other than the pastoral ministry."[100] In 1956 a "Lay School of Theology" was introduced for "a group of men and women from the city [of Rochester] wishing to enrich their understanding of the Christian faith."[101]

The coming and going of illustrious members of the CRDS faculty during these three decades was both significant and recurrent to the degree that it is both difficult and somewhat unnecessary to

---

94. *CRDS Bulletin* 28, no. 2 (May 1956): 22.
95. *CRDS Bulletin* 32, no. 1c, catalogue ed.: 40.
96. Ibid., 20.
97. Ibid., 41.
98. Ibid., 24.
99. Ibid.
100. *CRDS Bulletin* 26, no. 2 (May 1955): 63.
101. "The Report of the President," *CRDS Bulletin* 28, no. 2 (May 1956): 7.

completely chronicle. The arrival of two very different scholars during this period seems particularly significant, however, due to the way in which they epitomized the dynamic tensions that had long been at work in the CRDS formula for theological education.

The first of the men was Winthrop Hudson (1911–2001). He first came to CRDS in 1933 and was among the graduating class of 1937. From Rochester he went on to the University of Chicago, where he earned a PhD in church history in 1940. He was deeply affected by the Chicago School, which stressed the new sociohistorical approach to church history.[102] He was also deeply affected by the neo-orthodox theology that emerged on the American scene at that time and was well-represented at the University of Chicago. After pastoral service at Normal Park Baptist Church in Chicago from 1937 to 1942, he returned to CRDS to join the faculty as an instructor in church history, working in cooperation with Moehlman. After leaving in 1944 to return to teaching at the University of Chicago for three years, Hudson became a permanent fixture at CRDS where he was a popular teacher and eminent expert in the field of American Christianity. Through his efforts, the Divinity School's roots in the Baptist heritage and evangelical liberalism continued and received fresh expression.

Hudson's *The Great Tradition of the American Churches*, which was published in 1953, evidenced a deeply Baptist vision of the nature of the church. "The great tradition" mentioned in the title referred to "the voluntary principle in religion," which could be traced back to early American Baptists like Roger Williams and others. After a series of scholarly articles on American Baptist history and identity, Hudson's magisterial *Religion in American History* was published in 1965. It was a culmination of several decades of concerted research and became the standard text in that field for many years. His last major work was a popular anthology titled *Walter Rauschenbusch: Selected Writings* (1985), which introduced the core of the social prophet's writings to a new generation of readers.

The presence of William Hamilton (1924–2012) represented the other trajectory of the CRDS legacy—that of a liberal and progressive appropriation of the Christian faith that was deeply conversant with the current social climate and its challenges. Born in Evanston, Illinois, Hamilton was educated at Oberlin College, and after service

---

102. Norman Maring, "Winthrop S. Hudson: Church Historian," *Foundations* 28, no. 2 (April-June 1980): 130.

in the US Navy, he earned a master's degree at Union Theological Seminary in New York followed by a PhD in 1952 from St. Andrews in Scotland. Hamilton was a gifted and creative theologian whose passions included remaining current with and participating in new theological trends.

The shifting academic landscape that was tilting away from neo-othodoxy toward emergent Christian existentialism and rapidly moving to secular theology manifested at CRDS through special lectures by Paul Tillich and Rudolph Bultmann. Tillich's lectures in the autumn of 1956 and the spring of 1959 offered an interpretation of the social gospel that was infused with the eschatology of Christian existentialism. That same spring, Bultmann spoke at CRDS on the pressing question: "What Alienates Modern Man from Christianity?"[103] His lecture was then published in the *Bulletin* and summarized the modern scandal of Christianity in two main aspects: the misunderstanding and misrepresentation of the Easter event and the cross of Christ. "The resurrection is not an historical event," he urged, but an existential one which, like the cross, describes "the *understanding of self in the Christian faith.*"[104] These watershed lectures called for a wholesale reconstruction of the Christian message from the standpoint of contemporary existential philosophy and secular consciousness.

The future of Hamilton's own theological trajectory was foreshadowed in 1959 by his extensive article "Banished from the Land of Unity: A Study of Dostoevsky's Religious Vision through the Eyes of Ivan and Alyosha Karamazov."[105] Hamilton noted, "Ivan's picture of himself we immediately recognize as our self-portrait; the God that is dead for him is dead for us; and his Karamazov-God of tension and terror is often the only one we are able to find."[106] This new literary-theological focus seemed, almost eerily, to foreshadow the future theological developments at CRDS and the turmoil that ensued in the mid-1960s.

By 1959 President Saunders completed a full decade at the helm of CRDS and summarized it this way:

> The ten years have seen many changes. Even a casual glance at the future shows needs to be satisfied. Our program still calls for lifting the level of the amount of

---

103. Rudolph Bultmann, "What Alienates Modern Man from Christianity?" *CRDS Bulletin* 31, no. 2 (May 1959): 25.
104. Ibid., 27.
105. William Hamilton, "Banished from the Land of Unity: A Study of Dostoevsky's Religious Vison through the Eyes of Ivan and Alyosha Karamazov," *CRDS Bulletin* 31, no. 2 (May 1959): 55-80.
106. Ibid., 80.

support by ten thousand dollars each of the next two years that we may complete our plan for five additional faculty members. Capital needs include increased endowment money to enable us to continue our program of lifting faculty salaries, the money for a second unit (perhaps a cooperative house for women students).[107]

Saunders concluded his report with a prayer request: "Will all who have the interests of Colgate Rochester at heart pray for us that our devotion to Christ may be fervid and our expression of it wise and effective."[108] Upon Saunders's retirement, Dr. Gene E. Bartlett became president, and he guided the Divinity School through the next, tumultuous decade.

Who could have known the deep and tumultuous waters that lay ahead when the newly reunited, relocated, and reconstituted CRDS embarked upon its maiden voyage in 1928? In the next three decades the Divinity School sailed through uncharted waters made especially turbulent by national economic collapse, theological polarization and deep divisions in American Protestantism, a wholesale shift in the theological landscape, and still another world war. Dangerous and troubling undercurrents caused by racial segregation and the oppression of African Americans, women, and others continued almost unabated. The corporate life of CRDS showed the impact of these troubling times.

But it was also clear that the foundation of the Divinity's School's legacy held firm. The commitment to the Christian gospel, centered in the person of Jesus Christ, expressed as an evangelical liberalism that demanded both personal and social transformation, remained intact even though it was tested, strained, and sometimes assailed by conservatives and progressives alike. It was, however, a theological synthesis that required much grace and considerable balance to maintain. And the balance point between the evangelical and liberal components of this legacy seemed increasingly elusive as the century wore on.

CRCDS and its legacy were directly affected by the theological polarization of American Protestantism, which made evangelical liberalism seem untenable. It was deeply challenged by a social climate that continued to ignore, oppress, exclude, and disadvantage women, African Americans, immigrants, and many others—a situation that seemed to signal the failure of the social gospel. Yet, through all these challenges, the Divinity School and its prophetic legacy lived

107. Wilbour Saunders, "The Report of the President," *CRDS Bulletin* 30, no. 2 (May 1958): 18.
108. Ibid.

on, matured, and reinvented itself while striving to be faithful to the gospel of Jesus Christ as well as Jesus' mandate to be about the business of the kingdom of God.

11

Your Daughters Shall Prophesy: The Baptist Missionary Training School

The saga of the Baptist Missionary Training School (BMTS), open from 1881 to 1962, begins in the midst of what was then called "women's work" in late nineteenth- and early twentieth-century America. While this is not the place to detail that important history, it must be understood as the background over and against which the Baptist Missionary Training School was conceived and worked. In this context, three factors must be kept in mind: the first is the horrific social conditions in which many people lived on a regular basis. This situation was brought about by a deluge of spiritual, social, and economic problems that people tried to remedy. At the same historic moment that the post–Civil War Reconstruction failed to protect, equip, and enable newly freed men and women in the American South, and Native peoples were forcibly removed to barren western lands, deprived of their language, customs, and traditional livelihoods. At the same time, waves of destitute immigrants came to American shores from Europe, hoping to find a new life in the rapidly growing industrial cities of the East and Midwest. Chinese immigrants arrived on the West Coast (generally as indentured workers) to build a new civilization through their hard labor.

Christian women and, for the purpose of our focus here, Baptist women, were prominent among those whose faith, compassion, and commitment to making a better world placed them on the front line to address the social problems of their age. Women's efforts, however imperfect and deeply touched by the paternalism of those times, were carried out even under significant disadvantages. Social and culturally acceptable roles for women, even educated white women, in nineteenth-century America were severely restricted by the "Cult of true Womanhood."[1] It meant that women's opportunities were limited, in almost every case, to domestic life and specific duties associated with child rearing and keeping a home. Victorian women were viewed as paragons of virtue, both religious and civic, and shapers of the nation's future through their investment in the home and children, but the high pedestal upon which they stood was in equal parts both honorable and oppressive, since it set clear boundaries most women dared not cross.

The Christian church, and most especially the Baptist churches of this age, both shaped and reinforced the social segregation and oppression of its women with nearly the same neglect that was accorded to the challenges of African Americans and Native people. Women were silenced in public worship (1 Corinthians 14:34)[2] and deprived of religious authority, especially as it might imply equality with or authority over men (1 Timothy 2:12).[3] Hence, an unenlightened and conventional reading of the Bible both reinforced and exacerbated unjust social restrictions upon women by giving those restrictions the appearance of religious support and sanction.

Since Victorian culture decreed the home as women's domain, and ecclesiastical authority excluded women from meaningful leadership in their churches, it seems almost inevitable that the religious work of spiritually motivated and socially aware Baptist women would be in home missions. The resolutions passed at the organizational meeting of the Women's Baptist Home Mission Society (WBHMS) on May 24, 1877, reflected this development:

> Whereas it is a clearly revealed principle of the New Testament that our religious responsibilities are greatest in reference to those who are nearest to us; and as the evangelization of the people of our own country is not second to any Christian work which our divine Lord and Master has committed to the hands of American Christians, therefore,
>
> Resolved, that we recognize as one of the manifest leading of Providence, the formation of the Women's Baptist Home Mission Society in Chicago, to carry forward the work of Christian women for the evangelization of the heathen and semi-heathen people and homes in our country.[4]

---

1. Barbara Welter, Divinity Convictions (Athens: Ohio University Press, 1976), 21.
2. "Let your women keep silence in the churches: for it is not permitted unto them to speak" (KJV).
3. "But I suffer not a woman to teach, nor to usurp authority over the man, but to be in silence" (KJV).
4. The Women's Baptist Home Mission Society–1877 to 1882–Minutes of Annual and Special Meetings and Annual Reports of Corresponding Secretary during the First Five Years (Chicago: R. R. Donnelley & Sons, 1883), 2.

The phrase "home missions" should, in this case, be understood in a double sense; these women worked "at home" in their native land, not traveling abroad to spread the gospel, and worked in and through the restricted world of "the home," that is, through the domestic sphere, with both its limitations and opportunities.

By broadening the culturally accepted virtues of the "cult of domesticity," creative Christian women capitalized, built on, and extended the same social norms that restricted their more overt social action. It was in this climate that Christian home missions came to be understood as legitimate women's work. By the 1870s the Women's Baptist Home Mission Society organized and operated out of headquarters in Chicago, and their efforts were mirrored by a similar group, the Woman's American Baptist Home Mission Society, of Boston. The separate Baptist Women's Home Missions groups inched their way to a fruitful merger in 1910, all the while struggling for recognition by and independence from the national, male-dominated American Baptist Home Mission Society (ABHMS).[5]

The Chicago-based Women's Home Mission Society was led by Rumah Avilla Crouse (1836–1915). A native Chicagoan, Mrs. Crouse had a broad and effective background in reform efforts. She was, for example, instrumental in pioneering the kindergarten movement in Chicago as a Head Start–like preschool program for immigrant and underprivileged children. The Women's Society's financial strength and missional work depended largely on its ability to coordinate efforts with hundreds of local auxiliaries in Baptist churches throughout the country. The executive board of the WBHMS described its inception in this manner:

> In the rapid changes which time has wrought, both in the populations and the spiritual needs of our own country, there has arisen an imperative demand for enlarged plans and increased efficiency in the work of home missions. . . . The conviction is fast taking hope of the minds of all, that in the homes of the degraded populations of our country there is a work to be done second to no other, to which woman is specially adapted, and which most forcibly appeals to her sympathies and love—a work of lifting them from their degradation into the bright sunlight of Christian intelligence and purity.[6]

---

5. This long struggle is chronicled by Jewel Asbury, "A History of the Integration of the Woman's American Baptist Home Mission Society and the American Baptist Home Mission Society: A Case Study of the Oppression of Women," MA thesis, Colgate Rochester Divinity School, Bexley Hall, Crozer Theological Seminary, May 1983.
6. "Report of the Executive Board of the Women's Baptist Home Mission Society, for the Year Ending April 30, 1878," in *The Women's Baptist Home Mission Society*, 25.

The Women's Baptist Home Missions Society embraced the herculean task that lay ahead of them and made notable strides toward social reform almost immediately. Joanna P. Moore, one of the society's earliest and most able missionaries, offered this report:

> It was organized five years ago (1877), and now (1882) employs twenty-eight white and colored missionaries. Its work is not confined to the South. It has two missionaries in the far West, two with the Germans, two among the Mormons and Chinese, two among the colored people of eight different stations. Its great object is to reach the neglected citizens of the United States. This is done by its missionaries, of whom I am one, going from house to house with Jesus by our side, the Bible in our hands and the old story of Jesus and his love on our lips, telling it over and over again, till darkness and sin are gone. We do not wait for sinners to come to our churches, but go into all the houses we have time and strength to reach, for we know that among the rubbish of sin are some of the precious jewels that will shine in the Savior's diadem, and with God's help we will find them.[7]

This active and politically aware group of Baptist women spoke and acted prophetically against what they viewed as the injustice and oppression of their fellow humans. They spent their lives deeply involved in the plight of America's "degraded people" in ways that today would be termed "missional." They did not, as Joanna Moore reported, wait for people "to come to our churches, but go into all the houses we have time and strength to reach."[8] They were also willing to speak "truth to power" (to borrow a phrase from Martin Luther King Jr.), as was illustrated at their second annual meeting on May 27, 1879, when they passed a firm and formal resolution opposing current governmental Indian policy, in which "efforts are being made to open the Indian Territory to white settlers without the consent of the Indians and contrary to the solemn provisions of the Treaty of 1831–32."[9] Their resolution was announced to the newspapers and delivered in written form to President Grover Cleveland, as well as to each member of Congress, in both 1879 and 1880.[10]

The first annual meeting of the Women's Baptist Home Mission Society in Chicago, which was held on May 29, 1878, began by announcing the approval and support of their work by the parent national Baptist organization. Since the American Baptist Home Mission Society observed that the women had entered upon their

---

7. Joanna P. Moore, *In Christ's Stead: Autobiographical Sketches* (Chicago: The Women's Baptist Home Missionary Society, 1902), 133.
8. Ibid.
9. *The Women's Baptist Home Mission Society*, 4.
10. Ibid., 4, 8.

mission work "with the intention of only becoming a strong ally to this Society," the ABHMS welcomed the Women's Society as an associate agency in the enterprise of home evangelism.[11] Couched in this resolution, however, was the assumption that as "an associate agency," the women would not be full and equal partners.

Hence, approval by the male-dominated ABHMS came at a price: ultimate control of the women's society and its actions. A subsequent resolution made this clear: "We recommend that the Women's Society report to our Board the names of all their missionaries, their fields of labor, the work performed, and as far as possible the results achieved; also their receipts and expenditures, and that the same be incorporated in the annual report of our Board as the work of a coordinate organization."[12]

The original vision and plan for the Women's Home Mission Society stipulated that it was to be a mission for women, led by Baptist women, staffed by women, and predominately funded by women. The founding minutes made this clear: "As this Board is alone responsible for the financial prosecution of its work . . . it is fitting and necessary that it appoint its own missionaries and have command of its own money."[13] After working with the stipulations made by the ABHMS for about six months, the women's society declined them.[14] The women's society declared its own independence within the larger context of a cooperative relationship with the ABHMS.

The idea of a women's Baptist Missionary Training School had its birth in the information-gathering tour Mrs. Crouse made of the Home Mission stations in 1880. After her firsthand observations of the many hardships under which the women labored due to their lack of formal training, both in Bible study and professional skills, she issued a challenge to her executive board: "If they [the women missionaries] fail," she said, "you will only have yourselves to blame. . . . They need training and they need it now."[15] By the autumn of 1880, the formal plan drafted by the executive board appeared and was quite comprehensive. Mrs. Swift, acting as the corresponding secretary of the executive board, presented their "plan for the establishment of a Training School in Chicago, for ladies desiring to go

---

11. *The Women's Baptist Home Mission Society*, 2.
12. Ibid., 3.
13. Ibid., 27.
14. Ibid.
15. "Women's Baptist Home Mission Society," *Review and Prospectus of the Missionary Training School, 1881–1884* (Chicago: R. R. Donnley and Sons, 1884), 1.

as missionaries of the W. B. H. M. Society, where, for three or six months, they might receive courses of lectures in theology, medicine and domestic duties, also an opportunity be furnished them for doing practical missionary work, such as would await them on the missionary field."[16] It was also suggested that all women who applied for placement by the Women's Home Mission Society should be required to study at the school.[17]

In her speech before the annual meeting on May 24, 1881, of the Women's Baptist Home Mission Society, Mrs. Crouse observed an obvious difference between how male and female candidates for Christian service were treated. When a young man felt called to ministry, he was told, "Go to school and study to show thyself a workman approved." But when a young woman expressed a similar call to Christian service, she was told, in effect, "'Go to work,' and straightway have sent her to the field." In her musings about the deep irony of this situation, Rumah Crouse wryly concluded, "We have never been able to decide whether such a distinction resulted from a low estimate placed upon the importance of service woman feels called to render, or is to be interpreted as a virtual admission of her superior adaptability for Christian labor and Bible teaching."[18]

What was not directly mentioned in the board's report was the difficulty women missionaries experienced in acquiring adequate training in addition to the many rebuffs that often came their way because they lacked it. But Mrs. John H. Chapman remembered the dramatic success of their bold plan: "In May, 1881, Mrs. Crouse presented her thought to our Baptist organized societies. . . . Her dignity, her firmness, her well-poised character, and withal the favor in which she was held by the leaders of the denomination secured a hearing for her plan. The four years of successful effort that lay behind the Woman's Society held in check the ridicule that would else have been meted out by the skeptical."[19]

Once their plan was approved, Crouse and the executive board wasted no time. Within twelve weeks of its approval at the May

---

16. Ibid., 9.

17. Faith Coxe Bailey, based upon research done by Margaret Noffsinger Wenger, *Two Directions* (Rochester, NY: Baptist Missionary Training School, 1964), 5.

18. "Home Missions Lessons, Issued by the Women's Baptist Home Mission Society; Lesson II: 'The Women's Baptist Home Mission Society—The First Seven Years,'" 1894, in *The Baptist Missionary Training School Collection*, at CRCDS archives, Lesson II, 4.

19. Mrs. John H. Chapman, "History of the Baptist Missionary Training School," in *Alma Mater Memories: Being a History of the Baptist Missionary Training School—a Collection of Class Songs and Mottos, Prayer Songs and School Songs, Composed by the Students, 1881-1931* (Chicago: Baptist Missionary Training School, 1931), 8.

meeting, the plan for a training school was set in motion. With the grand total of $3,500 pledged (but not paid), the executive board rented a large house at 2338 Michigan Avenue in Chicago, which became the first home to the Baptist Missionary Training School as well as the Women's Baptist Home Mission Society.[20]

The Baptist Missionary Training School opened its doors on September 5, 1881, with a full sense of mission:

> The work is too responsible and too holy to be entrusted to novices. These women go forth in the name of God, to deal with the most momentous interests that concern humanity. Not every Christian knows how to lead sinners to Christ. . . . We believe that none should undertake to grapple personally with the giant evils which confront the Missionaries of the Society until she has proved her armor. While enthusiasm, consecration, and a tender sympathy with the victims of vice and degradation are indispensable to success, not less is a practical knowledge of certain lines of labor and methods of work.[21]

Looking back upon these sentiments from the distance of the seventieth anniversary of the school, President Robert Beaven described them as the "Magna Carta for all Christian training."[22]

Not only would these women missionaries gain "familiarity with the Bible and skill in applying its truths to the varied circumstances of all classes of people," but also they would embrace and fulfill the culturally sanctioned domestic aspects of women's work, which in the minds of many gave legitimacy to their distinctive training and subsequent service.[23] Hence, the missionary work of these Victorian-age women, which came to life through the domestic ideas of the era, went beyond them to the broader world of travel, witness, and teaching the Bible.

The inaugural class, in the fall of 1881, was comprised of ten students: "Six of them [were] those who had been in the work for more or less time, and four new applicants for appointment." The *Home Missionary Quarterly* stated, "Others are coming."[24] Mrs. M. M. Whaley was chosen as "Matron," whose task it was "to make it a home. . . . She knew how to comfort the homesick, to inspire the indolent, to repress the over-jubilant, to awaken the listless. She was a friend and helper in all the problems that a home presents."[25]

---

20. *Tidings* 8, no. 5 (January 1888): 12.
21. *Baptist Missionary Training School Bulletin*, 1908–1909, 7.
22. "From the President," *BMTS News* 5, no. 1 (March 1951): 1.
23. Ibid.
24. "The Training School," *The Baptist Home Missionary Quarterly* 3–4 (1881–1882): 125.
25. Chapman, "History of the Baptist Missionary Training School," 9.

Mary Burdette (1842–1907) was installed as the new school's first preceptress. Mrs. Chapman recalled she "was merciless in the rigor of her demands for efficiency and yet she was tender and forgiving to those whom she rebuked. Her mental vigor was of the quality that is 'communicable.'"[26] On December 1, 1881, Burdette was chosen as principal of the new school. The executive board explained, "Miss Burdette brought to her position a large and varied experience, as a teacher and Christian worker, and executive ability of a high order; and to her untiring devotion to the interests of the school is due much of its present prosperous condition."[27] She was a school teacher in Peoria, Illinois, from the age of sixteen and came to Chicago at thirty-six to begin working with the Women's Baptist Home Mission Society. After traveling as a recruiter and fund-raiser on behalf of the society, she accepted the position as preceptress at the fledgling BMTS before she reached the age of forty.[28]

Burdette's diverse background prepared her as she "crisscrossed the country" speaking about the BMTS's aims and needs, all while raising funds and recruiting students. A natural leader and insightful administrator, Burdette soon earned the nickname "the Little General." She was, as Bailey described her,

> highly intelligent, and her executive ability made her the moving, directing spirit . . . of the organizations which she served. She could be direct, yet she was not ruthless when she worked with people. She was quick to see the good in people, often discovering potentials hidden from others. . . . She had wit, humor and a quick repartee which was like an oasis to the students who more often than not were intensely serious as they thought about their unknown future.[29]

"The Little General" set high standards for herself and for the young women of the BMTS. "We want only the best material," she wrote, "women whom pastors and Sunday school superintendents felt they can ill afford to spare. A woman who has never been much account in her own church is not likely to be of much account anywhere as a Christian worker!"[30]

Veteran home missionaries like Jennie L. Peck and Joanna P. Moore[31] taught the new candidates skills like organization, planning,

26. Ibid.
27. Fifth Annual Report of the Executive Board of the Women's Baptist Home Mission Society, April 30, 1882, in *Minutes and Annual Meetings*, 19.
28. Ibid.
29. Bailey, *Two Directions*, 12.
30. Ibid.
31. The remarkable and prophetic ministry of Joanna P. Moore is detailed in chapter 12.

and stewardship of a small salary, while also taking courses.[32] The instruction was of good quality, mixing the academic with the practical, and "in spite of the crudeness made necessary by poverty, the school offered efficient and scholarly courses."[33] By the end of that first term, in December 1881, seventeen students entered placement and one returned for additional courses.[34]

The detailed description of the BMTS curriculum, which was published in the annual report of spring 1882, was comprised of the same three components laid out in the initial plan: lessons on Christian doctrine, biblical interpretation, and church history, as well as lessons on the work of Sunday schools and kindergartens, medical lectures by the faculty of the Women's Hospital of Illinois, and domestic arts, such as cooking, which was taught by the superintendent of the Chicago culinary school.[35] The course of study, which sounds quite ambitious for a term that ran only a few months, was clearly shaped by the expectations of what a nineteenth-century woman missioner should know and would be called upon to do. Perhaps it was the formal religious training that seems most out of place when viewed in that regard, because domestic arts and rudimentary medical care were tasks of the home, but advanced theological study was not. This same combination of domestic and evangelistic roles was voiced in Mary Burdette's description of "what our missionaries must know about and the variety of gifts they must possess."[36]

> To know how to cook, to clean, to keep home with neatness, and economy and to be able to teach that art to others; to sew, to mend, to visit, to minister; to prescribe for the sick, to comfort the afflicted; to soothe the dying; to feed the hungry and to clothe the ragged; to sustain industrial schools, Sunday schools, and conduct mothers' meetings; to teach manners and morals; to possess sanctified tact, self-control, and always show the spirit of the Master; to pray, to sing, to walk long miles if need be; to run and not be weary; to walk and not faint—this is the missionary's work.[37]

As the first annual report of the training school came to a close, its author, presumably Mrs. Swift, stated,

> The institution is still in its infancy, but it gives ample promise of vigorous growth and healthy development. . . . This is the only school of its kind among the

---

32. Bailey, *Two Directions*, 11.
33. Chapman, "History of the Baptist Mission Training School," 9.
34. "Fifth Annual Report of the Executive Board of the Women's Baptist Home Mission Society, April 30, 1882, in *Minutes and Annual Meetings*, 19.
35. Ibid.
36.
37. Chapman, "History of the Baptist Missionary Training School," 12.

denominations, and by birthright, as well as promise of a grand and honored future, it comes before you now for a blessing. Not that you may lay the parental
hand upon it and speak loving, appreciative words of its past brief history, or give
prophetic visions of its future greatness, but the fitting, needed blessing of such
financial aid as shall place it above present and future want.[38]

The report of the executive board, also from 1884, offered insight
about the progress of BMTS: "Under the careful management of the
Principal, Miss M. G. Burdette, this school has made most gratifying
advancement. Not only has [sic] a large number of pupils been enrolled, but the training given has been so systematized, and made so
thoroughly practical, that the most marked results have been achieved
in the preparation and training of the missionaries for the work to
which they have been called."[39] In fact, over the next few years, the
executive board reported, "With few modifications . . . the institution has been favored with continued prosperity and success."[40]

The twin messages of growing enrollment and usefulness on the
one hand, and the detrimental state of the current facilities on the
other, were significant concerns over the next few years. The minutes
of the twelfth annual meeting on May 13, 1888, for example, forged
the two concerns into one message: "This training School, in a small
building with many inconveniences, has, in nine years, enrolled in its
classes 149 students, the most of whom have become missionaries."[41]
A retrospective article penned by Burdette for *The Morgan Park Baptist Record* reported that a remarkable ethnic and cultural diversity
existed in the student body of BMTS from its inception: "From its
organization, September 5, 1881, to June 22, 1897," she wrote, "the
school enrolled 394 students. Of these 278 were English-speaking
students; 4 colored Americans; 46 Germans; 4 Swiss; 36 Swedes; 10
Danes; 6 Norwegians; 6 Mexicans; 2 Jews; 1 Hollander; 1 Icelander;
and 3 Bohemians."[42]

A change in leadership at BMTS also occurred during the 1888–
1889 academic year as Eliza Burke Harrington Morris (1837–1904)
replaced Burdette. *Tidings* stated, "With the beginning of the present

---

38. Ibid., 19-20.
39. "Seventh Annual Report of the Executive Board of the Baptist Women's Home Mission Society," March 31, 1884, in *Minutes and Annual Meetings*, 8.
40. "Eighth Annual Report of the Executive Board of the Women's Baptist Home Missions Society, for the Year Ending March 31, 1885," in *Minutes and Annual Meetings*, 30.
41. "Minutes of the Twelfth Annual Meeting of the Women's Baptist Mission Society, May 13, 1888," in *Minutes and Annual Meetings*, 6.
42. Mary G. Burdette, "Missionary Training School," *The Morgan Park Baptist Record*, 1987, located in the CRCDS archives.

school year, Miss Burdette, because of too onerous duties, in connection with other departments, tendered her resignation as preceptress and Mrs. C. D. Morris was unanimously elected to fill the vacancy. We are persuaded that no better choice could have been made."[43] Eliza Morris was a 1857 graduate of Mount Holyoke female seminary who traveled west to teach school on the American frontier in Ohio and Indiana. There she served with great effectiveness and married her husband, Charles David Morris, who was a Baptist minister. The WBMS board described her as "all love and honor. In her daily contact with the students she quietly impresses them with her beautiful Christian spirit, and her long and useful experience as a pastor's wife enables her to give them much practical instruction which will prove invaluable to them on any field of Christian labor."[44] "A creative and energetic educator, Eliza Morris "put her education and teaching experience to good use."[45]

By the academic year 1888–1889, the Training School Committee felt both the need and ability to move ahead with the plan for a new facility for BMTS. By May 1890, BMTS moved into new quarters at 2411 Indiana Avenue in Chicago. The spring "Report of the Executive Board of the Women's Baptist Home Missions Society," from March 31, 1890, succinctly stated, "The prophecy of the last year has been realized in the purchase of a house for the Training School, upon which there is not a dollar of indebtedness. To God be the glory and honor and praise; $20,000 will be necessary in the near future for needed modifications and additions and this also will the Lord give to us."[46] At the formal dedication services on December 10, 1891, Mrs. Chapman reported, "Some of us recall the expression of one pastor on this occasion, 'These women have done a great work but they have shortened their lives by many years by some of the hard service.'"[47]

Enrollment at BMTS continued to grow steadily. By 1890 twenty-nine students were entering for the fall term.[48] The annual report of the executive board for the academic year ending March 31, 1891, described continued growth both in the number of graduates and their opportunities for service:

43. *Tidings* 8, no. 10 (June 1889): 3.
44. "Annual Report of the Executive Board of the Women's Baptist Home Missions Society for the Year Ending, March 31, 1890," in *Minutes and Annual Meetings*, 17.
45. Bailey, *Two Directions*, 19.
46. Ibid.
47. Chapman, "History of the Baptist Missionary Training School," 9.
48. *Tidings* 10, no. 6 (February 1891): 11.

Fourteen students were graduated during the year, all of whom are rendering acceptable service as Christian workers, six among the Negroes of the South, one among the Indians, one among the Scandinavians, one among the Germans, one in Frontier work, one among Chinese, two church missionaries and one in a Home for the Friendless. Graduates from the Training School are not often found looking for employment. In fact, most of them are engaged before they complete the course, and for several years there has been a greater demand for church missionaries than the school has been able to supply. The class during the past year has enrolled 36 names. The present membership is 31, as many as can be accommodated until we have full possession of our property.[49]

An important curricular change was implemented in 1891: "the extension of the course of study . . . now requires for its completion two years instead of one as formerly."[50] This change not only allowed for more courses to be taken but also for them to "be arranged to avoid crowding."[51] Of equal importance is the fact that the new curriculum allows for more time in spiritual formation and practical work: so these students go forth from the classroom, week by week, and while, in imitation of the example of their Master, they teach the people many things pertaining to the Kingdom, they also, moved with his compassion, feed the hungry and seek to relieve the sick and suffering."[52] BMTS continued to operate under acute financial pressure, due largely to the limited size and disrepair of their facility. "The most pressing need," the board reported, "is about $4,000 more than is in hand, to make necessary alterations in the building during the summer."[53]

The early BMTS graduates established an amazing record of service to "the degraded and outcast" people of the late nineteenth century. Working among European immigrants at Ellis Island, New York, were Maria Rapp, Mary Melby, and Martha Troeck: "They knew how to locate friends and where to find milk for babies. Their pockets were filled with papers, books, picture cards, crackers, and apples for the children. For the parents, they carried books and Bibles. They comforted thousands. Letters from pastors 'out west' in South Dakota, and Minnesota, where the newcomers eventually settled, were their reward."[54] On the West Coast, Martha J. Ames

49. "Annual Report of the Executive Board of the Women's Baptist Home Missions Society, for the Year Ending March 31, 1891," in *Minutes and Annual Meetings*, 19.
50. Ibid.
51. Ibid.
52. Ibid.
53. Ibid.
54. Bailey, *Two Directions*, 19.

worked among Chinese immigrants for forty-six years. When she first arrived in 1889, "the prevailing American idea [was] that the Chinese were scarcely human and certainly had no souls."[55] Ames worked with her Chinese friends through the devastation and danger of the San Francisco earthquake and was quarantined with them during an outbreak of the bubonic plague. Her patient work with them, particularly through the school she established for their children, "won their love and respect. This was the start of the First Baptist Chinese Church of San Francisco."[56] In the urban centers of the East and Midwest, BMTS graduates "organized Industrial Schools" to teach women and children real-life skills like hygiene, reading, writing, rudimentary mathematics, cooking, and sewing and conducted religious meetings for lonely and destitute women: "In Chicago, there was Sophia Rausmussen '82 with the Danes and Norwegians, and Geisna E. Meir '82 with the German people. In Pittsburgh, there was Lyde Jenkins '04 with the Slavic and Hungarian people. Bertha A. Nicholet '04 worked with the French-speaking in New England; Ella G. Miller '02 with the Syrians and Russians."[57] Other BMTS women went west to work among Native Americans: Maryetta J. Reynolds, Sadie E. Bonham, Ida Schofield, and Mary McLean worked with the Comanches, Apaches, Cheyennes, and Arapahoes, where "they taught good housekeeping, they nursed the sick, and they brought the good news of God in Christ in ways in which the Indian men, women, and children understood."[58] Of particular note were the ministries of Mary McLean among the Hopi in Arizona and Isabel Crawford with the Kiowa in Oklahoma.[59]

BMTS women were continually forced to prove both the legitimacy of their call to service and the importance of their training for ministry. This ongoing challenge and their willingness to address it are chronicled all across the pages of their monthly magazine, *Tidings*. In April 1890, under the title "Our Ideal," for example, Mary E. McDowell urged the ladies to look to "the prophetic ideal" lauded for them in Psalm 144:12, which declared in part, "Our sons are plants fully grown in their youth, and our daughters as cornerstones,

---

55. Ibid.
56. Ibid., 29.
57. Ibid., 28.
58. Ibid., 27.
59. Ibid., 26-27.

sculptured after the similitude of a palace." In McDowell's mind, the prophetic ideal of Women's Home Missions infused the domestic standards of her age with the self-giving and transforming love of Christ. She prayed, "Great Sculptor hew and polish me, nor let / Hidden and lost Thy form within me lie. / Spare not the stroke! Do with me as Thou wilt! / Let there be naught unfinished, broken, marred; / Complete Thy purpose that we may become / Thy perfect image — / Thou, my God and Lord."[60]

Again, in July 1890, *Tidings* carried an article arguing for the scriptural legitimacy and continuing legacy of women's work. In a clever article, Mrs. I. E. Gurley of Troy, New York, observed that "not so long ago . . . one whose name every Baptist delights to honor uttered words . . . which were to the effect that woman in attempting to do public work as some of us are doing, cultivates in herself irreverence for the Scriptures. This irreverence is the actual effect which the speaker (or writer) had observed in such women as he knows who practiced public work."[61] Clearly, her unnamed antagonist fused "Paul's prohibitions" with the Victorian domestic ideal in order to forge a powerful weapon used to silence Christian women and deprive them of answering the legitimate call to Christian work. Mrs. Gurley answered this attack by also making recourse to the Scriptures: "As a Christian woman who desires above all things to order my life by God's holy Word . . . I undertook to learn what the Bible says of women's work, and I give you here some of the results of my search."[62] Thereupon, she examined the lives and work of Deborah, Priscilla, Ruth, and Hannah, concluding with the apostle Peter: "This is that which was spoken by the prophet Joel; And it shall come to pass in the last days, saith God, I will pour out my Spirit upon *all* flesh: and your sons and your *daughters* shall prophesy.' And again, 'On my servants and on my *handmaidens* I will pour out in those days of my Spirit, and they shall prophesy.'"[63]

The year 1904 was momentous in the history of BMTS. Mrs. Morris died suddenly that spring, just as the executive committee began to make plans to raise funds for a larger and more modern facility for BMTS. Prior to undertaking such a large, and potentially long, fund-raising campaign, BMTS needed both the permission and

60. Mary E. McDowell, "Our Ideal," *Tidings* 9, no. 8 (April 1890): 12–13.
61. Mrs. I. E. Gurley, "The Training School as Related to Women's Work," *Tidings* 9, no. 11 (July 1890): 12.
62. Ibid.
63. Ibid.; Acts 2:17 (KJV) is cited with emphasis added.

support of the parent body—the male-dominated ABHMS. Mrs. J. N. Crouse, chair of the women's society, was chosen in the absence of Mrs. Morris to make the appeal on behalf of BMTS; this was to take place before the annual meeting of ABHMS scheduled for May 1904 in Cleveland, Ohio.

Not quite as confident a public speaker as Eliza Burke Morris, Mrs. Crouse stepped anxiously to the lectern. Mary Burdette was seated just behind her for moral support. As she began her address, Crouse nervously knocked the pages of her intricately prepared message off the lectern and onto the floor. Fighting hard against the strong temptation to stoop over in front of the whole assembly to collect her pages and start again, she took a deep breath and began to speak from her heart:

> "I don't need notes to talk about Baptist Missionary Training School," she said. "What I want to say is fundamental. The work of the Women's Baptist Home Mission Society must not be handicapped by a mere lack of space for the applicants who are willing to enter service for their Christ. We need a new home for our school—more space for more girls, and all we want from you is permission to begin a campaign to raise $100,000 to buy property and erect a building."[64]

Permission was promptly granted, and the fund-raising campaign began.

On November 14, 1907, BMTS celebrated the laying of the cornerstone for a new facility. In the autumn of 1908, the school moved into its new, spacious, brick-and-Bedford-tone building located at 2969 Vernon Street. The new facility was designed to accommodate up to two hundred students. It included large and small lecture rooms, a library, hospital, reception hall, parlor, large dining area, and the students' residence hall. Fire protection was provided on every floor, and the architects, Pond and Pond, said that their design expressed "both domestic and religious atmosphere."[65]

Following the resignation of Elizabeth Church in 1909, Ina Shaw and Mathilde Dunning each served a short stint as principal of BMTS. More continuity was established under the leadership of Mrs. Mary Reynolds, who was principal from 1910 to 1914. Her stated twofold objective was "to achieve high standards of scholarship and stimulate the students to highest spiritual attainments."[66]

64. Bailey, *Two Directions*, 32.
65. Ibid., 36.
66. Ibid., 38.

Looking ahead to further growth, in 1913 the executive board of BMTS received a comprehensive study conducted by the American Baptist Board of Education. Among the signatories on the report filed on January 9, 1914, was Frank S. Padleford, who was instrumental in events leading to the reunion of Rochester Theological Seminary and Colgate Divinity School in 1928. The study commission made a number of challenging recommendations to enhance the academic quality and stability of BMTS by hiring five full-time, well-educated faculty, thereby decreasing reliance upon volunteer teachers and giving them a large teaching load of fifteen hours per week. Only high school graduates were admitted, and the two-year program was expanded to three years. A graduate program was developed to attract college graduates, and an endowment fund was established as well.[67]

In the face of the board of education's report, which was signed by five men, and its assessment, "the principal should preferably be *a man* who is a capable Bible student [who] is able to represent the school to the public,"[68] Mrs. Reynolds, who ably led the school since 1910, resigned at the end of the 1914 academic year. It was a clear signal that religious leadership by women was still not well-received beyond BMTS. Mrs. Reynolds was succeeded by the first male president in the history of BMTS, Dr. Warren P. Behan.

During Behan's presidency from 1914 to 1919, the school began another curriculum study, and the curricular upgrade envisioned and begun by Mrs. Reynolds went ahead with renewed gusto.[69] The *BMTS Bulletin* described two tracks or "two schools" available to incoming students: "1. The undergraduate school for students who have had High School training; this corresponds to three years of college work. 2. The Graduate School for students who have finished college, university or normal school courses."[70] Each student's program was organized under three majors or concentrations called "Vocational Courses": "1. For Home and City Missions—known as Course A. 2. For Church Workers—known as Course B. [and] 3. For Foreign Missionaries—known as Course C."[71]

---

67. Ibid., 39.
68. Ibid.
69. Margaret N. Wenger, "Through the Years of the Baptist Missionary Training School," typescript, bound but not published (Scranton, 1963), 65.
70. *BMTS Bulletin* (1915–1916), 27.
71. Ibid.

As the Fundamentalist-Modernist controversy raged in the American Baptist Church and many other Protestant denominations, theological turmoil also impacted BMTS from 1915 to 1916. One very vocal faculty member championed both sides of the debate and the student body was divided by the contention. Some students left school because of the ongoing contention. The board dismissed both polarizing faculty members and issued a position statement that affirmed the "fundamental truths" of the Christian message, as well as the enlightened and academic study of the Bible:

> We stand unitedly on the fundamental truths of the Deity of Jesus Christ, the inspiration of the scriptures, and the power and influence of the Holy Spirit. We endorse the policy of the school regarding the study and use of the Bible in the curriculum, and we approve the study of the Bible in the light of the historical, religious, social, political, and personal conditions out of which it emerged.[72]

During this year filled with controversy, enrollment dipped to a mere sixty-seven students, but by the 1916–1917 academic year, it was back up to eighty-nine. Student expenses were still quite low because, as the *Bulletin* reported, "There is no tuition fee." Hence, the estimate of student costs stood at $178.75 per year.[73] That same year Mrs. Clara D. Pinkham was hired as dean, in part because of the difficult situations that arose in a women's residential school led by a male president.

President Behan resigned in 1919 to become head of the Adult Department of the American Baptist Publication Society, and he was replaced by Mrs. Pinkham.[74] Mrs. Chapman described Pinkham as "a beautiful and gracious personality," and students who attended BMTS during her tenure "speak of the personal love she awakened and the lasting influence upon character and conduct that her teaching inspired."[75]

The *Bulletin* issued in 1919–1920 drew upon the immediate context of World War I to stress the importance of having "A Trained Womanhood for Spiritual Leadership":[76]

> The imperative demand for young men in war service, resulting in depletion of the present ranks of those now engaged in the various activities of the Christian ministry . . . lays upon womanhood the heavy, yet glorious burden of increasing the number of women recruits for spiritual service, so far as to fill these great gaps. . . .

---

72. Executive Board Statement, cited in Bailey, *Two Directions*, 41.
73. *BMTS Bulletin* (1915-1916), 24.
74. Wenger, "Through the Years," 69.
75. Chapman, "History of the Baptist Missionary Training School," 10.
76. *BMTS Bulletin* (1919-1920), 17.

Today is the day for recruiting young Christian womanhood for leadership in spiritual work.[77]

When Pinkham resigned the presidency in 1926, she was succeeded by Alice W. S. Brimson, a native Chicagoan. Brimson earned a bachelor of arts degree from Smith. She then returned to Chicago, where she received a master's degree from the University of Chicago; she was associated with WABHMS since 1919.[78] Under her leadership, the academic stature of the faculty and programs of BMTS significantly strengthened—new programs were added, such as a course of study for Graduate of Nurses' Training Schools, and fieldwork became increasingly organized under the leadership of a full-time director of fieldwork, Matilda Utecht.[79] The young women of BMTS were involved in practical service in Chicago, which helped them overcome their own prejudices and enabled them to work well in other venues: "Very soon industrial schools were started, evangelistic meetings, a kindergarten, clubs, mother's meetings. . . . We have yet to find even a few of our workers who have ever worked with the Negro who have not shown a growing faith in the race and a developing sense of justice in their attitude towards them."[80]

When Wall Street crashed the fall semester of 1929, BMTS enrollment plummeted to an all-time low of forty-two;[81] through hard work it climbed to 91.[82] It hovered in the range of eighty to ninety students for most of the 1930s and eventually returned to previous levels by 1937–1938.[83] When writing an article for the fiftieth anniversary of BMTS, Brimson reported,

> More than a thousand graduates serving around the world on mission fields, in Christian homes, in local churches, rise up this year to call their *alma mater*, blessed. They have been striving for two years to bring a Golden Gift adequate to express their appreciation. This gift is one of prayer for additional students in the School, 2000 lives linked to God, and last spring a fourth goal was added, that of raising $10,000 to make beautiful and worshipful the Morris Memorial Chapel in the building.[84]

Suzanne Rinck (d. 1997), who joined the staff as a field secretary in 1933, became one of the mainstays of the institution.[85]

77. Ibid., 17–18.
78. Wenger, "Through the Years," 73.
79. Bailey, *Two Directions*, 47. For more about Matilda Utecht, see Lee B. Spitzer, *Baptists, Jews, and the Holocaust: The Hand of Sincere Friendship* (Valley Forge, PA: Judson Press, 2017).
80. Chapman, "History of the Baptist Missionary Training School," 11.
81. *BMTS Bulletin* (1928-1929), 21.
82. Bailey, *Two Directions*, 47.
83. *BMTS Bulletin* (1937-1938), 8.
84. Alice W. S. Brimson, "The Baptist Missionary Training School," *Missions* (April 1931), 124.
85. *BMTS Bulletin* (1933-1936), 16.

Two major changes affected the shape and direction of BMTS in 1936. The first of these, which the school strove toward for many years, was when it became a four-year college, accredited by the state of Illinois to grant both bachelor of arts and bachelor of religious education degrees. The second major change came through a new charter, under which BMTS would function under the direction of its own self-sustaining board of directors, without direct oversight of WABHMS. This step gave BMTS more independence from the national church and allowed it to chart its own course more freely than it had in the past.

In 1936 Alice Brimson left BMTS to become executive secretary of WABHMS. She was succeeded by Jessie Dell Crawford. Crawford was a Boston University graduate who taught Christian education at both Denison and New York universities. When she accepted the BMTS presidency, she was already hard at work on her doctoral degree, which she completed during her tenure at the training school.[86] Soon after she assumed her new role at BMTS, Crawford was asked by the Women's Society what she needed to carry out her task. She provided them with a list of just two items: more money and a new building to house the growing Christian Center program that was both a training laboratory for the students and an extremely significant resource for ministry in their neighborhood. Both of these concerns, however, had bearing on her ultimate goal: receiving national accreditation for BMTS.[87] The process of fulfilling its valiant mission, while establishing greater academic and financial strength with the hope and anticipation of national accreditation, would become one of the main goals of BMTS for the next twenty years.

In 1943 Rev. (soon to be Dr.) Robert H. Beaven assumed the presidency of BMTS.[88] He was a graduate of Haverford College and Colgate Rochester Divinity School, where his father, Dr. Albert W. Beaven, was president.[89] Under his vigorous leadership, the quest for a new home for the school, which began under Crawford's tenure, was pushed through to completion. The facility at 2969 Vernon Avenue, which was dedicated in 1908, was cramped and worn out by its perpetual use. In 1943, for example, more than twenty-three distinct groups encompassing more than five hundred people met there each

---

86. Bailey, *Two Directions*, 48.
87. Ibid., 49.
88. Ibid., 54.
89. Wenger, "Through the Years," 86.

week.[90] By June 1945 a new facility at 510 Wellington Avenue became suitable for occupancy.[91] It was a six-story structure that housed the school's dining rooms, gymnasium, offices, infirmary, dormitories, libraries, president's apartment, penthouse, and prayer room.[92]

In the postwar years, enrollment grew dramatically as ninety-four women enrolled for the 1948 fall semester. By 1950 the enrollment stood at ninety-seven students.[93] As the newly established *BMTS News* began to publish photos of each graduating class, it became clear that BMTS educated and graduated African American women at the rate of one or two per year; among these early pioneers were Elefrida Powel (1950), Dorothy Sparks (1951), Mrs. Eugene Boyd (1952), Leola K. Johnson Hageman (1954), and Altha Bryant and Estelle Sparks (1955).

Ongoing financial challenges continued to plague BMTS, as President Beaven reported to the alumni in March 1952:

> The School has faced more than one crisis during the last 71 years and finds itself facing another at the moment. The challenge which has been thrust upon the Board of Directors by a $17,000 deficit which the School now faces is being met with real courage. . . . Certainly in the light of the sacrifices made by faithful women who founded the School, we cannot do less than make a real sacrifice in order that the future of the School will also be secure.[94]

By the following autumn, in 1953, the BMTS board approved a new $100,000 campaign to meet "the present and long-range financial needs of the School."[95]

The presidency of Robert Beaven was followed by Rev. Werner G. Keucher. A native of Pleasantville, New Jersey, he came to BMTS following service as a chaplain during World War II and several successful pastorates.[96] Keucher immediately took up the task of stabilizing the financial foundation of BMTS through contacts with the alumnae association and friends of the school; an 88 percent increase in regular support ensued. After concerted efforts the budget was once again balanced and a goal of maintaining five successive years "in the black" was set in preparation for national accreditation. The position of dean of the faculty was soon created, and Suzanne Rinck

---

90. Bailey, *Two Directions*, 51–52.
91. Ibid., 57.
92. *BMTS News* 1, no. 3 (April 1948): 1
93. *BMTS News* 4, no. 1 (October 1950): 4.
94. *BMTS News* 8, no. 3 (March 1952): 1.
95. *BMTS News* 9, no. 2 (January 1953): 1.
96. "BMTS Inaugurates New President," *BMTS News* 10, no. 1 (October 1953): 1.

was appointed to fill that post.[97] The *BMTS News* observed that "Miss Rinck brings to her new position a brilliant mind and a love for teaching the Bible and working with young people."[98]

Suzanne G. Rinck joined the BMTS staff almost immediately upon graduation in 1929 as field secretary. She trained for and was commissioned to do missionary service in Puerto Rico, but "in depression days when appointments were scarce as money, Suzanne Rinck came back to her alma mater to serve as Field Secretary instead of sailing to Puerto Rico as she had expected. The commission is still in her trunk."[99] Subsequently, she earned a bachelor of arts degree from Ottawa University and pursued additional graduate study at the University of Chicago, where she earned her master's degree.

Rinck served as instructor in courses like "New Testament," "Use of the Bible," and "Evangelism." Describing her own method for teaching the Bible, she reported, "It is taught in terms of God's original acts and in terms of God in Christ confronting man today in the experiences of his daily life. . . . It is taught that the students may know God in His judgment, His forgiveness, His renewal and His redemption."[100] A commemorative article in the *BMTS News* recalled that "her amazing knowledge of the Bible, coupled with her creative ability in presentation, made the subjects she teaches live in the hearts of her students and in their work."[101] The same article also lauded Rinck's work as registrar, in which "her careful guidance of each girl as she plans her course of study has also been important as students seek to equip themselves for service."[102]

It soon became apparent that accreditation by the newly formed American Association of Schools of Religious Education (AASRE) was necessary to ensure the credibility and future of the school. The accrediting agency pointed out what it considered several impediments to full accreditation; among these were "too few faculty member with advanced degrees, especially earned doctorates, salaries too low, and too little spent on instruction in comparison to other budget items."[103] Enrollment continued to decline into the mid-1950s, and the graduating class in the spring of 1957 was

---

97. Bailey, *Two Directions*, 59.
98. "Miss Suzanne G. Rinck, '29 Appointed Dean of Faculty," *BMTS News* 10, no. 1 (October 1953): 2.
99. "We Are Eighty—Illustrious Men and Women Serve on BMTS Faculty," *BMTS News* 17, no. 3 (March 1961): 2.
100. Ibid.
101. "Suzanne G. Rinck Completes 20 Years of Service on Faculty," *BMTS News* 2, no. 3 (June 1949): 3.
102. Ibid.
103. Bailey, *Two Directions*, 60.

comprised of only fifteen young women;[104] a similar size class followed again in 1958.[105]

Enough progress was made toward accreditation that by 1957 a site visit by the AASRE was arranged for the spring but was subsequently delayed when Keucher became critically ill and died that autumn.[106] After a hiatus of nearly a year, in which several acting chief administrators stepped forward to fill the gap, Pearl Rosser agreed to become the next president of BMTS in November of 1958.

Rosser was a 1927 graduate of the BMTS secretarial program. She earned a bachelor's degree from Denison University and took additional graduate training at Columbia, Union Theological Seminary, the University of Southern California, and Garrett Biblical Institute. She would be awarded an honorary doctor of divinity degree by Northern Baptist Theological Seminary in 1960 for her service to the church. Margaret Wenger summarized Rosser's legacy well when she wrote, "Her achievement for the denomination attested to that [of a] constant flow of new ideas."[107]

Under Rosser's leadership, BMTS sought to stabilize its course and once again seek national accreditation. But as she looked upon the task that lay ahead, Rosser told the crowd assembled for her installation that if the school were to succeed in its mission of preparing young women for efficient missionary service, five crucial matters must be addressed almost immediately: "They are—your need for accreditation, more students, producing graduates who can fill posts in the American Baptist world mission or who can undertake further specialized training, a larger resident faculty and adequate financial undergirding."[108] That low enrollments and the small number of full-time faculty continued to plague the school in 1958 was evident in "Miss Rosser's Column" of that autumn: "Our school is well begun. We number 63 students, of whom 30 are new. Our resident faculty and staff add 14 more. Other staff commute every day and several non-resident faculty members give us superb leadership."[109] The graduating class of 1959, however, was made up of only nine women,[110] and the incoming class of the fall of 1960 amounted to only twenty students.[111]

104. *BMTS News* 13, no. 4 (June 1957): 2–3.
105. *BMTS News* 14, no. 4: 2–3.
106. Bailey, *Two Directions*, 60.
107. Wenger, "Through the Years," 95.
108. Pearl Rosser, "Miss Rosser's Address," *BMTS News* 15, no. 3 (March 1959): 3.
109. Pearl Rosser, "Miss Rosser's Column," *BMTS News* 15, no. 1 (October 1959): 1.
110. *BMTS News* 15, no. 4 (June 1959): 4.
111. Pearl Rosser, "From the President," *BMTS News* 17, no. 1 (October 1960): 1.

After study commissions in 1959 and again in 1960, it was decided that pursuit of accreditation by the regional North Central Association (NCA) instead of the National American Association of Schools of Religious Education seemed more desirable. After thorough preparation and another self-study, the NCA site visit team arrived at BMTS in February 1961. In his summary report on behalf of the team, President Harold Richardson from Franklin College stated: "The school presents weaknesses of a long standing which indicate the extreme improbability that for a long time to come any North Central Association examining team would recommend the accreditation of the school."[112] Just weeks later a site visit by the Department of Fire Prevention of the city of Chicago indicated that the facility at 510 Wellington was unsafe from the standpoint of fire prevention and needed between $8,000 and $30,000 worth of new equipment if it were to stay open.[113]

As capital campaigns fell far short of the necessary structural renovations and costs associated with accreditation, the projected budget for the 1961–1962 academic year indicated that about $180,000 was needed to begin the fall term.[114] The women's society was not in a position to loan BMTS the necessary funds. As representatives of the BMTS board, the BMTS staff, and the Women's American Baptist Home Mission Society met together at 510 Wellington Avenue in April 1961, the situation looked so grim that it was decided that the fall program should be suspended: "that steps be taken to discover the direction in which the new program shall move."[115] As a way forward, in the "discover the direction" phraseology of the planning committee's report, Rosser suggested a merger with an already accredited American Baptist Seminary. The next day, Mr. Johnson, acting as chair of the committee, called Dr. Gene Bartlett, the president of Colgate Rochester Divinity School, to inquire whether CRDS might be interested in discussing some form of merger. Bartlett's reply seemed providential: "Not three days ago," he said, "we were thrashing out the future of the seminary's program for women. We came to the conclusion that something radically new and different had to be done. Yes, I'd like to talk to you."[116] As President Bartlett explained to the CRDS alumni, "The approach from BMTS matched

---

112. Bailey, *Two Directions*, 92.
113. Ibid.
114. Ibid., 93.
115. Ibid.
116. Ibid.

a growing feeling among us that we needed to come to terms with this matter of the theological education of women. . . . In the light of this awareness on our part, we took up the conversation."[117]

After a series of internal meetings on both sides of the question, it was decided that BMTS would terminate its undergraduate program at 510 Wellington Avenue, effective June 1, and both schools appointed teams to represent them on a committee charged with exploring the merger of the BMTS and CRDS. By the spring of 1962 a joint agreement for merger was drawn up that "recognized that each institution would continue as a separate corporation."[118] By the fall semester of 1962, BMTS relocated to the Rochester campus of CRDS.

The BMTS agreement with CRDS committed the two schools to a common mission: "To provide and furnish for Christian women opportunity for higher education which shall prepare them in the best way for efficient service for Jesus Christ and to provide and maintain courses of instruction in such departments as are necessary to attain their purpose."[119] The BMTS public relations office and its director, Margaret N. Wenger, moved to CRDS in December 1961.[120] Rinck became a member of the CRDS staff in September 1962, with duties in BMTS alumnae relations, field education, and instruction. On July 1, 1962, Rosser became the executive director of the Division of Program Planning of the American Baptist Convention, located in Valley Forge, Pennsylvania.[121]

In September of 1962, Colgate Rochester Divinity School announced "A Program of Graduate Education for Women," which would be "Continuing the historic purpose of Baptist Missionary Training School." The historic purpose of BMTS continued in a new form and on a new level. The prophetic legacy of BMTS women lives on not only in the vibrant and courageous female church leaders graduating from CRCDS but also in the fact that proceeds from BMTS and contributions given by its alumnae allowed the Divinity School to establish the Baptist Missionary Training School Chair of New Testament Interpretation. The most recent holder of this chair was Dr. Gay Byron, who occupied it from 2003 to 2012.

---

117. Gene Bartlett, "Letter to the Colgate Rochester Alumni," September 25, 1961, CRCDS archives, 2.
118. "Report of the Joint Committee on the Feasibility of the Proposed Merger of the Baptist Missionary Training School with the Colgate Rochester Divinity School," 10.
119. Agreement, dated 31st of May, 1962, between Colgate Rochester Divinity School, and "Baptist Missionary Training School . . . ," Item 7.
120. Wenger, "Through the Years," 277.
121. "New Appointments for Miss Rosser and Miss Rinck," BMTS News 18, no. 3 (March 1962): 4.

Daniel Hascall, whose concern for an educated clergy led to the founding of the Hamilton Institution (later Colgate Divinity School) (Source: *The First Half Century of Madison University (1819-1869) of the Jubilee Volume*, New York: Sheldon & Co., 1872, Public domain)

Jonathan Wade, first student at the Hamilton Institution, and later a missionary to Burma (Source: *The First Half Century of Madison University (1819-1869) of the Jubilee Volume*, New York: Sheldon & Co., 1872, Public domain)

Nathaniel Kendrick, a founder of the Hamilton Institution and its second faculty member (Source: *The First Half Century of Madison University (1819-1869) of the Jubilee Volume*, New York: Sheldon & Co., 1872, Public domain)

William Colgate, benefactor of the Hamilton Institution (Source: Colgate family papers, Special Collections and University Archives, Colgate University Libraries)

John Maginnis, professor of biblical theology and center of the controversy about moving the divinity school to Rochester (Source: Howard D. Williams, *A History of Colgate University, 1819-1969* New York: Van Nostrand Reinhold Company, 1969.)

John Wilder, a trustee of the Divinity School at Rochester (Source: American Baptist–Samuel Colgate Historical Library)

Henry Alvah Strong, newspaper publisher, treasurer of the board of trustees (Rochester), and father of Augustus H. Strong (Source: findagrave.com)

Ebenezer Dodge, professor and president of Madison University; president of Colgate Theological Seminary (Source: Colgate Special Collections and University Archives)

George W. Eaton, third president of Madison University (Source: Colgate Special Collections and University Archives)

James B. Colgate, a trustee of Madison University and a benefactor (Source: Howard D. Williams, *A History of Colgate University, 1819-1969* New York: Van Nostrand Reinhold Company, 1969.)

Samuel Colgate, a trustee of Madison University; a supporter of Madison Seminary (Source: Howard D. Williams, *A History of Colgate University, 1819-1969* New York: Van Nostrand Reinhold Company, 1969.)

Nathaniel Schmidt, professor of Semitic languages and literature; dismissed from Colgate for his views about the inspiration and inerrancy of Scripture (Source: Cornell Alumni Association. "Five Professors Retiring," *Cornell Alumni News* [May 19, 1932])

William Newton Clarke, professor of systematic theology at Colgate Theological Seminary and first American to write a systematic theology from a progressive point of view (Source: Colgate University Archives)

Ezekiel Gilman Robinson, professor of theology at Rochester Theological Seminary (RTS) (Source: Brown University Portrait Collection. Oil painting by Otto Grundmann)

Walter Rauschenbusch, father of the social gospel, in his later years (Source: Colgate Rochester Crozer Divinity School)

Strong Hall at Rochester Theological Seminary, named in memory of Henry Alvah Strong (Source: American Baptist Historical Society)

George Cross, professor of systematic theology and successor to Augustus H. Strong (Source: American Baptist–Samuel Colgate Historical Library)

Augustus H. Strong, president and professor of systematic theology at Rochester Theological Seminary, and his faculty, known as "the Big Five" (Source: American Baptist Historical Society)

Mordecai Wyatt Johnson, African American student at Rochester Theological Seminary (1913–16), who later became president of Howard University (Source: Richard I. McKinney, *Mordecai, the Man and His Message*. Washington, DC: Howard University Press, 1997.)

Charles D. Hubert, the first African American graduate of RTS (1912), who became Director of the School of Religion at Morehouse College (Source: *The Morehouse Alumnus*, July 1944. Found on http://www.wcrhubert.com/cd_hubert_frame.html)

Clarence A. Barbour, third president of RTS (Source: American Baptist Historical Society)

Ruth von Krumreig Hill, first woman admitted to RTS; also a graduate of the Baptist Missionary Training School (BMTS) in Chicago (Source: American Baptist–Samuel Colgate Historical Library)

Joseph H. Jackson, graduate of the newly unified Colgate Rochester Divinity School (CRCDS); secretary of the Foreign Missions Board of the National Baptist Convention and its president (1953–1982) (Source: Noah Genatossio, "Reverend Joseph H. Jackson (1900-1990)," (March 19, 2016). Retrieved from https://www.blackpast.org/african-american-history/jackson-reverend-joseph-h-1900-1990/. Image: Public domain)

George Cutten, president of Colgate University, who urged the merger of Colgate and Rochester theological schools (Source: Colgate Special Collections and University Archives)

Frank Padleford, John D. Rockefeller, Baptist layman, President of Standard Oil, and financial force behind the merger of RTC and Colgate Seminary. (Source: The Rockefeller Archive Center. Public domain.)

The historic campus of Colgate Rochester Divinity School (Source: American Baptist–Samuel Colgate Historical Library)

Helen Barrett Montgomery, scholar, educator, Bible translator; first woman president of the American Baptist Convention (1921) (Source: American Baptist Historical Society)

Howard Thurman and his classmates (Source: Crozer Collection, American Baptist–Samuel Colgate Historical Library)

Howard Thurman in his later years (Source: Howard Thurman Collection, Boston University Archives)

Conrad Moehlmann, professor of the history of Christianity, formative in Thurman's development as a theologian (Source: American Baptist–Samuel Colgate Historical Library)

Henry Burke Robins, professor of philosophy of religion and missions; formative in Thurman's theological development (Source: American Baptist–Samuel Colgate Historical Library)

The Samuel Colgate Memorial Chapel (Source: American Baptist–Samuel Colgate Historical Library)

Oren H. Baker, a pioneer in the field of pastoral counseling (Source: American Baptist–Samuel Colgate Historical Library)

Winthrop S. Hudson, church historian at CRDS and expert in the field of American Christianity (Source: American Baptist–Samuel Colgate Historical Library)

Rumah Alvilla Crouse, leader of the Women's Home Mission Society, based in Chicago, which founded the BMTS (Source: American Baptist–Samuel Colgate Historical Library)

Mary Burdette, "the Little General," preceptress (principal) of BMTS; a tireless recruiter and fundraiser for the school (Source: American Baptist–Samuel Colgate Historical Library)

Eliza Burke Harrington Morris ("Mother Morris"), second preceptress of BMTS (Source: Faith Coxe Bailey, *Two Directions*. Rochester, NY: Baptist Missionary Training School, 1964.)

Baptist Missionary Training School facility on Vernon Street in Chicago (Source: Faith Coxe Bailey, *Two Directions*. Rochester, NY: Baptist Missionary Training School, 1964.)

A class in religious education, BMTS (Source: *BMTS News*, American Baptist Missions Society)

Suzanne Rinck, supervisor of field work at BMTS and later dean of faculty there; dean of women at CRDS (Source: "Suzanne G. Rinck Completes 20 Years of Service on Faculty," BMTS News, Vol. 2, No. 3 [June 1949], 3.)

Pearl Rosser, president of BMTS (Source: Pearl Rosser, "Miss Rosser's Column," BMTS News, Vol. 15, No. 1 [Oct 1959], 1.)

Joanna P. Moore, missionary to freed African Americans in the Reconstruction-era South and graduate of BMTS (Source: Joanna P. Moore, *In Christ's Stead*. Chicago: Women's Baptist Home Mission Society, 1902. Public domain.)

Isabel Crawford, missionary to the Kiowa and graduate of BMTS (Source: Isabel Crawford, *Joyful Journey*. Valley Forge, PA: Judson Press, 1951.)

Gene E. Bartlett, president of CRDS in the 1960s (Source: American Baptist–Samuel Colgate Historical Library)

William Hamilton, CRDS professor and an originator of the "death of God" theology (Source: American Baptist–Samuel Colgate Historical Library)

Betty Bone Schiess, among the first women ordained as priest in the Episcopal Church (Source: http://www.womenofthehall.org/inductee/betty-bone-schiess/.)

Melanie May, who developed the program on women and gender at CRDS (Source: American Baptist–Samuel Colgate Historical Library)

Colgate Rochester students arrested for disrupting traffic during a protest about discrimination in housing (Source: Bill Vogler, "16 Arrested in Rights Protest," *Democrat and Chronicle*, April 16, 1964. Reprinted by permission of Democrat and Chronicle Media Group)

John David Cato, first African American professor at CRDS (Source: American Baptist–Samuel Colgate Historical Library)

Gardner C. Taylor, long-time trustee of CRDS and visiting lecturer in 1968-1969 academic year (Source: American Baptist–Samuel Colgate Historical Library)

Henry H. Mitchell, Martin Luther King Jr. Memorial Professor of Black Church Studies (Source: American Baptist–Samuel Colgate Historical Library)

Philander Chase, founder of Bexley Hall and Episcopal bishop of Ohio (Source: Library of Congress Prints and Photographs Division. Portrait by Matthew B. Brady. Public domain.)

Charles P. McIlvaine, second president of Bexley Hall (Source: Library of Congress Prints and Photographs Division. Brady-Handy Photograph Collection. Detail of portrait by Matthew B. Brady. Public domain)

Bernard John McQuaid, Roman Catholic bishop of Rochester and founder of St. Bernard's Seminary (Source: Robert F. McNamara, *St. Bernard's Seminary: 1893-1968*, Rochester: The Sheaf Press, 1968.)

John P. Crozer, benefactor of Crozer Theological Seminary (Source: History of Delaware County, Pennsylvania. Portrait by Henry Graham Ashmead.)

Henry Griggs Weston, first president of Crozer Theological Seminary (Source: Library Company of Philadelphia)

Henry C. Vedder, professor at Crozer, who expanded on the social gospel and weathered criticism from fundamentalists (Source: American Baptist—Samuel Colgate Historical Library)

George Washington Davis, professor at Crozer and a proponent of the historical method in biblical studies; Martin Luther King Jr. took many of his classes (Source: American Baptist—Samuel Colgate Historical Library)

William Roy McNutt, Crozer professor who emphasized practical theology and ministry (Source: Crozer Collection, American Baptist-Samuel Colgate Historical Library)

Samuel DeWitt Proctor, first African American student at Crozer Theological Seminary and one of its most distinguished alumni (Source: James R. Stewart Jr., Archives and Special Collections Librarian, F. D. Bluford Library, North Carolina A&T State University)

Ronald V. Wells, president of Crozer through the time of its merger with Colgate Rochester and Bexley Hall (Source: "Citation and Response," *The Voice*, Vol. 60, No. 4 [Oct. 1968].)

Martin Luther King Jr., graduation photo at Boston University (Source: Boston University Photography)

J. Pius Barbour, a Crozer alumnus and friend of Martin Luther King Sr.; he mentored Samuel DeWitt Proctor and Martin Luther King Jr. (Source: Calvary Baptist Church, Chester, PA)

Arthur R. McKay, first president of the newly formed Colgate Rochester Crozer Divinity School (CRCDS) (Source: American Baptist–Samuel Colgate Historical Library)

Johnny Ray Youngblood, who earned his master's degree from CRCDS and went on to a prophetic ministry at St. Paul Community Baptist Church in New York City (Source: American Baptist–Samuel Colgate Historical Library)

James H. Evans, first African American president of CRCDS (Source: American Baptist–Samuel Colgate Historical Library)

Beverly Roberts Gaventa, professor of New Testament and first woman granted tenure by CRCDS (Source: Baylor University)

Marjorie S. Matthews, first woman elected as bishop in the United Methodist Church, and the first woman to hold such a post in a mainline Protestant denomination (Source: General Commission on Archives and History, the United Methodist Church. Reprinted by permission.)

Shirley M. Jones, interim president of CRCDS and the first female chief administrator in the school's history (Source: American Baptist–Samuel Colgate Historical Library)

Thomas Halbrooks, who succeeded James Evans as president of CRCDS (Source: American Baptist–Samuel Colgate Historical Library)

Marvin A. McMickle, twelfth president of CRCDS (Source: American Baptist–Samuel Colgate Historical Library)

In the summer of 1963, Eaton Hall on the CRDS campus was converted into a "Women's Center" with residences for single women. Twenty-two women comprised the entering class. The new cooperative program was a large success, as CRDS President Gene Bartlett announced under the headline "Partnership Durable": "With the women's center full to overflowing we feel that ample confirmation is at hand for the importance of the women's program in the life of Colgate Rochester. We sincerely hope that it is fulfilling at the same time this historic purpose of the Baptist Missionary Training School."[122]

The BMTS saga is a luminous incarnation of the values that constitute the legacy of CRCDS. The significant role the school played in the "Baptist Education of Women"[123] was incalculable. There is an interior and exterior side to this story. As the founders and leaders of BMTS, among them Rumah Crouse and Mary Burdette, pushed through the ecclesiastical barriers that held women back and tried to make them subservient to men, they established a new way forward for all women that was based, at least initially, in women doing "women's work" as society and church understood it at the time. But in stretching women's traditional roles to the breaking point, by organizing new coalitions, by funding and establishing new institutions, missions, and publications, and by training women in a holistic and forward-looking fashion, BMTS furthered the cause of all women in America, not only in the churches but also in society.

Seen from the outside, BMTS women were prophetic trailblazers who embraced a missional understanding of ministry that lived up to the school's early motto, "Christ in Every Home."[124] They took the gospel of Jesus Christ into the homes of destitute immigrant people, from Europe as well as Asia, to oppressed African Americans, and to conquered and excluded Native Americans. As they went, these women took with them the liberating and transforming message of God's love and acceptance in Jesus Christ, as well as the practical tools necessary for making a better life and ultimately a better world. Joanna Moore's life and work among oppressed blacks in the post–Civil War American South and Isabel Crawford's ministry among the destitute and nearly destroyed Kiowa are but a sampling of the nearly

122. Gene E. Bartlett, "Partnership Durable," *Echoes: The Official Publication of the Alumnae of Baptist Missionary Training School* 58, no. 2 (Summer-Fall 1964): 1.
123. See William H. Brackney, *Congregation and Campus: Baptists in Higher Education* (Macon, GA: Mercer University Press, 2008), 140–64, for the larger context.
124. "Christ in Every Home" was the motto that appeared on each issue of *Tidings* from its inception. See, for example, *Tidings* 19, no. 5 (January 1900), https://babel.hathitrust.org/cgi/pt?id=nnc2.ark:/13960/t76t46r92&view=1up&seq=13.

twelve hundred missionary women who were educated, trained, and deployed in less than a century by the Baptist Missionary Training School. And so BMTS's record of women's inclusion, enablement, and missional deployment partook of the same spirit as the CRCDS legacy; it exemplified that legacy and powerfully expanded it.

12

Joanna P. Moore: Prophet of Racial Justice and Equality

Joanna P. Moore (1832–1916) was born in rural Clarion Country, Pennsylvania. "My mother was a Presbyterian," she remembered. "Therefore I committed their catechism as well as the Episcopal. I did not understand much of it, but I am glad that I learned both. They do teach the great fundamental truths of our religion."[1] She attended the Teacher's Institute in Clarion, Pennsylvania, and by 1852 was teaching school in Reedsburg, where she boarded with the John Corbett family.[2] She recalled,

> At night they took me with them to a revival meeting at Greenville. Here I was convicted of sin and led to see Jesus as my Savior, yet at the same time I remembered my childhood faith and it seemed as if I was reclaimed as a backslider. No one asked me to be united with the Baptist church, but I saw the converts baptized and asked, "Can this be the Bible way?" After much study of the Bible, I told my parents that I wanted to be baptized. They objected, especially my father. I waited one year for their consent. As it was not given, I obeyed what I thought was God's command, joined the Baptist church and it is the only church to which I have ever belonged.[3]

One or two years after her being "reclaimed," Moore heard a sermon on "Foreign Missions" by Sewell Osgood, "which brought almost as great conviction of sin to my soul as the meeting in which I was converted. I wept like a child. My soul burned with indignation toward all Christians. How could they neglect this last great

---

1. Joanna P. Moore, *In Christ's Stead: Autobiographical Sketches* (Chicago: The Women's Baptist Home Mission Society, 1902), 16.
2. Ibid., 10.
3. Ibid., 19–20.

command of our Lord and Savior [the Great Commission, Matthew 28:19-20], and yet say they loved Him?"[4] After the meeting, Moore joined Osgood in a soul-searching conversation about the potential of her becoming a missionary; "he said that I needed preparation," she recalled.[5] This ignited a desire for more education, but her path forward was delayed by several years. By 1856, however, she was able to return to school, "at New Bethlehem Pa., for six months. Most teachers in those days needed only to know the three Rs— 'Reading, Riting and Rithmetic.' There was also a little geography taught sometimes. I studied these at home, also algebra."[6]

In 1861 Moore went west, attending school at Belvidere, Illinois, during that summer. In the autumn she was able to secure a teaching position at Rockford Seminary. She stated, "The war that began in 1861 was then raging. Many of the girls in the seminary had laid aside their embroidery and were knitting socks and preparing bandages for the soldiers. I took no part in that. My spare moments were given to study or work."[7] On New Year's 1863, her disengagement came to an end: "I attended what they called a jubilee meeting," she said. "They said the black man was free and some shouted for joy. But to my ears there came with the shout of victory an undertone of sadness, a piteous cry for help. The next day, as I tried to study my lessons, there passed before my imagination a panorama of bondmen, tied down with cords of ignorance, superstition, and oppression."[8] Her conscience voiced the plea: "What can a man do to help such a suffering mass of humanity? Nothing. A woman is needed, nothing else will do."[9]

Later that same year, in February, Moore heard an account from a man who had just returned from a visit to "Island No. 10," located in the midst of the Mississippi River about thirty miles north of Memphis. She remembered, "He told us of his visit to that island, where were about 1,000 women and children in great distress. A Baptist minister had moved there and was in command of a colored regiment, who guarded the island. The speaker drew a very sad picture of their bodily suffering and their extreme ignorance."[10] She was

---

4. Ibid., 20.
5. Ibid.
6. Ibid., 21.
7. Ibid., 22.
8. Ibid., 23.
9. Ibid.
10. Ibid., 23.

deeply moved by his challenge to serve.[11] But her decision to go south was not immediate because her mind was flooded with questions: "What can I, a poor child, do? What kind of people are they? Why did God let them be slaves and shut the door of knowledge to them for so many years? Will they listen to me? . . . It will take an army to supply the needs of these people. What shall I do?"[12] She then wrote, "I asked myself and asked God a thousand questions and only got one answer: 'Go and see and God will go with you.'"[13] Before her school closed at the end of the term, Moore made her decision: "I did go, I did see, God did go with me and He went before me and cleared the way, and behind me as a rear guard. Duty was made plain, results glorious, and to-day I stop to shout 'Glory Hallelujah! I surely made a good bargain when I invested in the Negro race."[14] Beginning in November 1863 and up through 1868, Joanna Moore worked among those whom she called "the contrabands of war," the displaced persons—freed African Americans—who were made homeless and destitute by the Civil War. This was a full decade before the establishment of the Baptist Women's Home Mission Society (BWHMS) and well before there were established programs of help and funding mechanisms for working with these displaced persons.

The first day she arrived on Island No. 10, Moore found herself enmeshed in controversy and confusion. Two women were hauled before the commander of the base, Captain Benjamin Thomas, "to be punished for fighting and the fight was not yet over. Both were still in a most fearful rage calling each other terrible names."[15] Seeing Moore arrive, Thomas laughingly turned them over to her. "Miss Moore," he said, "I will turn this case over to you. Since you came here to make people good, try your hand on these women."[16] Moore recalled, "I do not know what I said, only I know they laughed at my earnestness, and I cried myself to sleep that night, as I did many another night that winter. Such a mass of suffering, sin, and ignorance as was gathered on that island sure no one ever saw before."[17] Visiting the shacks and tents in which these people were forced to live—often with as many as six to ten children in each dwelling—both broke

---

11. Ibid., 23.
12. Ibid.
13. Ibid., 24.
14. Ibid.
15. Ibid., 26.
16. Ibid.
17. Ibid.

the missionaries' hearts and bound them deeply to the refugees; they wrote down what each family needed so that their requests could be more specific and more urgent. Soon the "earnestness" of Moore and her newly arrived companion, Miss Baldwin, began to win the confidence and respect of those who so desperately needed their help. With no supplies on hand, they immediately began a letter-writing campaign: "We wrote hundreds of letters to our friends in the North [begging] for clothing, for the people were almost naked. Often we found children on the wharf with nothing on them but a part of a soldier's old coat. The women and children were free, but did not know where to go or what to do. They were taken by the soldiers on the boat, and as this was a 'contraband' camp, they were landed here."[18]

The refugees ate from a common pot in the center of each dwelling, and the fire beneath it was their only source of warmth in the middle of the winter. Moore and Baldwin began a Sunday school and conducted devotions and Scripture readings in each home, where the people heard stories from the Bible with the joy and wonder of those who had never heard its good news before—for they had not.

By April the whole colony was relocated to Helena, Arkansas. As Helena offered a stabler settlement of refugees, Moore transferred her base of operations to Home Farm, which was a contraband camp about three miles away. She remembered, "Here were gathered a great company of women and children and helpless old men. . . . There were no white people there, and no one was teaching or helping those people to a better life. I offered to go and live there. The other teachers called me presumptuous and crazy, but I went."[19] Soon Moore had the soldiers building her an "arbor and some rude seats"[20] where she taught various age groups by day and hosted family prayers in her cabin by night. She remembered well the healing power her participants' slave songs brought to those meetings: "Each retired with a sweet, glad song in all hearts, for it seemed, judging by the joy in my own heart. O, how I did enjoy each day there!"[21]

Moore's ministry in the Reconstruction-era South stopped for five years, during which Moore returned north to care for her invalid mother and to embark upon city mission work in Chicago. She reported, "Early in April 1869, I began work for the North Star Baptist

---

18. Ibid., 27.
19. Ibid., 29.
20. Ibid.
21. Ibid.

Church. I cannot remember with what success. But I find from an old record, that I made 2,292 visits in three months."[22] She also served at Shield's Mission of the First Baptist Church where she inaugurated "cottage meetings," where "a blessed work of grace began," and then in mission work of Eighteenth Street Baptist Church.[23]

Moore returned to the South in 1873 to start a vibrant mission in Louisiana. This was funded and sustained in part through connections and awareness she built during her stay in Illinois. Once again, she established a pattern of visiting house to house, teaching, reading the Bible, and evangelizing as she went, as well as "helping in every practical way."[24] When the Women's American Baptist Home Mission Society was established in 1877, Moore returned to Chicago to be commissioned as the society's first home missionary. She soon returned to Louisiana, working first in New Orleans, then Thibodaux, and later in Morgan City.[25] Soon Joanna Moore established a well-organized and flourishing ministry in New Orleans. In January 1879, Ms. Moore established a home for the homeless called Faith Home, which also served as the location for her school, lodging for Moore and visiting home missionaries, and a base of operations for her other ministries, such as caring for the poor, teaching the Bible, and helping people develop domestic skills.[26]

One of the important developments of Moore's work was when her ministry grew to the point that she trained local church women as home missionaries to join her in the work. Moore's monthly report from March 1880 stated,

> 59 women, from ten different churches, in one month, visited 693 families, read the Bible and prayed in 142 homes. Often they only talked to those visited without prayer and reading. Many of them could not read, but their talk was not idle gossip; often their mission was caring for the sick. They found 200 children who did not attend Sabbath school and brought into the school 120 of them; they found also 152 persons who didn't attend church, and persuaded 46 of them to attend at least once; most of them came oftener. They gave 140 garments to the poor, these garments were given to them by missionaries from supplies sent from the North. You see how we multiplied ourselves by the help of these women.[27]

Moore's work was effectual and encouraging to such a degree that she began to think and plan in even larger terms: "The result of

22. Ibid., 45–46.
23. Ibid.
24. Mary C. Reynolds, *Missionary Pioneers among the Negroes* (Chicago: Women's American Baptist Home Mission Society, n.d.), 10.
25. Ibid.
26. Moore, *In Christ's Stead*, 73.
27. Ibid., 130.

our work," she wrote, "was so encouraging that my constant prayer was that our plan of preaching the Gospel and saving souls along the way might spread all over the South." To this end, she made an exploratory trip in the spring of 1878: "I started on an exploring trip with Agnes Wilson, who shared Moore's intention to establish "a training school for colored women."[28]

Not surprisingly, Moore's missionary work in the Deep South brought danger to both herself and the people with whom she worked. Moore described in an issue of *Tidings* a horrifying visit by "The White League" to her school in Baton Rouge.

> On the morning of Nov. 20th we found a notice on our gate with pen picture of skull and cross bones pinned up with crape and signed "The White League." The notice stated that myself and teachers were ordered by the "White League" to close the school and leave the town or suffer the consequences indicated by the skull and cross bones. The reason assigned in the notice was the following: "You are educating the niggers up to think they are the equals of the white folks." Some of my pupils . . . saw the notice before we did, and were greatly alarmed. These poor colored people know too well what a skull and cross-bones means.[29]

After fervent prayer, Moore went directly to two lawyers, "influential citizens," whom she knew through her connection with local churches: "They said they would speak to the mayor and other officers and do their best to have me protected."[30] Later that same day she accidently met one of these men in town, "and he said that he was both surprised and gratified to find that I had the respect and confidence of the best people of Baton Rouge. He assured me that I would be protected and told me to go on with my school."[31] After worship time, based on Psalms 32:1 and 46, "the encampment of angels" and protection of God seemed ever more real to those at the "colored women's school," and Moore felt that she retired with "a very sweet thought of security in [her] heart."[32]

The next morning, while Moore and her students were at their devotions, she learned that the attack predicted the day before was not forestalled but rather relocated to an African American community about six miles away from her school in Baton Rouge, where a black pastor had been "almost whipped to death." When she visited the man, Moore

---

28. Ibid., 136.
29. Joanna P. Moore, "Persecuted but Not Forsaken," *Tidings* 10, no. 5 (January 1891): 10.
30. Ibid.
31. Ibid.
32. Ibid.

learned that without any warning being given, a band of white men with hideous masks on, came to his home on Tuesday night well armed, took him a short distance from his home and four men held him while five men whipped him. Meanwhile others stood with pistols ready to shoot his wife and children if they made any noise or came out of the house. . . . After they had finished the beating to their satisfaction, they brought him back to the house. A number of colored men had been treated in a similar manner, and one was shot dead.[33]

The horrible message sent by these acts of prejudice and brutality was, apparently, quite effective. "My school," Moore reported, "is closed, and I do not believe that I shall be able to open it again all winter. No husband will let his wife return if there be the least danger that she will be molested or harmed in any way."[34] Angered, frustrated, and disappointed, but not defeated, Joanna Moore and her colleagues decided to "remain in Baton Rouge and go forward with our work in this town and in the state unless the Lord should indicate by His Providence another line of action. It is not best for us to lay many plans. . . . All this is God's work and not mine. The battle is the Lord's and He keeps us sweetly trusting, because we are sure of success with such a Captain. Praise the Lord."[35]

Addressing the crucial topic in a piece she titled, "The Negro Problem from a Missionary's Standpoint," Moore wrote,

We hear much these days about the Negro problem. I've never seen a problem. I know exactly what to do for the white man, for the black man, and for all humanity. God has given His children a guide book which makes the path of duty very plain. But I do not quite understand what different classes of His children say. The Negro is often severely censured without a just cause.[36]

The real problem, as Joanna Moore rightly described it, was not at basis "a Negro problem" but a problem caused by the prejudices of white Christians who refused to see their black brothers and sisters as people who wanted and deserved those same rights they enjoyed. The way to remedy the plight of African Americans, as envisioned by Moore, was to free white people from their own bondage to greed and prejudice: "Together we will study our Bibles and see what is right and learn to love and respect each other, and thus live in peace. That is what the guide book teaches. . . . There is no problem before me, I know what to do. First, be good, loving, helpful and cheerful

---

33. Ibid.
34. Ibid.
35. Ibid.
36. Moore, *In Christ's Stead*, 252.

myself. Comfort others. Divide my last slice of bread with the hungry, cheer the fainthearted, tell them God lives and God loves."[37]

Joanna Moore and her associates gradually rebuilt their ministry in Louisiana, where she developed her "Fireside Schools," which brought Christian home education to black women and children. The object of these schools was twofold: "that the Bible shall be read daily and family prayer maintained with this reading, supplemented by other good books. Second, every one shall pass on to others the good they have learned."[38] Moore's Fireside Schools became the nucleus of her home missions work, and she produced a large body of literature to supply and direct it.

In a retrospective letter to "the White Baptist State Convention of Louisiana" she described her work and directly challenged their prejudices about her, a white woman, visiting black people in their homes:

> Thirteen years ago I came to New Orleans and began a new line of work that reaches home, the foundation of society. The home is my center of operation; there I can discover the needs of the people. My Fireside sermon reaches all the household. I can do more good spending a night in a home than in ten talks in public. . . . The colored people need help in their home life. If we can make all homes right, the nation will be right. All know that in order for me to do this effectually *I must go to the home*. And here is where I fear you many differ from me. However, I did not come to ask [your] advice on this subject. Long ago, before God, on my knees, with Jesus as my example, I settled on what should be my plan of work.[39]

Additionally, Moore inaugurated *Hope Magazine*, which came directly to her students with Bible lessons, along with other resources for family devotions. Soon "Sunshine Bands" were added to her Fireside Schools as a distinctive ministry for children. In Moore's "Word from the Field" report, December 1890, she wrote,

> When the children rose and told of their love to Christ and faith that their sins had been pardoned, I told them to go and tell mother and father how they felt. Tears were in all eyes, joy in all hearts, while the love of God was shed abroad and filled all our souls with the sweet peace of God. Angels in heaven rejoiced as they looked down into that little old school house on the poor neglected children, that Jesus who is no respecter of persons, took into His arms and blessed. Praise the Lord.[40]

Moore's work continued in Louisiana for a total of eighteen years. She then relocated to Little Rock, Arkansas, to start again, and in

---

37. Ibid., 253.
38. Reynolds, *Missionary Pioneers*, 11.
39. Moore, *In Christ's Stead*, 248.
40. Joanna P. Moore, "A Word from Miss Moore," *Tidings* 10, no. 4 (December 1890): 6.

1894 she planted a new work in Nashville, where she labored on another dozen years. In 1906 she finally returned to Chicago, finishing her course at the WABMHS headquarters and supervising her Fireside Schools movement. She continued to edit *Hope Magazine* until June 1911, when her growing weakness and ill health forced her to become its "honorary editor" as others took up that work.[41] As her fieldwork gradually came to a close, Moore published her memories under the title *In Christ's Stead*. It was dedicated to the women of WBHMS and became a textbook, field manual, and profound encouragement to them as they took over the ministries she so ably began. Looking back over her many years of sacrificial service, Moore wrote,

> Because of the comfort and help it has been to the neglected little ones of earth, I have never been a wife or mother. Now no true woman can say this without an undertone of regret, and yet, ever since the time I rocked the cradle for my little brothers and sisters, until today, the sunny face of childhood and the loving touch of little fingers, be they dark or fair, have kept the mother-love alive in my heart. But the children I saw were too many to be gathered into one mother-heart, therefore God gave me help through this Blessed Society, which during its twenty-five years has sent forth a thousand women with the love and patience of true motherhood, and those have saved a multitude of children of all races, from a life of sin and for a life of usefulness on earth and a home in heaven.[42]

Joanna Moore's selfless life and courageous ministry were an obvious fulfillment of the ancient prophecy "Your daughters will prophesy" (Acts 2:17). She incarnated the message and legacy of the Baptist Missionary Training School, as well showed what bringing the kingdom of God among God's children looked like in practical terms. In her, as in countless BMTS women who answered the call of the gospel, the evangelical-liberal, social gospel legacy that epitomizes the legacy of CRCDS took shape in real human terms.

---

41. Reynolds, *Missionary Pioneers*, 11–12.
42. Moore, *In His Stead*, iii.

13

Isabel Crawford: A Prophetic Presence with the Kiowa

Isabel Crawford (1865–1961) was born in Cheltenham, Canada. She was the fifth child of John and Sarah Hackett Crawford, who were Baptist missionaries from England. After serving several churches in the Toronto area, then teaching Bible and church history at the Canadian Literary Institute in Woodstock, Canada, John Crawford relocated his family, in 1879, to rural Manitoba. With support from Baptists in the Canadian East and the help of nine young church men, he constructed a small stone building near Rapid City, which he christened "Prairie College." The school was short-lived, however, and it closed three years later, collapsing under the weight of its own financial burdens and the desire of Canadian Baptists to consolidate their work in McMaster Hall in Hamilton.[1] From Manitoba, the Crawfords moved to St. Thomas, North Dakota, where John served a church for seven years and then retired to Wingham, Ontario, in 1890.[2]

Isabel (Belle) Crawford had little formal education as a child, due to the peripatetic nature of her father's ministry. She was homeschooled by her parents, and her father gave Belle instruction in the humanities and theology, while her mother, Sarah, taught her reading, writing, music, and painting.[3] By 1884 nineteen-year-old Crawford served as her father's assistant at the church in St. Thomas.[4] During these years she felt called to become a Christian missionary, but a serious illness

---

1. Robert G. Torbet, *A History of the Baptists* (Valley Forge, PA: Judson Press, 1950), 96.
2. Salvatore Mondello, "Isabel Crawford and the Kiowa Indians," pt. 2, *Foundations* 22, no. 1 (January–March 1979): 323–24.
3. Ibid., 325.
4. Ibid.

left her hearing-impaired and eventually totally deaf. Undaunted by the limitations of her gender, her disability, and her lack of funds, young Belle Crawford sold paintings and painting lessons to earn the $300 she needed to embark upon the two-year program at the fledgling Baptist Missionary Training School in Chicago.

Upon arriving in Chicago in 1891, Crawford described herself as having "two trunks, a castiron [sic] constitution, a Scotch backbone, and a fully developed Irish funny-bone."[5] The next day Crawford met Mary Burdette, the first preceptress of BMTS. She recalled Mary saying, "You are Isabel Crawford from Canada, I believe. I have your name here and have prayed for you every day since the Board voted to accept you as a student. You have come to prepare yourself for missionary service. I hope the Lord has called you and that you will bring great honor to His name. Let us kneel down and pray."[6] Crawford recalled, "It was the first time that I had ever heard *anyone* hint at the fact God calls women into full time Christian service as well as men."[7]

Her two years of missionary training with BMTS were formative for Crawford; but perhaps most influential, however, was her field-work among the urban poor in a ghetto called "the Black Hole" near the Chicago River. The BMTS women went out in pairs every Thursday, bringing food, clothing, and the gospel message of Christian love to the poor of the city. In this assignment she quickly learned there is nothing more important than "bearing the bread of life to the starving, but in the carrying of it we must be prepared for almost overwhelming obstacles." Belle was particularly moved by the plight of poor African American children she met in the Black Hole. "Poor children!" she poignantly asked in her journal. "Where are their helpers? Who is to tell them the way of life? They will never hear it at home any more than if they were in the heart of heathendom!"[8]

On June 8, 1893, Crawford laughingly reported that she "graduated from the Training School, not *with* degrees but *by* them—from a terror to a holy terror, from a holy terror to a missionary elect."[9] But her private journal struck a more somber note as she rededicated herself to Christ and his work: "It is Jesus Christ my Savior who

5. Isabel Crawford, *Joyful Journey: Highlights on the High Way* (Philadelphia: Judson Press, 1951), 41.
6. Ibid., 42.
7. Ibid., emphasis added.
8. Mondello, "Isabel Crawford," 328, quoting from Isabel Crawford's journal entry for May 9, 1893.
9. Crawford, *Joyful Journey*, 54, emphasis added.

loved me and gave Himself for me and I am only too glad to show my appreciation of the great love by honest active service and self-sacrifice." She felt prepared to "go out into life afraid of nothing and ready for anything."[10]

About the same time that Crawford graduated from BMTS, an appeal arrived from the Kiowa chief Lone Wolf. He wrote,

> You Christian people are like the summer. You have life and warmth and light. You have flowers and fruit and growth and knowledge. The poor Indians are like the winter. We have no growth, no knowledge, no joy, no gladness. Won't you share your summer with us? Won't you help us with light and life, that we may have joy and knowledge and eternal life hereafter?[11]

In response to Chief Lone Wolf's plea, the Baptist Home Missions board sent Rev. George W. Hicks, who was part Cherokee, and two recent graduates of BMTS, Isabel Crawford and Hattie Everts. Because she hoped for a foreign missions posting, Crawford was disappointed when her assignment among the Kiowa people of Oklahoma was announced. She recalled it "was a complete surprise and shock. I did not want to go to the 'dirty Indians' and nearly cried my eyes out over the thought of it." Although her initial reaction to the posting among the Kiowa was negative and tainted by popular prejudices about Natives, Belle soon became so attached to her adopted people that she wept bitterly when she left them. Having first nearly "cried her eyes out" because she was assigned to the Kiowa, "later," she wrote, "I nearly cried them [her eyes] back in again, because I didn't want to leave them. Such is life! . . . I gave in and went to the Kiowas. All I know is 'He drew me and I followed on' glad of the chance to spread the Good News anywhere."[12] Marilyn Whiteley reported that Crawford "became . . . a strong advocate for Indian rights."[13]

Crawford confided in her journal, "The secretary of the [mission] society had explained to her that, unlike foreign missionaries who were expected to learn the local language, missionaries among Native Americans worked with interpreters. 'Your being deaf wont [sic] interfere with your work.' "Why, I never thought being deaf any handicap; I just took it for granted."[14]

---

10. Mondello, "Isabel Crawford," 334, quoting from Isabel Crawford's journal entry for June 9, 1893.
11. Mondello, "Isabel Crawford," 335n.25.
12. Crawford, *Joyful Journey*, 55.
13. Marilyn Färdig Whiteley, *Preaching in Silence: Isabel Crawford and Indian Sign Language* (Wilmore, KY: Asbury Seminary, First Fruits, 2016), 22, https://place.asburyseminary.edu/cgi/viewcontent.cgi?referer=https://www.google.com/&httpsredir=1&article=1057&context=firstfruitspapers, accessed April 15, 2019.
14. Ibid., 23.

Isabel Crawford described her arduous journey from Chicago to Kiowa country as "a vivid change and strenuous training for what lay ahead."[15] She soon understood why Chief Lone Wolf wrote to BMTS pleading for "the summer" of Christian faith to be brought to the Kiowa. The once mighty nation appeared on the verge of extinction. She saw hardship, deprivation, and hunger everywhere she looked. Throughout the ensuing winter, Isabel and Hattie joined the Kiowa people in the hunger, cold, and deprivation of life on the reservation. Her unflinching good humor did not fail her, however, and despite not having potatoes, vegetables, or meat to eat for more than six weeks, "Old journal," she wrote, "I am so hungry and would eat you if you were beef."[16] The Kiowa, she observed, "know more about starvation that any other people on earth, I believe, and after this winter I have sympathy for them that will be ripe for action."[17] She also understood the true source of their hardships. The Kiowa "are poor," she noted, "because the white men have coveted and taken their land," and they "are weak because the white men have killed and hunted and frightened off all their game and buffalo."[18]

Crawford also saw that white gamblers and profiteers arrived at Elk Creek along with the government rations for Kiowas to sell them liquor and cheat them out of their food, clothing, and horses. "It is a perfect shame," she lamented to her journal. "Something ought to be done to protect those who are not wise enough to protect themselves."[19] While teaching at Little Bow's camp, she also saw that hopelessness and despair among the Kiowa gave rise to "ghost dancing" and the use of peyote, which induced hallucinations. While she taught and prayed with Kiowa women in one large tepee, their husbands lay in deep delirium in another nearby.[20]

Within a few days of her arrival at Elk Creek, Crawford's love and compassion for the Kiowa people forced her to lay aside the racial stereotypes she previously harbored. "Personally," she wrote, "I have never met a 'wild Indian' nor a 'naked savage,' but Indian ladies and gentlemen, rivaling us in good manners and modesty of dress, and outrivaling us in artistic talent in rugs, basketry, beadwork, pottery,

---

15. Crawford, *Joyful Journey*, 63.
16. Mondello, "Isabel Crawford," 30, quoting from Isabel Crawford's journal entry for March 30, 1894.
17. Ibid.
18. Ibid., 30, quoting from Isabel Crawford's journal entry for May 26, 1894.
19. Ibid., 29, quoting from Isabel Crawford's journal entry for January 6, 1894.
20. Ibid.

and painting, to say nothing of music, prose, poetry, and the universal sign language."[21]

The "universal sign language" proved to be of particular importance to Crawford's ministry. She recalled, "I could not speak the language. I could not hear it until an amazed Indian discovered that the contraption I hung around my neck was my conversation piece. . . . The interpreter alone bridged the gap until I could learn to read the graceful sign language that is understood by most Indians and some enterprising whites."[22] It was, perhaps, her own deafness that caused Crawford to realize more fully than other missionaries the importance of the universal sign language for her missionary work.[23] Soon she translated and paraphrased Psalm 23 into the Kiowa language:

> The Great Father above a Shepherd Chief is the same as, and I am His, and with Him I want not.
>   He throws out to me a rope. The name of the rope is "Love." He draws me, and draws me to where the grass is green and the water not dangerous; and I eat and drink and lie down satisfied.
>   Sometimes, it may be in a little time, it may be longer and it may be a long, long time, I do not know. He will draw me into a place between mountains. It is dark there, but I will pull back now, and I will be afraid not, for it is in there between those mountains that the Great Shepherd Chief will meet me—and the hunger I have felt in my heart all through this life will be satisfied.
>   Sometimes this rope is Love He makes into a whip, and He whips me, and whips me, and whips me, but afterward He gives me a staff to lean on.
>   He spreads a table before me and puts on it different kinds of food; buffalo meat, Chinamen's food, white men's food and we all sit down and eat that which satisfied us.
>   He puts His hands on my head and all the "tired" is gone.
>   He fills my cup till it runs over.
>   Now what I have been telling you is true. I talk two ways, not. These roads that are "away ahead" good will stay with me all through this life, and afterward I will move to the "Big Tepee" and sit down with the Shepherd Chief forever.[24]

Crawford's acceptance by the Kiowa was gradual but also deep and lasting. As she rode on horseback from encampment to encampment and sat with them by firesides, her presence was often met with surprise. "Hands were raised to mouth as each one showed astonishment to see the white woman there," she wrote. "Then some of them made the Indian signs: 'We like this. One Jesus woman among so many Indians, and no skeered [sic]. No Jesus man ever sat down with

21. Crawford, *Joyful Journey*, 62.
22. Ibid., 63.
23. Whiteley, *Preaching in Silence*, 20.
24. Crawford, *Joyful Journey*, photo insert between 152 and 153.

us. Jesus woman sit down, no skeered. That good. We thank you.' But the 'thank you' to Jesus and the Great Father is away ahead."[25] Soon Kiowa came from miles just to see her. "For days, by wagon and on horseback," Crawford writes, "Kiowas came, stood with hand on mouth, and chorused: 'Jesus woman all alone. No skeered.'"[26]

Crawford's program among the Kiowa included home visits, rudimentary medical care, preaching and teaching meetings, as well as sewing sessions for both men and women. The latter proved to be particularly effective because she helped them extend and supplement skills they already valued from their own culture. The sewing sessions also became the locus of Crawford's Bible lessons, which she often conducted in sign language. The beautiful quilts and other products that were developed in the sewing classes were sold to help raise funds for the church they hoped to build together.[27]

In May 1894, as Isabel Crawford prepared to leave for a visit with her family in Toronto and begin a lecture tour throughout Nebraska on behalf of the Kiowa, she received word that the Women's American Baptist Home Mission Society decided not to return her to Elk Creek because there were so few Natives there. Her Kiowa friends bid her a tearful farewell and said they would pray for her return.[28] She did return, however, and took several of her new Kiowa friends with her as she made speaking tours throughout the Midwest and cities as far away as Kansas City, Chicago, Indianapolis, and Dayton, Ohio, to raise funds to help provision the people, sustain her mission among them, and help build them a church.[29] In Omaha, Nebraska, Crawford told a church group that the Kiowa had come to "see Jesus through us," but "truly the view has been obstructed by the poor example that many white Christians present to them."[30] She concluded each of her messages with these words:

> It is only in the cross of the Lord Jesus Christ that the N. American Indian shall find riches, strength, and sight and I come to you tonight with a message from the God of heaven that you who are Christians stand no longer speculating on what policy is best for government to pursue but that you rouse yourselves up to that fact that it is only through the church of the Living God that they shall ever be raised from degradation here to sit in heavenly places above.[31]

25. Ibid., 64.
26. Ibid.
27. Whiteley, Preaching in Silence, 10.
28. Mondello, "Isabel Crawford," 33, quoting from Isabel Crawford's journal entry for May 13–June 17, 1894.
29. Crawford, Joyful Journey, 80–170.
30. Mondello, "Isabel Crawford," 31.
31. Mondello, "Isabel Crawford," quoting from her speech, "Our Indians," 32.

Crawford's many speaking tours and publications, such as "War: Whites against the Indians Since Colonial Times," established her as a leading advocate for the rights of indigenous people.[32] Coming as they did in the aftermath of the US Seventh Cavalry's massacre of more than three hundred Lakota men, women, and children at Wounded Knee, South Dakota, on December 29, 1890, Crawford's efforts helped turn the tide of public opinion toward the plight of native people.

At the end of her first year at Elk Creek, Isabel Crawford wrote back to Mary Burdette, "There have been no baptisms, three have confessed conversion."[33] But she won acceptance and earned the trust of many of the Kiowa. Even those who had formerly viewed Crawford with suspicion and anger began to welcome her and her message of love and acceptance. In one of her letters later that year, she reported,

> I feel satisfied that more progress has been made this year up to this time than was made all of last year. I feel thoroughly satisfied, and if the Indians will only stay here, when they come back next time, till we can have some special meetings with them, I think there will be some conversions. They are all so eager and willing to hear. Do you remember of my telling of an Indian who ordered us out of his tepee last year with a knife?[34]

Recounting the saga of her hasty retreat from the elderly Kiowa medicine man's violent anger the year before, Belle revisited Bopak during a serious illness: "I went to see him," she recalled,

> His eyes were very bad and he was shivering with the cold. I told him that Jesus always cured sick people when He was here, when they asked Him, and maybe He might cure him now, but I didn't know; but I did know He would cure his poor sick soul, that was worse than his body, if he really wanted Him to. Then I asked him if I might ask Jesus to save him. Then he said, "Yes."[35]

Crawford then walked around the campfire that separated them and took the man's hand, "laying my hand on the hand that, only a year ago, had drawn a knife on me, and I did pray for the poor, lost, sin and body sick soul."[36] As she began to rise from her knees, she

32. Isabel Crawford, "War: Whites against the Indians Since Colonial Times," Women's National Indian Association for 1901, from the US Department of the Interior Library, https://hv-proquest-com.ezp.lib.rochester.edu/historyvault/docview.jsp?folderId=002144-026-0446&q=&position=-1&numResults=0&numTotalResults=, accessed April 15, 2019.
33. Mary G. Burdette, *Young Women Among Blanket Indians: The Heroine of Saddle Mountain* (Chicago: R. R. Donelley & Sons, for the Women's Baptist Home Mission Society, 1898), 9.
34. Ibid.,18.
35. Ibid.
36. Ibid.

recalled, "he seized my hand and sobbed out some sentences. I asked the interpreter what he was saying, and he said: 'He's trying to pray.' I gave him a warm shirt, and ordered a cord of wood for him. He has been up to take dinner with me once since, and has not missed a single meeting. He never came last year, and scowled at us every time he saw us."[37]

She recounted a similar encounter with a Kiowa man who was formerly quite hostile to her presence and message and who then became "very much interested." "I made a personal appeal to him at the close of one of the meetings,"[38] Crawford recalled, and he said,

> "I will make a talk. I believe everything you have ever told me about the Christ, and I have put it all down in the bottom of my heart and think it over and over. I believe it because you know more than I do. You can read and see what Jesus says in his book, and I know what you say is true. I am glad you talked to me this way, and that you told me to pray, for I think that must be right. I want you to pray for me now." And I did pray for this anxious one, while he bowed his weary head and calmed his trembling lip, and I believe the dear Savior will answer in His own good time.[39]

Isabel was particularly disturbed by the plight of women in Kiowa society and made them a special focus of her ministry. After recounting several instances of women being bought, sold, raped, and beaten by their husbands or male members of the tribe, she concluded, "I have told you enough to let you know that Indian girls are all either sold, stolen, or given away, and to show you the great need of Christian women who will win the hearts of the mothers and try to instruct them in a better way."[40] At Easter, in the spring of Isabel's second year at Elk Creek, three Kiowa women, including Komal, the wife of Chief Lone Wolf, were baptized into the Christian faith.[41]

After she had worked at Elk Creek for two years, Crawford went farther into the interior of Kiowa territory to start a new work thirty miles distant at Saddle Mountain. She decided to relocate to Saddle Mountain since the camp at Elk Creek was already served by Rev. George Hicks and his wife. There was also a much larger group of Natives at Saddle Mountain who were not being served. She made the move in April 1896, without consulting the leaders of the Baptist

37. Ibid.
38. Ibid.
39. Ibid., 18–19.
40. Ibid., 26.
41. Ibid., 21–22.

Home Mission Society. News of Crawford's deep faith and personal courage preceded her. She was met by a Kiowa chief who told her,

> I am glad you have come to us. No white Jesus man ever "sat down" with us. You, one white woman, all alone among Indians and no scared—this is good. We like this. White people all afraid we scalp them. They do not know our hearts. The Great Father knows our hearts better than white men. He knows we are not bad. The Great Father told you we would be good to you and He came over here with you. We give you our hands, and our hearts are open for you to see. We have no one to help us about Jesus over here, and we all want you to stay and tell us, and we will listen with our hearts, and pretty soon some of us will be Christians.[42]

At Saddle Mountain, Crawford encountered many more people, some of whom were receptive to the message of the Christian gospel. Among them was Chief Hunting Horse and his brother-in-law, Lucius Aitsan, "who had been taught by missionaries and was ready to declare himself a Christian."[43] Lucius soon became a trusted interpreter for Crawford, a practicing Christian, and later a pastor among the Kiowa.

On the second Sunday she was at Saddle Mountain, Belle began her Bible study with the question, "'Are there any Christians here?' No hands. 'Would anyone like to give up the old roads and let the Holy Spirit teach the new road?' Two hands went up."[44] It was a beginning, though a humble one, initiated in large part by the Christian courage that allowed Crawford to go peacefully among those whom other whites feared. At the end of the session, when she invited the Kiowas to pray, "one said: 'Great God, our Father, you brought this leetle [sic] white woman here. This woman is your child. We are your children. We no more call her white woman, but sister. We have spoken."[45] A few days later, the Kiowa paid Belle the great compliment of giving her a Kiowa name. She explained, "They gave me, the 'no skeered white Jesus woman' an Indian name, *Gee-ah-ho-an-go-mah*, which means, 'She gave us the Jesus way.' May it prove prophetic!"[46]

Soon after arriving at Saddle Mountain, Crawford received word that her mother had died suddenly in Toronto. It broke her heart that she could not be with her mother and father at that difficult time,

---

42. Ibid., 38–39.
43. Mondello, "Isabel Crawford," 34.
44. Burdette, *Young Women*, 64.
45. Ibid., 65.
46. Crawford, *Joyful Journey*, 65.

and that she had no opportunity for a final farewell. As her sad news spread throughout the encampment, the Kiowa people gathered outside Isabel's door, silently waiting for her to emerge from within. When she came out, she found herself "surrounded by Indians, row on row, with bowed heads, wrapped in faded blankets and wearing their shabbiest clothing."[47] They came to mourn with her, in the manner prescribed by Kiowa custom:

> Quietly, the oldest Indian . . . came slowly forward and, putting his arm gently around me, pressed my aching head to his shoulder, and raising his hand, prayed this while the others silently wept: "O Great Spirit, our leetle Jesus Woman has lost her mother, and her heart is all broken to pieces. Gather it together again and put it back strong. You have given her to us, now we will take best care of her we know how. That is all. Domot has spoken."[48]

At the end of her third year with the Kiowa, Isabel reported, "The progress . . . has been greater than the two previous years put together."[49] But progress among the Kiowa was also severely hampered by government policy when, on July 1, 1901, their reservation in Oklahoma was opened to thousands of people who joined in the rush for free land. The situation became so dire at Saddle Mountain, due to the incivility of the white arrivals, that by August 21, 1902, Crawford slept with a revolver under her pillow to protect the Kiowa and herself.[50] Ironically, the Kiowa Christians became missionaries to the white Americans, as was evident in Lucius Aitsan's address to the new arrivals:

> The Great Father sent the only son He ever had to die for you. Why don't you love Him and give Him your hearts? Jesus came to this world to seek poor sinners. He did not come for only Indians or only black men or white people. He did not come to look for skins. He came to look for your hearts and mine and everybody's. We will pray for you that the Holy Spirit may show you the way.[51]

Isabel Crawford served with WABHMS for thirty-six years, both on the field and in administrative capacities. She was an innovative and independent thinker who served well but also at times frustrated Burdette and the society. One such instance occurred when she advocated for lay (diaconal) administration of the Lord's Supper if

---

47. Ibid., 67.
48. Ibid., 67.
49. Burdette, Young Women, 9.
50. Mondello, "Isabel Crawford," 39.
51. Isabel Crawford, Kiowa: The History of a Blanket Indian Mission (New York: Fleming H. Revell, 1915), 188.

ordained clergy were not available.[52] Church order, as interpreted by the WABHMS, allowed only ordained clergy to offer the Lord's Supper. But Crawford was more concerned about the spiritual life of the Kiowa people than ecclesiastical propriety and argued unsuccessfully that the Kiowa should be able to receive the Lord's Supper whether or not a clergyman was available to serve them.

In 1901 the American Baptist Home Mission Society (ABHSM) agreed to the US government's proposal of allowing each of the four American Baptist missions in Oklahoma 40 acres instead of the 160 acres the WABHMS negotiated for the Kiowa at Saddle Mountain. Not only did Crawford pointedly remind the male-dominated ABHMS that Saddle Mountain was under the jurisdiction of the women's society, but she also took the first train available—a freight train—and headed east to lobby the commissioner of Indian Affairs for immediate redress of the grievance. Through her efforts, the decision was reversed, and Saddle Mountain received the promised 160 acres, while the other three missions were forced to divide 160 acres between them.[53]

From 1908 to 1913, Crawford toured widely across the US, often donning Kiowa garb and demonstrating the international Native sign language she used so effectively to communicate the gospel to the Kiowa people.[54] She also worked among the people of the Iroquois nations in western New York prior to her retirement in 1930 due to ill health. But it was her work with the Kiowa that proved most significant for her, as well as for them. The Saddle Mountain Baptist Church, which she left behind, grew to more than one hundred members by the time of her departure on December 3, 1906.[55] The impact of her ministry is exemplified by a letter she received following her departure:

> I want to thank you for bringing God's message to Saddle Mountain. We were wild then and did not know how to live right. You taught us how to live right. You taught us how to live in houses, plant seeds, sew our clothes, and worship the true God in a church.
>
> Jesus lives in my heart every day. He never leaves me alone. All my Children are Christians, and my two sons are ordained ministers in Kiowa churches. I am still teaching my young people in Kiowa churches. . . . I am not too old or feeble for

---

52. Marilyn Färdig Whiteley, *More Than I Asked For: The Life of Isabel Crawford* (Eugene, OR: Pickwick, 2015), 85–99.
53. Mondello, "Isabel Crawford," 40.
54. Her rendering of Psalm 23, along with the Kiowa signs, was published as a fundraising pamphlet by the BMTS in 1915. See https://babel.hathitrust.org/cgi/pt?id=aeu.ark:/13960/t11n9wx25, accessed April 17, 2019.
55. Mondello, "Isabel Crawford," 40.

that, for I feel His guidance. I will be 103 years old in November, and the government is going to give me a beef or buffalo to feed my friends on that day. I wish you could be with us. Your brother in Jesus, Old Man Hunting Horse.[56]

The title of Isabel Crawford's autobiography, *Joyful Journey*, describes her life with the Kiowa. Her book is dedicated to her Kiowa friend and Christian brother Hunting Horse. Looking ahead to the Judgment Day, her Kiowa friends asked that Crawford be interred among them, "because," they said, "you can speak better than we can."[57] Isabel Crawford was buried in the Kiowa cemetery at Saddle Mountain, and the inscription on her tombstone reads, in Kiowa and English: "I dwell among mine own people."[58] In death as in life, she made the Kiowa people her own. It was a fitting finale to Crawford's service among those whom Jesus describes as "the least of these my brethren." "Verily I say unto you, Inasmuch as ye have done it unto one of the least of these my brethren, ye have done it unto me" (Matthew 25:40, KJV). Through her life and work among the Kiowa, Isabel Crawford lived out the prophetically transformative and inclusive ministry that epitomized the BMTS tradition and legacy. Her work both echoed and enhanced the BMTS legacy as well as that of CRCDS.

---

56. Crawford, *Joyful Journey*, 174–75.
57. Whiteley, *Preaching in Silence*, 25.
58. Ibid.

14

The Turbulent Sixties

Dr. Gene E. Bartlett (1910–1989) was "a unanimous choice for the presidency to succeed Dr. Saunders," reported CRDS board chair Arthur Stewart.[1] After time in the air force during the Korean conflict, Bartlett, a CRDS graduate, served several significant pastorates, including the large First Baptist Church of Los Angeles.[2] Dr. Bartlett was a widely published, nationally renowned speaker and preacher, fresh from delivering the prestigious Lyman Beecher Lectures on Preaching at Yale in the fall of 1960.[3] As it turned out, however, during the decade of his presidency, Bartlett's leadership and administrative acumen would be sorely tested, and the Divinity School's "long tradition of responsible theological education" would be seriously called into question. But these were the tumultuous 1960s, and controversy, tensions, and difficult confrontations were certainly in keeping with the tenor of the times.

It is difficult to summarize the decade, but many terms come to mind. African Americans and indigenous people asserted their God-given dignity and demanded civil rights and equal opportunity under the law, as did women and gay people. It was an era that started with unbounded optimism as the World War II baby boomers came of age. They rejected the conservative values and lifestyle of their Depression-era parents and created their own cultural expressions characterized by free thinking, new attire, looser morals, and lots of optimism about their ability to build a better world, all of which was played out against the sound track of the driving rhythms of rock-and-roll.

---

1. "Dr. Gene E. Bartlett Named President-Elect," *CRDS Bulletin* 32, no. 3 (March 1960): 1.
2. Ibid.
3. Gene E. Bartlett, *The Audacity of Preaching* (New York: Harper and Brothers, 1962).

In this context, much of the CRCDS tradition, like the historic emphasis upon a gospel-based progressive theology, socially engaged and inclusive of all people, would be both affirmed and called into question. The social gospel, epitomized by its prophetic patriarch, Walter Rauschenbusch, demanded a continued and sustained contact with an ever-changing world, its catastrophic needs and pressing demands. Women and African Americans, who had contributed significantly to the school since the opening years of the twentieth century, demanded the opportunity to move from the periphery and toward the center of the school's mission. True to its heritage, CRCDS was a Baptist institution of higher education, committed to training "scholarly pastors" for the Baptist churches, but other faith traditions were heartily welcomed as well. The tension that developed between being both Baptist and ecumenical would also prove to be a difficult one to maintain.[4]

The election of John F. Kennedy (1917–1963) as president in November 1960 signaled that a new era dawned. Kennedy was the youngest man ever to hold that office, and he and his wife, Jacqueline Bouvier Kennedy (1921–1994), were a photogenic couple. Their presence in the White House ushered in an era of good feelings, which the First Lady described as "Camelot"—borrowing the name of the idyllic kingdom of legendary King Arthur—looking back on the days with the optimism from before her husband's assassination just three years later on November 22, 1963.[5]

There were some hopeful signs of social change in the country. The US Supreme Court decision on May 17, 1954, for example, rendered the "separate but equal" statutes of the Jim Crow south unconstitutional. But changing real-life social situations, like choosing one's own seat on a public bus in Montgomery, Alabama, or trying to eat lunch at the café counter of Woolworth's in Greensboro, North Carolina, was still practically impossible without dangerous confrontations for African Americans. The Montgomery bus boycott, from December 5, 1955, to December 20, 1956, brought to national attention the courageous example of a black seamstress, Rosa Parks, who refused to relinquish her seat to a white passenger, and a young Crozer Seminary–educated black Baptist minister, Martin Luther King Jr., who brought a local civil rights violation to national

---

4. See chapter 15, "Ecumenical Patterns and Partners."
5. Theodore H. White, "An Epilogue for President Kennedy," *Life* 55, no. 23 (December 6, 1963): 158-59.

attention. King went on to organize the Southern Christian Leadership Conference (SCLC) in 1957 and became the most conspicuous leader of the African American struggle for full civil rights through nonviolent social change.[6]

The CRDS student newspaper, *Hilltop Views*, indicates that by 1959 the student body was talking about "The Negro in Rochester." An article by Harold Passer in the paper invited others to consider the reality of the black experience not far from campus: "Rochester has a serious Negro problem centered in housing." He was not optimistic about a quick solution either, because "it is doubtful whether anything will be done to alleviate the housing problem for Negros in Rochester until racial prejudice is reduced." He urged, "The churches of Rochester have a tremendous opportunity to influence their members to feel more kindly toward Negros, just how this opportunity should be taken advantage of is difficult to say but the opportunity is there."[7] In a subsequent edition of *Hilltop Views*, student Obadiah Williamson pointed out that there were at least two separate versions of the American dream, "one for whites and one for the Negro and other minority groups."[8] For the former, "the American dream" of life, liberty, and the pursuit of happiness amounted to unbounded opportunities, but for the latter it meant an opportunity to "stay in your place," as society had already defined that place for them. Williamson challenged his readers to be "truly liberal in their understanding of the American dream by bringing within its purview the excluded segments of our land and extending to them the full measure of freedom that is extended to free people in a free democracy."[9]

The question of race also began to gradually emerge in official publications and actions of CRDS. The *Bulletin* of June 1962, for example, reported a program that was under way to provide more scholarship funds and other opportunities for "Negro ministers."[10] But there is no report of the implementation of this or any other program related to racial inclusion, and the failure to address apparent inequities on campus would pay dire dividends in the future. The opening years of Bartlett's presidency at CRCDS seemed to mirror the Camelot-like climate of the Kennedy White House. Enrollments

---

6. See chapter 17, "Martin Luther King: Prophet of the Beloved Community."
7. Harold C. Passer, *Hilltop Views* 2, no. 6 (March 19, 1959): 5.
8. Obadiah Williamson, "The American Dream?" *Hilltop Views* 4, no. 1 (October 1960): 16.
9. Ibid.
10. *CRDS Bulletin* 34, no. 3 (June 1962): 8-9.

were strong and continued to increase, with the "record enrollment" reaching 165 students in 1962.[11] This record was then surpassed again in 1964 when the arrival of BMTS women increased full-time student ranks to 188.[12] The Divinity School was also on a sound financial footing; Frederick Pitrow's treasurer's report of June 1962 indicated an increase of annual reserves of over $365,000.[13] The arrival of BMTS women at the end of the same year brought five new faculty members to campus and added $645,750 to the CRDS coffers. The impending renovations to campus facilities and long-term income needed to sustain the larger faculty and programs also forced the Divinity School to embark upon a $600,000 development campaign,[14] and by the end of 1964 all but $96,000 of it had been received.[15]

The academic curriculum continued to evolve in response to the changing times. In May 1960 the academic dean, Milton C. Froyd, detailed three specific alterations that would go into effect the next fall. First, the "survey principle, by and large, was abandoned in favor of the principle of focus and depth." Second, "the curriculum was opened up to include larger freedom for electives." And finally, "this freeing of the curriculum in terms of electives now allowed sufficient flexibility of the student to concentrate in some depth in a particular field of interest."[16] New programs were proposed to enhance the Divinity School's appeal but also increased the size of its financial needs. A series of proposals for offering additional advanced degrees, including the PhD in conjunction with the University of Rochester, came to the curriculum committee of CRCDS and stalled because they stretched limited resources too far. As Winthrop Hudson's handwritten memo explained, "Instead of attempting to do many things in a mediocre fashion, it is much better to do a few things with distinction."[17]

Like much of the youth culture that surrounded it, CRDS seemed to be in search of its own identity. In one of his early columns in the *Bulletin*, President Bartlett urged the continuing relevancy of the ideal "scholar-pastor."[18] As the catalogues from 1962 onwards

11. *CRDS Alumni Bulletin* 35, no. 1 (October 1962): 1.
12. *CRDS Bulletin* 36, no. 3 catalogue ed. (January 1964): 81.
13. Frederic Pitrow, "Treasure's Report, June 18, 1962," *CRDS Bulletin* 34, no, 3 (January 1962): 3.
14. *CRDS Alumni Bulletin* 35, no. 1 (October 1962): 1.
15. *CRDS Alumni Bulletin* 36, no. 4 (March 1964): 1.
16. Milton C. Froyd, "Some Changes Affecting Curriculum," *CRDS Alumni Bulletin* 32, no. 4 (May 1960): 1.
17. Winthrop Hudson, "Curriculum Committee Minutes," c. 1965, CRCDS archives.
18. *The Thirty-Fifth CRDS Catalogue* (January 1965), 13.

explain, "From the very beginning this tradition has been character-ized by a spirit of open inquiry, an emphasis upon serious intellectual discipline in relation to biblical and theological subject-matter and a responsible involvement in the life of the church and the world on the part of both faculty and students."[19] The time-honored focus of becoming a "scholarly pastor," Bartlett suggested, was in danger of becoming "a cliché, a label without contents, without the addition of a well grounded sense of personal responsibility."[20]

At the turn of the century, the historic theological identity of CRDS—its evangelical liberalism—had been epitomized in differ-ent ways by Augustus Strong, William Newton Clarke, and Walter Rauschenbusch. It required a delicate balance point that was often difficult to maintain. In a previous chapter, I noted how the more recent efforts of professors Winthrop Hudson and William Hamilton epitomized the same theological tension in a different day. As strong currents of American theology swept beyond evangelical piety, through neo-orthodoxy, and on to the Christian existentialism and secular theology of the 1960s, the progressive aspect of the CRDS heritage flowed on with the tide. While concerted efforts were made to keep the Rauschenbusch legacy alive and vital, Saunders reported as early as May 1954 that "the change in theological climate" was no longer sympathetic toward that approach.[21]

In 1959 Hudson wrote a short essay for the student newspaper titled the "Evangelical Focus of Rauschenbusch," reminding his readers that the great social gospeler always considered himself to be somewhat of an evangelist.[22] But the 1960s evidenced a shift away from the Rauschenbusch legacy evident even in the Rauschen-busch lecturers selected in that period. The notable church historian Kenneth Scott Latourette, who presented the lectures on the one hundredth anniversary of Walter's birth in spring 1962, affirmed Rauschenbusch's evangelical roots in Pietism.[23] But the content of the lecture also suggests that Latourette had little interest in the man he was called upon to honor. Later Rauschenbusch Lectures had even less to do with that legacy.[24] Observing this same dismissive pattern in Baptist colleges, conservative commentator James Tunstead Burt-

---

19. *CRDS Bulletin* 34, no. 3, catalogue ed. (January 1962): 11.
20. Ibid., 6.
21. Wilbour Saunders, "The President's Report," *CRDS Bulletin* 32, no. 3 (May 1954): 6.
22. Winthrop Hudson, "Evangelical Focus of Rauschenbusch," *Hilltop Views* 3, no. 1 (October 22, 1959): 3.
23. Kenneth Scott Latourette, "Evangelicalism: Continuing Source of Social Reform," *CRDS Bulletin* 34, no. 3 (June 1962): 7.
24. *CRDS Bulletin* 36, no. 3, catalogue ed. (January 1964): 67.

chael connected it to a growing secularism he attributed to "Walter Rauschenbusch's social gospel, which was much more *social* than *gospel*."[25]

As early as the late 1950s, it was clear that another major theological shift was under way as Christian existentialism became the dominant theological tone. The same shift was also mirrored by events on the CRDS campus. In the autumn of 1957, for example, William Hamilton explained and defended existentialist Christology over and against two other modern alternatives at a forum on contemporary Christologies.[26] Further explorations into existential theology continued in "A Theologian at Easter," published in *Hilltop Views* in March 1959.[27] One month later, CRDS hosted lectures by the eminent Christian existentialists Rudolf Bultmann and Paul Tillich, which signaled the direction of the school's theological leaning.[28] An illuminating article, "An Honest Break: A Summary of the Areas of Conflict—Conversation between Conservatives and Non-Conservatives"[29] by CRDS student Dale Robinson, reflected the diverse theological landscape of the day as well as earnest conversations that were taking place all over campus.

Sensing the theological shift following his retirement, President Emeritus Wilbour Saunders addressed the graduating class of 1963 with a message titled "A Theological Rip Van Winkle."[30] Identifying himself as an advocate of the evangelical liberalism that was CRDS's hallmark for so long, Saunders recently awakened to find that a theological revolution had occurred, suggesting that the whole world had "succumbed to Secularism." Saunders urged his audience to join him in a "rear guard action" to preserve what was valid and potent in the older tradition.[31]

"Secular theology" led quickly to a "radical theology," which was indeed so secular that it was able to dispense with traditional "god-talk" and ultimately with belief in God. Soon Hamilton's "The Death of God Theology" appeared in *The Christian Scholar*[32] and was followed by his more popular exposition of the same theme, "The

25. James Tunstead Burtchael, *The Dying of the Light: The Disengagement of Colleges and Universities from Their Christian Churches* (Grand Rapids: Eerdmans, 1998), 439, emphasis added.
26. Jerry Freiert, "Christology," *Hilltop Views* 1, no. 2 (October 31, 1957): 4.
27. William Hamilton, "A Theologian at Easter," *Hilltop Views* 2, no. 7 (March 1959): 6–7.
28. "Convocation—March 30–April 1," *CRDS Alumni Bulletin* 31, no. 3 (March 1959): 3.
29. Dale Robinson, "An Honest Break! A Survey of the Areas of Conflict—Conversation between Conservatives and Non-Conservatives," *Hilltop Views* 4, no. 4 (April 1961): 2–4.
30. Wilbour Saunders, "A Theological Rip Van Winkle," *Colgate Rochester Bulletin* 35, no. 6 (June 1963): 58–64.
31. Ibid.
32. William Hamilton, "The Death of God Theology," *The Christian Scholar* 48, no. 1 (Spring 1965): 27–48.

Shape of a Radical Theology," published in *The Christian Century* in the autumn of 1965. Explaining the inner impulse of the death of God theologians, Hamilton wrote,

> It's really that we do not know, do not adore, do not possess, do not believe in God. It is not just that a capacity has dried up within us; we do not take all this as merely a statement about our frail psyches, we take it as a statement about the nature of the world and we try to convince others. God is dead. We are not talking about the absence of the experience of God, but about the experience of the absence of God.[33]

In October 1965, news about death of God theology exploded upon the American scene. Within two weeks, feature articles appeared in both *The New York Times* and *Time* describing, at length, the new theology of William Hamilton and three others. Hamilton's picture was carried prominently in both articles, as was his connection to Colgate Rochester Divinity School.[34] "Hamilton," wrote a *Time* reporter, "defines Christ not as a person or an object but as 'a place to be'—and the place of Christ, he asserts, is in the midst of the Negro's struggle for equality, in the emerging forms of technological society, and in the arts and sciences of the secular world."[35]

In April 1966 *Time* returned to the death of God theology with its provocative cover article blaring the question, "Is God Dead?" which also featured William Hamilton. It was the largest-selling issue of *Time* to date, and an estimated 4.5 million people read the article.[36] With theological controversy swirling all across the nation, Desmond Stone's "The Big Debate up on the Hill: Save Face or Save Faith?" appeared in the Rochester *Times-Union*.[37] It was quickly reprinted, in a truncated form, in the *CRDS Bulletin*.[38]

The maelstrom engendered by this new theology was probably not as great a shock and surprise "Up on the Hill" as it was to the general public. The article by Stone quoted President Bartlett as saying that "much of the ferment of the moment concerns the work of one man, Dr. William Hamilton, Professor of Christian Ethics and Theology."[39] Bartlett claimed that nineteen of the twenty full-time faculty of CRDS

---

33. Ibid., 31.
34. "New Theologians See Christianity without God," *The New York Times*, October 17, 1965, 85; "Christian Atheism: The God Is Dead Movement," *Time*, October 22, 1965, 61–62.
35. "Christian Atheism," 62.
36. "Toward a Hidden God," George Case (blog), https://georgecaseblog.wordpress.com/tag/toward-a-hidden-god/, accessed March 8, 2018.
37. Desmond Stone, "The Big Debate 'Up on the Hill,' Save Face or Save Faith," *The Times-Union*, December 3, 1965, 1b, 4b. The *Times-Union* article was front-page news in sec. B.
38. Desmond Stone, "The Big Debate 'Up on the Hill,'" *CRDS Alumni Bulletin* 38, no. 2 (December 1965): 1.
39. Ibid.

did not agree with Hamilton's position, and he assured his largely alumni readership, "There is a basic core of agreement among . . . faculty members. But though the amount of dissent is less, the degree of it is much sharper."[40] Bartlett also acknowledged that Hamilton's identification with the death of God movement "made it difficult for students to keep him in perspective."[41] He was, in other words, losing the student confidence and trust necessary for the work at hand.

Internally, the controversy ripped at the heart of CRDS. It pushed the theological balance of the Divinity School's historic evangelical-liberalism past the tipping point. It also threatened a fissure between two elements of its mission to develop scholarly pastors as the seemingly competing concerns of academic freedom and historic commitment to serving the Christian church painfully collided. On a personal level, it was even more difficult. Hamilton was both talented and well-liked by students and faculty. He also became the public face of the Divinity School, even representing it on national television.[42] Hamilton was, as Lloyd Steffen described him, "a jewel in the crown of up-and-coming American theologians; the most promising part of a traditional academic theological career was ahead of him."[43]

The stress and pain of the controversy is aptly illustrated in a note Bartlett wrote to Hamilton's parents from the midst of the maelstrom: "Let me say this to you as a friend and 'member of the family.' I have been very appreciative of Bill in these recent days. He has stood up under a great deal of challenges with a dignity which has made us all proud of him." Bartlett continued,

> These have been difficult days for him . . . we have tried to give every support we can. But I am sure there must be times when he feels standing quite alone and I wanted very much to stand with him at that point. But we have been grateful for his personal dignity in the matter. I do not agree with his position theologically, as you must imagine, but it is one which has to be faced with seriousness in this twentieth century.[44]

Almost immediately, Hamilton reported receiving death threats from those who thought that one death (the death of God) merited another—that of William Hamilton.[45]

---

40. Ibid.
41. Stone, "The Big Debate 'Up on the Hill,'" B1.
42. Gene Bartlett, "President's Report to the Board of Trustees of Colgate Rochester Divinity School," May 18, 1964.
43. Lloyd Steffen, "The Dangerous God: A Profile of William Hamilton," *Christian Century* 106, no. 27 (September 27, 1989): 844.
44. Gene E. Bartlett, to Mr. and Mrs. William M. Hamilton, dictated January 31, 1966, and mailed February 3, an unpublished letter from the CRDS archives.
45. Steffen, "The Dangerous God," 844.

As Bartlett stood before a public meeting requested by CRDS students on April 6, 1966, the practical question became "What arrangement within Colgate Rochester offers the best chance of affirming the essential values of identity on the one hand and freedom on the other?" The arrangement presented to the students that day was first presented to and approved by the executive committee of the board of trustees on January 19. It recommended that Hamilton should relinquish his academic chair, since the William Newton Clarke chair "be considered primarily responsible for Introductory and Systematic Theology" in an attempt to "affirm the identity of the School with its century old commitment to the Christian ministry." Hamilton stopped teaching the required introductory courses in theology and was replaced in that venue by a visiting professor, Dr. John Macquarrie. After working under the new arrangement for another year, Hamilton resigned his faculty position at CRDS. Looking back on these events a decade later, he remembered, "At that time . . . I saw my academic chair removed by my colleagues. No problem—one can teach standing up. I next observed that I was not to be allowed to teach the required introductory course. I got the message: death of God for me; death of Christian character for them. Fair exchange. The students, at least, were splendid."[46]

As the controversy boiled on for nearly two years, the volume of letters arriving from alumni, friends, and critics of the Divinity School was extraordinary. An examination of the correspondence retained in Bartlett's files suggests that negative replies predominated at a level of more than four to one. Several alumni reported they were not only dismayed but that their current financial support would cease and that they were removing the Divinity School from their wills. But a few correspondents lauded the way CRDS upheld the traditional Baptist principle of religious freedom. Bartlett asserted in 1967 that "there is no tangible evidence . . . that the school has suffered financially from this kind of involvement. In fact, gifts of regular support are ahead of those of the year before. This response," he said, "was a tribute to people who have supported the freedom of the school."[47] Taking the long view, however, William Brackney's assessment of the impact of the death of God controversy seems more

46. William Hamilton, "In Piam Memoriam—The Death of God After Ten Years," *Christian Century* 92, no. 32 (October 8, 1975): 873.
47. Gene Bartlett, "The Big Debate 'Up on the Hill," *CRDS Bulletin* 17, no. 2 (December 1965): 1.

accurate: "William Hamilton's career at Colgate Rochester had done deep damage even to the school's traditionally tolerant community of liberal Baptist support."[48]

On the national scene, Lyndon Baines Johnson (1908–1973) assumed the presidency following Kennedy's assassination. In many ways Johnson seemed to be the antithesis of the man he replaced, but he vowed to carry out the Great Society ideals of his fallen predecessor—and some notable steps were taken in legislation supporting education and public health. But President Johnson would also be remembered for his tardiness in acting on civil rights and for escalating US military involvement in Vietnam. By March 1965 a group calling themselves "The Rochester Area Professors Ad Hoc Committee on Vietnam" took out a full-page ad in the Rochester *Democrat and Chronicle* to ask, "Can we win in Vietnam?" Among the leaders were professors George Hall and William Hamilton of Colgate Rochester Divinity School; all told a dozen CRDS faculty were signatories.[49]

By 1967 more than five hundred thousand US soldiers fought in Vietnam, and with increased US involvement in Vietnam came increased social activism and protest. By December 1967 the number of young volunteers for the increasingly unpopular war dropped dramatically, making it necessary to institute a military draft. The draft added much fuel to the already smoldering fires of student protest and caused continuous conflict. And Student activism at CRDS also increased. In the spring of that year students instituted a "Fast Day for Peace," during which prayer and fasting was supplemented by anti-war literature, seminars, and soul-searching conversations.

On April 15, 1967, eight CRDS students participated in the "Spring Mobilization to End the War in Vietnam" in New York City.[50] The next spring the CRDS Student Committee hosted a full-scale Vietnam teach-in. More than three hundred people packed the campus auditorium to hear lectures and panel presentations both pro and con.[51] That same year more than thirty CRDS students were involved in staging events actively protesting the war in Vietnam,

---

48. William H. Brackney, *A Genetic History of Baptist Thought* (Macon, GA: Mercer University Press, 2004), 344.
49. "An Open Letter to President Johnson on Vietnam . . . Peace through Negotiation," *Democrat and Chronicle*, March 7, 1956, 117. The Colgate Rochester professors who signed the letter were James Ashbrook, V. E. Devadutt, Robert Eds, William Elliott, George Hall, William Hamilton, Harmon Holcomb, R. Lewis Johnson, Prentiss Pemberton, James A. Sanders, and John Charles Wynn.
50. Adele McCollum, "Students in Peace March," *CRDS Bulletin* 39, no. 4 (June 1967): 3.
51. Stuart Mitchell, "Students Stage Teach-In," *CRDS Bulletin* 40, no. 6 (May 1968): 3.

while others gave their time and efforts to the presidential campaign of "peace candidate" Senator Eugene McCarthy.[52]

The year 1967 was also the year of the Divinity School's sesquicentennial celebration. The celebrative convocation was held on March 29, 1967. Dignitaries and representatives from more than sixty-five institutions of higher learning and ecclesiastical communions marched in the grand procession.[53] On that occasion, Bartlett gave a reflective address titled "A Time to Challenge the Axioms," in which he looked both to the past to engage "in an enterprise of self-understanding and to the challenges of the future."[54] Bartlett stressed the new ecumenical context of Christian ministry, secularism, the difficulty of maintaining high academic standards in ministry, and the significance of the interconnection between personal religious experience and the pastoral office within a context where "many things in church seem to be dying."[55] Looking back upon a vibrant past and anticipating a challenging but glorious future, Bartlett also reminded his listeners, "After a century and a half a community of faith has ample ground to say, 'So long thy power that blessed me, Sure it still will lead me on.'"[56]

In the early 1960s, women began to take concerted strides toward greater social equality. The publication of *The Feminine Mystique* both signaled and impelled some of that change. In her work, Betty Friedan argued that equal opportunity and social equality for women are necessary for their own happiness and the betterment of society.[57] Following up on this attack against social inequality, Friedan, along with others, established the National Organization of Women (NOW) on June 30, 1966, to coordinate and organize women's fight for full equality. This event is generally taken to epitomize the emergence of "second wave" feminism; but actual social change emerged very slowly.

The article "Ministry Coeds," published by the *Democrat and Chronicle*, featured several CRDS women as "Students and Helpmates."[58] The article's subtitle, "Women 'Invade' CRDS,"

52. Ibid.
53. "Sesquicentennial Celebration, and Service of Worship: Colgate Rochester Divinity School," March 29, 1967, unpublished program from the CRCDS archives.
54. Gene Bartlett, "A Time to Challenge the Axioms," Colgate Rochester Divinity School, Sesquicentennial Celebration, March 29, 1967, unpublished document among the Gene Bartlett Papers, in the CRCDS archives, 1.
55. Ibid.
56. Ibid., 1–2.
57. Betty Freidan, *The Feminine Mystique* (New York: Norton and Company, 1963), xi–xx.
58. Mary McKee, "Ministry Coeds: Women 'Invade' Colgate Rochester as Students and Helpmates," Rochester *Democrat and Chronicle*, March 8, 1959, 71.

evidenced the presupposition that ministry and theological education were, properly, male-dominated spheres,[59] but it exemplified the stained glass ceiling faced by so many women in religious work. They were heartily welcomed into the work of the church but also relegated by tradition, hopes, perceptions, or aspirations to roles that would not lead to full participation and pastoral leadership.

In her November 1960 article in *Hilltop Views*, CRDS ministerial student Marita Drach indicated that she was tired of responding to the question "Why Am I Here?" as though that was a question women preparing for ministry needed to answer more frequently than their male counterparts.[60] She concluded that her decision to come to CRDS was made in the same way a male student's was and should be received as such.[61] But by 1998, Doug Mandelaro suggested "despite a 'stained-glass ceiling' that still prevents full equality with men, women have made tremendous progress in ascending the pulpits of America."[62] Dr. Melanie May, dean of women and gender studies at CRDS, stated, "Women are re-inventing the church" by choosing their own destiny and rejecting traditional power positions created by men; "they are finding a place."[63]

The emergence and growth of women's participation and leadership was also felt on the CRDS campus. This was due in part to the inclusion of the women from the Baptist Missionary Training School in 1962 in addition to the gradually changing reception of women and church work. Hence, the *Colgate Rochester Bulletin* of 1962 proudly announced the addition of "Graduate Professional Degree Programs for Women."[64] Suzanne Rinck, formerly of BMTS, was appointed "to assist in the establishment of the new program."[65] It was also announced that "the regular BD program is open to women seeking to enter the ordained ministry among those denominations for which such provision is now authorized."[66] By the fall of 1963, the Women's Center was solemnly dedicated in a service featuring a keynote address by the associate director of American Baptist Home Missions, Dr. Dorothy Bucklin,[67] and the long-running "News of

---

59. Ibid.
60. Marita Drach, "Why Am I Here?" *Hilltop Views* 4, no. 2 (November 29, 1960): 1–2.
61. Ibid., 20.
62. Doug Mandelaro, "Women in Pulpits Promise a 'Reformation' in Ministry," *Democrat and Chronicle*, July 17, 1998, 5.
63. Ibid.
64. *CRDS Bulletin* 34, no. 3, catalogue ed. (January 1962): 19–22.
65. "Miss Rinck Appointed," *CRDS Alumni Bulletin*, 34, no. 3 (March 1962): 2.
66. Ibid., 22.
67. *CRDS Alumni Bulletin* 26, no. 2 (December 1963): 2.

CRDS *Men* in the Field" column in the alumni edition of the *Bulletin* was replaced by the more gender-appropriate heading "News of Alumni in the Field."[68]

Tracking the enrollment of women across the decade indicates that initially the earlier pattern of one or two women graduated with a bachelor of divinity each year continued. After the merger with BMTS, however, the enrollment of women increased significantly, with seventeen women enrolled: six in the bachelor of divinity program, eleven in the master of arts, and eight "special students" in the entering class of 1962.[69] On May 23, 1966, the influx of BMTS women increased the graduation records, as twelve women graduated that year, but only two with a bachelor of divinity.[70] In 1969, the trend of women graduates with master's degrees doubling those with the bachelor of divinity was reversed, as five women were headed into pastorates or further study with the bachelor of divinity, and only one woman, Janice C. Skinner, pursued an educational ministry with her masters at the nearby Hillside Children's Center of Rochester.[71]

A growing awareness of both the CRDS heritage of educating women for ministry and the current need to celebrate women in that heritage was expressed in 1966, when the *Bulletin* ran a commemorative article titled "First Alumna of RTS Was BMTS Grad: The Story of Ruth von Krumreig Hill, Now a College Professor and Grandmother."[72] Ruth graduated from Shurtleff College and the BMTS with the intention of attending medical school. Upon her graduation from BMTS, however, she decided to teach school for several years to save up funds for medical school. In 1919 she attended a Student Volunteer Convention in Des Moines, where she met James Calvin Hill, a theological student from RTS. The sudden eruption of World War I and her need for additional studies delayed their marriage by another year. But their courtship continued. In 1920 Ruth joined her new husband as a student at RTS and as his copastor in the Baptist church in nearby Darien, New York. After serving with her husband in several pastorates, Ruth was ordained into the Baptist ministry after "having been rigorously examined by delegates from 47 Pittsburgh

---

68. *CRDS Alumni Bulletin* 36, no.1 (October 1963): 4, emphasis added.
69. *CRDS Alumni Bulletin* 25, no. 1 (October. 1962): 1.
70. *CRDS Catalogue*, 1967–1968, 77-78.
71. *CRDS/Bexley Hall Bulletin*, October 1969, 3.
72. "First Alumna of RTS Was BMTS Grad: The Story of Ruth von Krumreig Hill, Now a College Professor and Grandmother," *CRDS Bulletin* 38, no. 2 (March 1966): 3, 4.

Association Churches."[73] After several other pastorates, she relocated to the Chicago area, where she completed doctoral studies in theology at the University of Chicago. After working for many years as a social worker and then a college professor, Ruth Hill opened a counseling practice, making significant contributions to mental health work in both Florida and Minnesota. While the *Bulletin* article speaks clearly of the faith, dedication, and significant abilities of Hill, it says almost nothing about the challenges and significant barriers she overcame in pursuing her vocational path.

By December 1969 women not only had won a greater degree of acceptance at the Divinity School but also were insisting on acceptance and equal opportunity in church work beyond the school. A winter edition of the *Bulletin* reported: "CRDS/BH Woman Seeks Episcopal Priesthood." The article spoke about Betty Bone Schiess, who pursued the bachelor of divinity degree and ordination in the Episcopal Church. A strong advocate for racial equality, she participated in marches in the South, "including Selma, Alabama, and Jackson, Mississippi."[74] As she told a reporter, "I still believe in better opportunities for the Negro people, but I am even more committed to the cause of equality for women in the church."[75] After a long struggle, Schiess would be numbered among "the Philadelphia Eleven," who were the first group of women ordained as priests in the Episcopal Church, on July 29, 1974.[76] In 1994 she was inducted into the Women's Hall of Fame in Seneca Falls, New York, for her pioneering efforts in women's religious leadership.[77]

Writing in 1981, Jan Corbett noted, "Today more than 48% of the master of divinity candidates at the Divinity School are women—carrying on the tradition of . . . [BMTS]."[78] After interviewing female CRDS seminarians, Corbett got mixed reviews on the state of theological education for women. Susan Panck, a senior, reported hopefully: "At a recent seminarians' conference, we were amazed how far advanced men from our seminary were in using inclusive

73. Ibid., 3.
74. Lois Vosburgh, "CRDS/BH Woman Seeks Episcopal Priesthood," *CRDS/Bexley Hall Bulletin* 42, no. 2 (December 1969), 2.
75. Ibid.
76. Brenda Duncan, "Syracuses Betty Bone Schiess, One of the First American Femaile Epsicopal Priests, Dies," Syracuse.com, updated October 24, 2017, http://www.syracuse.com/news/index.ssf/2017/10/syracuses_betty_bone_schiess_one_of_first_female_american_episcopal_priests_dies.html.
77. "Betty Bone Schiess," National Women's Hall of Fame, https://www.womenofthehall.org/inductee/betty-bone-schiess/, accessed March 3, 2018.
78. Jan Corbett, "A School That Refused to Die," *The American Baptist* (March 1981).

language, and in accepting women as equals."[79] But Patricia Hunter, also a senior, pointed out, "We're still a minority because it's a male-dominated profession. . . . We're hit over the head with, 'Are you sure that you're really supposed to be here?'"[80] Corbett also noted, "Most [female] graduates of the present program plan to go into the pastoral ministry—a field which was rarely open to BMTS graduates. Times have changed; needs have changed; women have changed—and the BMTS has responded to these changes in its 100 years of history."[81] By September 1992 the Divinity School instituted a full-scale program women called Gender in Church and Society. Dr. Melanie May was chosen to develop and implement that program.[82]

Under President Johnson's leadership, the nation appeared to make small steps toward social change. But actual events and the stark realities faced by African Americans and other minorities belied that appearance. The leadership of Rev. Martin Luther King Jr. continued to be a galvanizing force for nonviolent civil rights activism. The March on Washington, which he orchestrated on August 28, 1963, and where he delivered his famous "I Have a Dream" speech, was instrumental in pressing Congress to pass the Civil Rights Act. This crucial legislation guaranteed all Americans equal opportunity in employment, housing, and other public facilities. But the bombing of the Sixteenth Street Baptist Church in Birmingham on September 15, 1963, which claimed the lives of four African American girls, seared the conscience of many Americans and caused determined protests and activism across the South.

The CRDS community was deeply aware and supportive of those struggling for civil rights all around them. In May 1960, for example, the faculty passed a series of resolutions supporting "the movement of non-violent resistance led by many students in the South against social injustices to which many of our fellow citizens are subjected."[83] At the same time, student resolve against racial oppression was evidenced in a feature article in the student newspaper by William Hugh Tucker, "A Look at Civil Rights."[84] A month later, Obadiah Wil-

79. Ibid.
80. Ibid.
81. Ibid.
82. Donna Jackel, "Dean Seeks to Close Religious Gender Gap with New Course," *Democrat and Chronicle*, September 22, 1992, 131. Interestingly, the University of Rochester had implemented its women's study major in 1984, and SUNY Brockport inaugurated the first full-scale women's program in 1975. Cf. Mary Ann Gallagher, "Women's Studies Gaining Ground," *Democrat and Chronicle*, August 24, 1975, 4B.
83. *Hilltop Views* 3, no. 6 (May 12, 1960): 2.
84. William Hugh Tucker, "A Look at Civil Rights," *Hilltop Views* 4, no. 1 (October 13, 1960): 6-7.

liamson interpreted the "American Dream," as it was experienced by black people in America: "There are two dreams," he wrote, "one for white and one for Negroes and other minority groups."[85] "The fight of the true liberal," Williams urged his readers, is one who refuses to accept this dualism as the status quo; rather she or he ought "to save and purify the dream from its already perverted character."[86]

The Divinity School had been racially inclusive since the turn of the twentieth century with the admission of African Americans since 1912, but they were admitted in limited numbers with an unwritten quota in place. Hence, there was a small but steady stream of influential black graduates, including most notably Mordecai Wyatt Johnson and Howard Thurman. While both men returned to campus for special lectures and acclaim, neither was made a permanent fixture of the Divinity School.[87] Paging through issue after issue of the *CRDS Bulletin*, one could not escape the impression that while it is packed with famous faces, such as Tillich and Bultmann, they were invariably white male faces. The same public face of the Divinity School was also reflected in the composition of its board of trustees, teaching faculty, and academic curriculum.

In the mid-1960s, student advocacy for civil rights and economic opportunity for minority people erupted forcefully in Rochester. On April 16, 1964, sixteen CRDS students, one of whom was African American, were arrested and charged with disorderly conduct for disrupting traffic and causing a public disturbance. The students were protesting housing discrimination in Rochester by pointing to a specific violation that had allegedly occurred at the Valley Court Apartments. On the Monday after Easter, Colgate Rochester students carried signs reading "Rochester—intelligent, virtuous and Silent" and "Rochester City of Wealth and Discrimination," while seven of the CRCDS men chained themselves together across Genesee Street as the others circled them with signs. The Rochester *Democrat and Chronicle* described this as "the first arrest of civil rights demonstrators in Rochester."[88] The students made a brief statement before they were hauled away to jail: "We are part of a continuous non-violent movement which has as its objective the elimination of all discriminatory structures in

---

85. Obadiah Williamson, "The American Dream?" *Hilltop Views* 4, no. 2 (November 29, 1960): 16.
86. Ibid.
87. "We Point with Pride," *CRDS Alumni Bulletin* 31, no. 7 (1958): 4.
88. Bill Vogler, "16 Arrested In Rights Protest," *Democrat and Chronicle*, April 16, 1964.

Rochester."[89] The students were charged with disorderly conduct, bail was set at $100 each, and since they gave 1100 Goodman Avenue as their residence, their "one phone call" came to CRDS and President Bartlett. They were paroled into his custody.[90]

By the end of the 1964–1965 academic year, in his "President's Report to the Board of Trustees," Bartlett pointed out how the presence of "nineteen Negro students" gave the school "a special sense of vocation."[91] This same report indicated that black student advocacy brought the question of race to the forefront: "Our Negro students have kept us aware of the urgency of the civil rights movement." "We have every evidence that the number of Negro students will continue next year at approximately the same level. We gladly accept our opportunity in this urgent contemporary area of church life."[92]

With the financial support of a Lilly grant, CRDS began a study on "Negroes in Theological Education," which was inaugurated by a special conference on the previous September 27. The two-day institute was attended by more than sixty students, welcomed keynote speakers from beyond campus, and offered many working groups. The two-day institute on the particular roles played by African Americans in theological education brought many influential guest lecturers to campus Among these notable guests was Rev. Wyatt Tee Walker of the Southern Christian Leadership Conference, who presented an address titled "The Changing Role of the Negro Church and Pastor."[93]

A few months later, in the long hot summer of 1964, urban violence erupted in Rochester. In his guest article "Anatomy of a Riot: Why Did It Happen? What Can We Do about It?" Arthur L. Whitaker, the African American pastor of Mt. Olivet Baptist Church, stated that "the racial disorder, violence, and lawlessness, which exploded in the city of Rochester, July 24–26, 1964, came as a 'rushing mighty wind,' with hurricane force. . . . The toll exacted for these three days of havoc and devastation included five deaths, the arrest of nearly 1,000 persons of both races, and property damage estimated at more than $1 million."[94] The racial tension behind the dreadful events was

---

89. Ibid.
90. Ibid.
91. Gene Bartlett, unpublished "President's Report to the Board of Trustees," May 14, 1965, 5.
92. Ibid.
93. George Hall, "Institute on the Negro and Theological Education," *CRDS Bulletin* 37, no. 1 (October 1964): 2.
94. Arthur L. Whitaker, "Anatomy of a Riot: Why Did It Happen? . . . What Can We Do about It?" *Democrat and Chronicle*, February 28, 1965, 3M.

the result of longstanding grievances within the African American community.[95] That African American frustration and disaffection with empty promises and social intransigence, which were eloquently voiced in King's *Why We Can't Wait*, were illustrated by the fact that the Black Power movement was born from the Student Nonviolent Coordinating Committee in June 1966.[96]

The Black Power movement made its voice heard in Rochester as an African American-based group, identified by the acronym FIGHT.[97] The organization sought equal employment opportunities from the city's largest industry, Eastman Kodak.[98] Militancy and advocacy for black rights, along with the potential for violent response to white oppression, was also seen in the emergence growing popularity of Afrocentric groups like the Nation of Islam. The latter group objected to the enslaving aspects of "white religion" and pursued a more authentic and separate black identity in Islam. The well-documented conversion of Malcolm Little (1925–1965) from Christianity to black pride, black nationalism, and pan-Africanism was well chronicled in *The Autobiography of Malcom X*, which tells of his becoming a minister in the Nation of Islam.[99] Malcolm's story was indeed the story of many African American people who struggled for pride, identity, and meaning in the face of overwhelming oppression. Just five days before he was murdered, Malcolm addressed "The Commission on the Negro and Theological Education—a student and faculty group at Colgate Rochester Divinity School."[100] While he was in Rochester, Malcolm X's home in New York City was bombed, which, in that sense, may have prolonged his life.[101]

The next academic year, 1966–1967, a new experimental course on The Negro, the Negro Church, and American Culture was added to the fall curriculum at CRDS. The course was taught in a seminar fashion, chaired by Professor Prentiss Pemberton, who was assisted by seven visiting black consultants. Among these guest lecturers were Dr. Nathan Wright, Dr. Gayraud Wilmore, Rev. Jessie Jackson, Dr.

95. Ibid.
96. Simon Hall, "The NAACP, Black Power, and the African American Freedom Struggle, 1966-1969," *Historian* 69, no. 1 (Spring 2007): 49.
97. The acronym FIGHT stands for Freedom, Integration, God, Honor, Today.
98. Jules Loh, "Rochester's Agony," *Democrat and Chronicle*, April 23, 1967, 4M.
99. Malcolm X and Alex Haley, *The Autobiography of Malcolm X* (New York: Grove Press, 1965).
100. William Hamilton reputedly recorded the speech and subsequently made a typescript, but unfortunately that speech is not extant.
101. Manning Marble, *Malcolm X: A Life of Reinvention* (New York: Viking Press, 2011), 420. Cf. Urla Hill, "Malcolm X: Black Leader's Ties to Area Are Recalled," *Democrat and Chronicle*, February 19, 1962, 67, 69.

Shelby Brooks, Dr. Gardner Taylor, and David Anderson. Twenty-six students participated in the new course, nine of whom were black.[102]

The murders of Martin Luther King Jr. and Robert F. Kennedy in early 1968 deeply shocked and shook the nation once again. They sent both the civil rights movement and the antiwar movement to new levels of outrage and desperation. The assassination of King acutely affected the hopes and fears of African Americans. The CRDS campus community was also deeply shaken and saddened, no one more so than the black students, several of whom knew King personally. Late into the night of King's murder, fourteen African American CRDS students came together to plan a common course of action. That meeting resulted in an early-morning phone call to President Bartlett asking permission to lead a special memorial service in the Divinity School chapel. Rev. Robert Eads recalled, "These men who had known Dr. King personally (one had been baptized by him and ordained by him . . . launched a nationwide effort to raise $800,000 to establish an endowed professorship and a scholarship program."[103] In six short weeks the students launched a nationwide campaign that enlisted the entire CRDS community, the community of Rochester, and major elements of the black church in America.

The June 1968 issue of the *CRDS Bulletin* introduced Rev. John David Cato "as the first black professor to be appointed to the Colgate Rochester Divinity School faculty. His specific professional role is that of Assistant Professor of Urban Studies and Chairman of the Black Church Ministry [program]."[104] "This appointment," Professor John Cato pointed out, "is a move in the direction of fulfilling our plan for scholarly, in depth instruction in Black Church studies."[105] Also in the fall of 1968, Gardner C. Taylor, African American pastor of the twelve-thousand-member Concord Church of Christ in Brooklyn, New York, and trustee of CRDS, was one of the three men appointed as visiting lecturers for the 1968–1969 academic year.[106]

Later, in November 1968, a special dinner was held to commemorate the life and work of Martin Luther King Jr. through the fund established in his honor. Among the nationally known African American dignitaries present were Dr. and Mrs. Martin Luther King

---

102. Ibid.

103. Robert H. Eads, director of the Department of Church and Ministry, CRDS, "Divinity Student's Drive Lauded," *Democrat and Chronicle*, May 25, 1968, 119.

104. "John Cato Appointed to Faculty," *CRDS Bulletin* 40, no. 4 (June 1968): 1, 3.

105. Ibid., 3.

106. "Visiting Lecturers Named," *CRDS/Bexley Hall Bulletin* 41, no. 1 (October 1968): 1.

Sr., president of the SCLC, Dr. Ralph David Abernathy, and internationally known singer Mahalia Jackson. Looking forward to the powerful impact of the scholarship fund and endowed chair to be established by the campaign, Abernathy declared, "They may have killed the dreamer, but I'll be dogged if they can kill the dream."[107]

On December 10, 1968, Bartlett received a letter from the CRDS Black Student Caucus. After cordially thanking the executive council and the board of trustees "for both the Bronze Plaque and the individual certificates of appreciation commemorating our role in the establishment of the Dr. Martin Luther King, Jr., Scholarship/Professorship Chair," the letter requested "that Colgate Rochester/Bexley Hall continue to become more aware of 'Black America's' need to be represented in the 'decision-making process.' Commensurate to these ends, we ask that the following requests be implemented":

1) 11 Black Men be appointed to the Colgate Rochester/Bexley Hall Board of Trustees; recommendations being suggested by the Black Caucus who will send representatives to insure Black participation. Effective March 1, 1969.
2) 3 Black Men be appointed to the Executive Council. Effective March 1, 1969.
3) 1 Black Man be appointed to each of the following Administrative Posts—Placement Office and Teaching Church. Effective September 10, 1969.
4) A total of 4 Black Professors be appointed to the five open faculty positions. Effective March 1, 1969.[108]

The letter closed on an ominous note: "Mr. President, in no uncertain terms, if these requests go unheeded, we the Black Caucus will use all means necessary to implement our demands."[109]

Bartlett replied to the Black Caucus letter on January 31, 1969:

I recognize our failure to keep you fully informed of the actions taken since that date and I would like to rectify the situation to some extent by including here a report of what has been done and of what is planned. If you find sufficient movement on our part to warrant such a meeting, I hope we can use the occasion for a mutual exploration of problems in an effort to work through an agreeable solution to them.[110]

After detailing the ways the Divinity School attempted to meet the student demands, Bartlett concluded on a pastoral note: "We are aware that these must be days of special strain for all of you. We assure you of our respect and our love in Christ. Let us pray for one

107. N/A, "Dr. Abernathy Underscores Importance of King Fund," Colgate Rochester Divinity School Bexley Hall Bulletin, vol. XLI, no. 2 (December 1968): 1-2.
108. "To President Gene Bartlett," from the Black Caucus, December 10, 1968, President Gene Bartlett Letter File, CRCDS archives "Black Caucus News Letter."
109. Ibid.
110. Ibid.

another that we may all have grace to see through the exciting possibilities which God has offered us in this community."[111]

As the campus community became more fully aware of the requests of the Black Student Caucus, a student committee drafted a letter urging the administration to "immediately respond; *not* by telling the Blacks why their demands are unreasonable and cannot be met, but by outlining *how and when* their demands will be met." It was signed by forty-four students.[112] That same day, Bartlett issued an "Administrative Newsletter," because the "students at last week's Conference on Curriculum requested a report in writing that would itemize the actions to date concerning a Black Presence on this campus."[113]

On February 27, 1969, a mimeographed "IMPORTANT NOTICE" was distributed across campus, announcing a community meeting scheduled for the next day in the campus auditorium. Issued over Bartlett's name, the notice stated, "At this time a full report will be given on the five demands submitted by the Black Caucus on December 12. Questions will be in order, and every attempt will be made to communicate facts. We urge your presence."[114] At the meeting, Bartlett said,

> I should like to make as clear as a commitment as I can: the administration, faculty and the trustees all are very much in accord with the intent and purpose of these demands. . . . We would also acknowledge that we are victims of a history which built structures which we are anxious now to replace. Just as fast as it is possible to do so we intend to replace those structures with new ones which more consistently express the mission we feel for this school.[115]

At another campus-wide meeting on February 28, Bartlett delineated what steps had been taken and tacitly admitted that the full slate of student demands could not be met by March 1. Shortly after that meeting, signs began appearing on chalkboards around campus: "No school till demands are met."[116] On March 2, 1969, the doors to

111. Gene Bartlett, "To the Black Caucus," January 31, 1969, President Gene Bartlett Letter File, CRCDS archives.

112. This letter does not seem to be extant in its original form. It is described and documented, however, in a chronology developed by Kenneth V. Dodgson in the spring of 2006, based on his access to several sets of files at that time. I am grateful for his work, which has preserved records that might otherwise be lost.

113. Gene Bartlett, "Administrative Newsletter," February 6, 1969, President Gene Bartlett Letter File, CRCDS archives.

114. Gene Bartlett, "IMPORTANT NOTICE," February 27, 1969, an unpublished document located in the Gene Bartlett papers in the archives of CRCDS.

115. Gene Bartlett, "Statement for Community Meeting, 1-2," President Gene Bartlett Letter File, CRCDS archives.

116. John McLoughlin, "Black Students Seize Seminary," *Democrat and Chronicle*, March 3, 1969, 1.

Strong Hall were chained shut, and the lockout began.[117] A handwritten sign on a chalkboard placed near the door said, "We will speak only to the executive committee [of the board of trustees]. School closed until our demands are met."[118]

The front page of the March 3 edition of the Rochester *Democrat and Chronicle* blared the headline "Black Students Seize Seminary." The *Times Union* reported, "The Colgate Rochester Sit-In" on its front page as well, and "Seminary's President Locked Out" was the bold headline in the local news section.[119] In both articles, Bartlett stressed the Divinity School's commitment to the concerns about black inclusion and participation epitomized in the students' demands, as well as his respect for the black student demonstrators and hope for a good resolution: "We feel we are dealing with men who are straightforward. They are our colleagues and they are men for whom we have great respect. We hope that this can be resolved through deliberation."[120] Later that same day, the Associated Press (AP) picked up the report filed by the *Democrat and Chronicle*. This led to the saga of the CRDS lockout appearing in AP newspapers all across the nation.

Mrs. Bartlett's handwritten notes after a series of meetings from March 4 to 7 indicate that an African American educator, John Cato, came to campus as a prospective faculty member and met with the faculty. The local trustees met in order to draft a reply to the recent demands, and at the same time Gardner Taylor had arrived from New York City. Bartlett hoped that Taylor would meet with the Black Caucus, but that did not transpire, since he suddenly had to return to New York. At about this time several area ministers also became involved in the stand-off. "Would they bring more confrontation or helpful mediation?" mused Mrs. Jean Bartlett's notes.[121]

Taylor was quoted as saying, "Whatever it takes, it must be done. Our being a race-oriented society, I believe crucial for identification and participation of black students to see their own color in positions

117. The CRDS students directly involved in the lockout were Joseph Davis, Thomas Diamond, David Garcia, James Garmon, James Goins, Raleigh Hairston, Pahle Hale, Melvin Hoover, James Hunter, Thomas Jordon, William "Charles" Larkin, Lorenzo Robinson, Bobby Saucer, James Swindell, Henry Thomas, Charles Walker, and John Walker. From "Honoring the Protesters of the 1969 Lock-Out," program from the 50th Anniversary of the Black Student Caucus: The Golden Gala, Colgate Rochester Crozer Divinity School, April 6, 2018.
118. "Colgate Rochester Sit-in," *Times Union*, March 3, 1969, B-1.
119. *Times Union*, March 3, 1969.
120. Ibid.
121. Jean Bartlett, "Notes Kept by JKB during the lockout," handwritten copy, entry for March 7, 1969, President Gene Bartlett Letter File, CRCDS archives.

of authority and esteem."[122] Taylor said he believed in the integrity of the black student protests: "I know them. I know their ideas. I think they have made reasonable requests."[123] After an unsuccessful attempt was made to contact Taylor, Dean George Hall offered a report on the recent meeting between Bexley Hall and the Black Caucus regarding the appointment of trustees. Mrs. Bartlett described the mood that followed these events as "Deep gloom."[124]

On March 9, Ralph David Abernathy arrived in front of Strong Hall and declared that the black seminarians occupying the building "have my full backing and cooperation."[125] "It takes a black to understand the background of the black church and the types of experiences they will face as they go out to perform their ministry," he stated.[126] "A lily-white board can't plan for these things, and we can't settle for tokenism anymore."[127]

The twelfth day of the lockout seemed uneventful, but negotiations and conversations continued behind the scenes. Both the faculty and student senate met later that same afternoon, and at a student meeting, Jean Bartlett reported some of the students "were upset that Gene [President Bartlett] didn't show more anxiety about getting back to class."[128] The same day, as hiring of several black faculty members was discussed behind the scenes, the *Times Union* ran a short article indicating that student opinion gradually shifted toward a desire to reopen the school.[129]

Perhaps in view of the gradually shifting student opinion against the lockout, and in view of the fact that most of their central demands were being met, the Black Caucus issued an undated statement: "We the members of the Black Caucus have decided to reopen Colgate Rochester/Bexley Hall Divinity School on Thursday [March 20] at 12:00 noon." "We felt we could be here forever and that the administration was not going to move. We didn't want to completely destroy the educational process. But," Charles Walker added, "we won't be satisfied until we rectify the business of arbitrary approval."[130]

122. Paul Haney, "Trustee Supports Protesters," *Times Union*, March 7, 1969.
123. Ibid.
124. Jean Bartlett, "Notes Kept by JKB during the lockout," handwritten copy, entry for March 9, 1969, President Gene Bartlett Letter, File, CRCDS archives.
125. Dan Lovely, "On Black Demands: 'Full Backing': Rev. Abernathy," *Democrat and Chronicle*, March 10, 1969, 12.
126. Ibid.
127. Ibid., 11.
128. Jean Bartlett, "Notes Kept by JKB during the lockout," handwritten copy, entry for "Thursday, March 13, 1969," President Gene Bartlett Letter File, CRCDS archives, 12.
129. "Students Want Classes to Resume," *Times Union*, March 14, 1969.
130. Dan Lovely, "Seminarians to End Sit-In," *Democrat and Chronicle*, Wednesday, March 19, 1969, 11.

Bartlett's "From the President" column in the *Bulletin* for March 1969 reported, "The ivory tower is leaning—or [is] perhaps occupied by a group of students with nonnegotiable demands. It affects almost all areas of the academic community, and the theological school is no exception. The thrust of the black students against structures which were born in a time of racial inequity is the most evident and most powerful protest. But the unrest touches almost all students and all the common life."[131] Bartlett continued, "Is there any basic theme which runs through it all? Yes, it seems to me there is. This generation of students is rebelling against decision-making which, while affecting their lives in major ways, leaves them out of the process."[132] Black Caucus student Joseph Davis of Buffalo offered an equally credible explanation: "What you end up with . . . [is] a liberal school with students putting into action what the school had taught them."[133]

"Where Are the Winners at the Divinity School?" was the title of an editorial in the *Democrat and Chronicle* on the day the lockout ended. As if answering that rhetorical question, Bartlett observed, "At this point in time, there are no winners in this sit-in, only losers."[134] But he remained hopeful and optimistic about the Divinity School's future:

> Confrontation can be redeemed. In these days we are working intensely to see that new dimensions come from the pain of our encounter. Today, I write in hope. . . . We have hope that the word of Ephesians will be fulfilled: "For he is our peace, who has made us both one, and has broken down the dividing wall of hostility." We believe passionately in that word. Better yet, we believe it is coming to pass.[135]

After four decades, Jean Bartlett recalled that her husband "thought he had good personal relations with the black students and he really cared about them and their plea for justice. I think the hurt that came was that we learned how little we had understood the depth of the anger and the alienation and their hurt. . . . We felt we had failed the black students in some ways."[136]

On November 10, 1969, Dr. Henry Heywood Mitchell was installed in the Martin Luther King, Jr. Memorial Professorship of Black Church Studies in an augural convocation celebrating and

131. Gene Bartlett, "From the President," *CRDS/Bexley Hall Bulletin* 41, no. 3 (March 1969): 2.
132. Ibid.
133. James Goodman, "17 Days of Confrontation," *Democrat and Chronicle*, March 4, 1984, 28.
134. "Where Are the Winners at Divinity School?" *Democrat and Chronicle*, March 19, 1969, 8.
135. Gene Bartlett, "From the President's Desk," *CRDS/Bexley Hall Bulletin* 41, no. 4 (June 1969): 2.
136. Barbara Zeller, "Race and Religion in Rochester, 1964 to 1969," unpublished MA thesis, Colgate Rochester Crozer Divinity School, December 2010, 71.

officially beginning the Black Church Studies program at CRCDS. The October 1969 edition of the *Bulletin* carried a feature article on the "Black Faculty" of the Divinity School, which highlighted the careers of Henry H. Mitchell, John David Cato, Frederick D. Jefferson, Joseph Pelham, and Gardner Taylor.[137]

The full impact of the lockout is difficult to gauge even at the analytical distance of these fifty years. If the angry letters filed by President Bartlett are anywhere close to being a representative sample, there was a significant and sustained negative outcry from reputed friends and alumni of CRCDS. One letter summarizes the sentiments of many: "Colgate Rochester died last year when it allowed itself to be taken over by a small irresponsible minority. If students and staff won't respect local laws how can they respect more demanding spiritual laws? No more of my hard earned money will go into the hands of soft spineless administrators."[138] John Walker, who was one of the student leaders of the lockout, said, "It is the opinion of most of the surviving Black Student Caucus that Dr. Bartlett's departure from the institution in 1969 was a forced exit due to his position that he took in support of Black Caucus demands."[139] Although Bartlett's personal correspondence betrays no hint of him being forced out, Jean Bartlett characterized the situation in this way: "His leaving the school was part of the price of the lock-out. He never was fired, but there were a lot of people giving their judgments that it would be better for the school if he left."[140]

It is also difficult to assess fully how much the angry withholding of funds and support might have hurt the Divinity School's financial strength; it clearly had a negative effect, as did other factors. Baptist historian William Brackney believes that the school was weakened by the combined effect of the death of God controversy and the lockout, both of which occurred at roughly the same time as the "unsuccessful mergers that crippled the school's financial standing by combining four facilities on one roster in the Rochester Theological Center."[141] Whatever the financial impact of these developments, the ongoing discussions about the merger of CRCDS with the socially

---

137. "Black Faculty," *CRDS/Bexley Hall Bulletin* 42, no. 1 (October 1969): 3.
138. Zeller, "Race and Religion in Rochester," 73.
139. Ibid.
140. Ibid., 74.
141. William H. Brackney, *Congregation and Campus: North American Baptists in Higher Education* (Macon, GA: Mercer University Press, 2008), 266–67.

conservative Roman Catholic St. Bernard's Institute were stalled because of the negative publicity generated by the lockout.[142]

The 1960s were tumultuous times, and in many ways events at CRCDS mirrored and were dramatically shaped by the convulsions of the larger society surrounding it. These developments both challenged and defined the identity of CRCDS. In a sense, the very public theological controversy that swirled around the death of God theology in the mid-1960s was a distant echo of the similar though less public transition that occurred at the beginning of the twentieth century when George Cross replaced Augustus Strong as the theological voice of the institution. In each instance, dramatic theological shifts were under way at the Divinity School. In each case, the school had taken a decided step toward the liberal side of the evangelical-liberal synthesis.

The challenges of this theological shift were compounded by the demands for greater inclusion and fuller participation by women and African Americans both in decision making and in curriculum. In each case, marginalized participants in the CRCDS vision asked the Divinity School to live up to its own prophetic message of equality and inclusion. As a result of these painful confrontations, a new, nationally known black church studies program was established and the foundation for a new Women and Gender Studies program was laid. These challenging events occurred at the same time the Divinity School was also searching for the balance point between its historical Baptist roots and new ecumenical mission in the face of the real-life challenges of mergers and new affiliations. It is to this latter situation we turn our attention in the next chapter as the Divinity School pursued new alliances and pioneered the concept of ecumenical theological education.

---

142. Robert F. McNamara, "Ecumenism and the Rochester Center for Theological Studies," *Rochester History* 52, no. 2 (Fall 1990): 18–19.

15

Ecumenical Patterns and Partners

At the outset of this study, we saw that the foundations of Colgate Rochester Crozer Divinity School were laid by thirteen men with $13 in 1817. They were thirteen Baptist men who worked and sacrificed mightily so that their Baptist tradition in particular, and the larger Christian church in general, would flourish under the leadership of a ministry that was well-educated and deeply devout. Over time, Christians of other faith traditions were gradually welcomed into that same mission. At the outset, however, the Divinity School saw itself as a Baptist enterprise, operated by and for Baptists.

Just as women and African Americans were welcomed into its community, although in small numbers beginning in the early twentieth century, while Baptists predominated by three to one or four to one, inclusion and participation in the student body was opened to Christians of all denominational backgrounds in the mid-1940s through the 1950s. The *Catalogues* and *Bulletins* not only lauded CRDS's ecumenical hospitality but also offered the demographics to prove it. During those years the school sought to both maintain its historic distinctiveness and embrace the inclusive spirit of an increasingly ecumenical age.

The language of the "The School and Its Purpose" statement, found in the thirty-first CRDS catalogue, demonstrated this attempt to balance the Divinity School's Baptist heritage with its growing ecumenical character. As if to reassure its Baptist constituency, the catalogue reported, "The school has its roots in the Baptist denomination . . . this responsibility must be taken more seriously than ever."[1] Over time, the historic emphasis of the Divinity School and its mission shifted from a primary concern about the particular role and contribution of Baptists and their heritage to a concerted embrace of the larger church as an ecumenical whole. Whereas in the earlier days all of the faculty and administrative leaders of both RTS and CDS were Baptists, by the middle of the twentieth century, CRDS claimed the freedom to draw upon the whole church for its leaders, faculty, and students. Hence, the catalogue reported: "All students have equal access to the resources of the Divinity School,"[2] and when the 1961 catalogue discussed "Its Purpose," ecumenism was given priority over denominational identity.[3]

Another indication of the growing ecumenical spirit at CRDS was signaled by the establishment of the Edwin T. Dahlberg Ecumenical Lectureship, through a $10,000 gift made by the Metropolitan Church Federation of St. Louis.[4] Dr. Dahlberg was pastor of Delmar Baptist Church of St. Louis and a longtime trustee of Colgate Rochester Divinity School. The lectureship established in his honor was intended to perpetuate Dahlberg's "ecumenical concerns and his dedication to peace, brotherhood, and the underprivileged people of the world."[5] Among the notable ecumenical leaders who presented the Dahlberg Lectures were Helmut Thielicke of the University of Hamburg, James McCord of Princeton Theological Seminary, and James Nichols, who presented a series of timely lectures on "Ecumenicity Since Vatican II."[6]

CRCDS Baptist church historian Winthrop Hudson epitomized the institutional attempt to retain a Baptist identity in the growing ecumenism of the age.[7] Others participated in this campaign for Baptist identity and historical roots, including Gene Bartlett, who published *These Are the Baptists*, as a pamphlet in 1972 and then as

---

1. *CRDS Bulletin* 33, no. 3, 1c, catalogue ed. (January 1961): 12.
2. Ibid.
3. Ibid., 12.
4. Gene Bartlett, "President's Report to the CRDS Board of Trustees," May 22, 1961, 6.
5. *CRDS Bulletin*, 36, no. 3, Thirty-Fourth Catalogue (January 1964): 66.
6. "Ecumenicity Since Vatican II Is Theme of Dahlberg Lectures," *CRDS Bulletin* 38, no. 2 (December 1965): 1.
7. Winthrop Hudson, *Baptist Concepts of the Church* (Valley Forge, PA: Judson Press, 1959); Hudson with Norman Maring, *A Baptist Manual of Polity and Practice* (Valley Forge, PA: Judson Press, 1963); Hudson, *Baptist Convictions* (Valley Forge, PA: Judson Press, 1963); *Baptists in Transition* (Valley Forge, PA: Judson Press, 1979); Hudson, "Interrelationships of Baptists in Canada and the United States," *Foundations* 23, no. 1 (January–March 1980): 22–41. During this same period, however, Hudson also demonstrated an ecumenical flair as he wrote *Understanding Roman Catholicism: A Guide to Papal Teaching for Protestants*, became an internationally known expert on English Puritanism, and penned the standard text on religion in America. See Norman H. Maring, "Winthrop S. Hudson: Church Historian," *Foundations* 23, no. 2 (April–June 1980): 132–42. Cf. Winthrop Hudson, *Understanding Roman Catholicism* (Philadelphia: Westminster Press, 1959), and John Corrigan and Winthrop Hudson, *Religion in America* (New York: Charles Scribner's Sons, 1961).

a chapter in the influential *Our Faiths* by Martin E. Marty.[8] But as the strongest current of American churchmanship was flowing away from denominational particularism and toward churchwide ecumenism, Colgate Rochester was swept along with it.

The Divinity School bathed in a worldwide ecumenical spotlight from August 17 to September 3, 1963, when the executive committee of the World Council of Churches met on its campus for ten days. From more than ninety nations came 201 religious leaders, representing more than 400 million Christians worldwide.[9] President Bartlett's welcoming remarks set the tone for the meetings: "Although we have retired to this hilltop we are very much aware the world is in ferment."[10] Later in the spring of 1964, in his annual report, Bartlett wrote: "We are confident that at no time in the history of the Divinity School have we had a more significant gathering of Christian world leadership on our campus. As a result of this meeting we have shared in one of the most significant moments of our time, we have won new friends around the world, and strengthened many ties within our own city."[11]

In the President's Report of 1965, Bartlett stressed the importance of accentuating the ecumenical nature of CRDS through forming new partnerships while maintaining its Baptist connection: "We believe we can cultivate relations with several denominations [while] at the same time reaffirming our continued affiliation with American Baptists."[12] Student enrollment for 1965 reflected this dual commitment to Baptist denominational identity and ecumenism, as the student body was comprised of 64 percent Baptists and 36 percent others.[13] These same statistics, however, also represented a significant change from twenty years earlier when Baptist students outstripped all denominations by more than three to one.

Following up on the growing ecumenical spirit and responding to recent American Association of Theological Schools (AATS) recommendations, on June 2, 1965, the administration circulated a draft document titled "Possible Forms of Theological Union." By October

---

8. Gene Bartlett, *These Are the Baptists* (Royal Oak, MI: Cathedral Press, 1972), and "These Are the Baptists," in Martin E. Marty, ed., *Our Faiths* (Royal Oak, MI: Cathedral Press, 1976).
9. "World Church Council Target: Woes of a World in Ferment," Rochester *Democrat and Chronicle*, August 28, 1963, 10; Desmond Stone, "On a Peaceful, Green Hilltop," *Times-Union*, August 27, 1963, B1. Cf. John E. Skoglund, "The World Council of Churches Central Committee in Colgate Rochester Divinity School," *CRDS Bulletin* 36, no. 1 (August 1963): 3–4.
10. Stone, "On a Peaceful, Green Hilltop," 1.
11. Gene Bartlett, "President's Report to the Annual Meeting of the Board of Trustees," May 18, 1964, 1.
12. Gene Bartlett, "Presidents Report to the Annual Meeting of the Board of Trustees," May 14, 1965, 14.
13. Ibid., 3.

25, 1965, the CRDS curriculum committee reviewed a "Preliminary Proposal for Oberlin Graduate School of Theology and Colgate Rochester Divinity School."[14] The heading of the document even suggested a name for the new Rochester consortium: The Center for Theological Study.[15] Among the potential strengths of this affiliation was "a major emphasis upon preparation of able Negro students for emerging leadership. Both Oberlin and Colgate Rochester have had significant involvement in this area."[16]

When "The Center for Theological Study—A Preliminary Proposal for Oberlin Graduate School of Theology and Colgate Rochester Divinity School" was presented to the faculty, controversy ensued. Handwritten notes on the margins of the official minutes, probably by Winthrop Hudson, reported discussion that made a strong case against a union of the Divinity School with the Oberlin Graduate School of Theology based in part on the different educational focus of the respective institutions, with one preparing pastors, while the other focused on graduate scholars, and denominational entanglements which might hinder CRDS.[17] Meanwhile, in their November meeting of 1966, the CRDS board approved opening conversations about affiliating with Bexley Hall, an Episcopalian seminary located on the campus of Kenyon College in Gambier, Ohio.

The Bexley Hall story begins in 1817, the same year the Madison Literary and Theological Institute was born in Hamilton, New York. The missionary Episcopalian priest and eventually bishop, Philander Chase (1775–1852), was the pioneer founder of Bexley Hall. He arrived in Ohio in 1817 with a compelling vision for evangelism and education in the West. After being ordained into the diaconate by the bishop of New York in 1798, Chase was sent to do missionary work throughout central and western New York, organizing parishes from Albany to Avon.[18] Within a year he was ordained, and he served pastorates in Poughkeepsie and New Orleans prior to arriving in Ohio in March 1817. He went to Ohio "without being called, sent, or subsidized by any missionary society or ecclesiastical authority."[19] On the edge of the American frontier, Ohio was undergoing rapid settlement.

---

14. "School," dated hypothetically because it was found in the folder of notes marked "Oct. 25, 1965." President Gene Bartlett Letter File, CRCDS archives, 1.
15. Ibid.
16. Ibid., 11.
17. Ibid., 3. I think the author of these notes was Winthrop Hudson, since they were in the file of the secretary of the Administrative Curriculum Committee. Committee minutes, October 1965, CRCDS archives.
18. Richard M. Spielmann, *Bexley Hall: 150 Years: A Brief History* (Rochester, NY: CRCDS/Bexley Hall, 1974), 7.
19. Ibid.

Observing this burgeoning unchurched community, Chase described himself as "feeling for their welfare" and "duty bound to do something in this humble sphere for the common good, in trying to remedy and prevent these dreadful evils, ignorance and irreligion."[20]

It soon became clear that "to institute a Seminary of learning . . . was wanted [i.e., needed]," and the newly elected and consecrated (February 11, 1819) Bishop Chase established a school in Worthington, Ohio, near Columbus. "This school of the Prophets was soon gathered," Chase's granddaughter, Laura Chase Smith, remarked, but "they did not look much like prophets or behave much like the statesmen or clergymen some of them would afterwards become."[21] Bishop Chase spent several months of 1823 in England, raising funds for the school, and he returned with "very liberal donations for the cause,"[22] a reputed $30,000.[23] By July 1825 the school relocated to Gambier, Ohio, and was incorporated as a "Theological Seminary of the Protestant Episcopal Church in the Diocese of Ohio."[24] In 1826 "the college lands, 4,000 acres, on both sides of the Kokosing [River], five miles below Mt. Vernon, were purchased from Wm. Hogg, Esq. of Brownsville, Pa., who made a generous donation . . . and . . . the site of Kenyon College was settled forever."[25] In December 1827, Chase applied for and was granted a "grant or donation of public lands, for the support and endowment of the said College."[26]

The theological seminary, formally established in 1824, "existed largely as an undergraduate college for the next half dozen years or so." The first seminary graduate, Nathaniel Stem, emerged in 1828 and was ordained to the ministry and served in Ohio for several years. Five future clergymen graduated from the school and were ordained to ministry while Chase was bishop of Ohio.[27] At the diocesan convention of September 1831, Chase resigned under pressure from Kenyon faculty and others due to his autocratic control over the diocese as well as the seminary and college. When asked to relinquish some of his control, Chase responded by resigning all of them.

---

20. Philander Chase, *A Plea for the West* (Boston: Samuel H. Parker, 1827), 3.
21. Laura Chase Smith, *The Life of Philander Chase: First Bishop of Ohio and Illinois, Founder of Kenyon and Jubilee Colleges* (New York: E. P. Dutton & Co., 1903), 197-98.
22. A. Banning Norton, *A History of Knox County, Ohio from 1799 to 1862 Inclusive* (Columbus: Richard Nevins, 1862), 418.
23. Spielmann, *Bexley Hall*, 10.
24. Norton, *History of Knox County, Ohio*, 419.
25. Ibid., 320.
26. Edward King, "Resolution of the Ohio Legislature," in Philander Chase, *The Star in the West, Or Kenyon College in the Year of Our Lord 1828* (Columbus: n.p., 1828), Internet archive, The Hathitrust, https://babel.hathitrust.org/cgi/pt?id=hvd.hn58xt&view=1up&seq=11, accessed September 12, 2019.
27. Spielmann, *Bexley Hall*, 14–15.

He soon moved to Michigan and then on to Illinois, where he was elected as the first Episcopal bishop and established another college.[28]

Following the abrupt departure of Chase, the Ohio Convention elected Rev. Charles P. McIlvaine (1790–1873), rector of St. Ann's Episcopal Church in Brooklyn, as both bishop of Ohio and president of the seminary. McIlvaine, who was educated at Princeton Seminary, brought with him a background in theological education that Chase lacked.[29] The unenviable tasks of gathering a faculty, developing a curriculum, and constructing the physical plant of the school fell to McIlvaine, but soon enough a teaching faculty and theological curriculum were in place.

The funds raised by Chase were quickly spent, and McIlvaine spent eight months in England raising funds for the seminary and gathering academic books for its library. He returned with $12,600, which was largely a gift from Lord Bexley, and nineteen hundred books; but indebtedness and current expenses cut so deeply into that major gift that Bexley Hall was not finished until 1844.[30]

The seminary enrollments significantly reflected the school's financial instability, ranging from four students in 1847 to ten in 1854. But even at this pace Bexley Hall was making its influence felt, and by 1850, a full one-third of the eighty clergy in Ohio were Bexley graduates.[31] On the eve of the Civil War, in 1859, at least one African American student, William Alston, was admitted. As the nation plunged itself into civil war, Bexley's enrollments increased dramatically, only to fall again after the war. By the time of President McIlvaine's death in 1873 enrollment dwindled to two students.[32] Internal conflicts between evangelicals and more liturgically minded members of the faculty also contributed to the decline. There were also several promising developments during the same period as Jay Cooke of Philadelphia (1866) and Sarah Lewis of Cincinnati (1867) made large financial gifts to Bexley Hall. These gifts formed the basis of endowed professorships in ecclesiastical history and systematic theology.[33]

Described as *A Born Again Episcopalian*, McIlvaine fit well with the revivalist theological style of Ohio and the American frontier.[34]

---

28. Ibid., 16–17.
29. Ibid., 19.
30. Ibid.
31. Ibid., 24.
32. Ibid.
33. Ibid., 25–30.
34. Thomas G. Grant, *A Born Again Episcopalian: The Witness of Charles P. McIlvaine* (Port St. Lucie, FL: Solid Ground Books, 2011).

His point of view was reflected in the "Matriculation Oath" that was developed in 1834 and signed by each entering student until 1959:

> We the subscribers, Students of the Theological Seminary of the Protestant Episcopal Church in the Diocese of Ohio, do solemnly promise with reliance on Divine Grace, that we will faithfully obey the laws and prosecute the studies thereof, endeavor to promote the reputation and interests of the Seminary, and make daily effort by pious reading, self-examination, and secret prayer, to cultivate religious and moral dispositions and habits, and grow in those graces which should characterize the Christian and the minister of the Cross.[35]

Louis Daniels described McIlvaine as "a man of striking personality," who became a polarizing through his staunch opposition to the Oxford Movement.[36] The Oxford Movement sought, as a corrective to the influence of revivalism, to restore the Anglo-Catholic liturgical and devotional customs and the theology of *via media* (middle way) within Anglicanism. Henry L. Richards, who knew and worked with McIlvaine in Ohio, remembered him as "a remarkable man. He had a good deal of religious fervor and enthusiasm, and a great horror of Popery."[37] Opposing the "Romish" style of Anglo-Catholics, he "was not the sort of man to govern his diocese with a velvet glove."[38] McIlvaine shaped the Ohio diocese after his own image, and as Rev. Charles Walworth reported, "We know by other testimony that some [clergy] left because the bishop made it too hot for them."[39]

When Bishop McIlvaine died in 1873, he was succeeded, as both bishop of Ohio and president of Bexley Hall, by Rev. Gregory T. Bedell (1817–1892). When he assumed the Bexley presidency in 1873, the school was in disarray; there was only one seminary student enrolled for 1874–1876. Bexley Hall was dealt a further blow in 1874, when Ohio was divided into two separate dioceses; but since neither diocese was directly responsible for supporting Bexley Hall, diocesan support became increasingly sporadic. When Bedell moved from Gambier to Cleveland in 1876, the seminary not only lost one of its three professors but also an active leadership.

Rev. William Andrew Leonard (1848–1930) was elected bishop by the Ohio Convention of May 1889, as well as president of Bexley Hall. Almost immediately, he took steps to reinvigorate the school. A

---

35. Spielmann, *Bexley Hall*, 19.
36. Louis Daniels, *William Andrews* (Cleveland, OH: Artcraft Printing, 1930), 37.
37. Clarence Walworth, *The Oxford Movement in America* (New York: The Catholic Book Exchange, 1895), 165.
38. Ibid., 162.
39. Ibid.

more moderate man than his predecessors, Leonard steered a middle course between the evangelicals and the ritualists. In his diocesan address of 1896, Leonard clearly stated that Bexley Hall would not be a narrowly partisan school under his leadership.[40] He apparently ironed out some of the differences between seminary and college, and the 1893–1894 catalogue reported, "Bexley Hall has now its complement of instructors, and is more fully equipped than at any time during the last twenty-five years. Its instruction is churchly and conservative, but does not shrink from discussion of those critical questions of the day, ignorance of which . . . is a disqualification as serious as it is inexcusable."[41] This deliberate balance between "churchly and conservative" and with a willingness to address "the critical questions of the day" would be the hallmark of the seminary for the next thirty years.[42]

The second fifteen years of Leonard's tenure was more tumultuous than the first half. Bexley Hall continued to struggle financially until 1923 when Samuel Mercer became dean and, along with Leonard, took an active role in fund-raising. Unfortunately, Dean Mercer's "grand vision" was too radical for President Leonard, and he soon departed for Trinity College, Toronto. He was replaced by Frederick Grant, who came to Bexley Hall with earned master's and doctoral degrees from Western Theological Seminary in Chicago.[43] Under Grant's leadership, more than $300,000 was raised or pledged for several important purposes, and the student body grew to a total of fifty-two.[44] Unfortunately, the harmony born in such remarkable successes was short-lived as seminary dean Frederick Grant and recently elected college president Pierce (who headed the finance committee of both schools) strenuously disagreed over how the recent influx of funds was to be shared by the college and the seminary. Grant resigned from Bexley Hall in July 1926. John Ludlow Pierce then stripped the dean's position of its independent authority when Charles Byer was "promoted" and moved into the office vacated by Frederick Grant.[45]

Dean Byer became the stabilizing force that guided Bexley Hall through several significant changes over the next fourteen years. During this time, the stock market crash also dramatically reduced the

40. Spielmann, *Bexley Hall*, 38–39.
41. Ibid.
42. Ibid.
43. Ibid., 50.
44. Ibid.
45. Ibid., 57–58.

seminary's already meager income, and as a result, by 1934 Bexley students were asked to contribute $100 per year toward their tuition.[46] Bexley Hall alumni continued to exert ecclesiastical leadership in the church well beyond their numerical strength; of the nine graduates in 1935, for example, two became bishops, and others took leadership roles of various kinds.[47]

In the midst of these pressures, in December 1934, wealthy Wall Street lawyer and Kenyon College trustee Wilbur Cummings wrote to President Pierce stating that Bexley Hall was "economically unsound" and should be merged with one of the denomination's "stronger seminaries" like General in New York City. Ohio bishop Warren Lincoln Rogers, who was also the president of Bexley Hall, responded at length to Cummings's letter, arguing that his proposed plan amounted to "the closing of Bexley Hall for no other reason than that Kenyon College needs some money to put on a bigger and better Kenyon program."[48] After almost three controversial years, the fate of Bexley Hall was addressed at the Ohio Convocation of 1937: a minority opinion that recounted the glorious history and financial viability of Bexley Hall was presented, and the convocation ultimately rejected the proposal to close the school. Bexley Hall then began planning a centennial celebration instead of a closing.[49]

After several false starts in the difficult years of World War II, Rev. Corwin Roach was selected to become dean of Bexley Hall in February 1942. The war also had a dramatic effect upon student enrollment, and by 1943–1945 the handful of remaining Bexley Hall students relocated to Virginia Theological Seminary in Richmond, along with Roach, to continue their work. At the Ohio Convention of 1945, Bishop Beverly D. Tucker presented a new proposal for the future of Bexley Hall based on a four-year plan, with the entire third year dedicated to parish work. This emphasis on practicality was folded into the seminary's traditional bachelor of divinity program and birthed a new program in rural ministry that led to the degree of master of sacred theology.[50]

Bexley Hall reopened at Gambier on October 8, 1945, with ten new students who were soon joined by two others returning from

---

46. Ibid., 60.
47. Ibid., 62–63.
48. Ibid., 65.
49. Ibid., 70.
50. Ibid., 77.

Virginia. The new programs, combined with the postwar flood of students, increased seminary enrollment through the 1950s. From a high of seventy-eight in 1952–1953 through the end of the decade to Roach's final year in 1957–1958, when there were forty-five full-time students, enrollments were large and stable. With the postwar years, however, came the challenge of housing married students, some with families, since housing and outside employment opportunities were severely limited in rural Gambier. Furthermore, increased enrollment did not result in significantly increased revenues, and funding remained a persistent problem. In 1954 the seminary was offered the suburban Akron home of industrialist Harvey Firestone as a site for relocation, but few at Gambier wanted to see the seminary move. Fifteen years later, under similar economic pressures, Bexley Hall relocated to Rochester as an affiliate of Colgate Rochester Divinity School.[51]

The late 1950s brought many changes in leadership at Bexley Hall. Perennial problems persisted, as Dean Robert Page clarified: "Bexley Hall has some pressing needs. I can put them in two words— *men* and *money*."[52] The 1958–1959 AATS accreditation visit was forestalled because there was little hope on campus of the seminary receiving accreditation. In 1959, after a thorough internal self-study, Almus Thorp accepted the deanship upon Page's retirement.

Dean Thorp worked diligently to rebuild the faculty, and by 1965 their ranks grew to ten full-time professors. Several fund-raising campaigns solicited $500,000 to replace the dilapidated library, only $200,000 of which was raised or pledged by 1965. At this point, it seemed to even some of Bexley's most ardent supporters that the school would close. President Franze Edward Lund's opening address for the fall semester of 1965 ended on an ominous note: "This may be the year of decision for Bexley, and Dean Thorp and I will face it together."[53] Just as a proposal to relocate Bexley Hall to Cleveland was submitted, other considered suggestions involved mergers with one of three other seminaries, including Colgate Rochester.[54] After a series of conversations and an all-day meeting on June 16, 1967, the study commission indicated a slight majority in favor of conversations

---

51. Ibid., 82–84.
52. Ibid., 86.
53. Ibid., 93.
54. Ibid., 96–99.

234 SCHOOL OF PROPHETS

with Colgate Rochester, and further discussions brought back a near unanimous vote in favor of a merger with Colgate Rochester.[55]

We now return to the original events under way at Colgate Rochester, where at the end of May 1967, CRDS President Gene Bartlett reported to the board that significant progress was made in preliminary conversations with Bexley Hall.[56] After "many months of work" the long-range planning committee of the CRDS board constructed a report replete with the details needed for full affiliation of Bexley Hall and Colgate Rochester. It suggested that, upon the approval of the respective governing boards, the Bexley program, along with six of their nine faculty and approximately twenty students, be relocated to the Rochester campus.[57] Within a matter of months, a twenty-page document titled "Modern Training for a Modern Ministry: A Proposal for a New Ecumenical Center for Theological Studies" was "Presented by Colgate Rochester Divinity School and Bexley Hall."[58] The report reveals that "the concept of a new center began to take shape several years ago as Colgate Rochester's board and administration sought new ideas to meet the growing needs of theological education. Colgate Rochester considered a number of other seminaries that might be invited to share its excellent campus at Rochester in the development of an ecumenical institution."[59] Colgate Rochester's newly established cooperative relationship with St. Bernard's Roman Catholic Seminary, located just twenty minutes from the Divinity School campus, was highlighted as an important dimension of the new endeavor, as was the need for greater inclusion of African American students and greater opportunities for interracial theological education and for the school to become "a real community."[60]

In the fall of 1967, Bartlett's "From the President's Desk" column in the *CRDS Bulletin* acknowledged what many of the alumni and friends of the Divinity School and Bexley Hall already knew: that "we are engaged in serious conversations with two other schools looking toward a center for theological studies."[61] In December 1967, both the Kenyon College and Colgate Rochester boards approved "the

---

55. Ibid., 99.
56. Gene Bartlett, "To the Board of Trustees: Report and Recommendation on the Affiliation of Bexley Hall," unpublished document, President Gene Bartlett Letter File, CRCDS archives.
57. Ibid., 6–10.
58. Ibid., 1.
59. Ibid., 3.
60. Ibid., 6–8.
61. Gene Bartlett, "From the President's Desk," *CRDS Bulletin* 40, no. 1 (October 1967): 2.

first steps toward affiliation."[62] Looking back upon five months of hard work, difficult conversations, and detailed planning, Bartlett observed, "We now know more clearly what we mean by the mind of Christ in which we find oneness in spite of differing traditions which reach back over centuries. We thought we were encountering one another; but the real encounter has been Christ. If for no other reason, the Center seems to us to be an act of obedience to God."[63]

In the spring of 1968, Bartlett issued a "Formula for the Future" in the form of a focus document that included both a history and a long-range plan for the new Center for Theological Studies (CTS) in Rochester. The new plan stipulated that Bexley Hall will move to the Rochester facility of CRDS in July 1968, and "at the earliest possible opportunity they will be joined by St. Bernard's Seminary presently located in Rochester but committed to a move on or contiguous to the Colgate Rochester campus."[64] Bartlett viewed the establishment of the CTS as a prophetic response to the new ecumenical climate of theological education: "So this is another time of reordering. . . . In such case, the new event has been the response to the changing time, the evidence of a new situation. So with the establishment of the Rochester Center for Theological Studies. It's a reordering of our theological education for the last third of the 20th century and, we believe, the opening of the 21st."[65]

On September 18, 1968, a feature article in the Rochester *Democrat and Chronicle* announced "New Rochester Theological Center Full of Firsts."[66] "After describing the affiliation of Colgate Rochester, which serves 15 different Protestant denominations, with Episcopalian Bexley Hall, it is pointed out that this was the first such union of theological schools at the seminary level, and the first instance of an Episcopalian institution with one from another communion." It was further noted that "these two schools will collaborate with the Roman Catholic, St. Bernard's Seminary . . . which will retain its campus."[67]

The catalogue language from 1962 remained more or less intact until 1968, when the catalogue explained, "The ecumenical emphasis

62. "President Bartlett Makes Progress Report," *CRDS Bulletin* 40, no. 2 (December 1967): 3.
63. Ibid., 4.
64. Gene Bartlett, "Formula for the Future," unpublished address/working paper, President Gene Bartlett Letter File, CRCDS archives.
65. Gene Bartlett, "From the President's Desk," *CRDS Bulletin* 40, no. 4 (June 1968): 2.
66. Mary Anne Ramer, "New Rochester Theological Center Full of Firsts," *Democrat and Chronicle*, September 15, 1968, 35.
67. Ibid.

is a central feature of the Colgate Rochester/Bexley Hall complex with its joint faculty and common curriculum. Colgate Rochester, funded by the Baptists, had grown increasingly interdenominational over the years until its faculty and student body encompassed a score of communions."[68] "As a consequence," the catalogue continued, "Episcopalians, Baptists, Roman Catholics, Presbyterians, Methodists, Lutherans, and many others are engaged side by side in theological education."[69]

The St. Bernard's story was also deeply woven into the ecumenical tapestry that became CRCDS. St. Bernard's Seminary began with the educational vision and herculean efforts of Bishop (Bernard) John McQuaid (1823–1909). The son of Irish immigrants from County Tyrone, John was born in Jersey City, New Jersey. After completing college at Chambly, Quebec, and seminary at St. John's, Fordham University, McQuaid was ordained into the priesthood on January 16, 1847, at St. Patrick's Cathedral, New York.

In 1853, the Archdiocese of Newark was established, and Rev. McQuaid was sent by Bishop James Roosevelt Bayley (1814–1877) to serve as rector of the Cathedral Church.[70] At the cathedral, McQuaid established a thriving academy that served more than six hundred pupils each year. He also played an instrumental role in the founding of Seton Hall College and Seminary in 1856 and served as president of Seton Hall for nearly a decade (1859–1868), while also maintaining his role at the cathedral. In these diverse roles, McQuaid earned the reputation of being a missionary-minded leader who wanted to extend and revitalize the church through the interconnection between Christian faith and education. As Henry Bowden noted, "His interest in Catholic education is the most significant characteristic of a distinguished clerical career."[71] In 1868, following the creation of the Rochester, New York, diocese, McQuaid was elevated to the office of bishop. He was consecrated bishop at St. Patrick's Cathedral in New York City on July 12 and then installed as bishop of Rochester on July 16, 1868. By 1870 he had opened St. Andrew's Preparatory School (a "seminary") and "completely organized a splendid

68. *Colgate Rochester Divinity School/Bexley Hall: Members of The Rochester Center for Theological Studies*, catalogue 1970-1971, 5.
69. Ibid.
70. Thomas F. Meehan, "McQuaid, Bernard John," *Catholic Encyclopedia*, www.catholic.com/encyclopedia/Bernard-John-McQuaid, accessed April 26, 2018; Henry Warner Bowden, "McQuaid, Bernard John," *The American National Biography*, https://www.anb.org/search?q=McQuaid%2C+Bernard+John+%281823-1909%29%2C+Catholic+bishop+and+educator, accessed September 12, 2019.
71. Bowden, "McQuaid, Bernard John."

parochial school system, taught by nuns and affiliated it with the State university."[72]

The initial vision for St. Bernard's Seminary was formed as early as 1878 when Rome inquired whether Rochester had a diocesan seminary. The response, that Rochester offered a "minor seminary," or a high school, but not a "major seminary" for training clergy, raised the obvious question of "Why not?" in Bishop McQuaid's mind. Then, in 1879, the long process of planning and fund-raising that finally enabled the purchase of a site in April 1887 began after the receipt of a major $5,000 gift from Rochester horticulturalist Patrick Barry[73] and a concerted fund-raising effort by the sixty-seven priests of the diocese. McQuaid's pastors contributed $41,500 out of their personal funds, and another $22,212.85 was raised through parish collections. When construction began in 1891, the financial sacrifice by both priests and congregants affected McQuaid so deeply that he lauded it in his inaugural message: "This deed has never been equaled in history. I need not praise them. God knows their hearts and reads their minds much better than I can, and He will reward them much better than I can."[74]

At the formal dedication services in August 1891, McQuaid explained why the new seminary would bear the name of St. Bernard: "St. Bernard was eminently a man of the people, one of them and laboring for them, and when the haughty barons of his day would trespass upon their rights, they found in St. Bernard a man who would stand up for them, [and] their rights. St. Bernard was a learned man, a student of all the deep questions of his time."[75] It was McQuaid's goal and vision that the seminary would exemplify the prophetic qualities of its eminent namesake. St. Bernard's Seminary opened on September 4, 1893, and about forty young men enrolled in the first class, most of whom were graduates of either St. Andrew's Preparatory Seminary of Rochester or the seminary at Troy, New York. The building fund, which began in 1879, reached $53,233.42 by opening day.[76]

The seminary building was state of the art in its day: "The rooms were pleasant and bright, with provision for good heating. The halls were designedly wide enough to serve as promenades when

72. Meehan, "McQuaid, Bernard John."
73. Robert F. McNamara, St. Bernard's Seminary: 1893–1968 (Rochester, NY: The Sheaf Press, 1968), 4–6, 8.
74. "St. Bernard's Seminary: An Address by the Bishop," Democrat and Chronicle, August 21, 1891, 8.
75. Ibid.
76. "St. Bernard's Seminary Opened Yesterday to Receive Its First Students," Democrat and Chronicle, September 5, 1893, 10.

the weather was bad. . . . There was adequate inside plumbing; that meant you could take a bath in a real indoor bathroom, and get a drink of good water without having to go outside."[77] The faculty was comprised of Fr. James Hartley, who taught moral theology; Dr. Edward Hanna, professor of dogmatic theology; Dr. Andrew J. Breen, professor of Hebrew Scriptures; Dr. Andrew Meehan, who taught liturgy and canon law; and Fr. Owen McGuire, professor of moral philosophy. Mr. Ludlow taught English and German, and Professor Eugene Bonn was music leader of the diocese.[78]

Bishop McQuaid became the seminary's "almost proverbial publicist," and enrollments continued to grow. By 1894 students came from dioceses as far away as New Orleans, France, and the Philippines. Soon the main building, which was built to house and serve sixty-eight students, was overcrowded.

In 1898 plans were laid to add a new three-story, fireproof building, with classrooms on the first floor, apartments on the second floor, and a large assembly hall on the third. A "New Building Fund" was established, and within two years, by the fall of 1900, Philosophy Hall was ready for occupancy.[79] In 1905 it was clear, once again, that St. Bernard's had outgrown its physical space, and in 1907 enough funds were finally raised to allow construction on the Hall of Theology. At this time, it was obvious that the chapel-refectory also required expansion, and so an annex was built.

Bishop McQuaid, even at eighty-three years old, was extraordinarily active in overseeing and implementing these projects, but over the summer of 1909 his health went into rapid decline, and he was barely able to participate in the dedication services for Theology Hall in August of that same year.[80] When serious illness returned during the Christmas season, the fiery founder of St. Bernard's Seminary passed away on January 18, 1909.

Bishop Thomas Hickey (1861–1940), who had been Bishop McQuaid's coadjutor since 1905, assumed control of both the Rochester diocese and of St. Bernard's Seminary. Dr. James Hartley (1860–1943) was named corector of the seminary by the aging McQuaid. When Hickey succeeded McQuaid as head of the diocese in 1909, he not

---

77. McNamara, *St. Bernard's Seminary*, 12.
78. Ibid., 13.
79. Ibid., 17–19.
80. Ibid., 19–20.

only saw fit "to continue the mild little priest in office but to bestow upon him the full title of rector."[81]

A native Rochesterian, born in Fairport, Hartley had attended both St. Andrew's and St. Joseph's Seminary in Troy, New York. Bishop McQuaid ordained him into the priesthood in 1885, and Hartley joined the work at St. Bernard's Seminary in 1893, first as professor of moral theology and then as corector. He was raised to the rank of domestic prelate, or monsignor, in 1914.[82] Under Hartley's leadership, the seminary continued to grow amid many changes.

Conflict came to campus in 1907 as Dr. Hanna, one of the original faculty of St. Bernard's, had his orthodoxy challenged due to an inquiry generated by his fellow St. Bernard's professor, Andrew Breen. Although no charges were sustained, Breen resigned from the faculty in 1908 in the midst of a theological climate full of the struggle against modernism. After Breen's resignation, Hanna's fidelity to the faith was then vindicated by his elevation to the episcopate in 1912.[83]

On August 15, 1923, Rochester's resident Roman Catholic bishop, Thomas Hickey, appointed Rev. D. Andrew Meehan (1867–1932) as rector of St. Bernard's. Under nearly a decade of his leadership, 1923 to 1932, the seminary charted a steady course toward new growth and development. Although Meehan implemented no major construction projects, he built the seminary from within. Hickey summed up forty years of ministry by Meehan, describing him as both a model and example "whose heart is close to that sacred heart of Jesus."[84]

Upon the death of Meehan in 1932, Fr. John Francis Goggin (1877–1964) led the seminary for the next sixteen years. Goggin, a native of nearby Palmyra, New York, was educated at Rome and served as professor of moral theology at St. Bernard's for twenty-nine years prior to taking his leadership role.[85] During his tenure as rector, virtually the entire faculty was rebuilt. In 1938 the seminary expanded its academic reach by also becoming the official seminary of the Syracuse Diocese. Because of these positive developments St. Bernard's successfully negotiated the difficult years of World War II,

---

81. Ibid., 24.
82. "Funeral for Prelate on Tuesday: Msgr. J. J. Hartley Rites Slated in Pro-Cathedral," *Democrat and Chronicle*, December 12, 1943, 21.
83. McNamara, *St. Bernard's Seminary*, 24–25.
84. "Cathedral Crowded to Capacity at Rites for the Rt. Rev. Msgr. Andrew B. Meehan," *Democrat and Chronicle*, February 4, 1932, 25.
85. "Professor Goggin Named Seminary Rector to Succeed Msgr. Meehan," *Democrat and Chronicle*, February 5, 1932, 19.

as well as the many challenges and restrictions it brought to religious higher education. A few curricular innovations, such as an accelerated program and a new course of study, were introduced in an attempt to address shortages in priestly leadership both at home and abroad just before Goggin retired from St. Bernard's Seminary in 1948.[86]

Bishop James E. Kerney, who served the Rochester Diocese from 1937 until his retirement in 1966, was replaced by the energetic and evangelistic bishop Fulton John Sheen. Described as "a Great Persuader" by the local press, Sheen was a significant personality on national radio and television when he came to Rochester as Kerney's replacement in 1966.[87] Sheen's long-running radio series "The Catholic Hour" (1930–1950) and various television programs like "Life Worth Living" (1951–1957) and "The Fulton Sheen Hour" (1961–1968) brought the attention of a national audience to Rochester and St. Bernard's Seminary. Reflecting the words of Pope John XXIII as he opened Vatican II by inviting the church to "open the windows and let in fresh air,"[88] St. Bernard's engaged three non-Catholics as nonresident instructors: Dr. Conrad H. Massa, professor of preaching; Dr. William Nelson, professor of fieldwork; and Rev. Michael Smith, professor of history; as well as nonresident lay instructors like Dr. Marvin Herrick and Dr. Earl Telschow, who taught pastoral psychology.[89]

Cooperation between St. Bernard's and Colgate Rochester began in the mid-1960s when the two schools cosponsored a series of public lectures on the Dead Sea Scrolls in April 1965. The internationally famous Dominican scholar Roland DeVaux was the featured speaker. A joint faculty dinner for professors from both institutions was held in his honor at the University Club.[90] A series of joint faculty meetings was proposed, which began when Sheen was installed as the new bishop of Rochester on December 15, 1966. A minor fire at St. Bernard's in April 1967 pushed the question of cooperation between the Rochester seminaries with more urgency as it was discovered that while the actual damage caused by the fire was rather slight, the facility itself was woefully behind code in terms of modern fire-prevention measures. It was determined that at least $300,000 was needed to

86. McNamara, *St. Bernard's Seminary*, 28.
87. Clifford Carpenter, "A Great Persuader," *Democrat and Chronicle*, October 27, 1966, 25.
88. Maureen Fiedler, "Vatican II: It's about Fresh Air," *National Catholic Reporter*, October 8, 2012, www.ncronline.org/blogs/ncr-today/vatican-ii-its-about-fresh-air.
89. McNamara, *St. Bernard's Seminary*, 67-69.
90. Robert F. McNamara, "Ecumenism and the Rochester Center for Theological Studies," *Rochester History* 52, no. 4 (Fall 1990): 11.

bring the facility into compliance.[91] After some preliminary consideration of rebuilding, Rector Joseph Patrick Brennan found himself in conversation with CRDS president Bartlett: "Why not move to our campus? We are just beginning to plan extensive changes."[92] Those changes involved the impending alliance between CRDS and Bexley Hall, which would then be agreed upon two months later, on June 16, 1967.

Sheen supported and pushed forward the cooperation between St. Bernard's and Colgate with characteristic gusto. His only proviso was that this would need to be an "integration with identity."[93] In other words, St. Bernard's, like the other affiliates, "would retain its own identity, its faculty, its curriculum, and its doctrinal convictions, while sharing the one locale and its academic, cultural, and domestic benefits."[94] Initially, the bishop advocated for a separate location nearby but not on the CRDS "hill." All plans, Sheen warned, were contingent upon the successful sale of St. Bernard's property.[95]

After some discussion, Brennan presented the consortium idea to Sheen, who, as bishop of Rochester, was ex officio head of St. Bernard's Seminary Corporation. Sheen was strongly attracted to the concept of an ecumenical seminary and began direct discussions about it with Bartlett. While the proposed "integration" of the three schools, and their cooperation in ecumenical theological education did not, as Sheen stressed, "interfere with the identity of the constituent schools," it did bring significant changes to St. Bernard's. One of these changes was the enrollment of "a Roman Catholic woman who was a member of the Sisters of the Cencale."[96] In the meantime, Eastman Kodak purchased St. Bernard's facilities, while the seminary's attempts to buy a new site fell through in November 1967. Upon these events, plans for the relocation of Bexley Hall to "the hill" and a formal proposal for affiliation between CRDS and St. Bernard's continued. The formal agreements were drafted and the new corporation for the Rochester Center for Theological Studies was in place by July 1, 1968, when Bexley Hall formally relocated its ministry to "the hill."[97]

91. Ibid., 12.
92. Ibid.
93. Ibid.
94. Robert F. McNamara, *The Diocese of Rochester in America 1858-1993*, 2nd exp. ed. (Rochester, NY: The Roman Catholic Diocese of Rochester, 1998), 545.
95. Ibid.
96. McNamara, *St. Bernard's Seminary*, 69.
97. Ibid., 15.

By the next spring, on April 11, 1969, the *Democrat and Chronicle* announced: "Merger with St. Bernard's Proposed." Bartlett made the announcement of an offer for full association between the three schools at the annual alumni convocation: "If our offer is accepted this will be the first time in our knowledge that such a thoroughly ecumenical community has been established."[98] But the rapid relocation of St. Bernard's to "the hill" hit a significant roadblock during the black student lockout at CRDS. The event dampened Sheen's enthusiasm for immediate implementation of that plan of affiliation.[99] Unfortunately, within a year, the three principal architects of the Rochester Center for Theological Studies passed from the scene; Bartlett and Sheen both retired, and Dean Almus Thorp of Bexley Hall was appointed to another post as director of the Episcopalian Board of Theological Education. These developments stalled full affiliation of St. Bernard's with CRDS and Bexley Hall, and for more than a decade the situation stood as when it was established in 1969.

By 1981, however, conversations restarted between Colgate Rochester/Bexley Hall President Larry L. Greenfield and Rector Eugene Lioi of St. Bernard's. The pressure of three successive years of deficits exceeding $100,000, in the face of falling enrollments, added fuel to the change.[100] On August 26, 1981, St. Bernard's and the Divinity School formally established their one-campus affiliation by signing an agreement that was valid for three years.[101] St. Bernard's Institute moved to the campus of Colgate Rochester/Bexley Hall beginning in the fall semester of 1981, and the two schools shared facilities, faculties, and curricula, and participated in cross-registration. Within two years, the St. Bernard's program thrived, with more than seventy full and part-time students, 52 percent of whom were women.[102]

The historic CRDS legacy of balance between evangelical and liberal traditions, which fused into an evangelical liberalism, with the time-honored identity of being both Baptist and ecumenical, seemed to be in danger of slipping away. Yet within a year of the establishment of the ecumenical Center for Theological Studies, the Baptist side of this equation would be accentuated through another merger, this time embracing Crozer Theological Seminary of Philadelphia.

98. "Seminary 'Merger' Proposed," *Democrat and Chronicle*, April 11, 1969, 20.
99. "Bishop Fulton Sheen, to President Gene Bartlett," June 5, 1969, St. Bernard's Seminary archives, cited in McNamara, "Ecumenism and the Rochester Center for Theological Studies," 17.
100. Stephanie Coulson, "St. Bernard's Makes Move Official Today," *Democrat and Chronicle*, August 26, 1981, 1.
101. McNamara, "Ecumenism and the Rochester Center for Theological Studies," 17-20.
102. John Hammond, "St. Bernard's Thrives at Colgate Rochester," *Democrat and Chronicle*, May 29, 1983, 24.

Crozer had deep roots in the "regular Baptist" tradition, reaching back to 1867, when its charter stipulated that seven of the twelve trustees and each professor "shall be a member of a regular Baptist church and amenable to the trustees, in matters of theological orthodoxy, morality, and capacity to teach."[103]

Within a year, a joint commission of representatives from Colgate Rochester Divinity School and Crozer Theological Seminary announced a "Tentative Draft" which thoroughly examined "Areas of Agreement in Principle Related to the Proposed Affiliation of Crozer Theological Seminary with Colgate Rochester Divinity School."[104] This fifteen-page agreement "in terms of *intent*, and of *principle*, paved the way for a rapid union of the two Baptist seminaries.[105]

One month later, the *Bulletin* ran the headline: "Crozer Seminary Affiliates with CRDS/BH." CRDS dean George B. Hall announced the union at the alumni banquet held at the annual meeting of the American Baptist Convention in Cincinnati. Speaking to a predominantly Baptist audience, Hall announced, "For those of you who are Baptists, it is one more way of reassuring you and ensuring that there will always be Baptist presence on the hill."[106] He then went on to say that Crozer would bring seven faculty members, 70 students, and its full library to Rochester, which would raise the Divinity School's enrollment to about 270, in the next fall semester.[107]

The Center for Theological Studies gave strong evidence to the prophetically inclusive dimension of the CRCDS legacy. The CTS remained intact for three decades, until 1998, when Bexley Hall relocated to Columbus, Ohio, reestablishing an Episcopal Church presence in Ohio by forming a partnership with Trinity Lutheran Seminary. After continuing operations both in Rochester and Columbus for several years, in 2008 the Rochester presence of Bexley Hall was discontinued due to falling student enrollments. After several years in Columbus, Bexley Hall entered into a cooperative relationship with Seabury-Western Theological Seminary of Chicago and relocated there in 2013 while continuing to retain its earlier relationships with Trinity Lutheran and other seminaries in Ohio.[108]

---

103. William H. Brackney, *Congregation and Campus: North American Baptists in Higher Education* (Macon, GA: Mercer University Press, 2008), 10, citing in part from the "General Laws of the Crozer Theological Seminary."
104. "Tentative Draft: Areas of Agreement in Principle Related to the Proposed Affiliations of Crozer Theological Seminary with Colgate Rochester Divinity School," May 15, 1970, unpublished typescript, CRCDS archives.
105. The Crozer story will be more fully developed in chapter 16.
106. "Crozer Seminary Affiliates with CRDS/BH," *CRDS/Bexley Hall Bulletin* 42, no. 4 (June 1970): 1.
107. "Tentative Draft: Areas of Agreement in Principle."
108. "St. Bernard's Names Its Second President," *Democrat and Chronicle*, June 21, 1993, 10.

By 2003 St. Bernard's remade itself once again. riding the crest of a $32 million fund-raising campaign by the Diocese of Rochester. The seminary was able to build a new $3 million state-of-the art facility in suburban Rochester and reconfigure itself as "St. Bernard's School of Theology and Ministry, a school for lay ministers on French Road in Pittsford."[109]

109. Diana Louise Carter, "Partners in Faith Campaign Aims for $50 Million by Year-End," *Democrat and Chronicle*, September 25, 2003, 19.

16

The Crozer Story

Chapter 15 discussed when the historically Baptist Crozer Theological Seminary, initially located in Upland, Pennsylvania, joined Colgate Rochester, Bexley Hall, and St. Bernard's Institute on "the hill" in 1970. We now pause to explore the proud and distinctive legacy that epitomized and accompanied Crozer when it came to Rochester. Like the Hamilton Institution, which became Colgate, and Rochester Theological Seminary, Crozer's inception was directly linked to the glaring need for educated Baptist pastors, but in eastern Pennsylvania, New Jersey, and the metropolitan New York area. Few Baptist ministerial students had either the finances or the academic preparation to qualify for admission at nearby Princeton or Yale.

The politics of particular churches made church-state relations and sectarian tests for admission controversial at that time, especially for Baptists, who "advocated liberty of conscience, the entire separation of church and state, believer's baptism by immersion, and a converted church membership—principles for which they earnestly contended from the beginning."[1] Hence, a few forward-looking Baptist pastors, such as Isaac Eaton of Hopewell, New Jersey, began mentoring candidates for ministry in their homes. Eaton's mentoring was supported by the Philadelphia Baptist Association, a cluster of twenty-nine churches that collaborated in service "for the education of youth for ministry."[2] Through their efforts, the sum of £400 was raised against the difficult backdrop of the impending American

---

1. Reuben Aldridge Guild, *History of Brown University with Illustrative Documents* (Providence, RI: Providence Press Company, 1867), 4.
2. Ibid.

Revolution. The Hopewell Baptist Academy was then established in 1756.[3]

While Hopewell Academy was short-lived, operating from 1756 to 1767, it led to the formation of the Philadelphia Baptist Association, followed by the establishment of both Brown and Columbia universities. The association "officially or unofficially, had attempted to establish a school of prophets, and twice had its project been diverted from its original aim into a mere college institution."[4] While the Hamilton Institution began to take shape in western New York, the members of the Philadelphia-based Baptist Education Association hoped to establish a Baptist theological seminary to serve their region.

In 1846 the Lewisburg University—subsequently renamed Bucknell in 1881—was established by a group of Pennsylvania Baptists who deemed it "desirable that a Literary Institution should be established in Central Pennsylvania, embracing a High School for male pupils, another for females, a College and also a Theological Institution."[5] The ardent Baptist layman and wealthy industrialist John P. Crozer of Philadelphia soon took an active interest in Lewisburg University, as well as other educational efforts in eastern Pennsylvania.

A descendant of Irish immigrants, John P. Crozer (1793–1886) was a farmer and carpenter by trade. Energetic and entrepreneurial, Crozer soon parlayed his meager earnings into part interest in a sawmill. Observing the rise of the textile industry, he bought used machinery and established a large mill in the Chester, Pennsylvania, area. One mill was soon followed by two larger ones. A self-educated man, Crozer was a firm believer in the importance of education. He established a school for the children of his factory workers. The school was forced to close in 1861 due to outbreaks of smallpox and scarlet fever. During the Civil War, the Upland facility was used first as a military training school and then as an emergency hospital.[6]

Crozer's philanthropic sentiments were amply demonstrated upon his death on March 11, 1866, when his extensive will ordered for the establishment of the "John P. Crozer Missionary Memorial Fund,"

3. *Historical Sketch of Crozer Theological Seminary: A Souvenir of the Thirtieth Anniversary of the Foundation of the Seminary* (Chester, PA: Printed for the Seminary, 1897), 9-10; "Hopewell Academy," *Historical Marker Database*, www.hmdb.org/Marker.asp?Marker=3197, accessed June 4, 2018.
4. *Historical Sketch of Crozer*, 10.
5. "Milestones," www.bucknell.edu/info-about-attending-bucknell/who-we-are/history-and-traditions/milestones, accessed June 4, 2018.
6. David A. MacQueen, *The Crozers of Upland* (Wilmington, DE: Serendipity Press, 1982), 1-24.

valued at more than $50,000, out of his bountiful estate.[7] The dispo-
sition of the Upland school property was still in question when, after
about three months after his death, a member of his family suggested
starting a theological seminary in Upland.[8] After making an onsite
visit and conferring with the Crozer family and the Philadelphia Conference of Baptist Ministers, a series of resolutions led to the relocation of the theology department of the University of Lewisburg to
Upland with substantial support from both the Crozer family and the
Philadelphia Baptists.[9] The Crozer family's support continued, reaching its apex on November 2, 1886, when eight Crozers endowed the
seminary with land, funds, and investments exceeding "the princely
sum" of $275,000.[10]

The official legal existence of Crozer Theological Seminary (CTS)
dates from April 4, 1867, when the Pennsylvania legislature granted
the newly formed board of trustees' articles of incorporation and a
charter.[11] Henry Griggs Weston (1820–1909) was called to become
the first president of Crozer Theological Seminary in 1868. Educated
at Newton Theological Seminary, Weston served several significant
pastorates prior to coming to Crozer. He was a gifted preacher and
writer who served as president of CTS for more than forty years and
published several significant books. Weston was a theological conservative with respect to the Bible, who had, in Norman Maring's words,
"a dogged belief in inspiration, without being able to define it."[12]

In a commemorative address, Weston's friend and colleague CTS
history professor Henry Vedder (1853–1935) said that President
Weston was "the creative mind" and "life-giving spirit" of the seminary: "The seminary, as a school of the prophets, is what he has made
it."[13] Under Weston's prophetic and able leadership Crozer became
one, if not the first, of the nation's integrated theological seminaries
when Henry Heywood Mitchell, "a young man of color," was admitted in 1876.[14] Racial inclusion was one of Crozer's hallmarks moving
into the modern era.

7. J. Wheaton Smith, *The Life of John P. Crozer* (Philadelphia: American Baptist Publication Society, 1868), 244-54, carries the full text of John P. Crozer's will.
8. Ibid., 255-56.
9. Ibid., 257-60, carries the text to two groups of resolutions passed and implemented at this time.
10. *Historical Sketch of Crozer*, 15.
11. Ibid., 18.
12. Norman H. Maring, "Baptists and Changing Views of the Bible, 1865-1918," in two parts, *Foundations*. I, no. 3-4 (October 1958): 1:58. Cf. William H. Brackney, *Genetic History of Baptist Thought* (Macon, GA: Mercer University Press, 2004), 369.
13. Robert A. Macoskey, "The Best of Pietism," *The Voice: The Bulletin of Crozer Theological Seminary* 59, no. 2 (April 1967): 34-35.
14. Ibid., 12.

Along with Weston, who also taught New Testament, George Dana Boardman Pepper was hired as professor of Christian theology. After serving at Crozer for fifteen years, he resigned to become president of Colby College in 1882. Howard Osgood served as professor of both Old Testament and church history and librarian. His resignation in 1874 was, as Stephen Reynolds described it, "the result of unpleasantness and tension,"[15] most of which revolved around complaints about his spending practices. As head of the library, Osgood tried to build a world-class collection for the fledgling seminary. Soon thereafter, in 1872, Lemuel Moss (1829–1904) was added to the faculty as professor of New Testament interpretation. The total enrollment for Crozer's first academic year, 1868–1869, was twenty; the next year, enrollment went up to thirty-six. The seminary's first commencement in June 1870 celebrated the graduation of eight students.[16]

The "General Laws of the Crozer Theological Seminary," published in the inaugural edition of the catalogue, asserted that the "object" of the school "shall be to furnish Theological instruction and training, to suitable candidates for the Christian ministry."[17] The seminary and course of instruction were divided into four departments: Interpretation of the Bible, Christian Theology, Church History, and Preaching and Pastoral Duties.[18] While admission was "open to all members of Christian churches, of any denomination,"[19] it was stated that each faculty member "shall be a member of a regular Baptist Church."[20] True to the missional posture of the school and the needs of the students, "no charge is made for tuition, room rent, fuel, light in the public rooms, or for the use of the library."[21]

Enrollment grew steadily in the first decade, leveling off at an average of forty-two students each year.[22] Following the departure of Professor Moss to the presidency of the University of Chicago and Professor Osgood to Rochester Theological Seminary (RTS) in 1874–1875, George Bliss joined the Crozer faculty as both librarian and professor of biblical interpretation, having been chair of Greek at the University of Lewisburg since 1849. Bliss was remembered

---

15. Ibid.
16. *Historical Sketch of Crozer*, 24-25.
17. *Catalogue of the Officers and Students of the Crozer Theological Seminary: Charter, General Laws, and Etc.* (Philadelphia: Markly and Son, 1869), 7-8.
18. Ibid., 7–8.
19. Ibid., 11.
20. Ibid., 8.
21. Ibid., 5.
22. Specifically: 1870-1871, thirty-five; 1871-1872, forty-two; reaching a high in 1878-1879 of forty-eight.

by one of his students as "a master in the art of teaching."[23] John S. Hutchinson was also added to the biblical interpretation faculty but left the following year. John C. Long then arrived in church history. Coming from the pastorate, Long began his Crozer career in the fall of 1875 and brought with him both significant learning and real-world experience that enlivened his classes. At this point, and up until 1877, the entire Crozer faculty consisted of only four professors. By 1878 the size of the faculty grew to five, with Weston also serving as president and Bliss as librarian. In that same year, Barnard C. Taylor was appointed as an instructor in Hebrew.[24] Elias H. Johnson, a 1871 graduate of RTS, also replaced Pepper in Christian theology.[25]

Soon the faculty grew to ten, including the addition of specializations in New Testament exegesis, Christian ethics, delivery of sermons, and physiology. But as enrollment began to slip under 40 students, the faculty soon returned to its earlier, leaner configuration of six full-time men with no visiting lecturers. It continued on at this smaller size, even when student enrollments rebounded and surged back up over 50 by 1888–1889, with 72 students in 1889–1890[26] and a new high enrollment of 103 in 1894–1895.[27] When Long died in 1890, he was replaced by Vedder, who was a graduate of the University of Rochester and RTS. A creative teacher and author of more than a dozen books, Vedder became one of the mainstays of the Crozer faculty. He epitomized Crozer Theological Seminary's evangelical liberalism, which was centered on the essentials of the Christian gospel and embraced social activism. In the face of growing conservativism in the American Baptist tradition, he refused to be silenced by fundamentalism.

While all students were strongly urged to complete college or university work prior to seminary, Crozer did not require a college diploma for admission. There was a missional rationale behind this decision, since "it is Crozer's desire to be helpful to the largest possible number of men who are studying to fit themselves for the ministry of the gospel, and its aid has never been refused to any man of good character who is able to profit by a course of study in even one of its departments."[28] In 1883 the American Baptist Committee

23. *Historical Sketch of Crozer*, 26–27.
24. *Crozer Catalogue*, 1878–1879, 5.
25. *Historical Sketch of Crozer*, 27–28.
26. *Crozer Catalogue*, 1889–1890, 14.
27. *Crozer Catalogue*, 1894–1895, 14.
28. *Historical Sketch of Crozer*, 29.

on Education reported that in fifteen years Crozer sent out nearly two hundred graduates, "many of whom are already occupying prominent positions." Five years later, a similar report noted, "In only twenty years this school of theological learning has become one of the largest and most controlling in our denomination . . . no theological seminary has won more shining honor."[29] By 1892 Crozer adopted the bachelor of divinity as its standard professional degree.

Another innovative development at Crozer was the establishment of the Crozer Extension Course in 1906. The Northern Baptists, like so many other Protestant communions dramatically shaped by the nation's western expansion and revivalist heritage, came late to producing a formally educated clergy. A report from the Pennsylvania Baptist Education Society from 1904 illustrated the dilemma: "When we have been laboring industriously sixty-five years to provide an educated ministry and now find out of the twenty-eight whom we usually ordain each year, scarcely one-fourth have had a full course in the schools, it is but reasonable to make some additional provision for the large number of unschooled men who are likely to be ordained during the next half-century."[30]

Extension courses of ministerial study emerged in response to this educational crisis, and the Crozer faculty developed a three-year program of private study. At about the same time, in 1906, Eli S. Reinhold, a banker from Mahanoy City, Pennsylvania, studying at Crozer to equip himself as a more effective Bible teacher, developed a plan for a seminary-sponsored extension program. Ultimately, "Mr. Reinhold resigned his lucrative position in the Bank, left his old associates in the business world and on smaller salary became, in 1907, the organizer and director of one of the best educational agencies connected with any institution of learning."[31] Upon the death of Reinhold in 1926, he was succeeded by Rittenhouse Neisser, who, along with Sarah Ogden, directed the Crozer extension program from 1926 until 1944. Upon Neisser's retirement, the extension program was led by Dean Charles Batten (1944–1954). The program underwent

---

29. Sandford Fleming, *American Baptists in Higher Education*, 6 vols. (Valley Forge, PA: American Baptist Board of Education, 1965), 2:6.
30. Albert L. Meiburg, "A Remarkable Ministry," *The Voice* 60, no. 2 (April 1968): 12, citing directly from the annual report of the board of managers of Pennsylvania Baptist Education Society (1904), which at that time was located in the Bucknell Library at Crozer Theological Seminary.
31. Milton G. Evans, "Professor Eli S. Reinhold, An Appreciation," cited in Meiburg, "A Remarkable Ministry," 12.

extensive revision in 1954–1955 by the Crozer faculty and was headed by Dr. Stephen Reynolds from 1957 onward.[32]

Crozer Seminary's second president, Milton G. Evans (1862–1939), not only succeeded Weston but also built upon and extended his work. Evans earned his baccalaureate degree from Bucknell University and his bachelor of divinity from Crozer in 1890. From that date forward he served his alma mater in various capacities until his retirement in 1933.[33] He joined the faculty in 1890 as professor of exegesis, and in 1893 was named professor in the fledgling field of biblical theology—the first such chair in the United States.[34] Quickly changing chairs and responsibilities as needed, Evans was named dean in 1905 and professor of Christian theology in 1906. By 1919 he changed his field of academic focus once again by assuming the role of professor of history of religion alongside his presidency. The Society of Biblical Literature states that "throughout the years he made constant contributions on Biblical and theological topics, chiefly through the weekly religious press and the less technical religious journals. His publications were of a practical nature though always based on accurate knowledge of the most recent scholarship."[35] His main work, *What Jesus Taught*, made a significant contribution to the scholarship of his day.[36] As a pedagogue, he helped turn the tide away from the older "textbook recital method" toward a newer approach based in original scholarship and critical thinking.[37]

It was as an administrative leader, however, that Evans made his greatest contribution to Crozer and theological education in his day. He not only provided the space, climate, and academic freedom that allowed colleagues like Vedder to venture into new and more progressive directions; he "set the style for Crozer to come." Evans encouraged, oversaw, and orchestrated the theological transition from Crozer's staunch Baptist conservativism toward the evangelical liberalism that began under Weston.[38] Evans's matriculation speech, which applauded Schleiermacher's modern approach to Christian theology, signaled that Crozer was undergoing the same theological shift from conservative Baptist-evangelical theology toward progressive

32. Meiberg, "A Remarkable Ministry," 14.
33. "Milton G. Evans," *Proceedings of the Society of Biblical Literature* 59, no. 1 (1940): iv.
34. Mack H. Langford, "The Second President: Milton G. Evans," *The Voice* 60, no. 2 (April 1968): 8.
35. "Milton Evans," v.
36. Milton G. Evans, *What Jesus Taught according to the Gospels* (Philadelphia: Judson Press, 1922).
37. Langford, "The Second President," 9.
38. Ibid.

evangelical liberalism that was also observed at Colgate Theological Seminary in the work of William Newton Clarke and at Rochester Theological Seminary in the person of George Cross. At Crozer this transition from "cautious conservativism" toward the more progressive modern or "liberal" viewpoint was contested:

> At Crozer there was the same cautious conservativism that was present at Rochester and Newton, although at all three institutions the younger men were restive. But even Elias Johnson and Henry G. Weston, who stood within the older camp at Crozer, recognized that the "religious dynamical" theory of inspiration advocated by Strong and Hovey [of Newton] was too easy a solution to the problems that had been raised to be either convincing or defensible.[39]

Crozer's systematic theologian, Elias Johnson, opted for a Christocentric approach to the question of biblical authority, reminiscent of the work of William Newton Clarke at Colgate, which did not seek support from mechanical theories of biblical inspiration and the dictation of an inerrant text. Johnson asserted that "the Bible is authoritative, because it bears witness to the central fact of God's revelation in Christ; and this witness is sufficiently clear to make preoccupation with theories of inspiration both fruitless and unnecessary."[40] At this same time, Weston wrote convincingly about the Baptist concept of church order, which could be briefly summarized as "a living Savior, a living church, an organic church, and a complete church."[41] As Crozer professors Jessie Brown and W. Kenneth Cauthen argued, "The liberal era [at Crozer] combined the historical approach with emphasis upon the priority of experience over dogma."[42]

Crozer's theological shift from cautious conservativism to progressive evangelical liberalism drew the attention and ire of conservatives in the Northern Baptist Convention at a time when fundamentalists tried to stem the tide of modernism at Baptist seminaries. When W. R. Riley presented his report on "Modernism in Baptist Seminaries" at a large conference on "The Fundamentals of Our Baptist Faith" in June 1920, he lamented that "many of the Baptist seminaries of the North are hot-beds of skepticism."[43] Later that same day,

---

39. Winthrop S. Hudson, "Shifting Patterns of Church Order in the Twentieth Century," *The American Baptist Quarterly* 30, no. 3/4 (Fall-Winter 2011): 325–26.
40. Ibid., 327.
41. Henry Griggs Weston, *Constitution and Polity of the New Testament Church* (Philadelphia: American Baptist Publication Society, 1895), 47–48.
42. Jessie H. Brown and W. Kenneth Cauthen, "Duty Bound to Question," *The Voice* 60, no. 3 (July 1968): 7.
43. *Baptist Fundamentals: Being Addresses Delivered at the Pre-convention Conference at Buffalo, June 21, and 22, 1920* (Philadelphia: Judson Press, 1920), 178–79.

when Jasper Cortenus (J. C.) Massee addressed the same assembly, he offered a sharp critique of the work of RTS theologian George Cross, as well as A. S. Hobart and Henry C. Vedder of Crozer. Massee urged, "All of Crozer needs a denominational disinfecting."[44] It was clear that dramatic theological changes were under way at Crozer, as with the progressive American Baptist seminaries like Rochester and Colgate, and at Crozer the career of Vedder epitomized this transition.

Born in the village of De Ruyter, New York, in southwest Madison County, Henry Clay Vedder was raised in the region known as "the burnt-over district," because evangelists came and went with such great frequency that the fires of religious revival never really subsided. This evangelical fervor profoundly shaped Vedder's life; one of his former students, Albert G. Williams, recalled hearing him give an account of his conversion experience, which was "vivid, heightened by the appeal to the fear of hell and retribution typical of that period. Unable to sleep following the evening service, the lad sought his mother, and with her insight and understanding, committed his soul's welfare to the care of Jesus Christ."[45] Looking back on that event, Vedder explained, "Though I had no spectacular conversion . . . for more than fifty years I have had an unbroken consciousness of deliverance from the power of sin through Jesus Christ, and of fellowship with him."[46] Vedder's career path was shaped by studies at both the University of Rochester and RTS, as he received both a bachelor of arts and bachelor of divinity in 1876. Upon graduation, Vedder worked on the editorial staff of *The Examiner* and then on the *Baptist Quarterly Review*. His journalistic career came to an end, however, when he accepted a call from Crozer Theological Seminary to chair the Department of Church History.

Vedder's early academic works, such as *Baptists and Liberty of Conscience*, evidenced his evangelical Baptist roots traced through the hallmark concept of "soul liberty," or liberty of conscience, from its earliest foundations.[47] *The Dawn of Christianity* expressed these same roots in addition to a growing passion for what would become the social gospel. Tracing the history and development of the early

---

44. Ibid., 181.
45. Robert B. Hanley, "Henry Clay Vedder: Conservative Evangelical to Evangelical Liberal," *Foundations* 5, no. 2 (April 1962): 136; cf. Dwight A. Honeycutt, *Henry Clay Vedder: His Life and Thought* (Atlanta: Baptist History and Heritage, 2008), 27.
46. Henry C. Vedder, "My Theological Emancipation," an unpublished address, in the American Baptist Archives; cited by Honeycutt, *Henry Clay Vedder*, 26.
47. Henry C. Vedder, *Baptists and Liberty of Conscience* (Cincinnati: J. R. Baumes, 1884), 9–12.

church from the teachings of Jesus onward Vedder noted, "What the religion of Christ is to every believer, that it has been and is to society—a power to transform life."[48]

Vedder's theological pilgrimage toward and perhaps beyond the social gospel was clearly evidenced in his *Socialism and the Ethics of Jesus* (1912). In that work he chronicled the history and development of socialism, noting its obvious parallels with the "social teachings of Jesus." Even the father of the social gospel, Walter Rauschenbusch, was surprised by Vedder's frankness. Writing in *The Standard*, Rauschenbusch remarked, "It was a matter of surprise and delight to me to find with what thoroughness and sympathy Doctor Vedder has dealt with the subject. I should not have picked him out as likely to be constitutionally predisposed to socialism, and I should be glad to buy another book in which he would describe how he arrived at his present convictions."[49] As *Socialism and the Ethics of Jesus* moved to a close, Vedder described the "Perils and Hopes" of the contemporary situation and concluded that, to its peril, the church lost Jesus' vision of the kingdom of God. But the hope for the future was bright, he urged, since Jesus' foundational concern can be recovered and expressed in workable alliances with prevalent social trends like democracy and Christian socialism.[50]

Two years later, Vedder's *Jesus and the Problems of Democracy* solidified his role as a leading religious social reformer. In the book, he traced the prophetic tradition of the great Hebrew prophets into the foundation of the gospel of Jesus Christ. Vedder summarized it in this way: "On its practical side is brotherhood. The content of this idea is large, but it cannot be supposed to mean less than these four things: equal rights for all, the supremacy of the common good, mutual dependence and service, and active good will to all."[51] These prophetic, gospel values, Vedder believed, both critiqued and empowered American democracy in the face of the myriad problems posed by the Gilded Age. Contemporary crises like social justice, poverty, "the woman problem," "the problem of the child," slums, crime, vice, disease, and lawlessness were each addressed in a salient chapter and followed by seven full pages of specific proposals

48. Henry C. Vedder, *The Dawn of Christianity, or Studies of the Apostolic Church* (Philadelphia: America Baptist Publication Society, 1894), 183.
49. Walter Rauschenbusch, "Professor Vedder's New Book on Socialism," *The Standard*, June 15, 1912, 1276.
50. Henry C. Vedder, *Socialism and the Ethics of Jesus* (New York: Macmillan, 1912). See especially 472ff.
51. Henry C. Vedder, *Jesus and the Problems of Democracy* (New York: Macmillan, 1914), 19.

and programs that could lead to substantive social change.[52] What was missing in Vedder's critique, however, was the recognition and redress of the glaring problem of racial prejudice and segregation in twentieth-century America.

That the theological transitions at Crozer in general, and in the work of Vedder in particular, angered conservative American Baptists was not surprising. Several aspects of Vedder's work became targets of conservative broadsides; most prominent among these were his modernist reading of the New Testament and willingness to stress the social gospel over the inerrant Bible and private gospel cherished by fundamentalists. Vedder titling his seminal work *The Fundamentals of Christianity* (1922) indicated his willingness to contest with the conservatives over the essence or "fundamentals" of the Christian message.

The conservative assault on Vedder's new theological trajectories began as early as 1914, when Curtis Lee Laws, editor of *The Watchman Examiner* and inventor of the term *fundamentalism*, reacted harshly to Vedder's attempt to liken the Protestant Reformation to the unwholesome social changes that stemmed from unbridled capitalism.[53] When Massee began his campaign to drum progressive Baptists out of the Northern Baptist schools and conventions, he published "An Open Letter to Northern Baptists," in which he urged those who disagreed with his own explication of "the fundamentals" of Baptist faith to "depart in peace. For this is our home and this is our name, and these are our priceless treasures of faith."[54] Vedder promptly answered Massee in the same journal by asking, "Must We Go—Where?" Vedder continued:

> The nerve of him! I have been a Baptist for no less than fifty years, and I hope I am not guilty of immodest boasting when I say that I have done my bit in making Baptist principles better known and more widely accepted, and in leading our people to take a more intelligent pride in our honorable history. . . . And so I say boldly to Dr. Massee and his ilk, "I am a Baptist, if any man is a Baptist. . . . If there is any 'departing' to be done, you will have to do it; for here I am and here I stay."[55]

By 1920 the editor of the Baptist *Western Examiner* urged that Vedder should be charged with heresy, and if those charges could not

52. Ibid., 388–95.
53. Curtis Lee Laws, "A New History of the Reformation," *The Watchman Examiner* 2, no. 35 (August 27, 1914): 1134.
54. Henry C. Vedder, "The Open Forum: Must We Go–Where?" *The Baptist: Published by the Northern Baptist Convention* 1, no. 39 (October 23, 1920): 1329.
55. Ibid.

be adequately answered he should be forced to resign from his position at Crozer.[56] Upon the publication of Vedder's *Fundamentals of the Faith*, Massee became the leading voice petitioning for his expulsion from Crozer. The trustees of Crozer replied to Massee's petition by pointing to the cherished Baptist belief in "soul liberty" and a biblical freedom from doctrinal standards of human invention: "Baptists have never formulated any standard of faith recognized among them as authoritative there has always existed great diversity of opinion both in the pulpit and in the teaching forces of their seminaries."[57]

The public acrimony and economic implications of the controversy surrounding Vedder's theological trajectory both shaped and hampered Crozer's message and mission. It caused Baptists and alumni who shared Vedder's progressive views to rally that cause, and through their efforts the school experienced renewed vigor. But in response to Crozer's unwillingness to expel Vedder, conservative Baptists in Philadelphia established Eastern Baptist Theological Seminary, which was chartered on April 28, 1925, on a staunchly conservative "Doctrinal Basis."[58] The theological trajectory that marked Vedder's work was continued by many successors within the Crozer faculty. The trajectory was also given clear and cogent voice in the *Crozer Quarterly*, established in 1924, which soon became one of the nation's chief expressions of progressive Protestant thought.[59] Reuben E. E. Harkness (1884–1972) succeeded Vedder as professor of church history at Crozer in 1927 and held that chair until his retirement in 1950. The Crozer philosophy of theological education was expressed in Harknesss's matriculation address of September 1935,[60] when he argued, "This Seminary . . . is not interested in theology, creeds, doctrines, and confessions of faith as such, nor is it concerned with establishing certain positions relative to theories of the Bible of Biblical interpretation. But it is interested in people, how they have lived, how they have found a worthier way of living, and how they may still find it."[61]

This same point of view was carried forward by Crozer professors like George Washington Davis, who served as professor of systematic

---

56. Hanley, "Henry Clay Vedder," 150-51.
57. Ibid., 153.
58. Cf. Robert A. Macoskey, "Henry C. Vedder: Historian Ahead of His Hour," pt 2, *The Voice* 60, no. 2 (April 1968): 19-21, for documents and discussions pertinent to these developments.
59. Brown and Cauthen, "Duty Bound to Question," 8.
60. Ibid., 7.
61. Ibid.

theology from 1938 to 1954. In his inaugural article for the *Crozer Quarterly* in 1939, Davis wrote, "Our thesis will be that the New Testament upholds the view that no matter what God does for man in Christ, until man responds to this divine initiative through a morally renewed life, salvation does not become a reality."[62]

A similar perspective was developed in the new methods and trajectories established by biblical scholars of the same era like Morton Scott Enslin, who served as professor of New Testament interpretation from 1924 to 1953, and James Prichard, professor of Old Testament from 1942 to 1954. Both men were leading exponents and practitioners of the historical method in biblical studies.

Dr. Evans's successor, President James H. Franklin, from 1934 to 1944 was the secretary of the American Baptist Foreign Mission Society and "brought to the seminary a world outlook and outreach."[63] Stressing the freedom of non-Western people to receive and follow Christ on their own terms, Franklin wrote, "It must be recognized that in many sections of the world there is a growing and encouraging tendency on the part of native Christians to claim their divine right to interpret Christ and the New Testament for themselves. . . . Baptists, if they are true to their 'historical contribution,' should find no difficulty in meeting such a situation."[64]

Franklin brought this same global, forward-looking attitude to his leadership at Crozer Theological Seminary. One of his first acts when he came into office in 1935 was to request that the faculty curriculum committee draw up a new plan of instruction, reflecting new educational ideas and philosophies. Within four months Dr. Cole and his committee returned with an eight-page, single-spaced document that advocated for and outlined a new model for theological education that was based in ministerial function. That document, issued in 1935, anticipated and shaped Crozer Theological Seminary's academic and practical course for the next twenty-eight years.[65]

Professor William Roy McNutt came to Crozer in 1928. He joined Cole and then replaced him as a shaper of the "new Crozer" that emphasized practical theology and ministry. When he first joined the faculty, Evans charged McNutt "to develop practical theology

---

62. Ibid., 8.
63. Robert C. Keighton, "An Arch Never Sleeps," *The Voice* 59, no. 3 (July 1967): 7.
64. James H. Franklin, "Baptist Missions in the New World Order," *Review and Expositor* 17 (October 1920), 396.
65. Edward E. Thornton, "Hints and Help, the Story of Practical Theology at Crozer, 1924–1947," *The Voice* 60, no. 3 (July 1968): 4–5.

with a parish-centered orientation and to cultivate good relationships with alumni and churches in the area, or as Evans said, 'to revive the Seminary in the hearts of the people.'"[66] This charge proved much more difficult than imagined, in large part because McNutt found that the prevailing emphasis among many of the faculty and students of the seminary could best be described as "our interest is *scholastic* wholly."[67] Ultimately, McNutt left the faculty due to "the long disagreement" between himself and Franklin, which "resulted in the dismantling of the practical fields of pastoral theology in recent years."[68]

Dr. Edwin E. Aubrey (1896–1956) succeeded Franklin in 1944 and served Crozer for five years. Aubrey came to Crozer from the University of Chicago, where he was professor of Christian theology and ethics from 1929 until his departure in 1944. His mark upon the seminary lay chiefly in the academic realm.[69] Although Aubrey was the author of many scholarly articles, his most famous work was *Present Theological Tendencies* (1936), which offered "a crisp, clear schematization of our present troubles and the chief theological and quasi-theological solutions for them."[70]

Notable African American church leaders, such as Samuel De-Witt Proctor and Martin Luther King Jr., epitomized the black contribution to the Crozer heritage. Proctor (1921–1997) grew up in Norfolk, Virginia, in the horrible inequities of racial segregation. To some degree, this precarious situation was counterbalanced by faith-filled memories of his grandmother, Hattie Ann Fisher, who rose from the oppression of slavery through a deep and abiding faith in God. "Grandma's intrepid confidence," he recalled, "rested on a single uncompromising notion: God created all people; any inequalities among us were due to unequal opportunity. From her we learned that hatred and vindictiveness were always destructive. 'No use of fretting and crying,' she would say, 'if you do your part, God will do the rest.'"[71] His grandmother's example, and many others from his family and the black church, instilled in young Proctor a call to

---

66. Ibid., 5.
67. Ibid., 6.
68. Ibid., 20.
69. Keighton, "An Arch Never Sleeps," 7.
70. Marshall Bowyer Stewart, "Present Theological Tendencies," *The Anglican Theological Review* 8, no. 3 (July 1936): 195 (a scholarly review of Aubrey's work). Cf. Brackney, *Genetic History of Baptist Thought*, 378–79.
71. Samuel DeWitt Proctor, *The Substance of Things Hoped For: A Memoir of African-American Faith* (New York: Putnam, 1995), 2.

service that would prove to be even larger than the bounds of the community of faith.

After a long and persistent struggle against segregation, injustice, and limited opportunities, Proctor gained admission to college but eventually left Virginia State University without a degree due to his outspoken opposition to the unjust and injurious hazing that was so much a part of fraternity life on campus. He found himself, instead, in the Naval Apprentice School, operated by the US Navy in the shipyards of Norfolk. Even then, however, Proctor recalled, "the ministry seemed to be following me."[72] At that time, under the guidance of D. C. Rice of Bank Street Baptist Church, Proctor found both a role model and direction. While he was at work one day soon thereafter, Proctor had a personal epiphany:

> One day I was at my workbench. . . . It was a tedious, mindless job. I was part way through the process when I had one of those flashes of insight, like Moses at the burning bush or Isaiah in the Temple. The truth did not come in segments; rather, like falling in love, it descended in one luminous, existential moment. Suddenly I knew that I would make any sacrifice, pay any price, endure any inconvenience to go back to school and prepare for the ministry. I had to find a place to serve that would nurture the faith of my people, challenge the pervasive injustice, and complete the task of those who died, laboring in the quarries where the rocks were hard indeed.[73]

It was a chance meeting with local white Baptist minister, Dr. Sparks White Melton, while Proctor was working as an elevator operator in a prestigious downtown department store that pointed Proctor toward Crozer Theological Seminary and helped him sustain the costs of getting there.[74]

When Proctor arrived at Crozer in September 1942, he "learned that I was the only black student there. In fact, I was the only black anything there! There was not a black janitor, cook, yardman, or even a black cat or dog. I was it!"[75] Not surprisingly, on the afternoon of that first day, he sought and found more familiar surroundings, as he "sneaked off campus and rode a bus into a black neighborhood. I walked around awhile and ended up getting a haircut from a black barber."[76] Through a strange string of events, Proctor found himself standing face-to-face "with a huge redhead from Fauquay-Varina,

---

72. Ibid., 41.
73. Ibid.
74. Ibid., 43.
75. Ibid. 44.
76. Ibid.

North Carolina, [who] . . . laid a big freckled hand on my shoulder. 'Hi ya doing, fella,' he said. 'I see you have a fresh haircut.' I admitted I had found a barbershop downtown," Samuel recalled. The large, white southerner "squinted his green eyes, poked his finger in my chest, and barked: 'Listen, I'm the barber here. I cut all the hair on this campus. And I'm gonna cut your hair too! If I catch you going downtown again, I'm gonna whip your ass. Heah me?"[77] Behind the tense confrontation and explicit threat of violence, young Proctor heard the strange combination of the racial status quo and progressive Christian ideals about racial equality that would epitomize his experience at Crozer. "It took several days," he recalled, "for me to absorb fully that a North Carolina white boy was going to be my barber."[78]

Proctor encountered racial stereotyping as he reported for his on-campus student employment at Crozer—assigned to work in the seminary kitchen. He wrote,

> My first thought was to give up on these white theologians and go home. But another part of my mind told me to stay right where I was and be the best kitchen help they ever had—and finish my academic work with honors. . . . I felt burdened at times and sometimes tears flowed freely. White people seemed to think I was without feeling, like a robot. And they were scholars of Jesus, who was so filled with compassion. It hurt—not the job itself, but how it had come to me.[79]

In the midst of "those days of doubt and confusion, of wandering and searching," Proctor found "safe harbor at the home of a local Baptist pastor named J. Pius Barbour. Dr. Barbour and his family always had a space for me at their table, and he always had time to sit with me for hours and debate the issues confronting me. . . . He understood my problem, having been a Crozer alumnus himself."[80] Barbour helped and mentored other black Crozer students in this same way, including young Martin Luther King Jr.[81]

Crozer Theological Seminary was also an academic challenge for Proctor, yet opened broader and refreshing vistas: "For me . . . listening to religious scholars who respected scientific data was a relief. Hearing them was like walking through a verdant forest with a mild breeze, birds singing and dancing on solid, ancient rocks. I loved it." Hence, he remembered, "My seminary took the plastic off the Bible,

---

77. Ibid.
78. Ibid.
79. Ibid., 45.
80. Ibid.
81. Ibid.

and made it a living book with a message infinitely stronger than I had ever dreamed possible. . . . The Crozer Theologians showed us how religion could have social and ethical application in the modern world."[82]

Proctor's Crozer experience also enabled him to see and embrace the religion of Jesus and clearly distinguish it from the current state of Christianity as practiced by so many white people:

> My seminary training helped me to see how orthodox, fundamentalist Christians, with its credulous literalism about the Bible, ended up as a religion unrelated to the travails of humans living in the real world. It was a religion that found reasons in the Bible to accept slavery and the subjugation of women; a religion that ignored Jesus, its Lord, and became comfortable with the rich; a religion that subjugated and exploited all of the darker skinned people of the world for the comfort of the whites; a religion that quietly endorsed militarism and bloodshed everywhere. In the hands of the fundamentalists, Christianity had become an embarrassment to Jesus.[83]

Proctor found himself deeply thankful for his seminary experience, which "delivered me from such views [about slavery and the role of women] while leaving my faith in God and the centrality of Jesus firmly in place. Intellectually and spiritually I had a bath, a new awakening. . . . I came out of seminary with a God more powerful, more worthy of praise than when I had entered. I came out with a Bible far more relevant to our spiritual quests."[84]

Upon completing his stellar academic career in the spring of 1945, Proctor recalled, "I left Crozer with a $2,500 John P. Crozer Fellowship to study social ethics at Yale University."[85] But a providential door opened to Proctor, as he found a way to transfer to Boston University and complete his PhD much closer to his family and church. Upon earning his PhD from Boston University in 1950, Proctor embarked upon an academic, pastoral, and professor career of extraordinary impact. In 1950 Dr. Proctor was invited back to Crozer Theological Seminary as a guest speaker. On that occasion, he wrote, "One of my old professors told be about a new student, a bright, promising alumnus of Morehouse College. . . . He was Martin Luther King. . . . It was immediately clear to me that I was talking to a prodigious candidate for leadership."[86] King and Proctor "stayed on

82. Ibid., 47–48.
83. Ibid., 48.
84. Ibid.
85. Ibid., 53.
86. Ibid., 70.

close touch" and ultimately became close friends and coworkers in the struggle for racial equality and social justice in America.[87]

At the same time that the Crozer curriculum was working out its balance between the academic roots and practical application of the Christian witness and ministry—emerging with a strong and persistent emphasis upon both dimensions—the theological landscape began to change dramatically as liberalism came under the criticism of the neo-orthodoxy epitomized by the work of Karl Barth (1886–1962) and many others. Just as the Crozer faculty reached a consensus in 1945–1946 that "we are in agreement that we are primarily interested in training men for the parish ministry,"[88] the Northern Baptist Convention, which was meeting in Grand Rapids, Michigan, at that same time, was riven by "polarized theological positions into separate camps [liberals and conservatives]," even as Baptist churches in the greater Philadelphia area aligned themselves as either "Crozer churches" or "Eastern churches."[89] The division was made along those same liberal and conservative theological lines.

The next Crozer president was Rev. Sankey Lee Blanton (1898–1974). He was educated at Wake Forest, Southern Baptist Theological Seminary, and Andover Newton. His chief contribution to the seminary was his ability to shepherd Crozer into "the present age."[90] With the growing tension between conservative and progressive Northern Baptists and the emergence of conservative Eastern Baptist Seminary literally across town from Crozer, Blanton sought to swing Crozer's focus and faculty toward a more conservative and centrist theological posture. Over the course of three years, the so-called Blanton exodus[91] resulted in professors Enslin, Pritchard, and Dean Charles Batten leaving Crozer for new and perhaps greater vocational opportunities. Martin Luther King Jr. subsequently wrote to a fellow student, Francis Stewart, that he believed that Blanton "was desirous of getting rid of these men from the very beginning. What the outcome will be I don't know. . . . I do hope that it won't be disastrous."[92]

---

87. Ibid., 70–71.
88. R. Melvin Henderson, "Interpreting the New Testament: Morton Scott Enslin," The Voice 60, no. 3 (July 1968): 16–17.
89. Ibid.
90. Keighton, "An Arch Never Sleeps," 7. William Brackney suggests that the intention of attracting progressive Southern Baptists to Crozer, not unlike the parallel development through Proteat at CRDS, was instrumental in Blanton's appointment (personal correspondence, June 16, 2019).
91. Patrick Parr, The Seminarian: Martin Luther King Jr. Comes of Age (Chicago: Lawrence Hill Books, 2018), 207.
92. Clayborne Carson and Tenisha Armstrong, eds., The Papers of Martin Luther King, Jr., 7 vols. (Los Angeles: University of California Press, 2014), 2:280, letter to Francis Stewart, July 26, 1954.

Among those who joined the Crozer faculty under Blanton's leadership was Dr. Kenneth ("Snuffy") Smith, who came as professor of applied Christianity in the fall of 1950. Smith epitomized the Crozer prophetic voice throughout its merger with Colgate Rochester/Bexley Hall in 1970, and he became a leading exponent and commentator on the life and legacy of Crozer's most illustrious and representative alumnus, Martin Luther King Jr.[93]

Ronald V. Wells followed Blanton's presidency, and he shepherded Crozer Theological Seminary from 1962 through its merger with Colgate Rochester/Bexley Hall in 1970. Wells was educated at Denison University and Crozer and then earned his PhD from Columbia in 1942. Coming from a broad range of personal experience, Wells exercised leadership in the development of an innovative and practical curriculum. Writing in October 1967, Wells sounds both prophetic and prescient as he explained, "A seminary is a place where serious study must be undertaken under diligent and rigorous programs of research, analysis, and problem-solving. Where careful self-scrutiny must go on. Where we can test safely new ideas. Where there is action. Only the seminary with clear, workable answers to the questions of how to justify its existence will survive."[94]

Looking back upon his years at Crozer, Wells recalled Martin Luther King Jr. saying that "it was in the classroom at Crozer he began to see the significance of nonviolence and the essential Judeo-Christian ethic for the eradication of the injustice and inequities suffered by the Negro community."[95] In response to the Crozer heritage of prophetic and progressive theological education, and more particularly as that heritage was embodied in the legacy of King, in 1962 "the faculty, administration, and Board of Crozer Seminary decided to create an experimental school for social change, growing out of this tradition but going beyond it in an emerging educational philosophy of professional leadership together with a wide variety of field work experience under trained supervision in areas of social community concern."[96]

The primary objectives of the "King School," as President Wells described them, were to help its students develop an understanding of

---

93. Kenneth L. Smith and Ira G. Zepp, *Search for the Beloved Community: The Thinking of Martin Luther King Jr.* (Valley Forge, PA: Judson Press, 1974).
94. Keighton, "An Arch Never Sleeps," 7-8.
95. Ronald V. Wells, "The Story behind the King School," *The Voice* 60, no. 4 (October 1968): 3.
96. Ibid.

the different theories and techniques of revolutionary social change with an emphasis upon nonviolence; to enable each student to develop his or her own philosophy of social change; to aid students in gaining the skills and techniques to deal with the problems of a world in revolution, and to produce in its students the desire and ability to "function responsibly as professional leaders in organizations and movements working for social change."[97]

As Wells summarized the final years of Crozer at its Upland campus, he noted a drastic change in educational climate during the final decade of the seminary at its historic location: "It was clear that there was no future for the traditional pattern of theological education inherited from the first half of the 20th Century and perpetuated in small independent seminaries."[98] Hence, Crozer mounted a concerted "search for a distinctive emphasis," which led to the development of new and exciting ventures in theological education.[99] Their many new educational ventures, Wells thought, could put Crozer on a stable footing over time, but the economic recession dashed any hopes for an institutional rebound.

The idea of merging Crozer with another seminary reemerged during informal discussions at the Crozer board of trustees meetings in June 1969. At that time, Wells was invited to have lunch with a leading trustee, Mr. Norman Baum, and the chairman—Mr. Crozer himself. Wells was surprised to hear Mr. Baum report, "Mr. Crozer and I think the time has come to merge Crozer with another Seminary."[100] In response, Wells said, "After serious reflection, I came to the conclusion that we needed to explore the possibilities of merger in an open spirit of investigation with no predetermined expectations. Thus we set about this exploration with both Andover Newton Theological School and Colgate Rochester Divinity School. . . . Andover Newton ultimately decided against more definitive talks. As talks continued with Colgate Rochester Trustees were involved and the final agreement formulated."[101]

"A Tentative Draft" of the formal agreement between Crozer and CRDS is extant in CRDS President Bartlett's files. It is a detailed plan describing the step-by-step consolidation of resources and faculties

---

97. Ibid.
98. Wells," "From the President's Desk," 3.
99. Ronald V. Wells, "The Final Years of Crozer Theological Seminary at the Upland Campus, Chester, Pennsylvania, 1962–1970," unpublished typescript, CRCDS archives, 1.
100. Ibid., 9.
101. Ibid.

of the two institutions. Described as an "agreement in principle," it ultimately was accepted by the executive committees of both boards of trustees and implemented with surprising dispatch.[102] Seven members of the Crozer teaching faculty were added to the CRDS staff, and sixty-five to seventy Crozer students relocated to Rochester in time for the 1970 academic year.[103]

Dr. Arthur C. McKay, a Presbyterian, assumed the presidency of the newly formed institution. CRCDS would continue the legacy of both its Baptist constituencies in embracing

> blackness. One-third of the trustees are black . . . six black faculty and more than 40 black students. Black and white coming together in shared power to talk together and live together and study together. To try as brothers and sisters in Christ to understand each other and how they can work together to change an unjust society. But that is not enough. To meet the special needs of the black church—needs too long ignored by most seminaries—the Martin Luther King Program of Black Church Studies was established last year.[104]

At the celebration of the affiliation of the schools, October 26–30, 1970, the Crozer legacy was aptly summarized: "Throughout its history the Seminary has sought to develop ministers both intellectually and socially aware. . . . The Seminary is formally affiliated with the American Baptist Convention, and for years has been ecumenical and inter-racial. . . . Crozer Seminary continues its historic legacy in a new and promising setting, as together the schools seek to meet the Church's challenging needs."[105] No one embodied this vison more effectively than Crozer's famous son, Dr. Martin Luther King Jr. It is to King's own prophetic contribution to the legacy of the school of prophets that we turn our attention in the next chapter.

---

102. "Tentative Draft: Areas of Agreement in Principle Related to the Proposed Affiliations of Crozer Theological Seminary with Colgate Rochester Divinity School," May 15, 1970, Gene Bartlett Letter File, CRCDS archives.
103. Wells, "From the President's Desk," 3.
104. Arthur C. McKay, "Continuity and Contemporaneity: The 1970 Annual Report," Colgate Rochester Divinity School, Bexley Hall, Crozer Theological Seminary," 4.
105. "The Celebration of the Affiliation of Crozer Theological Seminary with Colgate Rochester Divinity School and Bexley Hall," October 28–30, 1970; unpublished program, Crozer Collection, CRCDS archives.

17

Martin Luther King Jr.: Prophet of the Beloved Community

Born in Atlanta, Martin Luther King Jr. (1929–1968) learned lessons in the Jim Crow American South that were not taught in school. Of this experience, he wrote,

> I had grown up abhorring not only segregation but also the oppressive and barbarous acts that grew out of it. I had passed spots where Negroes had been savagely lynched, and had watched the Ku Klux Klan on its rides at night. I had seen police brutality with my own eyes, and watched Negroes receive the most tragic injustice in the courts. All these things had done something to my growing personality. I had come perilously close to resenting all white people. I had also learned that the inseparable twin of racial injustice was economic injustice.[1]

One early, vivid example of young Martin King's memories of the pain of racial prejudice illustrates the challenges of growing up black in America at that time. When he was fifteen-years-old, and a member of the Booker T. Washington High School debating society, he boarded a public bus and headed home from Dublin, Georgia, following a regional contest in that city. King's presentation, "The Negro and the Constitution," won him third prize in the debate. When the bus stopped in Macon, a large group of white passengers boarded the bus, and since there were no seats for some of them, the white bus driver ordered King, his teacher, Mrs. Bradley, and two other African American students to leave their seats and stand in the back of the bus. When they did not move quickly enough, the driver shouted at them, berated them with racial slurs, and loudly ordered them all to

---

1. Martin Luther King Jr., *Stride toward Freedom: The Montgomery Story* (Boston: Beacon Press, 1958), 77.

"Move on out!" King reported his response to this incident in a later interview: "Mrs. Bradley urged me up, saying we had to obey the law. . . . I refused to go to the back of the bus but the teacher pleaded with me. She said it would be advisable. . . . I had to stand all the way to Atlanta. . . .That night will never leave my memory. It was the angriest I have ever been in my life. . . . Suddenly I realized, you don't count, you're nobody."[2]

In the face of daunting social oppression, King's personal identity and religious consciousness were nourished by his deep roots in the black Baptist church tradition. As he recalls in his "Autobiography of Religious Development," written in the autumn of 1950 as an assignment for George Washington Davis's class at Crozer, King reported,

> The church has always been a second home for me. As far back as I can remember I was in church every Sunday. I guess it was inevitable since my father was the pastor of my church, but I never regretted going to church until I passed through a state of skepticism in my second year of college. My best friends were in Sunday School, and it was the Sunday School that helped me build the capacity for getting along with people.[3]

Two early religious experiences shaped young King's life. He wrote,

> The first was the death of my grandmother when I was about nine years old. I was particularly hurt by this incident mainly because of the extreme love I had for her. . . . She assisted greatly in raising all of us. It was after this incident, for the first time that I talked at any length on the doctrine of immortality. My parents attempted to explain it to me and I was assured that somehow my grandmother still lived. I guess this is why today I am such a strong believer in personal immortality.[4]

A second formative incident chronicled by King, from when he was a student, illustrated the intersection of race, religion, and the challenges of growing up as a black person in America. King recalled how his friendship with a white playmate from when he was six years old—one that lasted for over three years—came to a painful collapse as they prepared to enter school together. "The climax came," he remembered, "when he told me one day that this father had demanded that he would not play with me no more. I never will forget what a great shock this was to me. I immediately asked my parents about the

2. Patrick Parr, The Seminarian: Martin Luther King Jr. Comes of Age (Chicago: Lawrence Hill Books, 2018). 4–5.
3. Clayborne Carson and Tenisha Armstrong, eds., The Papers of Martin Luther King Jr., 7 vols. (Berkeley: University of California Press, 1992–2014), 1:361.
4. Ibid., 1:362.

motive behind such a statement. We were at the dinner table when the situation was discussed, and here for the first time I was made aware of the existence of a race problem."[5]

After a painful discussion of the race problem, including examples of the insults and injustices his own parents were confronted with because of it, young King recalled, "I was greatly shocked, and from that moment on I was determined to hate every white person. As I grew older and older this feeling continued to grow. My parents would always tell me that I should not hate the white [man], but it was my duty as a Christian to love him."[6] But this remained an ongoing challenge for King.[7]

In the fall of 1944, King entered Morehouse College in Atlanta, where his "concern for racial and economic justice was already substantial."[8] These Morehouse years "gave King a sense of direction and purpose; it also eased his antagonism toward whites . . . [and] at the same time, Morehouse professors inspired him with their frank discussions about race. They 'encouraged us in a positive quest for solutions to racial ills and for the first time in my life, I realized that nobody was afraid.'"[9] At Morehouse, Martin King found his roots and identity in the black church tradition both affirmed and challenged.

The passion for social change that King found in himself at Morehouse was palpable. Among the resources he studied while trying to imagine a way to improve "the lot of black folks in a white-dominated country"[10] was "Civil Disobedience" by Henry David Thoreau (1817–1862). Describing his own "pilgrimage towards nonviolence," King recalled, "During my student days at Morehouse I read Thoreau's essay 'Civil Disobedience' for the first time. Fascinated by the idea of refusing to cooperate with an evil system, I was so deeply moved that I reread the work several times. This was my first intellectual contact with the theory of nonviolent resistance."[11]

During his senior year in college, King decided to enter into Christian ministry, answering a call he felt "from my later high school days, but accumulated doubts had somewhat blocked the urge. Now

5. Ibid., 1:362.
6. Ibid.
7. Ibid., 1:362-63.
8. King, *Stride toward Freedom*, 78.
9. Stephen B. Oates, "The Intellectual Odyssey of Martin Luther King," *The Massachusetts Review* 22, no. 2 (Summer 1981): 303.
10. Ibid.
11. King, *Stride toward Freedom*, 78.

it appeared again with an inescapable drive."[12] "My call to the ministry," he continued, "was not a miraculous or supernatural something;
on the contrary it was an inner urge calling me to serve humanity."[13]
King also reported, "At the age of 19, I finished college and was
ready to enter the seminary. On coming to the seminary I found it
quite easy to fall in line with the liberal tradition there found, mainly
because I had been prepared for it before coming."[14] For King, at
Morehouse, "the shackles of fundamentalism were removed from my
body. That is why, when I came to Crozer, I could accept the liberal
interpretation with relative ease."[15]

King's interest in Crozer was stimulated by President Aubrey's
baccalaureate speech at Morehouse in 1945 during his second year
there. King's Morehouse mentor, Benjamin Mays, who studied under
Aubrey at the University of Chicago, also favored Crozer. King's bi-
ographer Patrick Parr asserts, "But a far greater influence came from
a family friend with a larger-than-life personality: Rev. J. Pius Barbour. Daddy King and Rev. Barbour likely crossed paths frequently
at major Baptist conventions, and ML, who was often dragged
along to these events from an early age, would have encountered
the gregarious 'northern' preacher throughout his childhood."[16] A
1936 graduate of Crozer, Barbour became pastor at nearby Calvary
Baptist Church in Chester. "Rev. Barbour not only knew Crozer's
course catalog," Parr noted, "he also knew each of the professors
at the school. Barbour was also a 'Morehouse man' (class of 1917),
and he understood ML's desire to leave the south to pursue a broader
educational perspective."[17]

About a month after beginning his studies, King wrote his mother,
Alberta Williams King, saying that he, like Samuel DeWitt Proctor,
became a welcome guest and younger colleague in the home of Rev.
Barbour: "I eat dinner at Barbour's home quite often," he wrote.
"He is full of fun, and he has one of the best minds of anybody I have
ever met."[18] In what sounds like a playful reply to a mother's ques-
tion about studies and social adjustments, King continued, "Since
Barbour told the members of his church that my family was rich, the

---

12. Carson and Armstrong, *King Papers*, 1:363.
13. Ibid.
14. Ibid.
15. Ibid.
16. Parr, *Seminarian*, 13.
17. Ibid.
18. Carson and Armstrong, *King Papers*, "To Alberta Williams King," October 1948, from Chester, PA, 1:161.

girls are running me down. Of course, I don't ever think about them; I am too busy studying."[19] While Martin King professed to being "too busy studying," his grades for his first year at Crozer were not stellar; he earned mostly Bs and Cs.[20]

Despite the great promise that Crozer held for young Martin Luther King, racial tensions were not absent from the Crozer campus. Soon after his arrival in the fall of 1948, King became involved in a heated confrontation with a white student, Lucius Z. Hall, from Hartsville, South Carolina, who had "the preconceived notions of a nineteenth-century southern white man. Lucius had no qualms about calling black students 'darkies' or appreciating the history of the Confederate flag."[21] Hall was also a practical joker who could not take a joke. When he was secretly pranked by several of the incoming students, Hall mistakenly assumed King's responsibility and confronted him with a loaded revolver while he sat studying at his desk: "'Martin . . . I'm gonna kill you.' Lucius said, his gun pointed and ready. "ML remained silent," Parr reported, "attached to his book like one would be to a shield."[22] It took more than an hour, and the careful intervention of several other students, white and black, to defuse the situation and convince Lucius Hall to give up his gun.[23]

By his second year in the seminary, King established a reputation as an exemplary student, earning all As in his courses senior year.[24] His written work evidenced that his studies also progressed well. A lengthy paper titled "The Significant Contributions of Jeremiah to Religious Thought," for example, which King wrote in that first semester for James Pritchard's Old Testament course, showed careful academic reflection as well as an ability to see prophetic vistas in the Bible that affect the modern age. In his view, the prophet Jeremiah exemplified what was best in "any religion"; "we must admit that men like Jeremiah are valuable to any religion. Religion, in a sense, through men like Jeremiah, provides for its own advancement, and carries within it the promise of progress and renewed power."[25] But there was also a steep price to pay by the social prophet, King observed, sounding prophetic as he asked, "What is societies [sic]

---

19. Ibid.
20. Carson and Armstrong, King Papers, chart titled "Courses at Crozer Theological Seminary," 1:48.
21. Parr, Seminarian, 20.
22. Ibid., 22.
23. Ibid., 20–24, for a fuller account.
24. Carson and Armstrong, King Papers, 1:48.
25. Ibid., 1:194.

reaction to such men? It has reacted, and always will react, in the only way open to it. It destroys such men. Jeremiah died a martyr."[26] Professor Pritchard assigned a B+ to King's research paper and added the comment, "You have made good use of the commentaries available to you and have written with enthusiasm in a convincing manner."[27]

About a year later, in the autumn of 1949, King took Dr. George Washington Davis's course Christian Theology Today. Davis was professor of systematic theology and a native of Pittsburgh whose father was involved in the unionist struggles in the city. His life experience drew him to RTS and the social activism of Walter Rauschenbusch. After earning his PhD in theology at Yale Divinity School, Davis began his teaching career at Crozer. In a letter he wrote to Davis while a doctoral student at Boston University, King averred, "I must admit that my theological and philosophical studies with you have been of tremendous help to me in my present studies. In the most decisive moments, I find your influence creeping through."[28] Of the 110 quarter hours of course work required for the Crozer's bachelor of divinity, King took 34 of them under Davis's instruction.[29] King's papers for Davis evidenced solid thought as well as a brutal honesty about religion and race; but they also showed a carelessness regrading formal academic citation that would follow him through the years.[30]

An evangelical liberal, Davis taught King theology and church history, having him read works like William Newton Clarke's *An Outline of Christian Theology* and the writings of Walter Rauschenbusch.[31] Walter Fluker identified the main theological themes of Davis's thought that most influenced Martin Luther King: "1) the existence of a moral order in the universe, 2) the activity of God in history; 3) the value of the personal; 4) the social character of human existence; and 5) the ethical nature of the Christian faith."[32] John J.

---

26. Ibid., 1:195.
27. Ibid., 1:181.
28. Kenneth L. Smith and Ira G. Zepp, *Search for the Beloved Community: The Thinking of Martin Luther King Jr.* (Valley Forge, PA: Judson Press, 1974), 20.
29. Ibid., 21.
30. See Clayborne Carson, Peter Holloran, Ralph E. Luker, and Penny Russell, "Martin Luther King, Jr., as Scholar: A Reexamination of His Theological Writings," *Journal of American History* 78, no. 1 (June 1991): 93–105; David J. Garrow, "King's Plagiarism: Imitation, Insecurity, and Transformation," *Journal of American History* 78, no. 1 (June 1991): 86–92; and Ralph Luker, "Plagiarism and Perspective: Questions about Martin Luther King, Jr.," *International Social Science Review* 68, no. 4 (Fall 1993): 152–60, for example.
31. Smith and Zepp, *Search for the Beloved Community*, 22–23.
32. Walter E. Fluker, *They Looked for a City: A Comparative Analysis of the Ideal of Community in the Thought of Howard Thurman and Martin Luther King Jr.* (Lanham, MD: University Press of America, 1989), 102. See also Smith and Zepp, *Search for the Beloved Community*, 21–31.

Ansboro further credits Davis with introducing King to theological personalism, which King pursued at length under his graduate professors at Boston University, and the central role *agape* plays in living the Christian faith. Davis's distinctive imprint upon King's theology of love was to merge it with Rauschenbusch's emphasis upon the corporate nature of all life.[33] Davis explained succinctly, "God intends all human life to achieve solidarity."[34] Here we find a distant echo of King's own concept of "the beloved community."

King wrote a research paper for Davis's course Christian Theology Today titled "The Sources of Fundamentalism and Liberalism Considered Historically and Psychologically." In his paper, King concluded, "It seems quite obvious that Liberal Theology resulted from man's attempt to answer new problems of cultural and social change. It was an attempt to bring religion up intellectually."[35] Fundamentalism stood in stark contrast to the contemporary emphasis and progressive attitude of liberalism. "Unlike liberalism," King explained, "fundamentalism is essentially a reactionary protest, fighting to preserve the old faith in a changing milieu."[36]

King wrote of the fundamentalist approach to the Bible: "The use of the critical method in approach to the Bible is to the fundamentalist downright heresy."[37] This approach failed to understand human personhood and the problems that plague human society. Against the fallen, flawed, and negative view of humans, King posited, "'Each human personality . . . is the object of divine love and holds in himself the possibility of a son of God' [quoting Theodore Sores, from *Three Typical Beliefs*]. This is essentially the liberal view toward man."[38] This project also received a B+ from Davis, along with a note: "You do not do justice to this. Think of what the psychological factors are which lie back of these two movements."[39]

King also encountered the writings of Walter Rauschenbusch during his second year at Crozer. "In the early 1950's I read Walter Rauschenbusch's *Christianity and the Social Crisis*," he later wrote, "a book which left an indelible imprint on my thinking."[40] King described its impact in this way:

33. John J. Ansbro, *Martin Luther King Jr.: The Making of a Mind* (Maryknoll, NY: Paulist Press, 1982), 15–18.
34. George W. Davis, "Some Theological Continuities in the Crisis Theology," *Crozer Quarterly* 27, no. 3 (July 1950): 218.
35. Carson and Armstrong, *King Papers*, 1:240.
36. Ibid.
37. Ibid., 1:241.
38. Ibid., 1:240.
39. Ibid., 1:236.
40. Martin Luther King Jr., *The Strength to Love* (Philadelphia: Fortress, 1963), 149.

> Rauschenbusch gave to American Protestantism a sense of social responsibility that it should never lose. The gospel at its best deals with the whole man, not only his soul but also his body, not only his spiritual well-being but also his material well-being. A religion that professes a concern about the souls of men and is not equally concerned about the slums that damn them, the economic conditions that strangle them, and the social conditions that cripple them, is a spiritually moribund religion.[41]

Rauschenbusch's emphasis on the whole person was clearly evidenced in King's *Stride toward Freedom*, where he asserted,

> The church must also become increasingly active in social action outside its doors. . . . It must take an active stand against the injustice that Negroes confront in housing, education, police protection, and in city and state courts. It must exert its influence in the area of economic justice. As a guardian of the moral and spiritual life of the community the church cannot look with indifference upon these glaring evils.[42]

Martin Luther King also strongly embraced Rauschenbusch's assertion that the kingdom of God is the center of Jesus' preaching and, therefore, that community is the aim and goal of Christian faith and practice. For Rauschenbusch, the purpose of Christianity is "to transform society into the Kingdom of God by regenerating all human relations and reconstituting them in accordance with the will of God."[43] This would become the foundational insight upon which King built his own concept of "the beloved community." But King's appropriation of Rauschenbusch was not blind to his "shortcomings."

King both critiqued and augmented the social analysis he found in Rauschenbusch. Over Christmas break of 1949, King studied *Das Kapital* and *The Communist Manifesto*. "In reading such communist writings," he intimated, "I drew certain conclusions that have remained with me as convictions to this day."[44] King's assessment was critical yet also affirmative: "In so far as Marx posited a metaphysical materialism, an ethical relativism, and a strangulating totalitarianism, I respond with an unambiguous 'no,' but in so far as he pointed to weaknesses of traditional capitalism, contributed to the growth of a definite self-consciousness in the masses, and challenged

41. Ibid.
42. King, *Stride toward Freedom*, 203.
43. Walter Rauschenbusch, *A Theology for the Social Gospel* (New York: Macmillan, 1917), 131.
44. King, *Stride toward Freedom*, 79.

the social conscience of the Christian churches, I responded with a definite 'yes.'"[45]

As he accepted and embraced the liberal tradition, King also critiqued and corrected some aspects of it. His critique of Rauschenbusch's theology came through King's close encounter with the writings of Reinhold Niebuhr in the Crozer Seminary course Christian Social Philosophy II, which he took under the direction of Dr. Kenneth L. Smith.[46] In Niebuhr's "Christian realism," King found a balance between the unguarded optimism of liberalism and the narrow rationalism of fundamentalism. He was particularly influenced by Niebuhr's assessment of the state of individuals and their societies:

> Niebuhr has extraordinary insight into human nature, especially the behavior of nations and social groups. He is keenly aware of the complexity of human motives and of the relation between morality and power. His theology is a persistent reminder of the reality of sin in every level of human existence. These elements of Niebuhr's thinking helped me recognize the illusions of superficial optimism concerning human nature and the dangers of a false idealism.[47]

While not losing his earlier optimism about human potential and his passion for social reform, King's was a chastened optimism: "While I still believed in man's potential for good, Niebuhr made me realize his potential for evil as well. Moreover, Niebuhr made me to recognize the complexity of man's social involvement and the glaring reality of collective evil."[48]

Another aspect of young King's thought that was affected by the theology of Reinhold Niebuhr was his critique of pacifism. King explored the idea of nonviolent social change as an expression of the Christian gospel after reading Thoreau's essay on civil disobedience at Morehouse. This trajectory continued at Crozer when several resources and people coalesced to continue his inquiry. "During my stay at Crozer," King wrote, "I was exposed for the first time to the pacifist position in a lecture by Dr. A. J. Muste. I was deeply moved by Dr. Muste's talk but far from convinced of the practicality of his position. Like most students at Crozer, I felt that while war could never be a positive or absolute good, it could serve as a negative good in the sense of preventing the spread and growth of evil force."[49]

---

45. Ibid., 82.
46. Cf. Smith and Zepp, *Search for the Beloved Community*, 71, and Carson and Armstrong, *King Papers*, 1:48.
47. King, *Stride toward Freedom*, 87.
48. Ibid.
49. Ibid., 83.

A second event occurred in the spring of 1950, when King heard an address on Gandhi and his nonviolent philosophy given by Mordecai Wyatt Johnson, who "had just returned from a trip to India, and to my great interest spoke of the life and teachings of Mahatma Gandhi. His message was so profound and electrifying that I left the meeting and bought a half dozen books on Gandhi's life and works." [50] King described the personal satisfaction he found in reading Gandhi's works:

> Gandhi was probably the first person in history to live the love ethic of Jesus above mere interaction between individuals to a powerful and effective social force on a large scale. Love for Gandhi was a potent instrument for social and collective transformation. It was in this Ghandian emphasis on love and nonviolence that I discovered the method for social reform that I had been seeking for many months. [51]

Still enthralled by Gandhi's philosophy of nonviolent social change, King wrote a research paper on it the next fall semester. [52] While this paper did not survive, one available paper from the second semester of his senior year on "War and Pacifism" clearly evidenced the impact of Niebuhr's critique of Christian pacifism. King concluded,

> It seems to me that we must recognize the presence of sin in man and that it can be done without seeing that there is also good. Since man is so often sinful there must be some coercions to keep one man from injuring his fellows. This is just as true between nations as it is between individuals. If one nation oppresses another a Christian nation must, in order to express love of neighbor, help protect the oppressed. This does not relieve us of our obligation to the enemy nation. We are obliged to treat them in such a way as to reclaim them to a useful place in the world community after they have been prevented from oppressing another. We must not seek revenge. [53]

Upon his own closer study of Gandhi's thought, King developed a new point of view by infusing it with his own ideas about the transforming power of Christian *agape*. His understanding of Gandhi's approach to nonviolent resistance carried King past an impasse he had found in Niebuhr's thought. He explained, "At first Niebuhr's critique of pacifism left me in a state of confusion. As I continued to read, however, I came to see more and more the shortcomings of his position. For instance, many of his statements revealed that he interpreted pacifism as a sort of passive nonresistance to evil expressing naïve

---

50. Ibid., 84.
51. Ibid., 84–85.
52. Smith and Zegg, *Search for the Beloved Community*, 45–46.
53. Carson and Armstrong, *King Papers*, 1:435.

trust in the power of love."[54] "My study of Gandhi," King recounted, "convinced me that true pacifism is not nonresistance to evil, but nonviolent resistance to evil. Between the two positions there is a world of difference. Gandhi resisted evil with as much vigor and power as the violent resister, but he resisted with love instead of hate."[55]

King was convinced that Niebuhr had misunderstood pacifism: "True pacifism is not unrealistic submission to evil power, as Niebuhr contends. It is rather a courageous confrontation of evil by the power of love, in the faith that it is better to be the recipient of violence than the inflictor of it, since the latter only multiplies the existence of violence and bitterness in the universe."[56]

King described his new understanding of pacifism as love in action as his "pilgrimage to nonviolence." He explained, "As I delved deeper into the philosophy of Gandhi, my skepticism concerning the power of love gradually diminished, and I came to see for the first time that the Christian doctrine of love, operating through the Gandhian method of nonviolence, is one of the most potent weapons available to an oppressed people in their struggle for freedom."[57]

During his years at Crozer, King's encounters with racial barriers and tensions continued as he formed a romantic relationship with a white woman, Betty Moitz, an art student at Moore College of Art, just across the river from Crozer. Betty was a frequent visitor to the Crozer campus because her mother, "Miss Hannah," was in charge of the seminary kitchen. In an interview given long after this time, Betty remembered, "One thing ML knew at age nineteen was that he could change the world."[58] Even beyond the challenges of their biracial relationship, they encountered further complications when King discovered that Moitz had seriously dated Kenneth Smith prior to his professorship at Crozer. Over time King was convinced, through the painful intervention of several friends, to end their romance. King's mentor, Rev. Barbour, was one of those who counseled strongly against their courtship. "He 'was a man of a broken heart,'" Barbour remembered. He never recovered."[59]

---

54. King, *Stride toward Freedom*, 86.
55. Ibid. 87.
56. Ibid., 88.
57. King, *Strength to Love*, 150.
58. Parr, *Seminarian*, 54.
59. Ibid., 154. For the text of this interview with Rev. Barbour, see David J. Garrow, *Bearing the Cross: Martin Luther King, Jr. and the Southern Christian Leadership Conference* (New York: William Morrow and Company, 1986), 41.

By the beginning of his senior year at Crozer, King began to gravitate to the idea of pursuing doctoral studies. He still intended to return to the South as a Baptist preacher of the gospel of social and economic justice, but he also hoped to fulfill that role as a preacher who evidenced both spiritual power and keen intellect. On January 11, 1951, Martin King received an acceptance letter from Boston University. His mentors and friends, professors Davis and Smith, advocated for Boston, and King's parents were glad when he decided to accept the offer a month later.[60]

When King graduated from Crozer Theological Seminary on May 8, 1951, it was, as Parr describeed it, "a day of honors . . . First his divinity degree, then the J. Lewis Crozer Fellowship, and the icing on the cake, the Pearl Ruth Plafker Memorial Award."[61] The latter was a $50 cash award given to "that student of the senior class who, in the judgment of the faculty, has maintained throughout his course of study in the Seminary a good academic record, and who has by his character and cooperation, made a distinct contribution to the community life of the campus."[62] The honor of the award meant much more than the $50 prize that came with it, and King set off for Boston with all the acclaim that Crozer could give him.

King went to Boston University intending to study theological ethics with Edgar S. Brightman. In his application King wrote: "My particular interest in Boston University can be summed up in two statements. First my thinking in philosophical areas has been greatly shaped by some of the faculty members there, particularly Dr. Brightman. For this reason I have longed for the possibility of studying with him. Secondly, my present professor is a graduate of Boston University, and his great influence over me has turned my eyes toward his former school."[63]

At Boston University, King took fifteen graduate courses that built upon the theological foundation that he laid while at Crozer.[64] Brightman's ill health and sudden death prohibited sustained contact with him, but a replacement was found in Professor L. Harold DeWolf, a leading theological exponent of Boston Personalism. King explained the lasting impact of these men: "This personal idealism remains

---

60. Parr, Seminarian, 171–78.
61. Ibid., 207.
62. Crozer Theological Seminary Annual Catalogue 42, no. 1 (January 1950).
63. Carson and Armstrong, King Papers, 1:390.
64. Smith and Zepp, Search for the Beloved Community, 99–100.

today my basic philosophical position. Personalism's insistence that only personality—finite and infinite—is ultimately real strengthened me in two convictions; it gave me metaphysical and philosophical grounding for the idea of a personal God, and it gave me a metaphysical basis for the dignity and worth of all human personality."[65]

In Boston Personalism, King also found an important corrective to Reinhold Niebuhr's pervasively negative view of human nature and potential. King described the impact of personalism on his thought in graduate school: "It was at Boston University that I came to see that Niebuhr had overemphasized the corruption of human nature. His pessimism concerning human nature was not balanced by an optimism concerning divine grace. He was so involved in diagnosing man's sickness of sin that he overlooked the cure of grace."[66] Leo Sandon summarized the impact of this view point upon the life and thought of Martin Luther King:

> Personalistic motifs are to be found in much of King's rhetoric, such as the "sacredness of human personality," "the legacy of dignity and worth," to which all persons are heir, and his frequent reference to "the moral laws of the universe." There is no theme more prominent in King's thought than his belief in the intrinsic dignity and worth of personality. This belief provided the theological and philosophical basis for his attack upon segregation.[67]

To his appreciation of personalism, King added the philosophical methodology of Georg Friedrich Hegel (1770–1831). He read *Phenomenology of Mind*, *History of Philosophy*, and *Philosophy of Right*[68] under the direction of Brightman, and perhaps also Peter Bertocci.[69] King found that "there were many points in Hegel's philosophy that I strongly disagreed with . . . there were other aspects of his thinking that I found stimulating. His contention that 'truth is the whole' led me to a philosophical method of rational coherence. His analysis of the dialectical process, in spite of its shortcomings, helped me to see that growth comes through struggle."[70] "His analysis of the dialectical process, in spite of its shortcomings, helped me to see that growth comes through struggle."[71]

---

65. King, *Stride toward Freedom*, 88.
66. Ibid.
67. Leo A. Sandon, "Boston University Personalism and Southern Baptist Theology," *Foundations* 20, no. 2 (April–June, 1977): 106.
68. King, *Stride toward Freedom*, 88–89.
69. Smith and Zepp, *Search for the Beloved Community*, 115.
70. King, *Stride toward Freedom*, 89.
71. Ibid.

Even in the midst of the challenges of the Montgomery bus boycott, King followed Hegel's analytical method to find "a third way" forward that neither acquiesced to racial injustice nor resorted to violence in the quest for equal rights. "The third way open to oppressed people in their quest for freedom," King observed, "is the way of nonviolent resistance. Like the synthesis in Hegelian philosophy, the principle of nonviolent resistance seeks to reconcile the truths of two opposites—acquiescence and violence—while avoiding the extremes and immoralities of both."[72] Applying this philosophy directly to the predicament of people of color in America, King concluded, "It seems to me that this is the method that must guide the actions of the Negro in the present crisis in race relations."[73]

With the formal portion of his doctoral studies behind him, in 1954 King stepped back into full-time pastoral ministry while completing his doctoral dissertation. He recalled,

> The major job that remained was to write my doctoral thesis. In the meantime, I felt that it would be wise to start considering a job. I was not sure what area of the ministry I wanted to settle down in. I had had a great deal of satisfaction in the pastorate and had almost come to the point of feeling that I could render my service in this area. I could never quite get the idea out of my mind that I should do some teaching, yet I felt a great deal of satisfaction with the pastorate.[74]

By January 24, 1954, King found himself driving from his parents' home in Atlanta to Montgomery, Alabama, to visit Dexter Avenue Baptist Church as its potential pastor. The next day, he preached a trial sermon before the congregation, "The Three Dimensions of Complete Life," and he felt that "the congregation was receptive."[75] One month later he received a written invitation to become the pastor at Dexter Avenue Baptist Church, as well as a call from a prominent church in Detroit. In response to these two offers, King recalled, "At this time I was torn in two directions. On the one hand I was inclined toward the pastorate; on the other hand, toward educational work. Which way should I go?"[76] After much soul searching, prayer, and deep conversation with his new wife, Coretta Scott King, the decision was made: "We agreed that, in spite of the disadvantages

72. Ibid., 208.
73. Ibid., 209.
74. Clayborne Carson, ed., *The Autobiography of Martin Luther King Jr.* (New York: Grand Central Publishing, 1998), 41.
75. Ibid., 43.
76. Ibid., 44.

and inevitable sacrifices, our greatest service could be rendered in our native South. We came to the conclusion that we had something of a moral obligation to return—at least for a few years."[77]

Martin Luther King preached his first sermon as pastor at Dexter Avenue in May of 1954. He told the congregation,

> I come to you with only the claim of being a servant of Christ, and a feeling of dependence on his grace for my leadership. I come with a feeling that I have been called to preach and to lead God's people. I have felt like Jeremiah, "the word of God is in my heart like a burning fire shut up in my bones." I have felt with Amos that the Spirit of the Lord is upon me, because he hath anointed me to preach the gospel to the poor, to heal the brokenhearted, to preach deliverance to the captives, and to set at liberty those that are bound.[78]

He soon completed his doctoral studies at Boston University, and with the acceptance of his PhD dissertation, "A Comparison of God in the Thinking of Paul Tillich and Henry Nelson Wieman," King graduated on June 5, 1955.

On December 1 of the same year, Mrs. Rosa Parks was arrested in Montgomery for refusing to relinquish her seat on a public bus to a white male. By the next morning, due to his role in the local National Association for the Advancement of Colored People (NAACP) and leadership in the African American community in Montgomery, King found himself deeply involved in the Montgomery bus boycott. It was a struggle that would begin the long process of bringing the evils of racial segregation and oppression to the attention of the nation for the purposes of redress and systemic change.[79]

The dire and dangerous events in those early days of "the struggle" in Montgomery became a sanctuary in which Martin Luther King found a renewed sense of God's presence in the midst of trial. After receiving yet another death threat by phone in the middle of the night, King was unable to sleep. Pacing the floor, he eventually went to the kitchen and heated a pot of coffee. "It seemed to me that all my fears had come down upon me at once," he recalled. "I had reached my saturation point."[80] In the midst of his despair, King turned his kitchen table into an altar before God:

---

77. Ibid.
78. Ibid., 46.
79. See, for example, Garrow, *Bearing the Cross*, 11–83, for a detailed account of the Montgomery bus boycott.
80. King, *Strength to Love*, 113.

My head in my hands, I bowed over the kitchen table and prayed aloud. The words I spoke to God that midnight are still vivid in my memory. "I am here taking a stand for what I believe is right. But now I am afraid. The people are looking to me for leadership, and if I stand before them without strength and courage, they too will falter. I am at the end of my powers. I have nothing left. I've come to the point where I can't face it alone." At that moment I experienced the presence of the Divine as I had never before experienced him. It seemed as though I could hear the quiet assurance of an inner voice saying, "Stand up for righteousness, stand up for truth. God will be at your side forever." Almost at once my fears began to pass from me. My uncertainty disappeared. I was ready to face anything. The outer situation remained the same, but God had given me inner calm.[81]

Three nights later, King's house was bombed while he led a rally in support of nonviolent resistance. Fortunately, his wife, Coretta, and their young daughter, Yoki, were unharmed, and the message went forth undaunted. The Montgomery bus protest, he told stamping, clapping crowds,

"is really noncooperation with evil. And the Christian doctrine of love is our regulating ideal. We must love our enemies in the sense of disinterested love for all mankind. For us, violence is both impractical and immoral. We must meet physical force with soul force, for unearned suffering is redemptive. We must not humiliate the white man, but win him over through our love for him and our faith in God. Our ultimate goal is not to gain a victory for 50,000 Negros, but to restore 'the beloved community.' For love not only avoids the internal violence of the spirit, but severs the external chain of hatred that only produces more hatred in an unending spiral; somebody must be willing to break the chain of hatred so that brotherhood can begin."[82]

King's conception of "the beloved community" became the ideal, the goal, and the mission of his struggle against racial injustice, economic oppression, rampant militarism, and violence in America. Walter Fluker described the roots of King's vision: "For him, the beloved community is synonymous with the kingdom of God. He draws upon several significant sources for his understanding of community. Most notable are personal idealism, evangelical liberal theology, and 'the black Christian tradition.'"[83] Announced and powerfully articulated many times and in many places for more than a decade, "the beloved community" permeates King's "I Have a Dream" speech, delivered on August 28, 1963, from the steps of the Lincoln Memorial before more than two hundred fifty thousand people at the March on Washington for "Jobs and Freedom." He told the multitude,

---

81. Ibid., 114.
82. Oates, "Intellectual Odyssey," 317, quoting directly from various King sources.
83. Fluker, *They Looked for a City*, 113-14.

I have a dream today. I have a dream that one day every valley shall be exalted, every hill and mountain shall be made low, the rough places will be made plain and the crooked places will be made straight and the glory of the Lord shall be revealed and all flesh shall see it together.

This is our hope. This is the faith that I will go back to the South with. With this faith we will be able to hew out of the mountain of despair a stone of hope.

With this faith we will be able to transform the jangling discords of our nation into a beautiful symphony of brotherhood. With this faith we will be able to work together, to pray together, to struggle together, to go to jail together, to stand up for freedom together, knowing that we will be free one day.

This will be the day, this will be the day when all of God's children will be able to sing with new meaning, "My country 'tis of thee, sweet land of liberty, of thee I sing. Land where my fathers died, land of the pilgrim's pride, from every mountainside, let freedom ring!" And if America is to be a great nation, this must become true.[84]

In his last major literary work, *Where Do We Go from Here: Chaos or Community?*, King's social-theological vision for the establishment of "the beloved community" remained intact, but his optimism, born in the experience of God's faithfulness and grace, was tempered by the stark Christian realism regarding the enormity of the task ahead. Here emerged the full scope of his vision; the civil rights struggle was a struggle for equality for all people, which included—and in fact, demanded—both economic justice for all Americans and a willingness to spurn militarism as a way of life. Naming the barriers that lay ahead, King declared, "For the evils of racism, poverty, and militarism to die, a new set of values must be born. Our economy must become more person-centered than property- and profit-centered. Our government must spend more on its moral power than on its military power."[85] Using the metaphor of a "large world house," he described both the values and the shape of "the beloved community" in our modern, technological age:

> We must rapidly begin the shift from a "thing"-oriented society to a "person"-oriented society. When machines and computers, profit motives and property rights are considered more important than people, the giant triplets of racism, materialism and militarism are incapable of being conquered. A civilization can flounder as readily in the face of moral and spiritual bankruptcy as it can through financial bankruptcy.[86]

As King's vision of "the beloved community" broadened, in the popular mind at least, to clearly include matters like poverty and war, his support began to wane. When he stressed that jobs, employment

84. Carson, *Autobiography of King*, 226–27.
85. Martin Luther King Jr., *Where Do We Go from Here: Chaos or Community?* (New York: Harper & Row, 1967), 142.
86. Ibid., 196–97.

opportunity, equal education, and the elevation out of poverty were all intimately related to "the struggle" for civil rights, popular support began to fade away. But when King attacked the war in Vietnam on April 4, 1967 (exactly one year before his murder), in "Beyond Vietnam," former allies from all across America deserted him. Yet he clearly saw the war as intimately related to the overall project of social reform:

> I watched this program broken and eviscerated as if it were some idle political plaything of a society gone mad on war. And I knew that America would never invest the necessary funds or energies in rehabilitation of its poor so long as adventures like Vietnam continued to draw men and skills and money like some demonic destructive suction tube. So I was increasingly compelled to see the war as an enemy of the poor and to attack it as such.[87]

When King was murdered in Memphis on April 4, 1968, he was leading a demonstration in support of the economic equality and working conditions of the city's sanitation workers. In a message shaped by the parable of poor Lazarus, who died at a rich man's gate (Luke 16), King told the Memphis workers and all America:

> And I come by here to say that America too is going to hell if she doesn't use her wealth. If America does not use her vast resources of wealth to end poverty and make it possible for all of God's children to have the basic necessities of life, she too will go to hell. . . .
> It seems to me that I can hear the God of the universe saying . . . "I was hungry and you fed me not. I was naked and you clothed me not. The children of my sons and daughters were in need of economic security and you didn't provide it for them. And so you cannot enter the kingdom of greatness." This may well be the indictment on America. And that same voice says in Memphis to the mayor, to the power structure, "if you do it unto the least of these my children you do it unto me."
> Having to live under the threat of death every day, sometimes I feel discouraged. Having to take so much abuse and criticism, sometimes from my own people, sometimes I feel discouraged. Having to go to bed so often frustrated with the chilly winds of adversity about to stagger me, sometimes I feel discouraged and feel my life's work's in vain.
> But there the Holy Spirit revives my soul again. In Gilead, there is a balm to make the wounded whole. If we will believe that, we will build a new Memphis. And bring about the day when every valley shall be exalted. Every mountain and hill will be made low. The rough places will be made plain, and the crooked places straight. And the glory of the Lord shall be revealed, and all flesh shall see it together.[88]

Martin Luther King's death occurred almost on the eve of his Poor People's Campaign, through which he planned for a "multiracial

87. Carson, *Autobiography of King*, 337.
88. Ibid., 353–54.

army of the poor" to present an "economic bill of rights" to Congress in Washington. King's economic agenda, as articulated in *Where Do We Go from Here?* included a revolutionary restructuring of the American economic system that included full employment and a guaranteed basic income for all Americans.[89] It, too, was deemed so radical that it cost him considerable support within the civil rights movement and especially angered wealthy white Americans.

As he prepared for what would become his final campaign, King drew upon themes based on his understanding of "the beloved community," to call upon America to turn from racism and economic oppression to embrace the luminous vision of its own democratic destiny:

> The American people are infected with racism, that is the peril. Paradoxically they are also infected with democratic ideals—that is the hope. While doing wrong, they have the potential to do right. But they do not have a millennium to make the changes. Nor have they a choice of continuing in the old way. The future they are asked to inaugurate is not so unpalatable that it justifies the evils that best the nation. To end poverty, to extirpate prejudice, to free a tormented conscience, to make a tomorrow of justice, fair play, and creativity—all these are worthy of the American ideal.[90]

Turning his attention to the community of faith, King urged fellow Christians to truly embrace the revolutionary character of the way of Jesus.

> The great tragedy is that Christianity failed to see that it had the revolutionary edge. You don't have to go to Karl Marx to learn how to be a revolutionary. I didn't get my inspiration from Karl Marx; I got it from a man named Jesus, a Galilean saint who said he was anointed to heal the broken-hearted. He was anointed to deal with the problems of the poor. And that is where we get our inspiration. And we go out in a day when we have a message for the world, and we can change this world, and we can change this nation.[91]

The evening before he was assassinated, April 3, 1968, Dr. King delivered a prophetic message at Mason Temple Baptist Church in Memphis. This sermon was called "Unfilled Dreams" because of its frank assessment of how little had been accomplished in the war against racism, poverty, and violence and how much remained to be done. The situation reminded him of Paul's unfulfilled desire to minister in Spain (Romans 15:24-28).

---

89. King, *Where Do We Go from Here?* 172-75.
90. Carson, *Autobiography of King*, 350-51.
91. Ibid., 351.

In Martin Luther King's view, the "unfulfilled dreams" of building a new America devoid of racism, poverty, and violence fit well into this same legacy: "Some of us are trying to build a temple of peace. We speak out against war, we protest, but it seems that your head is going against a concrete wall. It seems to mean nothing. And so you are left discouraged; you are left bewildered."[92] But delay did not signify defeat to King, and hope is rekindled by the presence of God in the midst of the struggle. He sensed the voice of God saying, "'It may not come today or it may not come tomorrow, but it is well that it is within thine heart. It's well that you are trying. You may not see it. The dream may not be fulfilled, but it's just good that you have a desire to bring it into reality. It's well that it's in thine heart."[93] After a quick survey of the struggle of good against evil throughout human history, the preacher concluded, "In the final analysis, God knows that his children are weak and they are frail. In the final analysis, what God requires is that your heart is right."[94]

King recounted the many struggles of people of faith who tried to do the will of God and pressed on, even under extremely difficult circumstances. The recent struggles of God's people for civil rights in Montgomery, Birmingham, and now in Memphis all fit into this same great panorama. Moving from diagnosis to prescription, the preacher looked to Jesus' parable of the Good Samaritan as a model for his listeners. Dr. King urged, "The question before you tonight . . . is not, 'if I stop to help this man in need, what will happen *to me?*' The question is, 'if I do not stop to help the sanitation workers, what will happen *to them?*' That's the question." The way forward was equally clear to King: "Let us rise up tonight with a greater readiness. Let us stand with greater determination. And let us move on in these powerful days, these days of challenge, to make America what it ought to be. We have an opportunity to make America a better nation. And I want to thank God, once more, for allowing me to be here with you."[95]

After recounting the bomb threats and extra security precautions that were associated with his recent flight from Atlanta to Memphis, King returned rhetorically to Moses' prophetic leadership of the Hebrew people to express his own sense of morality—stated with an

92. Ibid., 357.
93. Ibid.
94. Ibid., 358.
95. Ibid., 363.

utter directness that reflects a premonition of what lay immanently ahead of him:

> I don't know what will happen now; we've got some difficult days ahead. But it really doesn't matter with me now, because I've been to the mountaintop. And I don't mind. Like anybody, I would like to live a long life—longevity has its place. But I'm not concerned about that now. I just want to do God's will. And He's allowed me to go up to the mountain. And I've looked over, and I've seen the promised land. I may not get there with you. But I want you to know tonight, that we as a people, will get to the promised land.[96]

Martin Luther King's prophetic vision for God's people was encapsulated in his understanding of human life as "the beloved community." Fluker rightly termed this the "the single organizing principle of King's life and thought."[97] It was a vision for all people that was born in response to the African American experience of segregation and racial prejudice, and it was rooted in King's profound faith in God and developed through his formative educational experiences—perhaps most especially at Crozer Theological Seminary. Nurtured by his black Baptist roots, King was shaped by the evangelical liberalism of Crozer along with the social gospel. He was also a man of his own making who drew upon the teachings and example of Jesus and the Hebrew prophets, upon Rauschenbusch, Gandhi, Marx, and Hegel—and many others—to give both expression and significant extension to the prophetic Christian legacy which is the focus of this inquiry. King was not primarily a social reformer; he was a prophetic and pastoral Christian leader whose distinctive theological vision both fueled and impelled the impetus for making a better world, with God's help, by building "the beloved community." As he said so powerfully on the eve of the Montgomery bus boycott in 1955, "Our ultimate goal is not to gain a victory for 50,000 Negros, but to restore 'the beloved community.' For love not only avoids the internal violence of the spirit, but severs the external chain of hatred that only produces more hatred in an unending spiral; somebody must be willing to break the chain of hatred so that brotherhood can begin."[98]

---

96. Ibid., 365.
97. Fluker, *They Looked for a City*, 159.
98. Oates, "Intellectual Odyssey," 317.

18

The Prophetic Witness amid the Winds of Change

The ongoing struggles of the Divinity School from the early 1970s onward were directly connected to several seismic forces that both shook and reshaped the landscape of organized religion and theological education in North America. In one of his final "From the President's Desk" columns in 1969, CRCDS President Gene Bartlett asked if, after surviving the death of God, the Divinity School could survive the death of the church: "While the controversial phrase, 'God is dead' is rarely heard these days, there seems to be a successor, 'the church is dead.' . . . The signs of its death are listed: irrelevance, archaic language, loss of support, men leaving the ministry."[1] Bartlett's successor, President Arthur R. McKay, stressed the relevancy of CRCDS and its ability to meet these challenges in articles like "Colgate Rochester: Times Are Changing," but even those innovative measures did not stem the gradual decline.[2]

When Arthur McKay (1918–1989) assumed the presidency of the newly formed Rochester Theological Center after Crozer Theological Seminary joined Colgate Rochester and Bexley Hall in the autumn of 1970, he brought with him a wealth of leadership experience. The Divinity School opened in the fall of 1970 with a record enrollment of 270 students, but this growth was due more to the mergers than a resurgence of new seminarians.[3] Seven former Crozer faculty members joined the new Colgate Rochester Crozer Bexley Hall staff

---

1. Gene Bartlett, "From the President's Desk," *CRCDS/Bexley Hall Bulletin* 42, no. 2 (December 1969): 2.
2. Gene Kelly, "Colgate Rochester: Times Are Changing," *Democrat and Chronicle*, September 19, 1971, 99–103.
3. *CRCDS/Bexley Hall Bulletin* 43, no. 1 (October 1970): 1.

along with McKay.[4] Alongside the burgeoning faculty stood a growing administration as three new deans were appointed, with Bishop
Daniel Corrigan named dean of Bexley, Dr. Joseph Pelham as dean
of students, and Dr. R. Melvin Henderson, former academic dean at
Crozer, as dean of academic administration.[5] What financial gains
might have been made through the merger seemed to be almost immediately offset by dramatically increased salary costs.

In his inaugural address at CRCDS, President McKay expressed
his concern for the apparent "irrelevance" of the modern church.
As he articulated his ongoing vision for the Divinity School, McKay
explained, "Here in Rochester, we have a *vision*. We are a great
theological center being born, preparing men and women for sound
and imaginative ministry in the contemporary Church and Society."[6]
McKay used four main words to give substance to that "vision":
"ecumenical, pluralistic, worldly, and expensive."[7] It was perhaps
the last word that seemed to have the most impact on the school due
to the significant long-term expenses that came to the Divinity School
through the mergers and, at the same time, left it with an increased
faculty and staff. By 1971 the total budget rose to $1.8 million, which
reflected cuts of more than $90,000 from the budget of the previous
year. Among the many cost-saving measures was a yearlong freeze of
faculty, administrative, and staff salaries, and "steps have been taken
to limit spending to essentials."[8] Even in the face of these drastic
measures and an ambitious fund-raising campaign, the 1971–1972
budget carried a $290,000 deficit.[9]

The affiliation ceremonies, held October 26–30, 1970, celebrated the rich heritage of the constituent schools as being embodied
in Crozer, which "throughout its history . . . has sought to develop
ministers both intellectually and socially aware. . . . The Seminary is
formally affiliated with the American Baptist Convention, and for
years has been ecumenical and inter-racial."[10] Despite its rich legacy of inclusion, and with forty women enrolled for academic year
1970–1971, the Divinity School had not made significant progress

---

4. Ibid., 3. These were Jesse H. Brown (Old Testament), W. Kenneth Cauthen (systematic theology), R. Melvin Henderson (academic dean, professor of New Testament), Albert L. Meiburg (pastoral theology), Kenneth Lee Smith (ethics), Edward E. Thornton (pastoral theology), and Theodore Weeden (New Testament).

5. Ibid., "Three Deans Named," 3.

6. Arthur R. McKay, "From the President's Desk," *CRCDS/Bexley Hall Bulletin* 43, no. 1 (October 1970): 2.

7. Ibid.

8. Ibid.

9. "1971–72 Gift Goal: $315,000," *CRCDS/Bexley Hall Bulletin* 44, no. 1 (October 1971): 1.

10. "The Celebration of the Affiliation of Crozer Theological Seminary with Colgate Rochester Divinity School and Bexley Hall," October 28–30, 1970, unpublished program, Crozer Collection, CRCDS archives.

in placing women on the faculty and administrative team. To address these glaring omissions, the Divinity School Women's Caucus was formed and almost immediately a statement was issued by them: "Women in seminary have no opportunity to enter into dialogue with professional women in the field of religious studies and ministry, or to consider it a viable career possibility. Professional and competent women are needed as role models."[11] The next fall, a female theologian, Diane Tennis, was hired as visiting professor of theology. Dr. Tennis taught a class for women under the title Women's Role in Church.[12]

In March 1972, McKay announced the launching of the Martin Luther King Fellows in the Black Church Studies program. The three-year program was conceived and directed by Henry H. Mitchell, Martin Luther King Professor of Black Church Studies. Professor Mitchell noted, "This is a very imaginative approach to the development of new materials."[13] The thrust of the program was that each of the King fellows was committed to the authorship of some item to augment and enrich the bibliography in black church studies. Funded by a $113,990 grant from the Irwin-Sweeney-Miller Foundation, the program was inaugurated in 1972 and ran through 1974. The class of twenty African American pastor-scholars included many prominent church leaders, such as Ronald A. Carter, Joseph Clemmous, Philip Cousin, Jesse Douglas, Carroll Felton, James A. Forbes, Charles Hamilton, James Hargett, William A. Jones, Floyd Massey, Samuel McKinney, James J. Robinson, William J. Shaw, Julian A. Simpkins, and Wyatt Tee Walker, who graduated with the doctor of ministry degree in 1975.[14]

During this same time period, Johnny Ray Youngblood (1948–2009) graduated from CRCDS with a master's degree. Following his graduation, Youngblood was called to become pastor of St. Paul Community Baptist Church in Brooklyn, New York. Over the course of his long career, Rev. Youngblood's ministry grew St. Paul's from a membership of 84 to more than 10,000.[15] Youngblood's prophetic ministry embraced the full needs of all people, but his emphasis upon the role of black men in the African American community and church

11. "Women Request Changes," CRCDS Bulletin 43, no. 4 (June 1971): 1.
12. Ibid.
13. CRCDS Bexley Hall Bulletin 44, no. 4 (March 1972): 2.
14. "Minutes of Faculty Meetings," Colgate Rochester Divinity School Bexley Hall, Crozer Theological Seminary, August 1973-76, minutes for the meeting of May 7, 1975, 2.
15. "Letting Go, Gradually, of a Life Embracing Ministry," New York Times, July 11, 2009, A-12.

was particularly notable.[16] Hundreds of African American men came to faith or returned to the church through his various missional approaches. For example, "In 1987, he began the Eldad-Medad Men's Bible Study Class where men could search the Scriptures and fellowship together."[17] More than 150 men attended this ministry on a weekly basis. Youngblood served for many years on the CRCDS board of trustees and rose to national prominence because of his dynamic and prophetic ministry.

Beginning in the mid-1970s, several forces coalesced to cause the gradual decay of and occasional collapse of mainline churches and, along with the churches, the theological institutions of education that they supported and turned to for ministerial training.[18] The social and political crises of the 1960s and early 1970s, like the Vietnam War, the civil rights struggle, the sexual revolution, feminism, right to life, and political disillusionment, were, wrote James Wind of the Alban Institute, "just a few of the earthquakes that altered the religious landscape."[19] These shifts were both announced and chronicled by a veritable library of books and articles, beginning with *Why Conservative Churches Are Growing* (1972) by Dean M. Kelley.[20] Kelley stated, "In the latter years of the 1960's something remarkable happened in the United States: for the first time in the nation's history most of the major church groups stopped growing and began to shrink."[21]

This decline, reported by Kelley and many others, dramatically affected mainline denominations like the American Baptists, Episcopalians, United Methodists, and Presbyterians disproportionately, even while evangelical churches (which were more theologically and socially conservative) continued to grow steadily.[22] The steady numerical, and therefore financial, decline of progressive and ecumenical mainline churches continued for the next five decades; for example, three of the most dominant mainline churches lost 25 percent of their membership between 1965 and 1990, while others also steadily lost

16. *CRCDS Alumni Annual*, 1996, 2.
17. Ibid.
18. While there is no formal definition as to which Protestant churches constitute the mainline, the following eight are usually included: American Baptist Church, the Disciples of Christ, the Episcopal Church, the Evangelical Lutheran Church in America, the Presbyterian Church USA, the Reformed Church in America, the United Church of Christ, and the United Methodist Church. C. James Wind, "The Turbulent Ecology of Mainline Protestantism," *Theological Education* 44, no. 1 (2008): 29-34; see 29.
19. Ibid., 31.
20. Dean M. Kelley, *Why Conservative Churches Are Growing: A Study in Sociology of Religion* (New York: Harper and Row, 1972).
21. Ibid., 1
22. Ibid., 20-25.

members, but at a lessor rate.[23] Research by several groups indicates that while unanimous results are hard to come by, the trend of mainline decline and conservative growth continued unabated into the twenty-first century. For example, a "survey, which polled more than 54,000 adults, reported in March that the number of mainline Christians had slipped to 12.9 percent of Adult Americans—down from 17.2 percent in 2001 and 18.7 percent in 1990—as evangelical numbers grew."[24] Mainline Protestants declined at a much faster rate than any other major Christian group, including Catholics and evangelical Protestants.[25]

The hypothetical reasons for the decline of mainline churches while conservative ones grow are many and widely examined. While there is considerable debate as to the reasons for the decline of mainline churches, and corresponding growth of conservative churches, the numbers themselves are unequivocal.[26] While one is tempted to look to the religious disaffection that set in the 1960s or to theological differences for explanation of this pattern, Kelley's analysis of the sociological difference between "strong" and "weak" churches has more to do with "goals," "controls," and "communication."[27] Other studies point to matters like social advocacy and a willingness to address controversial issues: Ronald Simkins and Thomas Kelly report that "two issues have most notably distinguished Mainline Protestants and Evangelical Protestants since 1960: racial inequality and abortion."[28] To these must also be added the inclusion and role of LGBT people in the life of the church. Whatever its basis, the decline of the mainline or ecumenical churches, and a corresponding sociological and theological shift toward conservatism, seriously endangered the support which mainline seminaries, like CRCDS, were able to expect and receive from their historic constituencies.

President McKay's tenure at CRCDS amounted to a brief three years. Facing increased internal and external pressures, he returned

---

23. Robert Wuthnow and John H. Evans, *The Quiet Hand of God: Faith-Based Activism and the Public Role of Mainline Protestantism* (Berkeley: University of California Press, 2002), 6–7.
24. John Dart, "How Many in Mainline? Categories Vary in Surveys," *Christian Century* 126, no 12 (June 16, 2009): 13–14.
25. Michael Lipka, "Mainline Protestants Make Up Shrinking Number of U.S. Adults," Pew Research Center, May 18, 2015, www.pewresearch.org/fact-tank/2015/05/18/mainline-protestants-make-up-shrinking-number-of-u-s-adults.
26. Benton Johnson, Dean R. Hoge, and Donald A. Luidens, "Mainline Churches: The Real Reason for Decline," *First Things* 31 (March 1993): 13–18; see 13.
27. Kelley, *Conservative Churches*, 84, for a helpful chart delineating the characteristics of "strong" and "weak" churches.
28. Ronald A. Simkins and Thomas M. Kelly, eds.,"Religion and Identity," *Journal of Religion and Society*, supp. ser. 13 (2016), 163–64.

to the pastorate after the 1973 academic year.[29] A 1952 graduate of Colgate Rochester, Dr. Leon Pacala, was an American Baptist minister who was ordained for the ministry at nearby Pittsford, New York. He assumed the presidency of CRCDS/Bexley Hall in 1973 and continued in that role for seven years. He said "When the opportunity presented itself to come to Rochester, I found myself compelled by the prospects of coming to grips with the general issues surrounding professional education, and with those which are peculiar to seminary education." He also disclosed, "I should add that my devotion to the Divinity School as an alumnus played a strong role, perhaps stronger than I even now realize."[30]

When Pacala assumed the role of president, CRCDS/Bexley Hall had an enrollment of more than 200 and an incoming class of 109.[31] The combined schools had a full-time faculty of twenty men, including Gayraud S. Wilmore, who joined the staff in 1974 as Martin Luther King Jr. Memorial Professor and director of the Black Church Studies program. He was joined in the latter role by James H. Evans, who was hired in June 1980 as assistant professor of theology and black church studies.[32] By 1976, Beverly Roberts Gaventa joined the teaching faculty of CRCDS as professor of New Testament. The appointment was a momentous one for the Divinity School since it represented "the first full-time position with professorial rank to be held by a woman."[33]

In May 1977 the thirty-six-member CRCDS/Bexley Hall graduating class was reminded about the dramatic changes occurring all around them as they entered into the ministry of "a hard world." "It's is a world bounded by cynicism, indifference and yet it's the only world that you will minister," President Pacala told them.[34] By the end of Pacala's tenure, in the spring of 1980, the graduating class was comprised of twenty-seven men and sixteen women, thirty-four of whom earned master of divinity degrees.[35]

At thirty-eight, Dr. Larry L. Greenfield was the second youngest person elected to the presidency of the Divinity School when he

29. *CRCDS/Bexley Hall Bulletin* 45, no. 4 (June 1973): 1; cf. "McKay to Leave Divinity School," *Democrat and Chronicle*, April 14, 1973, 16.
30. "Interview with President Pacala," *CRCDS Bexley Hall Bulletin* 46, no. 1 (October 1973).
31. "Classes Begin for 200; 109 in Entering Group," *CRCDS/Bexley Hall Bulletin* 46, no. 1 (October 1973): 1.
32. "Evans Named to Faculty," *CRCDS/Bexley Hall Bulletin* 52, no. 2 (January 1980): 1.
33. "Woman Named to Faculty Post," *CRCDS/Bexley Hall Bulletin* 47, no. 3 (March 1975): 1.
34. "Graduates Urged to Balance Their Profession, Calling," *CRCDS/Bexley Hall Bulletin* 52, no. 4 (June 1980): 1.
35. Ibid.

assumed office in June 1980.[36] Heralding from Sioux Falls, South Dakota, Greenfield was a lifelong American Baptist. Educated at Sioux Falls and the University of Chicago Divinity School, he came into his leadership position at CRCDS after pastoral work in Chicago and serving on the faculty and as dean of the University of Chicago Divinity School.[37] In a telephone interview immediately following his election to the CRCDS/Bexley Hall presidency, he reflected upon the road that lay ahead of him: "I think the largest challenge I will face in Rochester is to make men and women of all ages aware that the ministry is the most meaningful, demanding, and fulfilling way to spend one's life."[38] At his installation, Greenfield described himself as one who had responded to "an awesome [call] and challenging honor." "This School," he said, "has chosen the faithful rather than the easy route. . . . The leadership role held by the School has had its costs, but I would hope in the years ahead that the School will continue to be willing to pay the price of being leaders in the American Baptist and Episcopalian traditions."[39]

The Divinity School's fluctuating student statistics reflected the challenging days ahead of it. In May 1982, 45 students, including 15 women, received a master of divinity degree, but that number was nearly cut by half in the next year when only 25 people graduated. Enrollments rebounded in the fall of 1983, when the total enrollment of 261 students was the highest level that it had reached in more than a decade.[40] The number of women attending the Divinity School continued to increase, and by academic year 1983–1984 the enrollment of women and men reached full equivalence.[41] But total enrollment continued on a downward spiral with 50 students graduating in 1986, 33 of whom were women.[42]

The growing presence of women in ministry in general and at the Divinity School in particular did not escape the attention of the public and figured prominently in a the Rochester *Democrat and Chronicle* feature article called "Women in the Pulpit."[43] Edward Lehman, a leading researcher in the field, attributed three practical considerations

36. "President Greenfield Responds to 'Awesome Call,'" *CRCDS/Bexley Hall Bulletin* 53, no. 1 (October 1980): 1.
37. Ibid.
38. Mary Hood, "Chicago Dean Named President of Divinity School," *Democrat and Chronicle*, August 13, 1980, 27.
39. Ibid.
40. "Opening Convocation 1983: 'More Light–More Students," *Bulletin from the Hill* 56, no. 1 (November 1983): 1.
41. Ibid.
42. "President Greenfield Wears Rauschenbusch Academic Robe at Commencement," *Bulletin from the Hill* 58, no. 3 (Summer 1986): 1.
43. Julia Vigaretti Hahn, "Women in the Pulpit," *Democrat and Chronicle*, August 25, 1985, 120.

that many keep men away from ministry: the end of the Vietnam War, with men no longer seeking to avoid the draft; economic rewards in the ministry not keeping pace with other fields; and "the prestige associated with the ministry has declined because society is more secular and religious criteria play a diminished role in people's everyday decision-making."[44] CRCDS faculty and students urged that women did more than "[fill] a vacuum. They are bringing a new perspective to the church's understanding of God and the Bible."[45]

The theological heritage of the Divinity School continued to be celebrated through special lectures. Church historian Jaroslav Pelikan, for example, presented the Rauschenbusch Lectures in 1983,[46] and in 1986, the sesquecentennial anniversary of the Divinity School was celebrated throughout the entire academic year with a series of special lectures and historical enactments of formative founders like Augustus Hopkins Strong, Helen Barrett Montgomery, and Walter Rauschenbusch.[47] Among the guest lecturers celebrating the King legacy in 1983 were Dr. Samuel Proctor and retired professor Kenneth ("Snuffy") Smith.[48]

In May 1984, Divinity School professor of theology and black church studies, James H. Evans, was named to the Martin Luther King Jr. Memorial Chair. "There is a great honor and responsibility which comes with the appointment," Evans said. He continued,

> The honor is to be associated with the name and legacy of an Afro-American spiritual genius. . . . The responsibility is to carry on the work which was initiated by the two previous holders of this position. Dr. Henry Mitchell and Dr. Gayraud Wilmore have distinguished themselves through their scholarship and active participation in the global mission of the Afro-American churches. To continue this tradition is my goal.[49]

Subsequently, Robert M. Franklin was named dean of black church studies,[50] and in the fifteenth annual celebration of the life of Martin Luther King Jr. in 1985, Rosa Parks, "the mother of the modern freedom movement in America," received the Divinity School's humanitarian award.[51]

44. Ibid., 121.
45. Ibid.
46. "Rauschenbusch Lectures Scheduled," *Bulletin from the Hill* 54, no. 1 (November 1984): 2.
47. "1986: An Anniversary Year: A Time to Make Use of Our History," *Bulletin from the Hill* 58, no. 2 (March 1986): 4–5.
48. *Bulletin from the Hill* 54, no. 2 (March 1982), 7–8.
49. "James H. Evans Appointed Martin Luther King, Jr. Memorial Professor," *Bulletin from the Hill* 56, no. 3 (June 1984): 1.
50. "Dean of Black Church Studies Announced," *Bulletin from the Hill* 57, no. 3 (June 1985): 3.
51. "Rosa Parks Receives King Memorial Award," *Bulletin from the Hill* 57, no. 2 (March 1985): 1.

The Divinity School's march from denominationalism toward ecumenism and religious pluralism continued in the 1980s. In his observation of the entering class of 1984, for example, reporter James Goodman noted, "What once was a largely Baptist divinity school now includes a student body represented by a diversity of denominations. This variety was encouraged by Colgate Rochester's combining an assortment of other theological schools over the past 25 years."[52] This observation was confirmed by President Greenfield: "Of the 260 students enrolled at Colgate Rochester, less than 25 percent are Baptists."[53] Noting "the name Colgate Rochester Divinity School/ Bexley Hall/Crozer Theological Seminary is so long that it cannot even be found on a sign at the campus complex," James Goodman was amused when Greenfield did not anticipate changing the school's name: "I think the title is so very important," the president said, "I think it's important in terms of our identity, that we keep this clumsy title, because it does describe what we are trying to accomplish."[54]

The tendency toward Christian ecumenism and affiliation, referenced by Greenfield, was aptly illustrated by the relocation of St. Bernard's Institute to the Colgate Rochester campus through agreements established in 1981. Stressing that St. Bernard's Institute continued to build upon the affiliations that were established in 1968, "We are committed to a double-edged sword—paying our way, but not underwriting the other institution," St. Bernard's directors Fr. Sebastian Falcone said. "St. Bernard's will, in effect, be 'paying guest' of Colgate Rochester," added CRCDS director of public relations, Rev. Charles Luckett.[55]

In the 1980s, waves of popular religion and American political conservatism resulted in a partnership between religion and politics through the birth of the Moral Majority led by Rev. Jerry Falwell. In a column titled "Questioning Moral Majority's Role in America," Dr. Greenfield and others challenged the heady blend of conservative faith and politics. "Nationalism is a form of religion, he said. And when you get religion and nationalism together, you limit the sovereignty of God. You bring God down to your size. But you'll pay for that fundamental sin. In the end, God will get you."[56]

---

52. James Goodman, "A School of Diverse Denominations: Colgate Rochester No Longer Mostly Baptist," *Democrat and Chronicle*, March 4, 1984, 27.
53. Ibid.
54. Ibid.
55. Stephanie Coulson, "St. Bernard's Makes Move Official Today," *Democrat and Chronicle*, August 26, 1981, 1.
56. Jim Meyers, "Questioning Moral Majority," *Democrat and Chronicle*, December 14, 1980, 3.

At the end of the decade, in 1989, Greenfield submitted his resignation, saying, "I've been here nine years and that's a long time for someone to be in one office. I wanted to do something else."[57] Thomas Richards, chair of the CRCDS board of trustees, credited Greenfield for developing a long-range plan for the school to increase enrollment and to make curriculum changes that would adequately reflect the changing composition of the student body and effectively integrate St. Bernard's Seminary into the Divinity School family.

Dr. Shirley M. Jones, who served as a trustee of the Divinity School since 1975 and as executive director of the America Baptist Board of Educational Ministries, was named interim president of CRCDS/Bexley Hall following the departure of Greenfield and prior to the election of Dr. James H. Evans. She was the first female chief administrator of the school in its 163-year history.[58]

Dr. James H. Evans was called next to the presidency of the Divinity School. Evans, who served as professor of theology and black church studies at CRCDS since 1979, was the first African American to take the helm of the Divinity School. He was selected from more than two hundred applicants. "My top priority," Evans said, "will be to promote the vision. It's a matter of moving beyond tolerance and beyond appreciation, to see that we need one another."[59] Evans also noted the irony that the Divinity School, which carries "a good deal of viability and marquee value on a national level, is not well known in the immediate area."[60] He also voiced pride in the Divinity School's rich heritage as one that includes "nationally recognized African American church leaders like Howard Thurman, Martin Luther King Jr., and James Forbes, as well as the social gospel emphasis of Walter Rauschenbusch, which continues to inspire an emphasis on the ethical dimensions of faith."[61]

A prominent exponent of black theology,[62] Evans frequently contributed to the local press articles and guest editorials addressing the religious dimension of national and local social issues.[63] Evans also

---

57. Diana L. Tomb, "Replacing 2 Top Administrators Is a Big Task Facing Divinity School," *Democrat and Chronicle*, June 17, 1989, 3.
58. The contributions of Shirley M. Jones will be chronicled in chapter 19.
59. James Goodman, "New Divinity School President Plans to Promote the Vision," *Democrat and Chronicle*, July 27, 1990, 46.
60. Kathleen Schwar, "At the Helm on the Hill," *Democrat and Chronicle*, December 1, 1990, 22.
61. Ibid.
62. James H. Evans, *We Have Been Believers: An African American Systematic Theology* (Philadelphia: Fortress, 1993; 2nd ed., 2012), and "Toward an Afro-American Theology," *Journal of Religious Thought* 40, no. 2 (January 1983): 39-54, among many other examples.
63. See, for example, "King Would Have Said 'No' to War," *Democrat and Chronicle*, Tuesday, January 15, 1991, page 9A and "The Narrow Political Vision of Religious Right Could Destroy the Union," *Democrat and Chronicle*, Sunday, December 22, 1985, page 15A.

put his theology to work as a playwright and avid golfer; he was the first black person to integrate the prestigious Oak Hill Country Club in Rochester.[64] Walter Earl Fluker, formerly professor of ethics at Vanderbilt University Divinity School, followed James Evans as dean of black church studies and the Martin Luther King Jr. Memorial Professor of Theology.[65]

In 1991, under the leadership of the new academic dean, Dr. William R. Herzog, the faculty began contemplating a new curriculum based in a series of interdisciplinary, team-taught courses to be taken in students' first year that would engage them in group reflection on crucial theological issues, including feminist/womanist theory and black church theology.[66]

In 1992 the Divinity School's Women and Gender Studies program was established under the leadership of Dean Melanie May. The Women and Gender Studies program connected with and continued the rich legacy of the many faithful women who stood in the CRCDS prophetic heritage, and most clearly those established by the women of the BMTS. The new program was inaugurated in a three-day event, "Stand Together in Hope."[67] Among the keynote speakers, including Dr. May, were Rev. Mercy Amba Oduyoye, deputy general secretary of the World Council of Churches, and alumna Rev. Betty Bone Schiess, who was one of the first women ordained to the priesthood in the United States.[68] The 1993 edition of the catalogue described Women and Gender Studies as one of "the signature programs" of CRCDS, which not only "embraces the inclusion of women into already extant offices and orders of ministry, but also the cultivation of women's uniquely creative gifts for ministry."[69]

Dr. May brought a broader emphasis to the Women and Gender Studies program than was seen in other women's studies programs, insofar as the "gender" aspect of it not only considered the formation of feminist/womanist perspectives but also explored the more foundational question of gender formation and human identity. As an obvious development of these more broadly defined gender studies

64. Scott Pitoniak, "Theologian to Integrate Oak Hill Club," *Democrat and Chronicle*, May 1991, 1. Evans's play, *Swamp Angel*, set in the life experiences of church folk in 1967 Detroit, was both performed and published. *Democrat and Chronicle*, September 24, 2001, 31.
65. "Four New Appointments Complete Administrative Team," *Bulletin from the Hill* 64, no. 1 (Winter 1991): 1.
66. "Divinity School Contemplates New Curriculum," *Bulletin from the Hill* 63, no. 1 (Winter 1991): 1.
67. "Women's Program a Reality," *Bulletin from the Hill* 65, no. 3 (June 1993): 3.
68. "Stand Together in Hope: The Inauguration of the Program in the Study of Women and Gender in Church and Society," May 1-3, 1993, conference program.
69. *The Divinity School, Rochester, New York, 1993-95 Catalogue*, 54.

and awareness, an Open and Affirming Student Caucus was formed at the Divinity School. Its mission statement reads in part:

> The Open and Affirming Student Caucus [OASC] enriches the lives of gay, lesbian, bisexual, transgendered, and questioning seminarians, together with persons who actively support them. By being a visible presence and engaging in dialogue and education, the OASC works in partnership with Colgate Rochester Crozer Divinity School as it lives out its commitment to be a safe, radically hospitable space in which LGBT students prepare for ministry in the 21st century.[70]

In 2013 the OASC was comprised of fifteen student members, for whom Dr. May served as faculty adviser. In a subsequent development, the Helen Barrett Montgomery Institute on Women in Church and Society was added to the Divinity School's panoply of special lectures in November 1995.[71]

Student enrollment at the Divinity School continued on a downward trend, despite innovative programs, curriculum, recruitment ventures, and programing, such as launching an evening master of divinity program in 1996. The entire graduating class was comprised of twenty-six students in 1996,[72] twenty-seven students in 1997,[73] and thirty students in 1998.[74] Meanwhile an ambitious capital improvement campaign had more than $6 million of its targeted goal of $11.7 pledged by the winter of 1998, and much needed renovations to Strong Hall were planned for that same summer.[75]

The Rochester Center for Theological Study began unraveling in 1999 when Bexley Hall left "the hill" and relocated in Columbus, Ohio. Bexley eventually joined with Seabury-Western and consolidated their operations in the Hyde Park district of Chicago in July 2016. During this same period, St. Bernard's Institute, which had, after long affiliation, come to "the hill" in 1981, remade itself once again, in 2003, by relocating to a smaller state-of-the art campus in suburban Rochester. Both of these developments had serious impact on the enrollment and financial health of CRCDS.

The Divinity School's declining enrollments and income forced a 20 percent reduction of staffing in 1999. The sixteen positions,

---

70. "Open and Affirming: The Student Caucus Joins Tradition of Activism on the Hill," *Bulletin of Colgate Rochester Crozer Divinity School* (Winter 2013), 11.
71. "First Annual Helen Barrett Montgomery Institute on Women in Church and Society Scheduled for November," *Bulletin from the Hill*, Fall 1995, 1.
72. "Graduates Told to 'Keep the Bread Fresh'," *Bulletin from the Hill*, Summer/Fall 1996, 1.
73. "Graduates Get 'Heart Answers'," *Bulletin from the Hill*, Summer/Fall 1997.
74. "Congratulations to the Class of 1998," *Bulletin from the Hill*, Summer/Fall 1998, 2.
75. James H. Evans, "The President's Column," *Bulletin from the Hill*, Winter/Spring 1998, 2.

mostly administrative staff, were eliminated as a cost-saving measure.[76] An unnamed senior staff person observed that the total enrollment of the Divinity School had declined by more than one hundred students in the last decade, without any reduction in support staff.[77] Evans noted, "Good decisions are always difficult ones and this has been no exception. The 'right sizing' of Colgate Rochester will cause some administrative and personal distress, but it will ultimately result in a stronger, more efficient institution."[78] At this time, the entire core faculty of the Divinity School was comprised of fifteen full-time scholars.[79]

Innovations and improvement in the curriculum continued at CRCDS: most notably, significant strides toward full inclusion of African Americans and women in the mission, curriculum, and leadership of CRCDS. But difficult decisions lay ahead. These were engendered, in large part, by the rapidly changing climate of church life and the status of theological education in North America. Major adjustments and course corrections lay ahead, but challenge and change were an ongoing reality in the CRCDS story. Reaching back to the meeting where thirteen men with $13 sought to establish a "school of prophets" in rural western New York, the Divinity School weathered the ups and downs of enrollments and financial stability, as well as the shifting tides of theological discourse.

But CRCDS would need to keep its eyes on the historic and prophetic mission of the institution and the heroic Christian service of its women and men in order to sustain its witness in the twenty-first century. Its hallmarks, like the evangelical-liberal theological perspective with a social gospel emphasis and the tension between its Baptist and ecumenical identity, required an acute sense of balance difficult to maintain in the new climate of the twenty-first century. Its longstanding emphasis upon diversity and inclusion was expanded and deepened as women and African Americans took a larger part in the instruction and governance of the school, and it was expanded to embrace LGBTI people and their struggle for equality and inclusion. CRCDS's legacy and ministry were whole and intact during these difficult days. Having remade itself many times done through the years, it and would be called upon do so again.

---

76. Doug Mandelaro, "16 Positions Cut at Colgate and Crozer," *Democrat and Chronicle*, October 13, 1999, 11.
77. Ibid.
78. Evans, "The President's Column," *Bulletin from the Hill*, Winter/Spring 1998, 2.
79. "The Core Faculty," *Bulletin from the Hill*, Fall 1995, 2.

19

Female Prophets Shattering the Stained Glass Ceiling

The story of women at CRCDS and its constituent bodies is deeply woven into the tapestry of our narrative. The labors of women like Rumah Alvilla Crouse, Mary Burdette, Joanna Moore, and Isabel Crawford transformed churchly women's work into the prophetic ministry of the Baptist Missionary Training School. This inspiring story includes Ruth Hill, who graduated in 1922 from Rochester Theological Seminary as the first woman awarded a bachelor of divinity degree. It reaches down through the nineteenth century and the early decades of the twentieth when women began to play an increasing role in the life and history of CRCDS.

Often, however, women's roles in the church were viewed as ancillary or supplementary to men's—serving as ministers' wives, pastoral assistants, educators, and sometimes as copastors. Very often these women did the same work as their male counterparts, performing at extraordinary levels amid challenges and artificial barriers that excluded them from more official and lucrative leadership positions. Women doing religious work often had their careers truncated by the stained glass ceiling of church laws, social customs, and religious prejudices that barred them from official recognition and advancement. One clear example, and yet exception, to this pattern was marked by the illustrious women of the BMTS who, upon being excluded from home and foreign missions, ostensibly because they were not well-trained, established and supported a fine training school of their own. When the male-dominated denominational hierarchy declined to support and deploy them, they supported themselves and went forward with or without the approval of the denominational hierarchy. The arrival of the BMTS women "on the hill" in 1962, along with their rich legacy of service and innovation, significantly enriched the CRCDS experience and heritage.

The exclusion of women from religious training and formal ecclesiastical leadership was a long-standing barrier that was gradually overcome, and CRCDS played an extraordinary role in that process. As we saw, in 1959 the Rochester *Democrat and Chronicle* deemed the appearance of women at CRCDS a newsworthy "invasion."[1] In 1960 a master of divinity student, Marita Drach, found it uncomfortably necessary to repeatedly "Why am I here?" since she enrolled in the Divinity School's ordination-track program—not as "a helpmate" to her husband.[2]

By 1971, visiting professor Dr. Diane Tennis taught a women's studies course, and in 1976 Beverly Roberts Gaventa joined the faculty full-time as professor of New Testament. In 1980 she became the first woman granted tenure by CRCDS in the school's long history. The presence of female faculty signaled growing institutional support for and recognition of an ever-increasing presence and contribution of women to the programs and mission of CRCDS. The inauguration of the CRCDS Women and Gender Studies program in 1992 marked a turning point in the Divinity School's attention to the inclusion, training, and deployment of women for ministry.

The current chapter highlights the careers and contributions of three CRCDS and Bexley women, whose lives embodied the prophetic legacy of the Divinity School on gender issues. Betty Bone Schiess, Marjorie Matthews, and Shirley M. Jones, for example, broke through the stained glass ceiling that hindered even the most capable Christian women from rising to the higher levels of ecclesiastical leadership.

The first of these women, Betty Bone Schiess (1923–2017), was one of the first female Episcopalian priests ordained in the United States. Bone earned a bachelor of arts degree from the University of Cincinnati, where she was active in religious work. After receiving her master's degree from Syracuse in 1947, she and her newly

1. Mary McKee, "Ministry Coeds: Women 'Invade' Colgate Rochester as Students and Helpmates," *Democrat and Chronicle*, March 8, 1959, 71.
2. Marita Drach, "Why Am I Here?" *Hilltop Views* 4, no. 2 (November 29, 1960): 1-2.

married husband, William A. Schiess, traveled abroad in Algiers for several weeks. This caused the couple to see the racial situation in the United States with new eyes, and as they arrived home they were determined, as she put it, "to do something about the plight of the Negro."[3] After taking an active role in the African American struggle for civil rights in the 1960s, Betty Schiess worked for the National Organization for Women (NOW).

In her autobiography, *Why Me Lord?* she reported:

> I had read the *Feminine Mystique* and, like many women in my generation, I felt this was our book, our life. To admit this publically was not easy. To say that we middle-class, middle-aged, married mothers were not "satisfied" sounded silly, trivial, in the light of the world's problems—most especially in the light of the ongoing struggle of blacks. We learned about how to go about "seeking remedy" from the leaders of the Civil Rights movements of the 1960's, but what business did we have applying it to ourselves.[4]

In this context of her finding a new identity and mission, Schiess found her call to ministry. Looking back, she wrote,

> As for a personal "call," this effort to relieve the Episcopal Church of its misogyny was, is, my call. A "call" is what prospective clergy are supposed to hear (best if it comes from God, but I have never dared presume that). If I ever wound up as the rector of a parish, I was arrogant enough to think that I could function as well as many clergymen whom I had seen. But it was never my ambition to be a Cardinal Rector (a good thing). My ambition was bolder. It was to change the Episcopal Church and the society it presumed to save.[5]

The transition from dedicating her life and energy to the black struggle for equality and the plight of women in the Episcopal Church seemed to be a natural one for Schiess. She was a strong advocate for racial equality and participated in several freedom marches in the Deep South.[6] As she said in an interview, "I still believe in better opportunities for the Negro people, but I am even more committed to the cause of equality for women in the church."[7] She summarized the plight of women in her own church by writing, "In working within the church, I found that women are more discriminated against than the Negroes. . . . I think this equally true in many other Protestant churches, but in our church, there is a difference. In other churches,

---

3. Lois Vosburgh, "CRDS/BH Woman Seeks Episcopal Priesthood," *CRDS/Bexley Hall Bulletin* 42, no. 2 (December 1969): 2.
4. Betty Bone Schiess, *Why Me Lord? One Woman's Ordination to the Priesthood with Commentary and Complaint* (Syracuse, NY: Syracuse University Press, 2003), 29.
5. Ibid., 34–35.
6. Vosburgh, "CRDS/BH Woman Seeks Episcopal Priesthood," 2.
7. Ibid.

it was apt to be 'de facto' discrimination. In our church it is a matter of church law."[8]

In 1969 Schiess enrolled in the Rochester Center for Theological Studies, and her struggle for ordination was reported in the *Bulletin*: "CRDS/BH Woman Seeks Episcopal Priesthood."[9] Historically, women were ordained as deaconesses, which was understood as standing in holy orders; but unlike their male counterparts, who were called deacons, deaconesses were denied the opportunity to be ordained as priests. Her experience at the Divinity School wholly supported her path and call: "If in the teachings at the Rochester Center for Theological Studies I had heard anything that suggested that women should not be ordained, and that this was a not-to-be-tampered with biblical truth, I would have left—unhappy, unsatisfied, maybe even disbelieving. But this was not the case."[10]

Upon examining the formal status of women's leadership in the Episcopal Church, Ms. Schiess found that only Canon #49, which stated that only males could read the Scripture lessons in its liturgical worship, excluded women. In fact, only that particular canon in all of church law even mentioned the word *male*.[11] Even the institution of that particular church law presupposed that at some one point, women had read the holy lessons when no males were available and others decided to put a stop to it. Following her scrutiny of the legal standing of the issue, Schiess concluded, "Not ordaining women was accepted as custom and the Episcopal Church paid great attention— much too much attention—to custom."[12]

In 1968 Betty Schiess believed that "it did seem remarkable that so far as I knew I would be the first woman in history to matriculate at an accredited seminary with the approval of the bishops, the parish, the Commission on Ministry, and the Standing Committee. Surely once this happened and if I completed seminary, the canons would allow it. I was wrong."[13] While church law did not formally bar women from ordination, church law and tradition, as her own bishop and others interpreted it, excluded them. It would be better, then, the bishop urged, "to wait until the canons specifically provided for ordaining women, otherwise the right to act as a priest might be

---

8. Ibid.
9. Ibid.
10. Schiess, *Why Me Lord?*, 44.
11. Ibid., 31.
12. Ibid.
13. Ibid., 39.

taken away from us at some future point."[14] Despite his warning, Schiess pressed ahead.

Although Schiess did not yet make a postulant for holy orders, which is the first major step toward the priesthood in her tradition, she remained hopeful. Her resident bishop, the Rt. Rev. George W. Barrett, had recently addressed an assembly in London saying, "If we reject the proposal to ordain women, we had better be very, very, careful of telling the world anything about racial discrimination."[15] By then she was dedicated to her course of action: "I was determined to spend the rest of my life trying to keep the church from sanctifying a separate space for women, where our voices stopped at the door of domesticity—where, as Josephine Butler, the great British feminist, had said so many years before, 'men work and women weep.'"[16]

By 1972, however, the church began to rethink its practice of having two separate categories for its deacons, and in November 1973 several women were ordained as deacons. But one month later, when they presented themselves for ordination, Bishop Paul Moore Jr. refused to lay his consecrating hands upon them, thereby depriving them of priestly ordination. Ultimately, and after a long struggle, Schiess was numbered among the first group of women to be ordained as Episcopal priests on July 29, 1974. The day was carefully chosen, as it was the Feast of Saints Mary and Martha on the church's liturgical calendar. Since the illegal service was held at the Episcopalian Church of the Advocate in Philadelphia, Schiess and her ten colleagues came to be known as "the Philadelphia Eleven."

These eleven female deacons were ordained as priests by two retired Episcopal bishops, Daniel Corrigan and Edward Wells, and one, Robert L. DeWitt, who had recently resigned from the episcopate. The three-hour service, which was punctuated by a pointed sermon on "The Priesthood of All Believers" by Harvard professor Charles V. Willie, was an act of ecclesiastical disobedience for the sake of conscience. Dr. Willie, an African American who was president of the House of Deputies of the Episcopal Church, resigned from his post as president in protest when the church refused to recognize the ordinations of the Philadelphia Eleven.[17] What followed was, for Schiess

---

14. Ibid., 40–41.
15. Ibid.
16. Ibid., 51.
17. Ibid., 85.

and the others, another two years of ecclesiastical "shunning,"[18] study commissions, and ecclesiastical wrangling until the general convention of the church affirmed and explicitly authorized the ordination of women to the priesthood in 1976.[19] There was, however, considerable debate about what to do about the "illegal ordinations" of the eleven women in Philadelphia in 1974. "As I understand it," Schiess wrote, "there was much effort to demand that we fifteen be reordained. Of course, none of us would have agreed to this. A compromise was agreed to which allowed our diocesan bishops to 'complete' us. My 'completion' took place in the chapel of St. Paul's Cathedral, Syracuse, New York."[20]

Reverend Schiess served as a chaplain at Syracuse University and Cornell University, as well as Grace Episcopal Church in Mexico, New York. She was an adviser to the Women in Mission and Ministry Commission of the Episcopal Church and received numerous awards for her efforts on behalf of the full equality of women. In 1994 she was inducted into the Women's Hall of Fame in Seneca Falls, New York, for her pioneering efforts. Schiess's testimonial read in part: "Through persistence, leadership and wisdom, Betty Bone Schiess led the successful effort to have women ordained priests in the Episcopal Church in America, elevating the position of women in the Church, and in society."[21]

Rev. Marjorie Matthews (1916–1986) began her ministry in 1959 as a part-time pastor in small United Methodist churches in rural Michigan. She was a second-career pastor who left behind a lucrative career as an administrative assistant to the president of a major auto parts manufacturer in order to answer a call to ministry. Matthews recalled facing staunch opposition in her pastoral role, during which other constituencies would tell her flock that "they were going to hell for having a woman minister."[22] Her marriage during World War II ended in divorce, and she raised her son alone. Marjorie entered college at the age of forty-seven, and upon graduation she chose to attend Colgate Rochester Divinity School because she was determined

18. Ibid.
19. "Syracuse's Betty Bone Schiess, One of the First American Female Episcopal Priests, Dies," Syracuse.com, updated October 24, 2017, https://www.syracuse.com/news/2017/10/syracuses_betty_bone_schiess_one_of_first_female_american_episcopal_priests_dies.html.
20. Schiess, Why Me Lord?, 109.
21. "Betty Bone Schiess," National Women's Hall of Fame, www.womenofthehall.org/inductee/betty-bone-schiess/, accessed September 12, 2019.
22. "Pioneer Marjorie Matthews 'knew the call,'" Worldwide Faith News archives, https://archive.wfn.org/2000/12/msg00031.html, accessed September 12, 2019.

to study theology in an ecumenical context. Matthew's warm and ecumenical spirit continued throughout her ministry. A vibrant hope that the community of faith would find deep unity in worship and mutual acceptance characterized her ministry: "The wisdom of ecumenicity," she wrote, "is to be found in the doing whatever it takes to keep moving forward toward that day of complete understanding and acceptance, not necessarily agreement."[23]

Bishop Matthews graduated from CRCDS with her master of divinity in 1970 and subsequently was named Alumna of the Year. Her official citation from that event recalled that Matthews "earned high marks on her field education evaluation form, which noted that the congregation installed a $500 loud speaker system just to better hear Rev. Matthews's soft voice during worship."[24] Her soft voice spoke loudly, however, regarding the need for full inclusion in the United Methodist Church (UMC) ministry. Matthews went on to earn two additional advanced degrees, including a PhD from Florida State University.

In reply to a questionnaire sent to her by CRCDS, Matthews wrote, "The task of the local church is an outreach of Christian love and fellowship. The task of the pastor is to instruct and guide [so] that he is no longer needed. The message is to help people discover for themselves the relevance of the Scriptures, and to find a meaningful existence in the knowledge and experience of God."[25] After illustrious pastoral service in churches of varying size, from eighty to seventeen hundred members, Rev. Matthews returned to Michigan, where she was appointed district superintendent for the Traverse District of the United Methodist Church. She was one of the first women to hold such a post in the UMC.

At the North Central Jurisdictional Conference of the UMC on July 17, 1980, held in Dayton, Ohio, Matthews was elected to the office of bishop by her colleagues in ministry. As Jean Caffey Lyles wrote on the editorial page of the *Christian Century*, "In many ways Marjorie Swank Matthews seems an unlikely figure to play the special role history has given her, that of being the first woman bishop of a major U.S. Protestant denomination."[26] She was elected in a

---

23. Marjorie S. Matthews, "The Wisdom of Ecumenicity," *Ecumenical Trends* 14, no. 4 (1985): 55.
24. Marjorie Matthews "1970 Alumna of the Year," unpublished document.
25. Alumni file, Marjorie Matthews, unpublished document.
26. Jean Caffey Lyles, "Editorial Comment: An Improbable Episcopal Choice," *Christian Century* 97, no. 26 (August 13-20, 1980): 779.

hotly contested election that ran into thirty separate ballots prior to arriving at the required majority vote. "The delegates who elected her," Lyles reported, "did not promise her a rose garden. Being the first woman anything is difficult. But as she said, many ballots before her election: 'I have never backed away from an open door God has put in my way. If God opens that door, I'll go through it.'"[27] She later wrote: "I believe my election to the episcopacy of the United Methodist Church was an act of the Holy Spirit moving in the church and in the world to open new avenues of service to women in the ecumenical relationship, and to open eyes, ears, and hearts for greater possibilities within our communities of faith, to the end that each of God's faithful children—man, woman, or child—may serve/worship God with all his or her being."[28]

As the first woman to serve as bishop in the United Methodist Church, and one of the first women to be so elevated in any church in North America, Bishop Matthews rightly saw her work as marking a beginning, not a culmination: "I do not . . . regard my election as the culmination of the feminist movement within the United Methodist Church. I still believe that recognition and acceptance of women clergy and the leadership of women in the entire church is an idea whose time was long over-due. There is a big job ahead for clergy persons everywhere, and a challenge to the church to remain faithful to the teachings of our Lord, Jesus Christ. I am committed to that challenge and struggle."[29] Despite having to overcome many obstacles in her ministry, Matthews summarized her calling quite simply: "to serve the church and to see progress in people's lives."[30] "Matthews's long years as a layperson and her experience in small churches may give her a valuable perspective on the grass-roots church that some of her colleagues in the episcopacy have lacked," noted Lyles.[31] Reflecting upon Matthews's prophetic life, Dr. Richard Tholin, academic dean at Garrett Evangelical Divinity School, remarked, "Her story is the story of women's struggle to adapt to new roles in the church."[32]

Dr. Shirley M. Jones epitomized the ever-increasing and influential roles CRCDS women played in theological education. An expert in theological education, Jones served on the Commission on

---

27. Ibid.
28. Matthews, "Wisdom of Ecumenicity," 55.
29. "Bishop Marjorie Matthews," unpublished document, CRCDS archives.
30. "Marjorie Matthews," *Democrat and Chronicle*, July 15, 2000, 15.
31. Lyles, "An Improbable Episcopal Choice," 780.
32. "Deaths in the News: Bishop Marjorie S. Matthews," *Chicago Sun-Times*, July 6, 1986.

Accrediting of the Association of Theological Schools, as well as the chief executive of Educational Ministries of the American Baptist Churches. She was a member of the CRCDS board of trustees for many years, beginning in 1975, and was chair of that body in the mid-1980s, until she was invited to become interim president of CRCDS following the departure of Dr. Larry Greenfield in 1989.

Dr. Jones's style of leadership was encapsulated in a document on "Trust Building," which she prepared for the board when she served as its chair. Describing the current situation as one in which the church and its institutions underwent dramatic changes, and seemingly no longer possessing the level of influence religious bodies once had in American life, she urged her hearers to "become the chief nurturing force, conceptualizer of the opportunity, value shaper, and moral sustainer of leadership."[33] She also called for "a new and dynamic relationship between the church and seminary if each is to be more fully what God called it to be and to do. It calls for trustees whose power lied in persuasion and example, rather than in domination and manipulation."[34]

In her homily delivered during the opening convocation of the 1989–1990 academic years, Dr. Jones delineated four fundamental tasks she believed would successfully carry the Divinity School forward through the immediate period of a transition in leadership and beyond it. She urged her listeners to engage themselves in four levels of listening: to "listen to and interact with the wisdom of the ages that is imparted in God's holy word and in the writing and teaching of scholars of the church";[35] and to "listen and wait for the voice of God in our lives.";[36] Opening ourselves to the integrity of Christian community, "we must listen to each other."[37] And finally, "[If] we . . . listen to the world without caring about those who suffer from injustice, poverty, and discrimination, our learning will turn out to be a meaningless void."[38]

In closing, Jones asked her listeners, "Will you join me during this year of transition to be active, attentive listeners to our God, to the wisdom of the ages that is imparted through the spoken and written word, to all the people in this community regardless of race, creed,

---

33. Shirley Jones, "Trust Building: The Board's Role in Church-Seminary Relationships," unpublished address, 7.
34. Ibid.
35. Shirley Jones, "Transitions: A Homily Presented at the Opening Convocation," *Bulletin* 61, no. 3 (Summer 1989): 4.
36. Ibid.
37. Ibid.
38. Ibid.

gender or theological perspective, and to the world?"[39] "That is my covenant with you," she pledged.[40]

Reflecting on her new role, Jones said: "I believe the preparation of future leaders for the church to be among the highest of Christian callings, and to serve as acting president of one of the finest institutions charged to carry out that ministry is indeed an honor."[41] Jones served with distinction for more than a year and was succeeded by James H. Evans. Jones was the first female chief administrator of CRCDS and one of the first women to become president of a major theological seminary in North America. Under her direction, a presidential search was successfully concluded, a provost was appointed, steps were taken toward the three constituent schools functioning under a single governing board, hallmark programs like those in women's studies and black church studies received renewed emphasis and support, and steps were taken toward a new curriculum that stressed the globalization of the Christian witness, in order to include voices from all around the world.[42]

At CRCDS, the prophetic words of Joel continued to come to pass, as God promised: "I will pour out my spirit upon all flesh; and your sons and your daughters shall prophesy, your old men shall dream dreams, your young men shall see visions: and also upon the servants and upon the handmaids in those days will I pour out my spirit" (Joel 2:28-29, KJV). These Spirit-empowered women expanded the Divinity School's legacy by bringing greater inclusion, opportunity, and equality for women, particularly women exercising leadership in the church and theological education. They opened holes in the ecclesiastical glass ceiling that were large enough for many other women to follow them toward full equality.

---

39. Ibid.
40. Ibid.
41. "Smooth Transition to Mark Change of Divinity School Leadership," *Bulletin* 61, no. 3 (Summer 1989): 1.
42. Shirley Jones, "The President's Column," *Bulletin* 62, no. 2 (Summer 1990): 2.

20

Finding a Prophetic Witness for the Twenty-First Century

In the spring of 2001, it was announced that Dr. G. Thomas Halbrooks would succeed James H. Evans as president of CRCDS. Evans announced his intention to leave his role as president in 1998, with a profound sense of divine call: "I attempted to resist," he said, "but I knew, as we all know that resistance is futile. God was calling me to do something else with my life."[1] The election of Thomas Halbrooks was the result of a long and careful search.[2] "I felt almost a sense of call, a sense of duty to do this," Halbrooks told reporter Jay Tokasz. "It was not as hard to say yes to coming here as it was to say no to Richmond [where he had been serving]."[3] In a short article, the Rochester *Democrat and Chronicle* captured the gravity of the situation at CRCDS: "G. Thomas Halbrooks is the new president of Colgate Rochester Divinity School. The school has fallen on hard times in recent years, but is looking to rebound under new leadership."[4]

Halbrooks came to CRCDS after serving as dean and cofounder of the Baptist Theological Seminary in Richmond, Virginia, which grew from three faculty members and 32 students in 1991 to an enrollment of nearly 300 in 2000.[5] Enrollments at Colgate Rochester were gradually falling for more than a decade. In 1984, for example, 275 students were enrolled at Colgate Rochester; by 2000, however, "the

---

1. James H. Evans, "The President's Column," *Bulletin from the Hill*, Winter/Spring 2000, 2.
2. "President -Elect Appointed," *Bulletin from the Hill*, Winter/Spring 2000, 1.
3. Jay Tokasz, "At Inaugural, Halbrooks Happy with Colgate Post," *Democrat and Chronicle*, April 26, 2001, 11.
4. "G. Thomas Halbrooks Is Taking on Challenge of Revitalizing Divinity School," *Democrat and Chronicle*, April 23, 2001, 9.
5. Doug Mandelaro, "Divinity School Picks Halbrooks," *Democrat and Chronicle*, December 16, 1999, 21.

number is 150, about a third of whom are studying for professional ministry."[6] President Halbrooks considered attracting more students to campus to be his top priority. "The more people we prepare [for ministry], the better we're doing our job. . . . But," he acknowledged, "getting there won't be easy."[7]

To more aggressively recruit new students, the position of vice president of enrollment services was created, and after a nationwide search, Robert Jones was selected to fill that capacity. Melanie May, formerly dean of the Women and Gender Studies program, joined the administrative team as vice president of Academic Life and dean of the faculty.[8] With a new comprehensive plan in place that would enable CRCDS to "define the future and identify goals worthy of achieving," Halbrooks was hopeful that the priorities of increasing funds and boosting enrollment could be met. "I am confident that with hard work and careful planning, with our new vice presidents, we can accomplish our goals," he said. "With the start of the new millennium, we have entered into a new era."[9]

When President Halbrook announced his retirement effective July 2005, enrollment, which had declined for many years, doubled to about 150. Spending was cut in half, to about $3.5 million per year, and donations amounted to more than $600,000 in 2003.[10] The teaching faculty shrunk to eight full-time persons, largely through attrition, and the Divinity School carried a budget deficit that neared $700,000.[11] The endowment, which was reported to stand at nearly $37 million five years earlier, stood at a value nearer $20 million because of the impact of a weakened stock market in the ensuing years.[12] Among the controversial cost-cutting measures implemented at this time was the transfer of most of the Divinity School's three hundred thousand–volume library to the University of Rochester. The move was estimated to save the Divinity School more than $300,000 a year, and an additional $45,000 would be raised by renting some of the Divinity School library space to the University of Rochester.[13] Urging that the transfer of books did not signal that the Divinity

---

6. Tokasz, "At Inaugural, Halbrooks Happy with Colgate Post," 11.
7. Ibid.
8. "New Administration Begins New Era," *Bulletin from the Hill*, Winter 2001, 1.
9. Ibid.
10. Matthew Daneman, "Divinity School Chief Plans July Retirement," *Democrat and Chronicle*, August 4, 2004, 9.
11. "Rochester Seminary President to Retire: G. Thomas Halbrooks," *The Christian Century* 121, no. 18 (September 7, 2004): 17.
12. James Goodman, "Divinity School Oks Book Transfer," *Democrat and Chronicle*, May 15, 2004, 15.
13. Ibid.

School was closing, board chair Rev. Ken Williams said, "We are cash poor and asset rich, and this is a way of ensuring we can get to a point of financial stability. The things we can control, we think are doing marvelously. Enrollment is up, and we have a strong and very productive faculty. We feel that we are in a revival. Closing the school is not an option we are considering."[14]

Rev. Eugene C. Bay succeeded Halbrooks, settling into his new post in January 2006. A former Rochester pastor at Third Presbyterian Church, Bay was lured out of retirement by Divinity School trustee John Wilkinson, who said, "He's the right person at the right time."[15] Acknowledging the challenges that lay ahead, Bay pointed out that enrollments were on the rise and fund-raising increased significantly. "I've come not simply to help this institution to survive, but to thrive," said President Bay. Implying that more changes were forthcoming, Bay noted, "The future may not be the same as the past, and should not be anyway."[16] He said that his "priorities include[d] discussions with other schools about joint academic programs as well as leasing some divinity school property."[17]

During Bay's four-year tenure, the Divinity School received one of its largest single monetary gifts in recent years: $1.35 million, from long-time CRDS trustee Thomas Gosnell in honor of his father. The gift established the Arthur J. Gosnell Chair of Christian Ethics.[18] Also in 2006 Ithaca College's Physical Therapy Center became a tenant on the ground floor of Strong Hall. Under the terms of a ten-year lease, income from the rent was earmarked to help stabilize the Divinity School's sagging budget.[19] Two years later, through the generosity of a $4 million gift, the Divinity School's Trevor-Eaton dormitory was renovated and opened as Hope Lodge and Hospitality House. It "provide[d] 35–40 hotel-style rooms and suites for out-of-town cancer and organ transplant patients and their families staying in the area while receiving specialized medical care."[20] At this time, there were only seven full-time faculty at the Divinity School, and student enrollment began to decline again.[21] Upon Bay's retirement, Wilkinson

14. Doug Mandelaro and Rich Armon, "Divinity School Forced to Sell Some Treasures," *Democrat and Chronicle,* January 16, 2003, 1.
15. Matthew Daneman, "Former Pastor Chosen to Lead Colgate Rochester," *Democrat and Chronicle,* January 11, 2006.
16. Ibid., 11.
17. Ibid.
18. Matthew Daneman, "$1.35 Million Donated to Divinity School," *Democrat and Chronicle,* August 22, 2006, 3.
19. Matthew Daneman, "Divinity School Gets Tenant," *Democrat and Chronicle,* April 3, 2006, 17.
20. Chris Swingle, "Golisano Funds Hope Lodge," *Democrat and Chronicle,* July 17, 2008, 13.
21. CRCDS, *2007-2009 Catalogue,* 100-101.

stated, "We are deeply grateful to Gene Bay for his leadership over the past four years. . . . he has helped right the school's financial situation and put us in the position to move ahead into a bright future. Gene Bay's contribution to CRCDS cannot be overstated."[22]

Following the retirement of Bay, effective June 2010, the Rt. Rev. Jack M. McKelvey, retired bishop of the Episcopal Diocese of Rochester, was appointed interim president. An active member of the CRCDS board of trustees since 2000, President McKelvey said, "I look forward to serving the school and the task of theological education in this important way. Having served on the school's board and in my role as bishop, I know that the school is needed more than ever by the church, and in particular, the church in Western New York."[23]

In May 2011, the CRCDS announced the appointment of Dr. Marvin A. McMickle as the Divinity School's twelfth president. He was a faculty member at Ashland Theological Seminary, as well as senior pastor of the Antioch Baptist Church in Cleveland, Ohio. The *Democrat and Chronicle* announced, "Rev. Marvin A. McMickle brings to his new job as president . . . the skills of a well-known pastor who has not only been active in community affairs but also has authored a dozen books."[24] McMickle was born in Chicago and graduated from Aurora College and Union Theological Seminary. He did additional graduate studies at Columbia University prior to earning his DMin from Princeton Theological Seminary and PhD from Case Western University. McMickle "hope[d] to be a president who [would] direct the seminary toward a broader engagement with society and to put people in the ministry for the 21st century."[25]

A distinguished church leader and theological educator, President McMickle is expert in homiletics and black church studies, as well as being a widely appreciated speaker and preacher on the national stage. Following the prophetic path established by presidents Greenfield, Evans, and others before him, McMickle was an active contributor to local religious and social discourse through guest editorials[26] and

22. CRCDS board of trustees report, as quoted by the Episcopal News Service, "Jack McKelvey Appointed Interim President of Colgate Rochester Crozer Divinity School," Episcopal Church, May 14, 2010, https://www.episcopalchurch.org/library/article/jack-mckelvey-appointed-interim-president-colgate-rochester-crozer-divinity-school.
23. Ibid.
24. James Goodman, "Colgate Rochester Crozer Divinity School Announces New President," *Democrat and Chronicle*, May 16, 2011, 13. Among McMickle's timely monographs on prophetic preaching are *Where Have All the Prophets Gone? Reclaiming Prophetic Preaching in America* (Cleveland: Pilgrim Press, 2006), *Pulpit and Politics* (Valley Forge, PA; Judson Press, 2014), and *Be My Witness* (Valley Forge, PA: Judson Press, 2016).
25. Ibid.
26. See, for example, McMickle's *Democrat and Chronicle* columns "Catastrophe Knows No Color" (September 10, 2017), "Reflections on the S@#* Hole Nations" (January 21, 2018), and "Church Leaders Silent in Wake of Scandals" (February 4, 2018).

blogs in the "Let's Talk"[27] column of the *Democrat and Chronicle*. Deeply appreciative of the CRCDS legacy, he said,

> It is out of this radical discipleship that we passionately teach. CRCDS is proud of our Progressive Christian heritage and our commitment to the social gospel. Our mission is to prepare women and men for ministry that is pastoral, prophetic, and learned. We recognize that ministry today is complex and demanding and the voice of CRCDS is vital to the life of the Church.[28]

McMickle is particularly adept at connecting the rich legacy of the Divinity School as a school of prophets to the larger task of prophetic preaching and living. In reply to the rhetorical question "What is prophetic preaching?" Dr. McMickle wrote,

> Prophetic preaching shifts the focus of a congregation from what is happening to them as a local church to what is happening to us as a society. Prophetic preaching then asks the question: "what is the role or appropriate response of our congregation, our association and our denomination to the events that are occurring within our society and throughout the world?" Prophetic preaching points out those false gods of comfort and of a lack of concern and acquiescence in the face of evil that can so easily replace the true God of scripture, who calls true believers to the active pursuit of justice and righteousness for every member of the society.[29]

Among the interesting and inspiring developments at CRCDS in recent years were the continuation of the long-established lectureships associated with the school's multiple histories, including the Stanley I. Stuber, J. C. Wynn, Martin Luther King Jr., Gene Bartlett, Howard Thurman, Mordecai Wyatt Johnson, LGBTI, and Helen Barrett Montgomery endowed lectures. Among the prominent guest lecturers in recent years have been Rev. Jimmy Creech (LGBTI issues, 2012), Rev. Jeremiah Wright (African American experience, 2014), Dr. Alan Boesak (faith and justice, 2014), Dr. Leonard Sweet (future of the church, 2016), Dr. Christopher Evans (Rauschenbusch legacy, 2017), Mr. Tim Ternes (Saint John's Bible, 2018), and Rev. Brae Adams (Christian faith and the LGBTI experience, 2018).

A second venture was the development of a veterans' temporary housing program, in cooperation with the Veterans Administration and Housing and Urban Development, by converting twelve units of

---

27. See, for example, "There is a Sense in Which the Events That Have Unfolded in Ferguson . . ." and "We Celebrate the Names of Susan B. Anthony and Fredrick Douglass . . ." at DemocrateandChronicle.com/opinion.
28. Marvin A. McMickle, "Welcome to Colgate Rochester Crozer Divinity School," CRCDS, www.crcds.edu/about-crcds/our-story/, accessed July 21, 2018.
29. Marvin A. McMickle, "Prophetic Message," in *New Interpreter's Handbook of Preaching*, ed. Paul Scott Wilson (Nashville: Abingdon, 2008), www.theafricanamericanlectionary.org/pdf/preaching/PropheticPreaching_MarvinMcMickle.pdf.

Andrews Hall into housing for veterans attempting to make the difficult transition back into the American mainstream.[30] Additionally, celebrating the fiftieth anniversary of the historic civil rights lockout focused the community's attention upon the interface between Christian faith and issues of inclusion and equality. "We've got to keep listening to people who say they belong to the church but the church doesn't belong to them," Dr. McMickle said.[31] Damond Wilson, student president of the Black Student Caucus, who sponsored a gala banquet during the celebration, also remarked: "At the base of what they were doing was being able to have their voice heard, and that definitely is life-changing, because in this day there are definitely situations where people's voices aren't being heard."[32]

Despite the prophetic vision and rich legacy of CRCDS, the Divinity School continued to struggle with declining student enrollments and financial shortages. It operates with five full-time and four part-time faculty and an enrollment of roughly 115 students, less than half of what it was thirty years ago and most of whom are commuters.[33] The current, full-time faculty is comprised of Mark Brummitt in Old Testament, Jin Young Choi in New Testament, Melanie Duguid-May in theology, David Yoon-Jung Kim in ethics, and John R. Tyson in church history, in addition to Marvin McMickle in black church studies, and Stephanie Sauvé in practical theology, who split administrative and instructional duties. Two scholars, Dr. David Yoon-Jung Kim and Dr. Jin Young Choi, are of Korean descent and bring a global and postcolonial point of view to the ongoing work of the seminary.

In 2016 Ithaca College elected not to renew its ten-year rental agreement with CRCDS and relocated its physical therapy program to the campus in Ithaca, New York. This development ended an important income stream for CRCDS. Shrinking graduating classes continued the Divinity's School saga of dwindling enrollments with a total of thirty graduating students in May 2012, for example.[34] "The world of theological education has already changed dramatically. Long gone are the days when only 22–25-year-old males enrolled

---

30. David Andreatta, "As Enrollment Declines, Seminary Offers 12 Beds For Homeless," *Democrat and Chronicle*, September 27, 2012, B4.
31. Justin Murphy, "Demanding Change: Divinity School Marks Anniversary of Historic Civil Rights Lockout," *Democrat and Chronicle*, April 3, 2018, A1.
32. Ibid., A5.
33. Andreatta, "As Enrollment Declines, B1.
34. "The Class of 2012," *Colgate Rochester Crozer Bulletin* (Summer 2012), 4.

full-time in seminary, took classes exclusively on campus, in-person, during the daytime with the expressed goal of one day becoming a pastor or perhaps a missionary," McMickle observed. "Now, the overall number of people attending seminary has changed, but, importantly, so has who attends seminary, how they attend seminary and where and when they take classes. . . . Even the reasons why people attend seminary have shifted."[35] At the same time, the Divinity School also faced nearly $2 million of deferred maintenance on its aging facilities.[36]

Dr. McMickle opened the 2014–2015 annual report with the prophetic words from RTS President Augustus Strong, written in 1900:

> We cannot be absolutely sure than any earthly instrument is necessary to God. Times change, and methods change with them. Our part is to do our work, to stand by the institutions Christ has put into our charge, to make them, by our liberality, our teaching, our influence, what they ought to be. The present is ours; the future belongs to God. We trust that the Seminary shall abide so long as the world stands. But, after all, the Seminary is but a means to an end. That end is the progress and triumph of the Kingdom of God.[37]

Seen in this light, certainly the beautiful CRCDS campus, on "the hill above Highland Park," is but a means to an end—the same end outlined so well by Strong. In the face of mounting shortages, and a largely second-career, nonresidential, and significantly female student body, the decision was made to sell its historic campus and relocate to a more modern, right-sized, and cost-effective campus elsewhere in Rochester. The move was a strategic one, designed to direct the Divinity School's funds away from facilities management and more directly toward its historic mission and current ministry. McMickle stated that "this is a wonderful opportunity for us to be in a new facility to get out of the real estate management business and have a space we can operate in for many years to come."[38] Reiterating the CRCDS's permanence in Rochester, the president reported that the school has no plans to close: "We will be around for another 200 years."[39]

The original relocation plan, which included the purchase of the campus property by a real estate development firm for the purposes of

---

35. Marvin A. McMickle, "This Is Truly an Exciting Time at Colgate Rochester Crozer Divinity School," *Colgate Rochester Crozer Bulletin* (Summer/Fall 2016), 4.
36. James Goodman and Brian Sharp, "Divinity School Selling Campus: To Rent New Facility," *Democrat and Chronicle*, March 10, 2017, A3.
37. Marvin A. McMickle, "Message from the President," *CRCDS Annual Report: 2014-15*, 2.
38. Goodman and Sharp, "Divinity School Selling Campus," A3.
39. James Goodman, "Trustees OK Divinity School Campus Sale," *Democrat and Chronicle*, May 18, 2018, A4.

building a luxury hotel and allowed CRCDS to rent back a portion of the redesigned space, did not come to fruition. As Steve Orr reported, "Sale of the verdant hillside home of Colgate Rochester Crozer Divinity School to a struggling local start-up company has been canceled—but school officials say a new buyer has been lined up."[40] But the two-year hiatus between the announced sale of the campus and the restart of the relocation of the Divinity School paralyzed student recruitment, enrollment, and donations. Speaking on behalf of the administration, chief operating officer Tom McDade Clay summarized the situation: "Right now, we are in discussions with the new buyer and internally—about where to locate, both short-term and long-term."[41] On August 29, 2018, however, President McMickle announced: "I am delighted to report that the Trustees have voted to relocate CRCDS to a new 'home' at 320 North Goodman Street in Rochester, beginning with the Fall 2019 semester."[42] Located in the heart of Rochester, the new state-of-the-art educational facility of CRCDS more effectively reflects the needs of the twenty-first-century seminary student.

It is said that the past is like a distant mirror that allows us to see ourselves more clearly—see who we have been, who we are, and who we ought to be. Let it be so for the saga of this school of prophets. While this bicentennial history of Colgate Rochester Crozer Divinity School draws to a conclusion, in the summer of 2019, its proud legacy and effective mission do not come to an end.

CRCDS will live on as the rich legacy and pertinent mission of its constituent schools finds still another incarnation in new people and in a new location. Its future is as audacious as the hopefulness of thirteen men, who with God's help and $13, thought they could build a new school and offer a better future for their church, their region, and their world. It is as pertinent as the evangelical liberalism of Augustus Strong, William Newton Clarke, and Henry Griggs Weston, who sought to combine the eternal gospel of the Christian past with the forward-looking attitudes of a new and present age. It is as socially aware as Walter Rauschenbusch's and Henry Vedder's stinging critique of America's growing economic disparity. It is as racially inclusive and prophetically transformative as the contributions

---

40. Steve Orr, "New Buyer Arises for Divinity School Property," *Democrat and Chronicle*, May 9, 2018, A6.
41. Ibid.
42. Marvin McMickle, "Exciting News from President McMickle," e-blast press release, August 29, 2018, https://www.crcds.edu/exciting-news-from-president-mcmickle/, accessed September 23, 2018.

of Mordecai Wyatt Johnson, Howard Thurman, Samuel Proctor, and Martin Luther King Jr., who clearly saw the injustices of their own society and invited people of faith to join God in building a better world—a beloved community—instead. This legacy is seen time and time again in the selfless dedication of women like Rumah Avilla Crouse, Ruth Hill, Mary Burdette, Joanna Moore, who gave themselves unreservedly to God and to the care of those whom Jesus called "the least of these my brethren," even when both church and society placed barriers in their way. It is seen in the trailblazing efforts of women like Rev. Betty Bone Scheiss, Dr. Shirley M. Jones, and Bishop Marjorie Matthews. It is seen in the vibrant spirituality of Ebenezer Dodge, William Newton Clarke, George Cross, Howard Thurman, and Milton G. Evans, and others who looked to the enduring message of Jesus to find the essence of true religion as well as the values that drew people of faith together instead of dividing them and driving them apart.

The Divinity School's two-hundred-year-old prophetic, Christian legacy was well stated and richly reaffirmed by its current faculty in a "Curriculum Preamble" that describes the vision of the faculty and staff of CRCDS for its students, programs, and new future:

Confessing that Jesus Christ is the Good News of God who transforms both persons and societies—
    We are rooted in biblical faith and in the lived traditions of the church.
    We are shaped by the witness of the Social Gospel movement, by the traditions of the Black Church, by the voices of women in church and society, and by Christian responses to religious pluralism and issues of gender, each as critically interpreted and embodied by those who both cherish the past and are open to the future.
    We are committed to the ministry as we engage the theological disciplines in an ecumenical Christian community of teaching, learning and worship that prepare students for Christian ministries that are learned, pastoral and prophetic.
    We are committed to theological education that embodies acts of radical hospitality, in our classrooms, and in chapel, in our churches and communities.
    We seek the integrity of living faith and intellectual inquiry by which women and men are prepared for local, national, and global Christian ministries dedicated to a life-giving future for all God's people.[43]

---

43. *CRCDS Catalogue*, 2017-2019, 10.

Afterword

"We equip women and men for careers in ministry who are learned, pastoral, and prophetic". This phrase sits at the heart of the mission statement of Colgate Rochester Crozer Divinity School; the school where I served as President from 2011-2019. Being learned, pastoral and prophetic is what our recruitment literature promotes. It is what our curriculum and faculty provide. It is what I said to the eight entering classes during new student orientation during my tenure. It is what I reinforced to eight graduating classes at commencement. It is what we hope and expect from our alumni as they approach their ministry whether inside the local church or beyond.

The notion of equipping persons for a ministry that offers a prophetic critique of the church and of the broader society is nothing new for CRCDS. This was baked into the DNA of the school long before I or anyone currently affiliated with the school ever stepped on campus or ever stood before students in a lecture hall. More than one-hundred years ago, Walter Rauschenbusch who was both an alumnus of the school and one of its most distinguished professors spoke to the mission of what was then Rochester Theological Seminary by saying, "we breed prophets here". This mission statement by Rauschenbusch is the basis for the title of this book by John Tyson; School of the Prophets: The History of Colgate Rochester Crozer Divinity School.

This book traces the history of CRCDS over its two-hundred years of providing theological education. Founded in 1817 in Hamilton, New York and offering its first classes in 1819, this book serves to mark the school's bicentennial. John Tyson guides the reader through the institutional mergers, the physical relocations, the ecumenical partnerships, and the theological shifts that have occurred over those two hundred years. The school moved from Hamilton, NY to Rochester, NY in 1850 where Rochester Theological Seminary was already operating. Colgate Theological Seminary would merge with Rochester Theological Seminary in 1928 to become Colgate Rochester Divinity School.

In 1962 the Baptist Missionary Training School that prepared women for careers in various fields of service left Chicago and moved onto the campus of CRCDS. In 1970 Crozer Theological Seminary of Chester, Pennsylvania (the alma mater of Martin Luther King, Jr) merged with CRDS to form Colgate Rochester Crozer Divinity School (CRCDS). The book examines the years when Bexley Hall Episcopal Seminary and St. Bernard's Roman Catholic School of Theology also operated on the campus of CRCDS.

The book confronts the many theological debates that have occurred and keep occurring during the school's existence. William Newton Clarke will be found arguing for a theology that requires both personal salvation and social engagement. Walter Rauschenbusch will introduce the Social Gospel as a result of his years in pastoral ministry among the marginalized persons in New York City during the so-called Gilded Age when wealth disparity was even more extreme than it is today. Tyson points out how the faculty dealt with the rise of biblical criticism and the scientific method of textual analysis, and how that methodology sent shock waves through the church and through seminaries and divinity schools across the country.

This book examines the debates that surrounded the admission of women and of African Americans into the student body of the divinity school. It sheds new light on the claim that "God Is Dead" set forth by William Hamilton in the mid-1960s. It looks at the black student unrest in 1968 that resulted in the "lockout" of 1969 when the black students took over Strong Hall as a way to dramatize their demands for the addition of black scholars to the faculty, the appointment of black persons to the Board of Trustees, and the expansion of the curriculum to include courses in the history and polity of black churches in the United States. That lockout gained all those things, and it also resulted in the first Black Church Studies Program in the United States. That led to the creation of the Martin Luther King, Jr. Fellows program which was a Doctor of Ministry Degree program directed by Henry Mitchell. That program brought together some of the leading black pastors in the country, and the doctoral dissertations generated by that group formed the core of the scholarly research and literature that informed other Black Church Studies programs across the country for years to come.

A discussion of a School of the Prophets is made complete by Tyson when he examines the Women and Gender Studies Program which began in the 1980s under the initial leadership of Melanie Duguid May. This program has a dual focus, first of advocating for women who seek careers in the ministry. It also does that same work of advocacy and education for and concerning persons in the LGBTQ community whose aspirations for ordination into a ministry career remain one of the defining issues for the 21st century church around the world.

Twice each year, in the Fall and Spring Lecture Series CRCDS offers academic lectures to the broader Rochester community that intentionally include a focus on issues of race, gender, and sexual orientation. This unabashed support for racial minorities, women, and LGBTQ persons has long been part of the mission and ministry of CRCDS. Rather than simply writing or talking about such issues, this school has designed its curriculum, shaped its admissions standards, approached its hiring policies, and geared its public pronouncements with these issues being front and center!

I am especially grateful to John Tyson for accepting the assignment given to him by the school to prepare this study of the history and evolution of CRCDS. Tyson is a world-renowned church historian with a particular expertise in Methodist studies in general, and with a lengthy list of publications, lectures, and scholarly articles focused on the work of John and Charles Wesley in particular. This book shows all the signs of an historian at work. He has uncovered first-hand reports about the school and its most noted faculty and students. He has secured helpful photographs and other images. At points, the reader will find themselves sitting in on a faculty meeting where curriculum and enrollment issues are being discussed. At other times, it is as if the reader is sitting in on a Trustee meeting where issues of building construction, institutional mergers, and fundraising challenges are being discussed. After eight years as president of this school, I can attest to the fact that these kinds of conversations and debates continue to this day.

Other church historians will be helped by noting the methodology that Tyson has employed in doing his research. Other seminaries and divinity schools will find in this book a roadmap on how to navigate the constantly changing theological and cultural environment in which seminaries have to operate. All readers will be helped by his discussions about noted African American alumni including Mordecai Johnson, Howard Thurman, and Martin Luther King, Jr.

The book is not without its harsh analysis of how the school has been forced to adjust to the shifting terrain of theological education from 1819 to the present. In fact, while this book was being researched and written, CRCDS was once again on the move to a new physical location. Its home since 1928 was built as residential school that served primarily single, white male students who were bound for careers as pastors in American Baptist Churches. Today, CRCDS has within its student body persons from over thirty separate Protestant denominations and other Independent Church movements. Its once crowded dormitories are no longer needed since the school consists largely of commuter students who rarely enroll on a full-time basis.

Like many other seminaries and divinity schools in this country, CRCDS is having to reimagine and redefine how it will go about accomplishing its mission. However, one thing will never change. CRCDS will always be a school that "equips women and men for ministry in the local church and beyond who are learned, pastoral, and prophetic". Now in its third century of life, CRCDS continues to be a School of the Prophets.

Marvin A. McMickle, PhD
President (retired)
Colgate Rochester Crozer Divinity School 2011–2019

Appendix

Chronology of Main Events

Colgate Theological Seminary (Hamilton Institute), Rochester Theological Seminary, Baptist Missionary Training School, Bexley Hall, Crozer Theological Seminary, and St. Bernard's Institute

1815
- Daniel Hascall begins to teach candidates for ministry in his home in Hamilton, New York.

1817
- Episcopal Bishop Philander Chase, founder of Bexley Hall, arrives in Ohio.
- Thirteen "ministers and brethren" meet in the home of Samuel Payne to establish "a school of prophets" to train candidates for the Baptist ministry.
- Baptist Educational Society of the State of New York forms.
- The Payne family's farm in Hamilton is proposed as the location for the school.
- New York Baptist Theological Seminary group is established in New York City.

1818
- Philander Chase is elected Episcopal bishop of Ohio.

1819
- Chase establishes a school in Worthington, Ohio.
- Jonathan Wade enrolls as first student at Hamilton Literary and Theological Institute.
- Hamilton Literary and Theological Institute is granted a charter from New York State.

1820
- Hamilton Literary and Theological Institute opens with 10 students and one instructor.

1821
- Nathaniel Kendrick joins the Hamilton faculty.

1822
- Jonathan Wade, Hamilton's first graduate, becomes missionary to Burma.

1823
- New York City Baptist Theological Seminary group begins to support Hamilton.
- New York City Theological Seminary group transfers its library to the Hamilton Institute, and with the merger of the two groups, William Colgate transfers his support to Hamilton.

1824
- The Episcopal Diocese of the State of Ohio resolves to establish a seminary for the Protestant Episcopal Church.

1825
- Ohio Episcopalians purchase a large tract of land with funds donated by English Admiral Lord Kenyon Gambier.
- Chase's school relocates to Gambier, Ohio, as the Theological Seminary of the Protestant Episcopal Church in the Diocese of Ohio.
- Kenyon College is established out of the funds raised for the Episcopalian seminary in Ohio.

1826
- Hamilton Institute builds its first building, "the stone academy."

1827
- West Hall, a second building for the Hamilton Institute, is proposed.

1828
- Nathaniel Stem is the first graduate from what would become Bexley Hall.

1829
- The academic course of study at Hamilton Institute is increased from two years to four years; in 1832 it would be extended to six years.
- West Hall is completed at Hamilton Institute.

1832
- Charles P. McIlvaine is consecrated as the second Episcopal bishop of Ohio and becomes the second president of both Kenyon College and Theological Seminary.
- More than one hundred students enroll in the Hamilton Institute.

1833
- Kenyon College introduces a full seminary program and begins building a theological faculty.

1834–1835
- The Hamilton Institute introduces its collegiate course, and the academic program is extended to eight years.

1839
- Kenyon College and the Ohio seminary establish separate administrations and programs.
- Construction begins on Bexley Hall to house the Ohio Episcopalian Seminary
- The Hamilton Institute admits students who do not have ministry as their chief aim.

1844

- McIlvaine completes the construction of the seminary building in Ohio, naming it Bexley Hall in honor of its substantial English donors.

1846

- Enrollment at the Hamilton Institute increases to 146 students, and the school receives a university charter from the Board of Regents of the State of New York.
- The Bexley Hall facility is completed.
- The collegiate division of the Hamilton Institute separates from the theological seminary and is chartered as Madison University.

1847

- The relocation of the Hamilton Institute to Rochester, New York, is first proposed.
- Hamilton professor John Maginnis, trustees Elisha Tucker and John Wilder, and pastor Pharcellus Church meet in the First Baptist Church of Rochester to make plans for the relocation of Madison University to the city of Rochester.

1847–1850

- The "removal controversy" occurs; Rochester Theological Seminary and University of Rochester are born through schism at Hamilton Institute.

1850

- The "removal controversy" is resolved as the Supreme Court of New York State denies the petition of the Rochester faction to move the school to the city.
- The University of Rochester and Rochester Theological Seminary are established as new institutions by emigres from Hamilton and interested parties in Rochester, supported by the newly chartered New York Baptist Union.
- Stephen Taylor leaves Bucknell University to become president of Madison University and Seminary.
- George Eaton, Edward Turneyn, and Philetus Spear join Hamilton faculty.
- The University of Rochester and Rochester Theological Seminary open in the former City Hotel with 66 students enrolled in the university and 24 in the seminary.

1850–1860

- McIlvaine's leadership and association with the evangelical revival in the West brings increased growth to Bexley Hall.

1851

- The German department of RTS is established to meet the needs of immigrant people.

1853

- Ebenezer Dodge, future formative president of the institution, is called to Madison University as professor of New Testament interpretation.
- Ezekiel G. Robinson is called to RTS as a professor of Christian theology.

1854

- The enrollment of Madison University climbs to 216 and is larger than prior to the relocation controversy.

1856

- George Eaton becomes president of Madison University and Seminary. He serves in this role until 1868.

1857

- Samuel Colgate and James B. Colgate, the sons of William Colgate, join the Madison University board of trustees. Samuel takes a particular interest in the affairs of the seminary.
- John Price Crozer, a Philadelphia industrialist, establishes a normal school in "the Old Main."

1858

- Augustus Rauschenbusch, father of Walter, joins the RTS faculty as director of the German department.

1860

- Ezekiel G. Robinson becomes the first president of RTS.

1861

- Students from the Episcopalian seminary in Virginia transfer to Bexley Hall due to war.
The University of Rochester builds its first building.

1866

- John Price Crozer dies. His family decides to establish a theological seminary in his memory.

1867

- Crozer Theological Seminary is granted a charter by the state of Pennsylvania.

1868

- Henry Griggs Weston is named the first president and main professor of Crozer.
- RTS faces severe financial crisis; President Robinson returned from sabbatical in Europe to lead a fund-raising campaign to save the school.
- John McQuaid is installed as episcopal head of the newly created Rochester Diocese of the Roman Catholic Church.

1869

- Rochester Theological Seminary moves into its own facility, Trevor Hall.
- Ebenezer Dodge becomes president of Madison University (Colgate Theological Seminary).
- Joanna P. Moore begins her extensive ministry among freed blacks in the Deep South.

1870

- McQuaid establishes St. Andrews Preparatory Roman Catholic School in Rochester.

1872

- Augustus Strong comes to RTS as president and professor of systematic theology.

1874

- The Episcopal Church of Ohio is divided into two separate dioceses, which drastically reduces support for Bexley Hall.

1874–1875

- Bexley Hall has only one student.

1876

- The first black student enrolls at Crozer Theological Seminary.

1877

- Crozer grows to 42 students, taught by six faculty members.
- Rumah Alvilla Crouse (and many others) establish the Baptist Women's Home Mission Society in Chicago.

1878

- The Roman Catholic diocese of Rochester discusses starting a theological seminary.

1879

- Roman Catholics purchase seminary site in Rochester.

1880

- Rockefeller Hall is erected at RTS.
- The Baptist Women's Home Mission Society founds a missionary training school for women.

1881

- The Baptist Missionary Training School (BMTS) launches in Chicago, with Mary Burdette as principal.
- Moore comes to BMTS as an instructor and student.

1886

- Walter Rauschenbusch graduates from the English department at RTS.
- Augustus Strong, Baptist theologian at RTS, publishes his magisterial *Systematic Theology*.
- Rauschenbusch accepts a call to Second Baptist Church in New York City.

1888:

- Mary Eliza ("Mother") Morris becomes head of BMTS.

1889

Andrew Leonard is elected Episcopalian bishop of Ohio and president of Bexley.
The theological seminary at Kenyon College changes its name to Bexley Hall.

1890

- BMTS moves into its new facility on Indiana Avenue in Chicago.
- Madison University, formerly the Hamilton Institute, changes its name to Colgate.
- William Newton Clarke joins the faculty of Colgate Theological Seminary.
- Leonard's efforts bring significant growth to Bexley Hall.
- Crozer becomes the first theological seminary to establish a chair in biblical theology.

- Moore begins her Fireside Schools and *Hope Magazine*.
- Henry Clay Vedder becomes professor at Crozer.

1891

- St. Bernard's Roman Catholic seminary is formally dedicated and opened.
- The BMTS curriculum is extended from one year to two.

1892

- The BMTS program of study is increased to two years, and enrollment grows to 84.
- "The Brotherhood of the Kingdom of God" meets in Rauschenbusch's apartment.

1893

- BMTS alumna Isabell (Belle) Crawford begins her ministry among Native Americans.
- St. Bernard's new Lake Avenue facility is completed.

1897

- Walter Rauschenbusch joins the faculty of RTS.
- BMTS announces that since its inception the school trained 394 women as missionaries.

1898

- William Newton Clarke of Colgate Theological Seminary publishes *Outlines of Theology*.

1902

- Walter Rauschenbusch accepts the chair of Church History at RTS.

1904

- Coburn Hall, the 12,000-volume theological library at Bexley Hall, is dedicated.

1905

- The New York State Board of Regents authorizes RTS to grant the bachelor of divinity degree.
- Thomas Hickey becomes coadjutor with McQuaid, and James Hartley becomes corector of St. Bernard's Seminary.

1906

- Bexley Hall revises its curriculum into a form that remains intact for nearly fifty years.
- Strong publishes his magisterial *Systematic Theology*.

1907

- BMTS breaks ground for its new facility on Indiana Avenue.
- Walter Rauschenbusch publishes his epoch-making *Christianity and the Social Crisis*.
- Crozer Theological Seminary implements an extension course.
- Colgate Theological Seminary establishes its Italian department.

1909

- The teaching faculty of the BMTS receives salaries for the first time.
- Milton G. Evans becomes president of Crozer.

1910

- BMTS plans to increase its program to three years and adds a graduate department.
- The BMTS alumnae organization issues its first edition of its newsletter, *Echoes*.

1912

- Charles Hubert, an African American student, graduates from RTS with the bachelor of divinity degree.
- Augustus Strong retires, and progressive James Stewart serves as acting president of RTS. George Cross, Conrad Moehlman, Henry Burke Robins, and Ernest Parsons come to RTS.
- Rauschenbusch publishes *Christianizing the Social Order* as the sequel to his previous work.
- Henry C. Vedder of Crozer publishes *Socialism and the Ethics of Jesus*.

1914

- The Kenyon College trustees establish a standing committee on the theological seminary.
- John Behan becomes the first male president of the BMTS.
- Vedder's *Jesus and the Problems of Democracy* causes controversy among fundamentalists.

1915

- Clarence Barbour is named the third president of RTS.
- Mordecai Wyatt Johnson graduates from RTS with the bachelor of divinity degree.
- The Bexley Hall facility is renovated after a funding campaign netted $50,000, but the cost of the renovations grows to more than $80,000.
- Theological controversy over fundamentalism and modernism at BMTS results in the dismissal of faculty members on both sides of the issue.
- William Newton Clarke of Colgate publishes *The Ideal of Jesus*.

1917

- Rauschenbusch publishes his seminal work, *A Theology for the Social Gospel*.

1918

- George Cross publishes *What Is Christianity?* as a wholesale remaking of Christian theology.

1919

- The RTS board of trustees votes to admit women on equal standing with men in all programs.
- President Richard Cutten of Colgate opens a conversation about merging CTS and RTS.
- Clara Pinkham becomes president of the BMTS.

1920

- Fundamentalists attack RTS; the assault reaches its height in 1929.

1922

- Ruth Hill, an alumna of the BMTS, graduates from RTS with her bachelor of divinity degree.

- Colgate Theological Seminary grows to five full-time faculty and enrolls 45 students.
- Andrew Meeham is named rector of St. Bernard's Seminary.
- Conservative Baptists call for the expulsion of Vedder from Crozer.

1924

- The first edition of the *Crozer Quarterly* is published.
- Professor Steward Cole brings progressive education to Crozer.

1926

- Howard Thurman graduates as valedictorian of his RTS class.
- Bexley Hall has largest enrollment ever.
- Colgate, Newton, and Rochester theological seminaries discuss consolidation.
- The Bexley Society is organized.
- Alice Brimson becomes head of the BMTS.
- Mordecai Wyatt Johnson becomes president of Howard University.

1927

- The Supreme Court clears the way for the merger of Colgate and RTS.

1928

- Colgate and Rochester seminaries formally unite.
- Colgate Rochester Divinity School (CRDS) moves to the former RTS site.
- John D. Rockefeller pledges $1,250,000 to CRDS.
- W. R. McNutt pioneers the study of practical theology at Crozer.
- The Ayers and Trevor endowed lectures are established at CRCDS.

1929

- Albert W. Beaven is named president of CRDS.
- *The Colgate Rochester Bulletin* begins as "the voice of the prophets."
- A new curriculum is put in place at CRDS, which would guide the school for more than two decades.
- The Great Depression hit Bexley Hall particularly hard.
- BMTS enrollment drops to an all-time low of 42 students.
- Suzanne G. Rinck joins the BMTS staff as supervisor of fieldwork.
- The Rauschenbusch Lectures in Applied Christianity are established at CRDS.

1931

- The cornerstone for Strong Hall lays other buildings on the new CRDS campus.

1932

- New CRDS facilities are formally dedicated. Helen Barrett Montgomery and CTS alumnus Harry Emerson Fosdick are among those who address the gathering.
- The Ambrose Swasey Library is dedicated and named for its donor; it combines 55,000 volumes from RTS with more than 7,000 from Crozer.
- CRDS opens its fall term with an enrollment of 142 students.
- The August Wilheim Neander Theological Library is added to the Ambrose Swasey Library.
- John Groggin becomes rector at St. Bernard's.

1933
- Mordecai Wyatt Johnson delivers lectures at CRDS.

1934
- James H. Franklin becomes president of Crozer, a position he holds until 1944.
- Crozer students are placed in clinical pastoral training, one of the first programs in the nation.
- Kenyon College trustees suggest closing Bexley Hall for financial reasons.
- Reinhold Niebuhr delivers the Rauschenbusch Lectures at CRDS, which are subsequently published as his *Principles of Christian Ethics* in 1935.

1935
- Crozer's curriculum committee rejects the new practical studies–based model of theological education (the functional model) in favor of the traditional classical model.
- Plans for the merger of CRDS and Auburn Theological Seminary are explored and then discontinued.

1936
- The Samuel Colgate Memorial Chapel on CRDS's Highland Park campus is dedicated.
- The first meeting of the American Association of Theological Schools (AATS) is held at Crozer.
- BMTS expands programs to offer two separate bachelor of arts degrees and establishes its own separate board of directors for greater independence.
- Jessie Crawford becomes head of the BMTS.

1937
- *The CRDS Bulletin* begins publication as a quarterly alumni newspaper.
- The proposed merger of CRDS with Auburn Theological Seminary is abandoned.
- A commission, chaired by Bishop Strider, recommends either the closing or merger of Bexley Hall.

1938
- Ohio Bishop Beverly Tucker rejects plans to downgrade or close Bexley Hall.

1939
- BMTS becomes a four-year college and hires a full-time director for fieldwork.
- The CRCDS alumni fund drive is instituted following a 20 percent decrease in endowment income.

1940
- Plans to strengthen the basis of Bexley Hall are halted by the coming of war.

1942
- Conrad Roach becomes dean at Bexley Hall, a position he holds for eighteen years.
- Beaven announces CRDS is facing a severe financial crisis.
- Winthrop Hudson joins the CRDS faculty.

1943
- Bexley Hall, with only nine students, temporarily relocates to Richmond, Virginia.
- Albert Beaven dies suddenly.
- Robert Beaven begins a decade as president of BMTS.
- *The CRDS Bulletin* is replaced by bimonthly *Alumni News Bulletin*.

1944
- Edwin McNeill Poteat is inaugurated as the third president of CRDS.
- CRDS summer session is developed to meet the needs of wartime students.
- CRDS begins the process of achieving national accreditation.
- BMTS acquires property at 510 Wellington Avenue in Chicago to begin a new facility.
- Howard Thurman establishes The Church for the Fellowship of All People in San Francisco.
- Edwin Aubrey becomes president of Crozer, a post he holds until 1949.

1945
- Bexley Hall leaves Virginia and returns to its original location in Gambier, Ohio.
- Tucker launches an innovative four-year plan to improve Bexley Hall.
- Crozer's innovative pilot program for field education is rejected by the administration.
- Samuel DeWitt Proctor graduates from CTS.

1948
- Martin Luther King Jr. enrolls at Crozer.

1949
- Wilbour Eddy Saunders begins his eleven-year tenure as CRDS president.
- The Samuel Colgate Historical Library is moved to CRDS.
- The German department of RTS moves to Sioux Falls, South Dakota, where it reopens as North American Baptist Seminary.
- Howard Thurman publishes *Jesus and the Disinherited*.
- Sankey Lee Blanton becomes president of Crozer.

1950
- CRDS trustees approve a sweeping new curriculum program.
- The RTS centennial launches with more than $60,000 already in hand.
- The national Episcopal Church financial campaign gives Bexley Hall funds for facilities.
- Samuel D. Proctor earns his PhD at Boston University Divinity School.
- Kenneth ("Snuffy") Smith joins the faculty of CTS.
- Martin Luther King Jr. reads Rauschenbusch's *Christianity and the Social Crisis*, which leaves "an indelible imprint" on his thinking.

1951
- Martin Luther King Jr. graduates from CTS.

1952

- The Fifth Annual CRDS Ministerial Conference reaches an attendance of more than one hundred pastors.
- Bexley Hall enrollment reaches a historic high, causing problems in housing married students.

1953

- The shortfall between the CRDS endowment income and operating budget ($45,000) is raised through an annual giving program.
- William Hamilton joins the CRDS faculty as professor of systematic theology.

1954

- CRDS president Wilbour Saunders announces a dramatically changing theological climate in which the social gospel is no longer valued.
- Bexley Hall declines relocation to the Firestone mansion in Akron, Ohio.
- Martin Luther King Jr. becomes pastor of Dexter Baptist Church, Montgomery, Alabama.

1955

- BMTS alumni and friends contribute $55,000 toward building a new chapel.
- Practical ministry studies and pastoral experience becomes required of all CRDS students.
- Martin Luther King Jr. graduates with his PhD from Boston University.
- Rosa Parks is arrested for refusing to relinquish her seat on a public bus, setting off the Montgomery Bus Boycott, in which King takes leadership.

1957

- A study by the Lilly Foundation recommends separate boards for Bexley Hall and Kenyon College, as well as an equitable division of assets.

1958

- Pearl Rosser becomes president of BMTS.
- Dean Robert Page of Bexley Hall reports a dire shortage of "men and money."

1959

- Almus Thorp becomes dean of Bexley Hall.
- CRDS president Wilbour Saunders announces the end of "a decade of growth."
- Christian existentialist theologians Rudolph Bultmann and Paul Tillich lecture at CRDS.
- The *Democrat and Chronicle* publishes "Ministry Co-eds," featuring CRDS women.

1960

- The CRCDS endowment is valued at more than $5 million.
- A curriculum revision at CRDS allows for more elective courses and more flexibility.

1961

- Edwin T. Dahlberg Ecumenical Lectureship (endowed lectures) are established at CRDS.
- Gene E. Bartlett becomes president of CRDS.
- The BMTS board votes to adapt the school's mission to a graduate-level program.
- A study commission reports that the financial status of BMTS is untenable; merger plans with CRDS are explored.

1962

- The merger of BMTS and CRDS is finalized, and BMTS relocates to the CRDS facility.
- Suzanne Rinck is named dean of women at CRDS.
- CRDS has $365,000 in reserve, even as five new faculty are added.
- The Upland Institute for Social Change is established at Crozer and soon becomes the Martin Luther King, Jr. School.
- Ronald V. Wells is named president of CTS.

1963

- Martin Luther King Jr. gives his "I Have a Dream" speech.
- The central committee of the World Council of Churches meets on the CRCDS campus.
- CTS and Chester Hospital join hands in a clinical pastoral education (CPE) program for Crozer.
- The financial deficit at Bexley Hall reaches almost $75,000.
- Eaton Hall at CRDS is transformed into a Women's Center.

1964

- CRDS institutes a study on "Negroes in Theological Education."
- Sixteen CRDS students are arrested for civil disobedience in protesting segregation.
- William Hamilton publishes on the death of God theology.

1965

- An ecumenical Rochester Center for Theological Studies is first proposed.
- Dean Thorp announces the coming of "a year of decision" for Bexley Hall.
- The death of God controversy brings national attention to CRDS.
- Malcolm X addresses a student and community group on the CRDS campus.
- The Philadelphia College of Nursing relocates to the Crozer campus.
- St. Bernard's and CRDS host joint lectures by Roland DeVaux.

1966

- Fulton Sheen is installed as Roman Catholic bishop of Rochester.
- The Negro, the Negro Church, and American Culture course is offered at CRDS.
- St. Bernard's and CRDS begin a program of faculty get-togethers for the two schools.
- The Bexley Hall board of trustees begins to study relocation of the school.
- *Time's* "Is God Dead?" cover and article features William Hamilton of CRDS.
- Bexley Hall task force recommends the relocation of the school to CRDS.

1967

- Martin Luther King Jr.'s *Where Do We Go from Here: Chaos or Community?* is published.
- The relocation and merger of CRDS and Bexley Hall is approved by trustees, and the formation of the Rochester Center for Theological Studies (CTS) is announced.
- King's "Beyond Vietnam" speech links issues of race, poverty, and violence in a way that loses him a significant amount of popular support.
- William Hamilton leaves CRDS to take a position at the New College in Sarasota, Florida.
- A fire at St. Bernard's results in an invitation from Bartlett to relocate to "the hill."

1968

- Martin Luther King Jr. delivers his "I Have Been to the Mountain" speech on April 3.
- King is murdered in Memphis, Tennessee, on April 4; CRDS students and faculty hold a commemorative service for him.
- CRDS students stage a teach-in in protest of the war in Vietnam.
- John D. Cato, the school's first African American professor, is appointed.
- Bexley Hall students and five faculty relocate to CRDS in Rochester.
- The academic year opens with CRDS, Bexley Hall, in affiliation with St. Bernard's.
- Gardner Taylor is named as a CRDS trustee and gives a series of guest lectures.
- The Rochester Center for Theological Studies is launched.
- CRDS holds a banquet in honor of Martin Luther King Jr., which features nationally known African Americans like Ralph David Abernathy and Mahalia Jackson.
- A group of black CRDS students make institutional and curricular demands.
- The Crozer Foundation is formed to give financial support to the School of Nursing and the Martin Luther King, Jr. School for Social Change.

1969

- The CRDS/Bexley Hall trustees discuss the matter of greater inclusion of black trustees to properly represent the Divinity School's commitment to racial inclusion.
- Two days of faculty meetings examine the question of the inclusion of black faculty and curriculum without reaching firm conclusions.
- The seminary is locked out by a group of black CRDS students.
- With the pending sale of the Lake Avenue property, St. Bernard's announces it will relocate to the CRDS campus.
- Henry H. Mitchell is named to the Martin Luther King professorship at CRDS/Bexley Hall.
- The student lockout dampens Bishop Fulton Sheen's enthusiasm for St. Bernard's relocation to the CRDS campus.
- Samuel Crozer and Norman Baum of the Crozer Seminary board of trustees suggest to President Wells that it is time to consider a merger with another school, and CRDS is chosen.

1970

- A women's caucus is formed to address the needs and concerns of seminary women.
- Formal services celebrate the affiliation of CRDS/Bexley Hall and Crozer.
- CRCDS/Bexley Hall President Gene Bartlett announces his resignation.
- CRCDS/Bexley Hall opens the fall semester with a record enrollment of 270 students, including 7 faculty and 65 students coming from Crozer.
- Arthur McKay becomes president of the newly formed CRCDS/ Bexley Hall.
- Kenneth ("Snuffy") Smith joins the faculty of CRCDS/Bexley Hall and is one of the chief proponents of the legacy of Martin Luther King Jr.

1971

- Diane Tennis, a visiting professor, is the school's first female professor.
- CRCDS/Bexley Hall announces a $290,000 budget deficit.
- CRCDS/Bexley Hall replaces the bachelor of divinity degree with the master of divinity.
- The CRCDS annual fund reaches its goal of $315,000.
- Hays H. Rockwell is named dean of Bexley Hall.
- Henry H. Mitchell becomes Martin Luther King, Jr. Professor of Black Church Studies.
- The King Fellows Program begins and continues through the 1974 academic year.
- St. Bernard's Seminary is granted American Association of Theological Schools accreditation.

1972

- Best-selling book *Why Conservative Churches Are Growing* by Dean M. Kelly is published; it details a dramatic shift in the American theological climate.

1973

- Leon Pacala becomes the new president of CRDS/BH/CTS.
- The New York State Board of Regents approves the new, innovative CRCDS Doctor of Ministry program.

1974

- Gayraud S. Wilmore Jr. becomes the Martin Luther King, Jr. Professor and Dean of Black Church Studies.
- Betty Bone Schiess is ordained (irregularly) to the priesthood of the Episcopal Church.
- Bexley Hall trustees pass a resolution in favor of the full ordination of women.
- Pacala asserts "the plight" of the Divinity School due to enroll-ment and financial crisis.

1975

- CRCDS trustees appoint a committee to explore the financial undergirding of the school.
- The Divinity School observes 125 years of theological education in Rochester.

- The total income of the school exceeds $1 million for the first time.

1976

- A six-year, $7 million campaign launches.
- Beverly Gaventa joins the faculty as the first full-time tenure-track woman on staff.
- The Kresge Foundation donates $100,000 to the Forward Fund for facilities renovation.
- The Mordecai Wyatt Johnson Institute of Religion is established at CRCDS.

1977

- Richard H. Mansfield Jr. is installed as the tenth dean of Bexley Hall.
- "Center Days," celebrated on Ash Wednesday, brings the faculty and students of St. Bernard's and the Divinity School together for worship and celebration.

1980

- Pacala resigns as president of the Divinity School.
- James H. Evans joins the faculty as professor of theology and black studies.
- For the fifth consecutive year, income for the Divinity School exceeds $1 million.
- Marjorie S. Matthews becomes the first woman elected bishop in the United Methodist Church and the first female bishop of a mainline denomination.
- A CRCDS graduating class of 43 students signals the beginning of declining enrollments.
- Larry Greenfield becomes president of CRCDS/Bexley Hall.

1981

- A three-year covenant agreement brings St. Bernard's Institute to "the hill" under the leadership of Sebastian Falcone.

1983

- William Peterson is appointed dean of Bexley Hall.
- Kenneth L. Smith is appointed dean of Crozer to enhance both ties to the former institution and bolster Baptist presence.

1984

- The Consultation on Collegiality is founded to engender the full partnership of women in theological education.
- James H. Evans becomes the Martin Luther King, Jr. Professor of Black Church Studies.

1985

- The Divinity School governing board adopts a policy of divestment in South Africa.

1986

- Robert M. Franklin Jr. is inaugurated as dean of black church studies.

1987

- BMTS alumnae begins a campaign to endow a faculty chair with an initial goal of $600,000.

1988

- Grants are received to put Ambrose Swasey Library rare books online.
- The Lilly Endowment funds two grants to explore attracting students from new contexts.
- Curriculum revision study emphasizes globalization.
- A new long-range planning committee is established, and consultants are brought in.
- A new chapel organ is contracted and built by Karl Wilhelm of Quebec.

1989

- Larry Greenfield resigns after a nine-year presidency.
- Shirley M. Jones is named interim president, is the first woman to hold this office at CRCDS, and is among the first to do so in the nation.

1990

- Evans becomes the first African American president of CRCDS.
- The design for a unified board of trustees for the Divinity School is suggested.
- The annual operating budget rises to nearly $4 million.

1991

- Walter E. Fluker is named dean of black church studies and brings the Howard Thurman research and works project to the Divinity School.
- New curriculum highlighting black church studies and women's and gender studies is implemented.

1992

- The Women and Gender Studies Program (one of the nation's first) is inaugurated under the leadership of Melanie A. May, dean of women's studies.
- Jessie Jackson addresses the CRCDS during commencement via telephone connection from the scene of riots in Los Angeles.
- The Divinity School governing board adopts the unified, single-board plan.

1993

- Evans initiates the development of a new strategic plan for the future.
- ATS accreditation is granted for a 10-year period.
- Concerted efforts are made to bring campus facilities in line with the Americans with Disabilities Act.
- The Capital Campaign Committee faces the needs of new technology and the library.

1994

- A lengthy study and revision of the CRCDS curriculum is undertaken.

1995

- A new strategic plan for the Divinity School is presented.
- The academic year opens with community-building events.

1996

- A graduating class of 26 students signals an ongoing decline in enrollment.

1998

- Bexley Hall relocates to Columbus, Ohio, where it affiliates with Trinity Lutheran Seminary.

1999

- Declining enrollments and increased operational costs force a 20 percent reduction in CRCDS staff.

2001

- G. Thomas Halbrooks is announced as the next president.

2003

- St. Bernard's Institute builds and occupies its own new facility on French Road, Rochester.

2005

- Halbrooks announces his retirement, and the Divinity School faces a $700,000 deficit.

2006

- Eugene C. Bay becomes president of the Divinity School.
- Ithaca College's physical therapy program takes up residency in the first floor of Strong Hall, bringing much needed additional income to the Divinity School.

2008

- The Gosnell Endowed Chair of Christian Ethics becomes fully funded.
- Hope Lodge is established in the renovated Trevor-Eaton Hall through a $4 million gift.

2010

- Bay announces his retirement as president of the Divinity School.
- Jack McKelvey is appointed interim president.

2011:

- Marvin A. McMickle is appointed as the twelfth president of CRCDS.

2012

- Andrews Hall is renovated into 12 units of temporary housing to help transition returning veterans back into the community.
- A graduating class of 30 students signals a continuing decline in enrollment.

2013

- Bexley Hall moves from Columbus to Chicago, where it merges with Seabury-Western Theological Seminary.

2016

- Ithaca College leaves Strong Hall, taking with them an important income stream.
- McMickle reports more than $2 million in deferred maintenance on the physical plant.

2017

- Enrollment in the doctor of ministry program enrollment reaches 60 students.

2018

- The Black Student Caucus hosts a gala celebration commemorating the 50th anniversary of the student lockout.
- A new strategic plan is adopted, proposing the sale of the campus to offset nearly $2 million in deferred maintenance on the physical plant.
- A strategic plan calls for a greatly expanded doctor of ministry program, setting a goal of 50 students by 2018.
- McMickle announces the impending sale of the 1100 S. Goodman Street campus and the relocation of the Divinity School.
- Space at 320 North Goodman Avenue, in the heart of Rochester, is leased as the new site of CRCDS.

2019

- Following extensive renovations, CRCDS takes up residence in its new state-of-the art facility at 320 North Goodman Avenue, Rochester.

Selected Bibliography

Bulletins, catalogues, reports, minutes of meetings, and other archival materials are cited in the footnotes of this work, as are newspaper reports.

Adams, S. W. *The Memoirs of Rev. Nathaniel Kendrick D.D. and Silas N. Kendrick*. Philadelphia: The American Baptist Publication Society, 1860.

Ansbro, John J. *Martin Luther King, Jr.: The Making of a Mind*. Maryknoll, NY: Paulist Press, 1982.

Asbury, Jewel. "A History of the Integration of the Woman's American Baptist Home Mission Society and the American Baptist Home Mission Society: A Case Study of the Oppression of Women." MA thesis, Colgate Rochester Divinity School, Bexley Hall, Crozer Theological Seminary, May 1983.

Aubrey, Edwin E. *Present Theological Tendencies*. New York: Harper and Brothers, 1936.

Bailey, Faith Coxe, based upon research done by Margaret Noffsinger Wenger. *Two Directions*. Rochester, NY: Baptist Missionary Training School, 1964.

Baptist Fundamentals: Being Addresses Delivered at the Pre-Convention Conference at Buffalo, June 21 and 22, 1920. Valley Forge, PA: Judson Press, 1920.

Barnes, Sherman B. "Walter Rauschenbusch as Historian." *Foundations* 12, no. 3 (July 1969):

Bartlett, Gene E. *The Audacity of Preaching*. New York: Harper and Brothers, 1962.

———. *These Are the Baptists*. Royal Oak, MI: Cathedral Press, 1972.

———. "These Are the Baptists." In *Our Faiths*, edited by Martin E. Marty. Royal Oak, MI: Cathedral Press, 1976.

Beaven, Albert. *The Lift of a Far View*. Valley Forge, PA: Judson Press, 1936.

Brackney, William H. *Congregation and Campus: North American Baptists in Higher Education*. Macon, GA: Mercer University Press, 2008.

———. *A Genetic History of Baptist Thought*. Macon, GA: Mercer University Press, 2004.

Bronson, B. F., ed. *The First Half Century of Madison University (1819–1869) or, The Jubilee Volume Containing Sketches of Eleven Hundred Living and Deceased Alumni with Fifteen Portraits of Founders, Presidents, and Patrons. Also The Exercises of the Semi-Centennial Anniversary*. New York: Sheldon and Co., 1872.

Burdette, Mary G. *Young Women among Blanket Indians: The Heroine of Saddle Mountain*. Chicago: R. R. Donelley & Sons, for the Women's Baptist Home Mission Society, 1898.

Burtchael, James Tunstead. *The Dying of the Light: The Disengagement of Colleges and Universities from Their Christian Churches*. Grand Rapids: Eerdmans, 1998.

Carson, Clayborne, ed. *The Autobiography of Martin Luther King, Jr.* New York: Grand Central Publishing, 1998.

———. *The Papers of Martin Luther King, Jr.* 7 vols. Berkeley: University of California Press, 1992.

Carson, Clayborne, Peter Holloran, Ralph E. Luker, and Penny Russell. "Martin Luther King, Jr., as Scholar: A Reexamination of His Theological Writings." *The Journal of American History* 78, no. 1 (June 1991): 93–105.

Chapman, Mrs. John H. "History of the Baptist Missionary Training School." In *Alma Mater Memories: Being a History of the Baptist Missionary Training School—a Collection of*

Class Songs and Mottos, Prayer Songs and School Songs, Composed by the Students, 1881–1931. Chicago: Baptist Missionary Training School, 1931.

Chase, Philander. *A Plea for the West*. Boston: Samuel H. Parker, 1827.

———. *The Star in the West, Or Kenyon College in the Year of Our Lord 1828*. Columbus: n.p., 1828. Internet archive, The Hathitrust, https://babel.hathitrust.org/cgi/pt?id=hvd .hn58xt&view=1up&seq=11.

Clarke, Emily, ed. *William Newton Clarke: A Biography*. New York: Charles Scribner's Sons, 1916.

Clarke, William Newton. *The Ideal of Jesus*. New York: Charles Scribner's Sons, 1911.

———. *Sixty Years with the Bible*. New York: Charles Scribner's Sons, 1909.

Cole, S. C. *The History of Fundamentalism*. New York: Smith, Inc., 1931.

Crawford, Isabel. *Joyful Journey: Highlights on the High Way*. Valley Forge, PA: Judson Press, 1951.

———. *Kiowa: The History of a Blanket Indian Mission*. New York: Fleming H. Revell, 1915.

Cross, George. *The Theology of Schleiermacher: A Condensed Presentation of His Chief Work "The Christian Faith."* Chicago: University of Chicago Press, 1911.

———. *What Is Christianity: A Study of Rival Interpretations*. Chicago: University of Chicago Press, 1918.

Cross, Whitney R. *The Burned-Over District: The Social and Intellectual History of Enthusiastic Religion in Western New York, 1800–1850*. Ithaca, NY: Cornell University Press, 1950.

Daniels, Louis. *William Andrews*. Cleveland: Artcraft Printing, 1930.

Dart, John. "How Many in Mainline? Categories Vary in Surveys." *Christian Century* 126, no. 12 (June 16, 2009).

Davis, George W. "Some Theological Continuities in the Crisis Theology." *Crozer Quarterly* 27, no. 3 (July 1950).

Dodge, Ebenezer. *The Evidences of Christianity and an Introduction on the Existence of God and the Immortality of the Soul*. Boston: Gould & Lincoln, 1869.

———. *Lectures in Theology*. Hamilton, NY: University Press Print, 1883.

Dodgson, Sally. "Rochester Theological Seminary: 1850–1928." *American Baptist Quarterly* 20, no. 2 (June 2001): 114–29.

Douglas, Crerar, ed. *Autobiography of Augustus Hopkins Strong*. Valley Forge, PA: Judson Press, 1981.

Eaton, George W. "Historical Discourse Delivered at the Semi-Centenary of Madison University, Wednesday, August 5th, 1869." In *The First Half Century of Madison University (1819–1869) or, The Jubilee Volume Containing Sketches of Eleven Hundred Living and Deceased Alumni with Fifteen Portraits of Founders, Presidents, and Patrons. Also The Exercises of the Semi-Centennial Anniversary*, edited by B. F. Bronson. New York: Sheldon and Co., 1872.

Evans, Christopher. *The Kingdom Is Always but Coming: A Life of Walter Rauschenbusch*. Waco, TX: Baylor University Press, 2010.

Evans, James H. "Toward an Afro-American Theology." *Journal of Religious Thought* 40, no. 2 (January 1983): 39–54.

———. *We Have Been Believers: An African American Systematic Theology*. Philadelphia: Fortress Press, 1993; 2nd ed., 2012.

Evans, Milton G. *What Jesus Taught*. Valley Forge, PA: Judson Press, 1922.

Fleming, Sandford. *American Baptists in Higher Education*, 6 vols. Valley Forge, PA: American Baptist Board of Education, 1965.

Fluker, Walter E. *They Looked for a City: A Comparative Analysis of the Ideal of Community in the Thought of Howard Thurman and Martin Luther King Jr*. Lanham, MD: University Press of America, 1989.

———, ed. *The Papers of Howard Washington Thurman*. 4 vols. Columbia: University of South Carolina Press, 2009– .

———, and Catherine Tumber, eds. *A Strange Freedom: The Best of Howard Thurman on Religious Experience and Public Life*. Boston: Beacon Press, 1998.

Foreman, Edward, ed. *The Centennial History of Rochester*. New York: Rochester Public Library, 1931–1932.

———. *The Centennial History of Rochester, New York*. Rochester, NY: J. P. Smith Co., 1934.

Foster, Frank Hugh. *A Genetic History of the New England Theology*. New York: Russell & Russell, 1963.

———. *The Modern Movement in American Theology*. Reprint ed. Freeport, NY: Books for Libraries Press, 1969.

Fountain, C. H. *The Denominational Situation: Should Our Schools Be Investigated?* Plainfield, NJ: n.p., 1921.

Franklin, James H. "Baptist Missions in the New World Order." *Review and Expositor* 17 (October 1920): 389–401.

Freidan, Betty. *The Feminine Mystique*. New York: Norton and Company, 1963.

Furniss, N. F. *The Fundamentalist Controversy, 1918–1931*. New Haven, CT: Yale University Press, 1954.

Garrow, David J. *Bearing the Cross: Martin Luther King, Jr. and the Southern Christian Leadership Conference*. New York: William Morrow and Company, 1986.

———. "King's Plagiarism: Imitation, Insecurity, and Transformation." *The Journal of American History* 78, no. 1 (June 1991): 86–92.

Giles, Mark S. "Howard Thurman: The Making of a Morehouse Man, 1919–1932." *Educational Foundations* 20, no. 1–2 (Winter–Spring 2006): 105–22.

Goodwin, Mary E. "Racial Roots and Religion: An Interview with Howard Thurman." *The Christian Century* 90 (May 9, 1973): 533–35.

Grant, Thomas G. *A Born Again Episcopalian: The Witness of Charles P. McIlvaine*. Port St. Lucie, FL: Solid Ground Books, 2011.

Guild, Reuben Aldridge. *History of Brown University with Illustrative Documents*. Providence, RI: Providence Press Company, 1867.

Hall, Simon. "The NAACP, Black Power, and the African American Freedom Struggle, 1966–1969." *The Historian* 69, no. 1 (Spring 2007): 49–82.

Hamilton, William. "The Death of God Theology." *The Christian Scholar* 48, no. 1 (Spring 1965): 27-48.

———. "In Piam Memoriam—The Death of God after Ten Years." *Christian Century* 92, no. 32 (October 8, 1975): 872–73.

Handy, Robert. "The Ecumenical Vision of William Newton Clarke." *Journal of Ecumenical Studies* 17, no. 2 (January 1980).

Hanley, Robert B. "Henry Clay Vedder: Conservative Evangelical to Evangelical Liberal." *Foundations* 5, no. 2 (April 1962).

Hardin, Shields T. *The Colgate Story*. New York: Vantage Press, 1959.

Harding, Vincent. "Dangerous Spirituality." *Sojourners*. January–February 1999.

Henry, Carl F. H. *Personal Idealism and Strong's Theology*. Wheaton, IL: Van Kampen Press, 1951.

Historical Sketch of Crozer Theological Seminary: A Souvenir of the Thirtieth Anniversary of the Foundation of the Seminary. Chester, PA: Printed for the Seminary, 1897.

Honeycutt, Dwight A. *Henry Clay Vedder: His Life and Thought*. Atlanta: Baptist History and Heritage, 2008.

Howe, Claude L. *The Theology of William Newton Clarke*. New York: Arno Press, 1980.

———. "William Newton Clarke: Systematic Theologian of Theological Liberalism." *Foundations* 6, no. 2 (1963).

Hudson, Winthrop S. *Baptist Concepts of the Church*. Valley Forge, PA: Judson Press, 1959.

———. *Baptist Convictions*. Valley Forge, PA: Judson Press, 1963.

———. *Baptists in Transition*. Valley Forge, PA: Judson Press, 1979.

———. "Interrelationships of Baptists in Canada and the United States." *Foundations* 23, no. 1 (January–March 1980): 22–41.

———. *Religion in America*. New York: Charles Scribner's Sons, 1961.

———. "Shifting Patterns of Church Order in the Twentieth Century," *The American Baptist Quarterly* 30, no. 3/4 (Fall–Winter, 2011): 320–37.

————. *Understanding Roman Catholicism: A Guide to Papal Teaching for Protestants*. Philadelphia: Westminster Press, 1959.

Hudson, Winthrop S., with Norman H. Maring. *A Baptist Manual of Polity and Practice*. Valley Forge, PA: Judson Press, 1963.

"An Interview with Howard Thurman and Ronald Eyre." *Theology Today* 38, no. 2 (July 1981).

Johnson, Benton, Dean R. Hoge, and Donald A. Luidens. "Mainline Churches: The Real Reason for Decline." *First Things* 31 (March 1993): 13–18.

Johnson, E. H. *Ezekiel Gilman Robinson: An Autobiography: With a Supplement by H. L. Wayland and Critical Estimates*. New York: Silver, Burdett, and Co., 1896.

Kelley, Dean M. *Why Conservative Churches Are Growing: A Study in Sociology of Religion*. New York: Harper and Row, 1972.

Kelly, Robert. *Theological Education in America*. New York: George Doran Co., 1924.

King, Martin Luther, Jr. *The Strength to Love*. Philadelphia: Fortress, 1963.

————. *Stride toward Freedom: The Montgomery Story*. Boston: Beacon Press, 1958.

————. *Where Do We Go from Here? Chaos or Community*. New York: Harper and Row, 1967.

Laws, Curtis Lee. "A New History of the Reformation." *The Watchman-Examiner* 2, no. 35 (August 27, 1914).

Luker, Ralph. "Plagiarism and Perspective: Questions about Martin Luther King, Jr." *International Social Science Review* 68, no. 4 (Fall 1993): 152-60.

Lyles, Jean Caffey. "Editorial Comment: An Improbably Episcopal Choice." *Christian Century* 97, no. 26 (August 13–20, 1980).

MacQueen, David A. *The Crozers of Upland*. Wilmington, DE: Serendipity Press, 1982.

Malcolm X and Alex Haley. *The Autobiography of Malcolm X*. New York: Grove Press, 1965.

Marble, Manning *Malcolm X: A Life of Reinvention*. New York: Viking Press, 2011.

Maring, Norman H. "Winthrop S. Hudson: Church Historian." *Foundations* 23, no. 2 (April–June 1980): 132–42.

Matthews, Marjorie S. "The Wisdom of Ecumenicity." *Ecumenical Trends* 14, no. 4 (1985).

May, Arthur. *A History of the University of Rochester 1850–1962*. Rochester, NY: University of Rochester Press, 1977.

McKelvey, Blake. *Rochester on the Genesee: The Growth of a City*. Syracuse, NY: Syracuse University Press, 1973.

McKinney, Richard I. *Mordecai: The Man and His Message*. Washington, DC: Howard University Press, 1997.

McMickle, Marvin A. *Be My Witness*. Valley Forge, PA: Judson Press, 2016.

————. "Prophetic Message." In the *New Interpreter's Handbook of Preaching*, edited by Paul Scott Wilson. Nashville: Abingdon, 2008.

————. *Pulpit and Politics*. Valley Forge, PA: Judson Press, 2014.

————. *Where Have All the Prophets Gone? Reclaiming Prophetic Preaching in America*. Cleveland: Pilgrim Press, 2006.

McNamara, Robert F. *The Diocese of Rochester in America 1858–1993*. 2nd exp. ed. Rochester, NY: The Roman Catholic Diocese of Rochester, 1998.

————. "Ecumenism and the Rochester Center for Theological Studies." *Rochester History* 52, no. 2 (Fall 1990): 21–22.

————. *St. Bernard's Seminary: 1893–1968*. Rochester, NY: The Sheaf Press, 1968.

"Milton G. Evans." *Proceedings of the Society of Biblical Literature* 59, no. 1 (1940).

Minus, Paul M. *Walter Rauschenbusch: American Reformer*. New York: Macmillan, 1988.

Mondello, Salvatore. "Isabel Crawford and the Kiowa Indians." pt 2. *Foundations* 22, no. 1 (January–March 1979): 28–42.

Moore, Joanna P. *In Christ's Stead: Autobiographical Sketches*. Chicago: The Women's Baptist Missionary Society, 1902.

Moore, LeRoy. "The Rise of American Religious Liberalism at the Rochester Theological Seminary, 1872–1928." PhD diss., Claremont Graduate School, 1966.

Niebuhr, Reinhold. *An Interpretation of Christian Ethics*. London: SCM Press, 1936.

————. *Moral Man and Immoral Society*. New York: Charles Scribner's Sons, 1932.

———. *The Nature and Destiny of Man*. 2 vols. New York: Charles Scribner's Sons, 1941–1943.

Norton, A. Banning. *A History of Knox County, Ohio from 1799 to 1862 Inclusive*. Columbus, OH: Richard Nevins, 1862.

Oates, Stephen B. "The Intellectual Odyssey of Martin Luther King." *The Massachusetts Review* 22, no. 2 (Summer 1981): 301–20.

Parr, Patrick. *The Seminarian: Martin Luther King Jr. Comes of Age*. Chicago: Lawrence Hill Books, 2018.

Pitts, Bill. "Personal and Social Christianity in Rauschenbusch's Thought." *American Baptist Quarterly* 26, no. 2 (Summer 2007): 138–60.

Proctor, Samuel DeWitt. *The Substance of Things Hoped For: A Memoir of African-American Faith*. New York: Putnam, 1995.

Ramsey, William. *Four Modern Prophets*. Atlanta: John Knox Press, 1986.

Rauschenbusch, Walter. *Christianity and the Social Crisis*. New York: Macmillan, 1907.

———. *Christianizing the Social Order*. New York: Macmillan, 1913.

———. *Dare We Be Christians?* New York: Beacon Press, 1914.

———. *Prayers of the Social Awakening*. Boston: Pilgrim Press, 1910.

———. "Professor Vedder's New Book on Socialism." *The Standard*, June 15, 1912.

———. *The Social Principles of Jesus*. New York: Association Press, 1916.

———. *A Theology for the Social Gospel*. New York: Macmillan, 1917.

Reynolds, Mary C. *Baptist Missionary Pioneers among the Negroes*. Nashville: Sunday School Publication Board, n.d. Various dates are given; the book possibly was published before 1900.

"Rochester Seminary President to Retire: G. Thomas Halbrooks." *Christian Century* 121, no. 18 (September 7, 2004): 17.

Rosenberger, Jesse. *Rochester: The Making of a University*. Rochester, NY: University of Rochester Press, 1927.

———. *Rochester and Colgate: The Historical Backgrounds of Two Universities*. Chicago: University of Chicago Press, 1925.

Rossol, Heinz. "More Than a Prophet." *American Baptist Quarterly* 19, no. 2 (June 2000): 129–53.

Sandeen, Ernest R. *The Roots of Fundamentalism*. Grand Rapids: Baker Book House, 1978.

Sandon, Leo A. "Boston University Personalism and Southern Baptist Theology." *Foundations* 20, no. 2 (April–June 1977).

Schiess, Betty Bone. *Why Me Lord? One Woman's Ordination to the Priesthood with Commentary and Complaint*. Syracuse, NY: Syracuse University Press, 2003.

Sharpe, Dores Robinson. *Walter Rauschenbusch*. New York: Macmillan, 1942.

Simkins, Ronald A., and Thomas M. Kelly, eds. "Religion and Identity." *Journal of Religion and Society*, supp. ser. 13 (2016).

Skoglund, John E. "Edwin Dahlberg in Conversation: Memories of Walter Rauschenbusch." *Foundations* 18, no. 3 (July 1975).

Smith, J. Wheaton. *The Life of John P. Crozer*. Philadelphia: American Baptist Publication Society, 1868.

Smith. Kenneth L., and Ira G. Zepp. *Search for the Beloved Community: The Thinking of Martin Luther King Jr.* Valley Forge, PA: Judson Press, 1974.

Smith, Laura Chase. *The Life of Philander Chase: First Bishop of Ohio and Illinois, Founder of Kenyon and Jubilee Colleges*. New York: E. P. Dutton & Co., 1903.

Smith, Luther E. *Howard Thurman: Mystic as Prophet*. Lanham, MD: University Press of America, 1981.

Spielmann, Richard M. *Bexley Hall: 150 Years: A Brief History*. Rochester, NY: Colgate Rochester Crozer Divinity School, Bexley Hall, 1974.

Stackhouse, Max *The Righteousness of the Kingdom*. Nashville: Abingdon, 1968.

Steffen, Lloyd "The Dangerous God: A Profile of William Hamilton." *Christian Century* 106, no. 27 (September 27, 1989): 844.

Stewart, Marshall Bowyer. "Present Theological Tendencies." *The Anglican Theological Review* 8, no. 3 (July 1936).

Strong, Augustus H. *Christ in Creation and Ethical Monism*. Philadelphia: Roger Williams Press, 1899.

———. *Historical Discourse Delivered as a Part of the Exercises in Connection with the Celebration of the Fiftieth Anniversary of the Rochester Theological Seminary*. Rochester, NY: E. B. Andrews, 1900.

———. *Lectures on Theology*. Rochester, NY: E. R. Andrews, 1876.

———. *Miscellanies*. Vol. 2, *Chiefly Theological*. 2 vols. Philadelphia: Griffith & Rowland Press, 1912.

———. *One Hundred Chapel Talks to Theological Students*. Philadelphia: Griffith & Rowland Press, 1913.

———. *What Shall I Believe?* New York: Fleming H. Revell, 1922.

Thurman, Howard. *The Creative Encounter: An Interpretation of Religion and the Social Witness*. New York: Harper and Brothers, 1954.

———. *Deep River and the Negro Spiritual of Life and Death*. 2nd ed. Richmond, IN: Friends United Press, 1975.

———. *The Luminous Darkness: A Personal Interpretation of the Anatomy of Segregation and the Ground of Hope*. New York: Harper and Row, 1965.

———. "Mysticism and Social Action." *The A.M.E. Zion Quarterly Review* 92, no. 1 (October 1980).

———. *With Head and Heart: The Autobiography of Howard Thurman*. New York: Harcourt, Brace, Jovanovich, 1979.

Torbet, Robert G. *A History of the Baptists*. Valley Forge, PA: Judson Press, 1950.

Tull, James. *Shapers of Baptist Thought*. Macon, GA: Mercer University Press, 1972.

Vedder, Henry C. *Baptists and Liberty of Conscience*. Cincinnati: J. R. Baumes, 1884.

———. *The Dawn of Christianity, or Studies of the Apostolic Church*. Philadelphia: American Baptist Publication Society, 1894.

———. *The Fundamentals of Christianity*. New York: Macmillan, 1922.

———. *Jesus and the Problems of Democracy*. New York: Macmillan, 1914.

———. "The Open Forum: Must We Go—Where?" *The Baptist: Published by the Northern Baptist Convention* 1, no. 39 (October 23, 1920).

———. *Socialism and the Ethics of Jesus*. New York: Macmillan, 1912.

Wacker, Grant. *Augustus Strong and the Dilemma of Historical Consciousness*. Macon, GA: Mercer University Press, 1985.

Walworth, Clarence. *The Oxford Movement in America*. New York: The Catholic Book Exchange, 1895.

Welter, Barbara. *Divinity Convictions*. Athens: Ohio University Press, 1976.

Whiteley, Marilyn Färdig. *More Than I Asked For: The Life of Isabel Crawford*. Eugene, OR: Pickwick, 2015.

———. *Preaching in Silence: Isabel Crawford and Indian Sign Language*. Wilmore, KY: Asbury Seminary, First Fruits, 2016.

Williams, Howard D. *A History of Colgate University*. New York: Van Nostrand Reinhold, 1969.

Wind, C. James. "The Turbulent Ecology of Mainline Protestantism." *Theological Education* 44, no. 1 (2008): 29–34.

Wuthnow Robert, and John H. Evans. *The Quiet Hand of God: Faith-Based Activism and the Public Role of Mainline Protestantism*. Berkeley: University of California Press, 2002.

Zeller, Barbara. "Race and Religion in Rochester, 1964 to 1969." Unpublished MA thesis, Colgate Rochester Crozer Divinity School, December 2010.

Index

338